THE
PERENNIAL
CARE
MANUAL

THE PERENNIAL CARE MANUAL

A Plant-by-Plant Guide: What to Do & When to Do It

NANCY J. ONDRA

PHOTOGRAPHY BY **ROB CARDILLO**

Storey Publishing

The mission of Storey Publishing is to serve our customers by
publishing practical information that encourages
personal independence in harmony with the environment.

Edited by Carleen Madigan and Gwen Steege
Art direction by Dan O. Williams
Book design by Patrick Barber/McGuire Barber Design and Dan O. Williams

Cover and interior photography by © Rob Cardillo, except © AGSTOCK/Arlyn Evans
    (soldier beetle), 105; © AGSTOCK/Jack Clark (lacewing), 105; Wikimedia, 109 top;
    © cfgphoto.com, 117 bottom; © GAP Photos Ltd., 203; © Rosemary Kautzky, 112, 113, 114;
    © Saxon Holt/Photo Botanic, 140.

Indexed by Christine R. Lindemer, Boston Road Communications

Printed in China by R.R. Donnelley
10 9 8 7 6 5 4 3 2 1

Library of Congress Cataloging-in-Publication Data

Ondra, Nancy J.
  The perennial care manual / Nancy J. Ondra.
      p. cm.
  Includes index.
  ISBN 978-1-60342-150-8 (pbk. : alk. paper)
  ISBN 978-1-60342-151-5 (hardcover w/ jacket : alk. paper)
  1. Perennials. I. Title.
SB434.O53 2009
635.9'32—dc22
                          2009001531

CONTENTS

Foreword

PERENNIALS. For so many gardeners, they represent the heart of a garden: hope, regeneration, longevity, and ease of maintenance. From experience, though, we know that nothing is as simple as it appears to be. So, in our insatiable quest to master the art of perennial gardening, we devour a variety of books on the subject, hoping to gain enough knowledge to be able to handle most of the situations that will inevitably occur when planting, growing, and maintaining these stalwarts of the garden.

I can think of no one more capable and well equipped to guide and teach gardeners how to design, plant, and maintain a perennial garden than Nancy Ondra. She is one of the most talented, passionate, experienced, and curious gardeners I have ever known. Nan is a true lover of plants. Nothing thrills her more than experimenting with new specimens and plant combinations, and observing how they grow and thrive in her own garden. Nan's garden, her own laboratory and living landscape, transforms itself year to year with a pageantry of annuals and bulbs. But always at the base of the garden, holding the design together, are perennials. Nan has had years of experience tilling her own soil, digging and creating garden beds and planting them with a plethora of wide-ranging plant material. Yet, she is never satisfied. With an insatiable curiosity, Nan is constantly seeking new and better ways of gardening so that she, as well as her readers, can garden in the most efficient manner possible with excellent results.

The Perennial Care Manual, written in a conversational and personal style, invites you into Nan's world, where she, step by step, shows readers what to do and how to do it. From the moment you sink into the text of this book, you'll know that you are in the hands of an expert. Nan generously shares information, teaches skills, and offers encouragement — all with a dose of passion and curiosity — to help you move forward in immersing yourself in the world of perennial gardening.

— Fran Sorin
Author of *Digging Deep: Unearthing Your Creative Roots Through Gardening*

Welcome!

GORGEOUS PERENNIAL GARDENS don't just happen. Behind every bloom-filled border is a grubby, sweaty gardener with muddy knees, chipped fingernails, and sore muscles — and a big smile, too. So, what's that goofy gardener smiling about, anyway? For the uninitiated, the reality of what it takes to create and maintain a great-looking garden appears to be an endless string of tiresome tasks and dirty jobs. But true gardeners know that the real fun of gardening is in the *process* — the planning, the planting, the nurturing, and the learning. If we end up with a pretty garden along the way, that's terrific. Chances are, though, that once we get a garden looking just right and everyone tells us how perfect it is, we'll decide we want to take it apart and try something else or turn our attention to starting a brand new border from scratch. Maybe it doesn't make sense, but it doesn't really need to: It's just what we do.

It's undoubtedly possible to be a successful perennial gardener without ever picking up a gardening book or magazine. After all, learning by doing is an important part of the gardening tradition. But the urge to acquire information in any way possible also seems to be a key trait that all gardeners share. We love reading about new plants to grow, hearing about interesting techniques to try, and picking up great ideas for helping our gardens thrive. Sometimes, we just need a quick rundown of a plant's preferred growing conditions so we can figure out where to put it; other times, we're seeking more in-depth advice to solve a problem. And if we can find all of that information in one place, so much the better! Well, that's what this book is all about.

❧ Looking for in-depth information on techniques that can help you garden smarter? Turn to Part One: Perennial Care Basics, starting on page 3. You'll find detailed advice on everything from planning an easy-care perennial garden to planting, watering, mulching, and pruning, as well as propagating your favorites and dealing with problems you may encounter along the way.

❧ Need to know the best time to plant, move, divide, or fertilize a particular perennial? Flip to its entry in Part Two: Plant-by-Plant Perennial Guide, starting on page 121. There, you'll find a rundown of what needs to be done season by season, along with growing tips to help you select the ideal site, figure out what problems it's likely to have, and choose the best way to propagate it. This kind of information is also handy to review *before* you buy a new perennial, so you can have an idea of how much maintenance it's going to need and be aware of potential problems it may have (or cause).

You know, there's something special about the perfect cover, clean pages, and crisp smell of any newly acquired book, and it can be tempting to treat it carefully to preserve its perfection as long as possible. But to my mind, the very best gardening books are those that actually get *used:* their covers are a bit rumpled, the edges are mud-smudged, the pages are dog-eared, and the margins are filled with scribbled notes. It's my hope that this book will meet that fate at your hands, instead of sitting neatly on a shelf somewhere. Think of it just like your favorite trowel or prized pair of pruning shears: as a tool to help you create a gorgeous perennial garden and have a wonderful time along the way.

Nancy J Ondra

PART ONE
PERENNIAL CARE BASICS

Ready for in-depth information on the various techniques you can use to get your perennial garden off to a super start and keep it growing strong? To find out how you can minimize the garden chores you *don't* like to do so you have more time for the fun stuff, turn to Creating an Easy-Care Perennial Garden, starting on page 4. This chapter also covers the down-and-dirty details on preparing a new site for planting, selecting the best perennials for your yard, and sprucing up older gardens that could use some help.

When it's time to really get growing, see Caring for Your Perennials, starting on page 22. You'll learn about planting and transplanting, watering, fertilizing and soil-building, mulching, and caring for perennials through the winter months. When the urge to create a new bed or border hits, come here to find out how to propagate your perennials with a variety of simple techniques, so you can fill that space with great plants without spending a fortune.

Keeping Up Appearances, starting on page 68, covers the grooming and maintenance techniques that keep your perennials looking their best: staking, pinching, dividing, and more. It also includes ideas for dealing with the debris that inevitably piles up from all that snipping and trimming throughout the year.

While good planning and routine care go a long way toward keeping your perennials in peak form, you'll probably have to deal with occasional damage or disorders. In Troubleshooting Perennial Garden Problems, starting on page 94, you'll learn how to figure out just what's happening, and you'll find environmentally friendly ways to deal with it so you can get back to the business of enjoying your glorious garden!

OPPOSITE Many plants, like *Sedum rupestre* 'Angelina', can be easily propagated simply by digging a small plug from an established clump.

Chapter One

CREATING AN EASY-CARE PERENNIAL GARDEN

A PLACE FOR DESIGN

When you're thinking about creating a new garden, there are all kinds of design aspects to consider: colors, textures, fragrance, seasonal interest, and so on. In the excitement of all this planning, it's easy to overlook a less thrilling but equally important consideration: how much time and energy will you need to take care of this new garden? Any planting takes some amount of maintenance, of course, but the time you spend puttering around in your garden is supposed to be fun, not an endless series of boring chores. Decisions you make at the planning stage can make a big difference in the amount, frequency, and type of care your garden needs to look its best over its lifetime.

Learn about Your Site

For most of us, the process of creating a new garden starts with choosing the site. Maybe you know what *kind* of garden you'd like: a woodland garden in your tree-shaded side yard, perhaps, or a four-season foundation planting to add curb appeal to your front yard. Or, you might wish to create a border based on your favorite colors or in a particular style. Whatever your inspiration, the process starts with observing the site you have available. Once you have a fairly good handle on how much light it gets, and what the soil is like, you can more readily select perennials that are naturally adapted to those conditions — and in the long run, that means healthier, better-looking plants with less work on your part.

❧ Sun and shade. As a very general rule, a "full sun" perennial needs at least 8 hours of sun a day; a "light shade" perennial needs 6 to 8 hours of sun; a "partial shade" perennial needs roughly 3 to 6 hours of sun; and a "full shade" perennial grows fine with less than 3 hours of direct sun. Simple, right? Unfortunately, it's not quite that easy!

❧ When and how much light. Knowing *when* your plants will get sunshine matters just as much as *how much* they get. A site with 4 hours of morning sun and 4 hours of late-afternoon sun technically qualifies as full sun, but the intensity of the light at those times of the day may not meet the needs of sun-worshipping perennials. Conversely, a site that's blasted by 2 hours of midday sun, with no direct light for the rest of the day, may fry a full shade perennial. Generally speaking, a site with morning sun and afternoon shade is fine for plants in the "partial shade to full shade" range, while a site with morning shade and afternoon sun works for most "light shade to full sun" perennials.

Keep in mind that in any given site, light levels can change dramatically throughout the year. For instance, a spot that's flooded with sunshine through the spring months may quickly turn into deep shade once overhanging trees leaf out and stay that way through the rest of the growing season. That's why you'll often hear the advice to observe light levels over the course of an entire growing season before you choose plants for a particular site. If you decide not to follow that advice — and to be fair, few of us can wait that long once we've set our mind to garden planning — be prepared to adjust your design over the first season or two, as you see how the perennials

Dealing with Deep Shade

For the most part, perennials are very adaptable, and you'll find that they can survive (even if they don't thrive) in a wide range of light levels. Deep shade is one exception because plants need at least *some* light to grow. If you have a spot with dense, all-day, year-round shade, you might be better off covering it with mulch or paving and making a sitting area out of it, rather than struggling to grow perennials there. A site that gets full sun in the spring but full shade the rest of the year can be well suited to early blooming perennials for a shot of early color, at least. Or, you may also want to experiment with woodland plants that naturally grow in these tough conditions.

you don't want to be stuck with extra watering chores all summer, a site that gets a few hours of afternoon shade may be a better choice than one in full sun. Conversely, some perennials typically recommended for shade can grow well in more sun where the soil doesn't dry out completely.

You can get a rough idea of your soil type by crumbling a handful of moist earth and rubbing it between your fingers:

– **Sandy and gravelly soils** feel gritty; these tend to drain quickly, so you'll want to look for perennials that are touted as being drought-tolerant or well suited for dry soil.

– **Clay particles** are very tiny and cling together tightly, giving the soil a somewhat sticky feel. They hold water tightly, too, so they are often moist to wet. When they do dry out, though, soils that are high in clay tend to be hard and difficult to dig.

– **Silty soil** feels smooth between your fingers. It normally includes varying amounts of clay and sand, so it tends to drain reasonably well but still hold some moisture in the root zone: the often-recommended "moist but well-drained garden soil."

Tree roots can also play a big role in soil moisture levels. Where their roots are abundant — and especially when they are close to the surface, as with many maples (*Acer*), for example — the soil can be very dry, regardless of whether it's sandy, silty, or clayey.

Admittedly, this is all a rather simplistic overview of what is actually a complex set of interrelated factors. Besides your soil's sand, silt, and clay content, issues such as its nutrient balances, organic matter level, pH (acidity and alkalinity), and biological health all influence how well your perennials may perform. If you're so inclined, you can have many different tests performed on your soil before you plant, either through your state soil testing laboratory or a private lab. In most cases, though, simply knowing if you're facing any extreme conditions (very wet, bone dry, tightly compacted, and so on) is good enough. If there is already lawn and other plantings around your home and they look alright, you can probably assume that you

LOCATION, LOCATION, LOCATION *Where* you live also influences how light affects your plants. A perennial that thrives in all-day sun in northern gardens may suffer greatly with that much light in a hotter area. Southern gardeners may find that perennials touted as needing full sun — like crocosmia — grow just fine with morning sun and shade for part or all of the afternoon.

adjust to the available conditions. Plants that wilt dramatically without extra watering may appreciate a somewhat shadier site (or some shade from a taller companion), while those that lean toward the light or flop altogether may need more sun.

❖ Soil considerations. The amount of moisture your soil holds can have a major influence on how your perennials adjust to the sun or shade they get. Some plants, such as ligularias (*Ligularia*), can wilt dramatically in afternoon sun unless their soil is constantly moist (and sometimes, even if it is wet). So, if your soil isn't dependably moist and

have "average, well-drained" soil and choose your perennials accordingly. Other gardeners in your area can be an invaluable resource for more detailed information about the particular traits of your local soil types, as well as practical advice on what you need to do to succeed with perennials there.

❖ Climate considerations. Before deciding on specific perennials for your yard, you'll also want to familiarize yourself with the general climate conditions of your area. For gardeners, one of the most widely recognized climate-related factors is the "hardiness zone," commonly based on the USDA Plant Hardiness Zone Map. (You'll find a copy of this map on page 355.) This map divides the United States and Canada into 11 zones based on average annual minimum temperatures, so it's essentially a guide to whether a particular plant is likely to survive a typical winter in your area.

THE ROOTS OF THE MATTER Fighting with tree roots can be a frustrating battle, especially when they're paired with heavy shade. Look for a more hospitable planting site, if possible, or else be prepared to spend a lot of time carving out planting pockets and then providing supplemental water and fertilizer to get your perennials established there.

You'll frequently see a range of recommended hardiness zones given in plant descriptions in books, magazines, and catalogs, and on pot tags, too.

Winter temperatures are just one factor, though. Snow, for instance, is an excellent insulator for dormant perennials, often allowing them to survive the winter much more easily than they could in unprotected gardens in somewhat milder areas. Summer heat and humidity, too, have a definite influence on the vigor of some perennials. The AHS Heat Zone Map divides the country into 12 zones, based on the average

KEEPING YOUR COOL A generous layer of snow can be a real boon for perennial gardens. If you can depend on a blanket of the white stuff through the winter in your area, you may be able to succeed with plants that wouldn't otherwise survive in your hardiness zone.

number of days per year over 86°F (30°C). Heat zone ratings are not used nearly as frequently as hardiness zones, however, so it can take a bit of research to find the ratings for perennials you may be interested in trying.

Settling on a Size

There are two factors to keep in mind when deciding how big to make a new garden: how much work it will take to create and how much time you'll need to maintain it. It seems obvious that a large garden would take more work than a small garden, but that's not always the case. Yes, a large border demands a lot more effort than a small bed at planting time, and a larger quantity of mulch and initial watering as well. But if you

fill that big border with good-sized clumps of ornamental grasses and other sturdy, long-lived perennials, it'll take far less day-to-day fussing over the long run than a smaller one filled with tiny starts of more demanding plants. Still, there are some practical limitations to the ultimate size of any garden, including how much space you actually have available, how much help you have (if any) to get the site ready for planting, and how many plants you have on hand or can afford to buy to fill the space.

Even if you've already settled on a size and shape in your mind, it's easy to get carried away once you start digging, so it's wise to stake out the perimeter of the area *before* you begin. If you've planned your garden on paper, you have a head start; simply transfer the outline and dimensions from your plan to the ground. For those of you who prefer to design "on the fly," experiment with different outlines using stakes and string, then set out the still-potted plants (or use buckets or boxes as placeholders) to try out spacings and placements.

Plan Ahead for Access

Good garden planning is more than just creating great-looking combinations. It also takes into account how you're going to reach your perennials to take care of them.

❋ Beds and borders. Generally speaking, the term "border" is used for a garden that runs along the edge of something — next to a fence, for instance, or against a wall, or along a walkway — while a "bed" is a geometric or free-form area that's not tied into any particular feature. What you call your garden isn't nearly as important as making sure that it includes easy access to all of the plants without your having to step on any of them or on the soil. If you can reach in from only one side of the area, the maximum width is about 3 feet (90 cm); if you can reach in from two sides, figure a maximum width of about 6 feet (1.8 m).

In larger beds and borders, you'll thank yourself later if you include some kind of access path at the design and installation stage. It doesn't

THE BEST OF BOTH All-gravel paths look and sound great and offer excellent drainage, but they can also shift underfoot and make it tough to push a wheelbarrow or narrow-tired garden cart. To get the benefits without the drawbacks, consider a path that pairs gravel with timbers to hold the stones in place.

need to be large — roughly 18 to 24 inches (45 to 60 cm) wide is usually fine — but the footing should be as sturdy as a regular garden path. Trying to balance on teetering stepping stones with pruning shears in one hand and a bucket in the other can lead to disasters for both you and your perennials if you lose your footing.

❋ The paths to success. The paths you use to navigate around your property also affect how hard or easy it's going to be to maintain your gardens. Winding, circuitous routes can be interesting to stroll along but a bother when you're trying to get a debris-laden wheelbarrow from one point to another. Also, keep in mind that it's practically

SPREAD OUT THE WORK Can't create your entire dream garden right now? Consider digging and planting just the back one-third or one-half of the area first, then dig and plant the front one-half of the border next year. Or, start at one end of the area, then dig and plant it in sections as time and money allow.

impossible to push a full wheelbarrow along a gravel path, so consider a firmer surface for main paths, at least. (It doesn't have to be paving; even a bark-chip path is better than loose gravel!) And on sloping sites, watch out that you don't create wheelbarrow-inaccessible areas with flights of steps, if you can possibly avoid it. You may be able to deal with a single step, though it won't be easy, but shifting a wheelbarrow or cart up two or more steps simply isn't practical, unless the design of the steps includes some kind of ramp along the side for the wheel.

Easy-Care Planning Pointers

Whether you're designing your garden on paper or making it up as you go along, keep these additional maintenance-related tips in mind.

❧ It's all about you. Each of us has garden chores we enjoy and others we loathe. If you know (or can guess) what you do and don't like to do, you can plan your garden and choose plants accordingly. If you hate dragging hoses around, for instance, try siting your new planting close to your house for easy access, or concentrate on perennials that are touted as being drought-resistant, or use lots of mulch, or employ some combination of those strategies.

❧ Choose bedmates carefully. "Mixed" borders — plantings that include shrubs, vines, annuals, and other plants besides hardy perennials — offer lots of visual interest, and they're invaluable where it's important to have something to look at all year long. Remember, though, that each of those different plant groups has some specific needs of its own, and that can complicate maintenance matters a bit. Well-planned gardens that include only perennials can also offer multiseason interest, with the added benefit of easy cleanup.

❧ Keep it simple. Plantings based on large groupings of a few perennials generally simplify maintenance, because you need to consider the needs of only those particular plants. Few of us have the discipline to create only mass plantings, however. Gardeners tend to like variety, and lots of it, which is great fun from an aesthetic aspect but often way more complicated from a mainte-

EASY CLEANUP When you grow perennials by themselves, late-fall or early-spring cleanup is as easy as whacking everything down close to ground level. A scythe, string trimmer, trimmer–mower, or brush mower makes garden cleanup go quickly — a huge help in large-scale borders, especially.

nance standpoint. (Obviously, trying to remember the needs of 30 different plants takes a lot more brain space than just a half-dozen or so!) As a compromise, consider keeping your "one-of-this, one-of-that" gardens in a side yard or back yard, with larger masses of dependable, easy-care perennials in your front yard or other areas where it's important for the gardens to look good even if you can't fuss with them frequently.

❧ Spacing out. Plant spacings recommended on pot tags or in books are usually based on the size of the plants after a few years, which is fine if you

Temporary Fillers

You've virtuously planted your new perennials at their "proper" spacings, and now you have a bed or border with lots of bare soil between those little plants. While you're waiting for them to fill in, why not add some extra color (and cover the soil, too) with some annuals? There's no need to spend lots of money on these short-term fillers; try these tips:

❈ Include a few fast-growing tender perennials (perennials that are killed by winter cold in your area) to add height or fill ground space for the first year or two. Tender salvias (*Salvia*), sweet potato vines (*Ipomoea batatas*), and cannas (*Canna*) are a few easy-to-find options.

❈ Tuck in seeds of annuals that sprout readily when sown directly in the garden, such as castor beans (*Ricinus communis*), cosmos, four-o'clocks (*Mirabilis jalapa*), nasturtiums (*Tropaeolum majus*), and sunflowers (*Helianthus annuus*).

❈ Use inexpensive filler annuals such as pansies (*Viola* × *wittrockiana*), snapdragons (*Antirrhinum majus*), and sweet alyssum (*Lobularia maritima*).

❈ Don't overlook vegetables and herbs, either, such as basil, hot peppers, lettuce, and parsley. They make great fillers, and you can even harvest from them — an extra bonus.

A SWEET SOLUTION Sweet potato vines (*Ipomoea batatas*) come in a number of foliage shapes and colors, and they can fill lots of space quickly once the weather heats up.

don't want to deal with dividing or moving your perennials any more than absolutely necessary. The tradeoff is that your new garden will probably look sparse for the first few years, and weeds may invade the empty spaces between the clumps. You can get around that by using lots of mulch or, better yet, filling those spaces with bushy or trailing annuals for the first few years. (See Temporary Fillers, page 12 for details.) Another option is to set the perennials closer together (at about one-third to one-half of the recommended spacing) for a more immediate effect, with the idea of moving some of them out again in a year or two.

❧ Don't forget the edge. A freshly dug garden automatically has a clean-looking edge, so it's easy to forget that you're going to need to keep that edge maintained somehow. Lawn grass can

KEEP 'EM SEPARATED Installing some kind of edging strip will go a long way toward keeping your lawn from creeping into your perennials. Plus, it will give your garden a tidy, well-maintained look without the need for tedious hand edging or trimming.

quickly leap into the loose garden soil, and the perennials within will spill outward, making it necessary for you to hand-trim around them. A thin plastic or metal strip may fix the problem to some extent, but it isn't much of a barrier to creeping plants; instead, consider an edging that's 4 inches (10 cm) wide or more, made out of concrete pavers, cut stone, brick, or something similarly hard wearing. That way, you can run the wheels on one side of your mower on top of the edging and cut a neat edge each time you mow.

PLANTING PREP

Drawing a garden on paper or in your imagination is one thing; actually getting the site ready for your perennials is quite another. Your new garden is hopefully going to be in place for a long time, so it's worth taking the time to prepare the site and get if off to a great start.

Getting Rid of Grass

Unless you're starting a garden around a just-built house, there's probably already grass or weeds (or both) growing in the space where you want to put your plants. Do *not* think that you can simply dig the grass into the soil, and then plant right away! Doing that does not kill the grass and weeds; it merely chops them up into thousands of pieces that will resprout and creep around quickly in the loosened soil. Trying to weed turf grass out of perennial clumps — and particularly out of ornamental grasses — is a nightmare no one needs to deal with.

The most obvious option is to remove the grass altogether. You could use a sharp spade held almost horizontally to cut the roots just under the soil surface, then remove the chunks of sod. Planning on getting rid of a *lot* of grass? Consider renting a power-driven sod cutter or hiring someone with one of these tools to strip off that turf in a jiffy. Pile the sod chunks soil-side-up in an out-of-the-way spot, and they'll decompose into nice, fluffy soil in a year or two. Or turn them over and use them as the base layer for a new raised bed.

Another route is to mow the grass and weeds as low as you can, then smother them. If you're not in a hurry to plant, you could cover the mown area with layers of newspaper (roughly 10 sheets thick), or with sheets of cardboard if you have tough creeping weeds or grass, and then top that with 4 to 6 inches (10 to 15 cm) of shredded bark or some other mulch. If you

A GARDEN WORKOUT A manual sod cutter takes lots of energy to use, but it's a handy tool to have on hand if you plan on doing a lot of garden-making. Whether you use a sod cutter, a spade, or some other tool, the idea is to cut deep enough to get the grass crowns and a good part of the surface roots, but not so deep that you take away lots of topsoil, too.

do this in fall, it's probably best to wait until the following fall to plant; if you start smothering in spring, you can usually plant in fall, or definitely the following spring.

Ready to get growing *now?* Mow and spread the newspapers over the site, then build a raised bed on top.

Building the Bed

Once the site is clear, you have another decision to make: are you going to loosen the existing soil, pile more soil on top to make a raised bed, or use some combination of those two approaches? Unless large rocks make it impractical, loosening the exposed soil is generally a good way to start. You can hand-dig it with a shovel or spading fork or use a rotary tiller to loosen the top 8 inches (20 cm) or so of soil. If you want to boost your soil's organic matter, spread 1 to 2 inches (2.5 to 5 cm) of compost or aged manure over the site and work it in as you dig or till. If you wish to loosen clayey or compacted soil permanently, try digging or tilling in a ½- to 1-inch (12 to 25 mm) layer of a gritty material, such as PermaTill or Profile (also sold as Schultz) Clay Soil Conditioner. As you prepare the site, work from one end to the other or from the middle outward, so you're not walking on the soil you've already loosened.

Some gardeners choose to raise the level of the planting area somewhat above the level of the surrounding soil. This gives the perennials extra rooting room if the existing soil is very rocky, tightly compacted, or otherwise too difficult to dig. Raised beds also tend to drain more quickly than ground-level gardens, so they're useful if you're trying to grow a wide range of perennials in a normally wet spot.

Usually, a raised bed is surrounded by a frame or low wall, made from stones, timbers, or some other material, to hold the soil in place. If you've already loosened the existing soil, topping it with an additional 4 to 6 inches (10 to 15 cm) of topsoil is good enough; if you didn't dig at all, try for at least 8 inches (20 cm) of topsoil. Or, try a "layering" technique, using some topsoil along with various types of organic matter: grass clippings, shredded leaves, aged manure, compost, and the like. Spread the topsoil and whatever organic materials you've chosen on top of each other

RAISING THE ROOTS Filling the frame of your raised bed with loose, weed-free topsoil alone creates fine conditions for many perennials. For those that thrive in richer soil, mix compost, mushroom soil, or aged manure with the topsoil (roughly 1 part organic matter to 2 to 4 parts of topsoil). Besides boosting fertility, the organic matter will hold more moisture, so the bed won't dry out as quickly.

in layers about 2 inches (5 cm) thick; the order doesn't really matter. A series of layers that starts out 1 foot (30 cm) thick will settle to roughly 6 inches (15 cm) deep after a few months and offer great rooting conditions for perennials.

SELECTING EASY-CARE PERENNIALS

You've found the perfect site for your new garden, and you've worked out a size and shape that allows you easy access for maintenance. Now, keep up the good work by putting as much care into your plant choices as you put into all of your other garden-related decisions!

Making Wise Buying Decisions

Of all the ways you can save time on garden maintenance, the most important one is also the simplest: base your plantings on perennials that are well suited to the growing conditions that your site and region have to offer. No matter how much you want to grow a particular plant, if it needs sun and dry soil and you can offer it only a shady, damp spot, it's likely that neither one of you is going to be happy.

Fortunately, many common garden perennials can adapt to a wide range of growing conditions. These time-tested favorites may not be as thrilling as the latest cutting-edge introductions, but they've proven their ability to survive in a variety of sites, climates, and care regimens over many years. They also tend to be less expensive, so you can buy more of them or start with larger pots to get a more immediate effect. A beautiful border filled with common but healthy and vigorous perennials is typically much more of a landscape asset than a collection of rarities that look fantastic in photographs but less than appealing in an average home garden.

So, remember: Unless you've already chalked up a number of years of gardening experience and can easily separate hype from reality, those gorgeous, glossy plant catalogs are *not* your friends when it comes time for choosing the major part of your perennial purchases. Books and magazines can be somewhat more impartial, but unless they're written for your specific region by someone with a lot of personal gardening experience there, they may not address unique local challenges you might face when selecting and growing perennials.

When it comes to figuring out which perennials will look the best with the least amount of fussing from you, your best bet is to draw on the experience of other gardeners in your area. As you're driving around, make a mental note of the perennials that are performing well in other people's yards. For a close-up look, go on all the local garden tours you can find and talk to the people who actually care for the plantings. Gardeners tend to be a friendly and generous lot, sharing their opinions on plants, tools, and techniques — and often actual plants, as well — with anyone who cares enough to ask. Gardening blogs and online gardening forums are other great ways to connect with gardeners who have practical experience with conditions similar to yours.

Despite our best intentions, most of us succumb to at least a few impulse plant purchases

HOLD IT! Instead of adding impulse plant purchases directly to your garden, consider growing them in a holding bed for a year or more, so you can learn about their needs first. It's also a great way to "bulk up" perennial seedlings or tiny mail-order purchases.

every year without doing our homework first. Experimenting with new plants is a great way to expand your gardening skills, after all (and to have something to impress gardening friends with, too, if you enjoy a little horticultural one-upmanship). It's fine to tuck these treasures into existing borders, if they're big enough to hold their own, but it's usually not wise to base a major part of a new garden on plants you've never grown before. If they perform poorly, the whole garden may look terrible, and you may create a serious maintenance headache for yourself as well. Instead, consider setting up a separate holding area, where you can give unplanned acquisitions a little extra care and attention until you see how they behave. For more information on building and using these mini test gardens, see Making the Most of Holding Beds on page 67.

Fuss-Free Perennial Features

Even after separating out the perennials that aren't well suited to your site and climate, you'll still have dozens to hundreds of suitable perennials to choose from. To whittle down your options, look at obvious features, such as height, flower color, length of bloom time, foliage features, and so on. But don't forget to consider their maintenance needs, as well. Here's a rundown of some features that can cut down on the time you spend doing some of the less-fun gardening chores.

❖ **Don't like to spray?** Seek out perennial species and selections that have proven to be resistant to diseases that are common in your area. They still may show some symptoms, but they're far more likely to look respectable all season even without spraying.

❖ **Bored with deadheading?** If you find removing dead flowers a tedious task, avoid perennials that tend to need frequent deadheading to look tidy. Instead, consider those that have attractive seed heads, can get by with a single mid-season shearing, or are "self-cleaning," meaning that their dead blooms drop off on their own.

❖ **Overwhelmed with off-season cleanup?** Cutting down all of your perennials at one time is a big job and leaves you with a mountain of

FOLIAGE AND FLOWERS Concentrating on perennials with great-looking leaves may seem like an obvious way to minimize deadheading chores, but that's not always the case. These plants produce flowers, too, but their blooms are typically removed in favor of the foliage, so you won't be saving yourself much work in the long run.

debris to deal with. One alternative is to base your borders on perennials that offer winter interest, in the form of interesting seed heads, long-lasting leaves and stems, or evergreen foliage. Then spread out your cleanup sessions into smaller chunks through the winter months, cutting down only the plants that have started to lose their good looks.

REWORKING ESTABLISHED GARDENS

No matter how carefully you plan them, all gardens need a little (or a lot) of tweaking as they mature. Some of the perennials may not have performed as well as you'd hoped; others may have grown larger or wider than you expected. There may also be some plants that look great but take more attention (in the form of watering, staking, and so on) than you want to invest. Maybe you overlooked some creeping weeds for a season or two and now have a serious problem to fix. Or perhaps you skimped on soil preparation at planting time and now want to do a more thorough job. There are also all kinds of design-related reasons you might want to make changes, such as fine-tuning color combinations or adding textural contrast. In any of these cases, the solution may be as simple as shifting a few clumps around or as drastic as clearing out everything and starting from scratch.

Evaluating Existing Plantings

A couple of times during the growing season, take a stroll around your yard with a notebook. Look at each border with a critical eye, and make notes about what you'd like to change and what really needs to be fixed. It's also a good idea to take photos of each bed and border from a couple of different angles. That way, you'll know exactly what needs to be done in fall or early spring, and you'll have a visual record of where each plant is, even if your perennials are dormant then.

Generally speaking, newly planted gardens shouldn't need major reworking for the first 4 to 5 years, unless you deliberately set your perennials close together at planting time or you made some poor design decisions at the outset.

You can fix many design or maintenance problems by leaving some of the perennials in place and dividing, moving, or replacing some others. If you want to do some major soil improvement or completely change your plant choices or planting style, or if there's a major problem with creeping perennials, self-sown seedlings, or weeds, then it's worth digging up everything, enriching the soil with organic matter, loosening it up with soil conditioners (if needed), and then replanting.

WORTH WAITING FOR Many perennials need to be in place for at least three years to settle in, fill out, and look their best, so don't be in a hurry to consider them a disappointment.

Smart Strategies for Reworking Beds and Borders

Exactly how you approach doing minor fine-tuning or major renovations depends on your available time and energy. You might choose a systematic approach, completely digging up and replanting one garden each year, or doing one in spring and one in fall. Or, you might prefer to tackle only individual plants or small sections, so you spread out the work over a longer period. Either way, here are some tips to help you get the most out of your efforts.

❖ On-the-spot soil improvement. When you dig up a perennial to move or divide it, or when you dig a new planting hole in an existing bed, add a shovelful or two or compost to the hole and mix it into the soil a bit before replanting.

❖ Clean and quarantine. If creeping perennials or weeds have tangled themselves into clumps of plants you want to keep, lift the good clumps, wash off the soil, and carefully pick out all of the weed roots you can find. Unless you are positive you have gotten all of the weeds, consider planting the cleaned-up clumps in a "quarantine" bed (separate from your other gardens) for a season or two. Repeat the cleaning process if the creepers reappear; otherwise, you can move the clumps back to your garden once you're sure they're weed free. If perennial clumps get inextricably intertwined with weeds, you may be best off discarding them and starting with new plants.

❖ Smother the spreaders. In areas where creeping plants have taken over, you could try digging out all of the root pieces you can find, but you'll likely miss a few and the weeds will be back in no time. Instead, cover the area with a sheet of cardboard (or newspaper, in a layer roughly 10 to 20 sheets thick), then top it with about 6 inches (10 to 15 cm) of mulch and let it sit for a full year or two before replanting.

❖ Keep seeds under cover. A similar smother technique can help in areas where self-sown perennials or annual weed seedlings are a problem. But

CULLING ALL VOLUNTEERS! A few self-sown seedlings can be welcome, but an overabundance is a maintenance problem. To prevent future "volunteers," make sure you remove the seed heads of problem plants.

in this case, you'd use a thinner newspaper layer (roughly 5 to 10 sheets thick). Remove the perennials and dig compost or other organic matter into the soil before replanting, if you need to. Then cover the soil between the plants with newspaper topped with 1 to 2 inches (2.5 to 5 cm) of mulch.

❖ Get edgy. While you're reworking or renovating, it's worth taking the time to add some sort of edging strip to minimize tedious trimming and give your garden a sharp, neat outline. (See Don't Forget the Edge on page 13 for more information.)

❖ Know when to give up. If there's an area of your yard where you simply can't get perennials to thrive, no matter how hard you try, then it may be time to try something else. Consider covering the spot with mulch, gravel, or decking and using it for a sitting area, for instance, or set a collection of pots or a special garden ornament there.

Watch Out for Problem Plants

IT NEVER FAILS: We do everything we can to get our perennials off to a good start, and we spend the first few years worrying about them not growing as fast as we'd hoped. Then, we start worrying about those that are *too* vigorous: the spreaders that are crowding out their companions, and the self-seeders whose seedlings pop up all over the place.

BAD BOYS While you can still find purple loosestrife (*Lythrum salicaria*) sold as a garden perennial, this prolifically self-sowing nonnative is considered seriously invasive in wetlands and is classified as a noxious weed in many parts of the United States. Spike gayfeather (*Liatris spicata*) can be a suitable (and safer) substitute.

❖ Creepers. Aggressive perennials aren't always bad. In fact, some can be a real blessing in the right site. With those that spread by creeping roots, the trick is to save them for tough sites where less vigorous perennials simply won't thrive — dry shade, for instance, or hot, dry slopes. In these difficult growing conditions, "problem" perennials can look great without the extra pampering that less vigorous plants would require. Or, you could combine all of your spreading perenni-

als into one border and let them fight each other for space. Digging up and dividing the clumps every year or two, growing them in containers, or planting them in beds surrounded by paving or another hard surface are other possibilities. If you really want to keep a creeper in your regular garden, you could try surrounding it with some sort of barrier to keep its roots contained, such as a bottomless pot or bucket sunk nearly to its rim in the soil.

❖ Self sowers. Perennials that self-sow prolifically are both easier and trickier than creepers to deal with. The basic solution is simple: remove the flowers before they produce seed, and you'll never get any seedlings. That's not always as easy as it sounds, though. Unless you check your perennials every day or two, you may not notice that the flowers have formed seed before it's too late to cut them off. And sometimes, you want to leave the seed heads because they are interesting to look at.

The most challenging aspect of dealing with self-sowing perennials is that you often don't know if they're going to be a problem for a few years. You may notice just one or a few seedlings in the second or third year and be pleased to have them. Then one spring, you start noticing the volunteers appearing *everywhere*, and you're stuck trying to weed them out of your beds, borders, and paving. For the most part, it's just one of those things that make gardening such an interesting and unpredictable experience. But if you have advance warning that a particular perennial *might* be a problem, you can take steps to prevent it from getting out of hand. You'll find tips on coping with the creeping or seeding habits of specific perennials in the individual plant entries in Part Two, starting on page 121.

❖ Invasives. We gardeners are also becoming more aware that the plants we choose to grow can have an impact beyond our own yards. They may not cause a problem in our own gardens, but their seeds can sprout and grow in woodlands, along waterways, and in other natural areas, crowding out the native plants and interfering with natural ecosystems. As with

GOING TO SEED Beware of some plants, like maiden grass (*Miscanthus sinensis*) that have decorative seed heads but self-sow too prolifically.

aggressive perennials, these invasive plants may be a serious problem in some conditions and regions and perfectly well behaved in others. The responsible approach is to familiarize yourself with the garden plants that are considered invasive in your area. (One good resource is the Plant Conservation Alliance's Alien Plant Working Group. Turn to Resources, page 355, for the Web site.) If you find out that a perennial you already have or want to buy is considered a problem, think about replacing it with a similar but noninvasive option.

Chapter Two
CARING FOR YOUR PERENNIALS

PLANTING AND MOVING PERENNIALS

Of all the skills it takes to grow a garden, planting and transplanting are the two most important skills you need to learn. Obviously, you need to know how to get new plantings into the ground to get your beds and borders growing in the first place. Then, once your perennials are in the ground, there are any number of reasons why you may want or need to move them. So whether you're starting a garden for the first time or fine-tuning your transplanting skills, let's dig in and start putting those perennials in their place!

Perennial Planting 101

Once you've prepared the soil where you're going to start a new garden, you're at the fun part: actually getting your plants in the ground! Read on for the scoop on setting out new container-grown and bare-root perennials.

❋ **Getting ready to plant.** Whenever possible, plan your planting for an overcast day, ideally just before rain is due, to reduce the stress on your plants.

To make sure the rootballs of container-grown perennials are thoroughly moist, lower each plant — pot and all — into a bucket or tub of water and hold it down so the water covers the surface of the growing mix. Bubbles will rise as water replaces the air in the rootball. Once no more bubbles are visible (usually anywhere from 1 to 10 minutes, depending on the size of the pot and how dry the growing mix is), remove the pot from the water. If the plant was very dry, you may want to do this step the day before planting, then repeat it on planting day; otherwise, just let it drain for a minute or two before moving on to the next step.

top growth

crown

rootball

The *crown* of a perennial is the point where the roots join the top growth. Usually, the crown should be about the same level as the soil surface after planting.

When you're starting with plants growing in individual containers, it's fine to set them out onto the prepared soil in the places where you want them; in fact, that's a great way to fine-tune their spacing and arrangement before planting. You could even go ahead and dig all of the planting holes once you're satisfied with their placement. Don't be tempted to remove all of your perennials from their pots at the same time, though. It's best to plant them one at a time, so the exposed roots won't have time to dry out.

For bare-root perennials, remove the packing material, then soak the roots in a bucket of warm water for an hour or two just before planting. (If you're planting several different bare-root

Planting and Transplanting Calendar

🔵 Spring (March–May)

In general, the spring months are prime time for planting and transplanting, especially for perennials that bloom in summer and fall. Early to midspring, in particular, is fine for transplants and potted plants of all sizes and particularly good if you're starting with small plants (those grown in cell packs or small pots, for example). Early to midspring is also the best time for setting out bare-root perennials, but late spring can be fine if the plants weren't available sooner or if conditions weren't right for planting.

Exactly when you can start in spring may vary widely from year to year, depending on the temperature (you'll need to wait until the ground thaws, at least) and the amount of rainfall (you can start working earlier in a dry spring than a wet one). Loose, sandy soil tends to dry out and warm up relatively quickly if the season is mild, letting you start as soon as early March. If your soil tends to be clayey and the spring is cool and rainy, you might have to wait as late as mid- or even late April to begin planting and transplanting.

Frost isn't an issue if you're planting or transplanting perennials that have been outdoors during the winter. But if you've started seedlings indoors or purchased perennials that have been in a warm greenhouse, which encourages them to produce leaves and even flowers several weeks before they'd start sprouting outdoors, you'll want to protect them from freezing temperatures. For more information on helping them to make the transition outdoors, see Handling Hardening Off, page 64.

⚙ Summer (June–August)

Mid- to late summer can be a good time to plant or move perennials that flower in spring or early summer and then mostly or completely die back to the ground — such as Oriental poppy (*Papaver orientale*) and common bleeding heart (*Dicentra spectabilis*).

In the case of actively growing plants, it's ideal to finish planting and transplanting tasks before early summer, but if you *really* need to, you can keep setting out container-grown plants and moving established clumps of many perennials through this period. To improve your chances of success, try to wait until the start of a rainy — or at least cloudy — spell that's predicted to last for several days. When rain is lacking, be prepared to pay close attention to watering, so the soil doesn't dry out. Providing temporary shade during hot, sunny weather is a big help, too. Cutting back the top growth of transplants by about one-half reduces water loss through the leaves, offering another way to improve your odds of success.

perennials, soak each kind in a separate container so you don't get them mixed up.)

❈ Planting perennials from cell packs. Plastic "cell packs" have long been familiar to gardeners who grow annuals, and sometimes you can find perennial seedlings sold in them, too. They offer a relatively inexpensive way to start a new garden, but the individual plants are small, so most will take a season or more to fill out and flower well. You have two options: plant them at the proper spacings (1 to 2 feet [30 to 60 cm] apart for most), and then fill in among them with low-growing annuals or mulch, or set them relatively close together (8 to 12 inches [20 to 30 cm] apart) to get a more immediate impact, and then plan to move some to another area in a year or two to prevent overcrowding.

🍁 Fall (September–November)

In many parts of the country, the fall months offer perfect planting conditions. The usually mild temperatures make it a pleasure to be out digging, rainfall tends to be more dependable, and the combination of warm soil and cooler air encourages your perennials to put their energy into producing new roots instead of foliage and flowers. This season is an especially good time to plant or move spring-bloomers so they'll be settled in and ready to grow as soon as winter is over.

Exactly how long into fall you can continue planting container-grown perennials and transplanting established clumps varies widely. One rough guideline many gardeners like to use is to finish up about 6 weeks before the ground starts to freeze. If you're not sure when that happens in your area, try to finish by early September in Zones 1 and 2, mid-September in Zones 3 and 4, late September in Zone 5, late October in Zone 6, and mid-November in Zone 7. South of there, soil freezing is rarely an issue, so you can keep planting through the winter months.

Like all gardening rules, these times are flexible, depending on your local conditions. In areas that tend to have a dependable blanket of snow from late fall or early winter to late winter, for example, you may continue planting and transplanting until the snow starts to fall, knowing that it will protect them from the winter freezing-and-thawing cycles that can push unprotected perennials right out of the soil if they haven't had time to form new roots. In areas with alternating cold and mild spells but without snow cover, it's a good idea to finish planting and transplanting as early as possible, and to provide a protective mulch for the first winter.

Mail-ordered bare-root plants may not arrive until mid- or late fall, but you don't have to wait until then to prepare their new homes. Get the holes ready earlier in the fall, while the weather is still pleasant, then you can quickly pop them into the ground when they finally do arrive.

❋ Winter (December–February)

If you live where snow constantly blankets the ground all through the winter, your work is done until spring. Otherwise, take a stroll through your garden once a week or so (especially during warm spells), and make sure none of your new fall plantings have been pushed out of the ground. If they have, gently push them back into the soil, if possible; otherwise, pile more mulch around them to keep the roots from drying out until you can replant properly in spring.

To remove a perennial seedling from a cell pack, hold its top growth with the fingers of one hand while you use the other hand to pull off the plastic cell it's in. It's likely that the roots will be circling around the outside of the growing mix; carefully tease them loose with your fingers or with the point of a pencil to straighten them out a bit. If they are very tightly wound, you may want to snip each side of root mass with garden shears, cutting about ¼ inch (6 mm) deep, to stop the circling and encourage new roots to grow outward. Set each plant in its hole so the crown is about even with the soil surface, then pull the soil back around the roots and use moderate pressure to firm the ground around the plant with your fingers.

❖ Planting potted perennials. Most perennials are sold in square or round plastic pots that range in size from about 4 inches (10 cm) to 12 inches (30 cm) across. If you're working with small pots or those with very thin sides, you can loosen the rootball by squeezing the sides with your fingers or hands. With larger or thicker pots, lay the plant on its side and gently tap or roll the pot with your foot to help release the rootball. If you can't easily remove a plant by cradling the base of the plant and the top of the rootball with one hand and sliding off the pot with your other hand, you may need to slit the sides of the pot to get it off. (Most perennials can survive a few tugs on their leaves, and they'll recover even if a few leaves get broken, but if you pull too hard on the top growth and end up snapping the top off right at its base, you'll set the plant back severely and possibly even kill it.)

LEFT To judge the planting depth for a bare-root perennial, lay a stake across the top of the hole to show the final soil level. If needed, add or remove some soil from the mound you've made in the center of the planting hole to ensure that the crown will sit at the right height.

RIGHT If the roots of pot-grown perennials are too tightly matted to loosen with your fingers, use a sharp knife to cut slashes about ½ inch (12 mm) deep every few inches (cm) around the rootball, and on the bottom, too.

With your fingers, ruffle all sides of the rootball to loosen any circling roots and knock off any loose growing mix. Set the rootball in the planting hole, then add or remove soil under the rootball to get the plant sitting at the right height. You generally want the crown — where the roots join the stems — about even with the soil surface. If the bed you've prepared is very loose and fluffy, though, set the crown about ¼ inch (6 mm) higher to allow for settling. Push the soil back around the roots to fill the hole, then firm it using moderate pressure with your hands. (Instead of filling the hole all in one step, some gardeners prefer to fill the hole it only halfway, then add enough water to make the soil soupy. Give it a minute or two to soak in, then finish filling the hole.)

❖ Planting bare-root perennials. Dig a planting hole as you normally would, then replace some of the loosened soil to make a mound in the center. Set the crown (center) of the plant on top, add or remove soil so the crown will be about even with the soil surface (or about 2 inches [5 cm] lower, if you're planting peonies), and spread the roots out as evenly as possible on the sides of the mound. Replace the soil to fill the hole, and firm it using moderate pressure with your hands.

❖ **Aftercare for newly planted perennials.**
Unless you've perfectly timed your planting project to end just before a steady rain starts, water all newly planted perennials as soon as possible. In hot, dry weather, keep a watering can handy to give each perennial a drink before moving to the next plant, then water the whole bed thoroughly as soon as you're finished planting. If it's relatively cool and cloudy out, you can wait to water until you're all done planting the bed or border. Keep watering regularly (roughly once or twice a week during dry weather) through the first growing season. Mulch can also benefit new plantings; so can light doses of organic fertilizers for spring to midsummer plantings. (For more details, see Watering Your Perennials on page 30, Fertilizing and Soil-Building on page 36, and Choosing and Using Mulches on page 41.)

Moving Your Perennials

In the excitement and exhaustion of preparing a new bed or border and planting perennials there for the first time, it's tough to imagine ever wanting to dig them up again — but it's almost

THE KINDEST CUT If you must move plants while they're actively growing (like this rumex), cutting them back to about one-half their original height can help reduce some of the stress of transplanting. Remove any remaining flower buds, as well.

inevitable that you will. You may find that the area is getting more or less light or is wetter or drier than you anticipated, making it necessary to move some of the plants to a site they're better suited to. You might decide to shift some plants around to fine-tune the design or experiment with combinations you didn't think of at planting time. And you'll need to divide most perennials every few years, which usually involves digging them up and results in extra pieces that you can plant elsewhere in your yard or share with friends.

It's easy to be intimidated by the thought of disturbing an established perennial and taking the chance that you might somehow kill it in the process. This is especially true if you've seen lists of perennials that supposedly "hate" to be moved

LIFTING A PERENNIAL CLUMP Digging in a circle that's 2 to 4 inches (5 to 10 cm) farther out from the outer edge of the crown is usually about right. If that makes a root ball too large for you to carry, divide the clump to create smaller sections that you can move comfortably.

— usually those with long or easily broken roots, such as balloon flowers (*Platycodon*), columbines (*Aquilegia*), hollyhocks (*Alcea*), lupins (*Lupinus*), and poppies (*Papaver*), to name just a few. But if it's a matter of the plant growing in a poor spot, you're often better off trying to move it than leaving it in place to die a slow death. And enough gardeners have had success moving these "do not disturb" perennials that it's worth trying yourself, as long as you can accept that yes, it *might* die. Chances are that it won't, though.

When moving any perennial, your odds of success are usually greatest if you move it within a few weeks of its bloom period ending. That's why fall planting is so popular with many perennial gardeners: the transplants have several months to settle in and produce new roots, so they're in prime form to grow normally next spring. Moving them just *before* they start growing (February to April for most perennials) can be all right, too. The least ideal time to move perennials is when they're fully leafed out — and particularly when they're blooming — but it's possible to succeed even then if you're willing to provide some special attention afterward. Any transplanted clump may not grow quite as tall or bloom quite as well as usual during the first year or two after the move; it may even skip flowering altogether. But if it's in a good site, it should eventually return to its former glory — and maybe even look and bloom better than ever.

❖ Getting ready for the move. The same conditions that make for good planting weather — an overcast or drizzly day just before a rainy spell — are also ideal for transplanting. The day before you plan to transplant, water the clumps thoroughly. And to minimize the time the clump will be out of the ground, make sure its new site is ready for it *before* you dig it up. Don't skimp on the size of the planting hole: make it about as deep and ideally twice as wide as the rootball you plan to put in it. (You'll have to estimate that, since you haven't actually dug the rootball yet, but a hole that's roughly 18 to 24 inches [45 to 60 cm] across and 6 to 8 inches [15 to 20 cm] deep is usually about right for an established perennial clump.)

❖ Digging and moving the plants. Generally speaking, the more soil you take with the roots at transplanting time, the less damage they'll suffer

and the more quickly the plant will recover. Large rootballs are heavy, though, and may be difficult to move. So usually, it's a matter of compromise: dig a rootball you can easily carry for most perennials, and try for a somewhat larger one for perennials that have a reputation for disliking transplanting.

Most gardeners use a shovel for transplanting because its curved blade will naturally cut downward and toward the center of the plant, creating a roughly rounded rootball. If you must use a spade, insert it into the soil at about a 45-degree angle, so each cut will meet at about the same point below the soil surface. Either way, insert the blade of the tool as smoothly and deeply as you can in one pass to cut the roots as cleanly as possible. A rootball that's 6 to 8 inches (15 to 20 cm) deep works fine for most perennials.

Once you've worked your way all around the plant with your shovel or spade, lift out the rootball and pull it to the side of the hole. Divide it now, if you wish (see Dividing Your Perennials on page 84 for details). Lift and carry the plant to its new home, knocking off as little soil as possible in the process. Set the clump or division into the center of the hole, adding or removing soil as needed to have the crown of the plant at the same level it was growing before. Push some of the soil back around the roots, add enough water to create a soupy mix, and then let it drain for a minute

MADE FOR SHADE Transplants moved to sunny sites benefit from some temporary screening. Set a lawn chair or laundry basket over each clump, or drape a light sheet over a tomato cage, to supply light shade for the first few days.

or two before replacing the rest of the soil. Settle the soil around the clump by pressing firmly with your hands.

Transplanting only one clump at a time is the best approach. That way, each plant is out of the ground for only a few minutes. If you can't replant immediately, set the clump in a plastic shopping bag, place it in a shady spot, and keep the soil moist. Most perennials can last a few days this way. If the plant's new home won't be ready for a week or more, planting it in a pot or holding bed may be a better option.

❖ Aftercare for transplants. If you've transplanted in early spring or fall, your perennials may hardly know they've been moved; just water them thoroughly once after planting and again during dry spells for the rest of the growing season. Actively growing plants need watering every few days for the first week or two, and then weekly watering during dry spells through the rest of the season. Providing some shade for the first few days can also help minimize wilting.

WATERING YOUR PERENNIALS

Ah, the eternal gardening question: Should I water, or should I wait? Trying to decide which plants to water, when to do it, and how much to give them can be enough to keep your head spinning if you take it all too seriously. Yes, there are times when you'll need to supply water beyond what Mother Nature provides, but it doesn't have to be a life-or-death dilemma: just use your common sense and remember that most perennials are tough enough to survive even when their growing conditions aren't ideal.

Sunny slopes tend to be dry, providing ideal conditions for perennials that appreciate good drainage, such as lavenders (*Lavandula*) and butterfly weed (*Asclepias tuberosa*).

Keep Watering Chores to a Minimum

Unless you actually enjoy spending your summers worrying about watering, it just makes sense to do everything you can to reduce the need for it in the first place. Here are some sensible ways to save yourself time and effort — and save a precious natural resource as well.

❖ **Choose perennials adapted to your area.** Reducing watering needs is one of the best reasons to build your gardens around native perennials: plants that have adapted over the millennia to the soil and weather conditions that are common in your area. Each perennial you choose that can withstand a wetter-than-usual year without rotting and a drier-than-average year without withering away is one less plant you need to worry about, no matter what the weather.

❖ **Make the most of your site.** Even in a small yard, there are likely to be some spots that are a bit drier or wetter that others. In areas that tend to be dry — slopes, beds along sidewalks and driveways, borders right next to the house, or the spot where the roof overhang blocks the rain-

fall — stick with perennials described as being drought tolerant or liking very well-drained soil. Grow moisture-loving plants in sites that naturally tend to be damp, such as areas near gutter downspouts.

❖ Group perennials with similar watering needs. Make your life a whole lot easier by keeping moisture-loving plants closest to the house, where you can keep an eye on them and easily reach them if they need water. Farther out is fine for perennials that can survive moderate dry spells; if you have to drag a hose out to them once or twice a summer, it's not a big burden. Drought-tolerant plants are ideal for the parts of your yard farthest from the house, and for areas where it's simply not practical to water.

❖ Prepare the planting site carefully. Skimping on soil preparation before planting can cost you a lot of watering time in the long run. When you prepare a whole planting area, loosening the soil and adding compost or other organic matter, you provide ideal conditions for the roots of your perennials to spread deeply and widely. The same perennials set into small, individually dug holes (particularly in sites with tight, clayey soil) are likely to have much more limited root systems, and they'll be more dependent on you for watering during even short dry spells.

❖ Plant and transplant at the right time. The longer a plant stays in one place, the more roots it has, and the farther they can spread to seek out moisture. Perennials that have been in one spot for a full growing season or longer usually need watering far less often than those planted or transplanted during the current year.

❖ Apply appropriate mulches. Bare soil can lose a lot of moisture to evaporation, especially during sunny, breezy weather — just when your plants need it most. Covering the ground between your plants with some kind of mulch shades the soil, reducing the amount of water lost. Chopped leaves, compost, and other organic mulches also add some humus to your soil as they decompose, improving its ability to hold moisture.

WATER OR WAIT? Go to the root of the matter to judge if you should water your perennials or not. If the top 3 to 4 inches (7.5 to 10 cm) of soil are dry, it's time to irrigate.

Deciding When to Water

You'll often hear the rule of thumb that perennials need 1 inch (2.5 cm) of water, from either rainfall or irrigation, every week. That's fine advice — for some perennials, in some areas, and at some times of the year. The truth is, plants don't follow set schedules, so routinely dumping that much water on established perennials once a week may be more likely to harm them than help them. How often and how much you should water really depend on one thing: How dry is the soil?

Sometimes, the plants themselves will tell you. If they wilt a bit in the afternoon but perk up in the evening, they can probably wait a day or two for water. If they are still wilted the next morning, though, you'll need to water them as soon as possible (ideally, that morning). Depending on the "wilt factor" isn't the most accurate way to go, but it's quick and good enough in most cases. A far better approach, though, is to actually look below the soil surface. Brush any mulch off of the soil in one spot, then dig down 3 to 4 inches (7.5 to 10 cm) with a trowel. If the soil is dry down that far, it's a good idea to water as soon as possible. If only the top 1 to 2 inches (2.5 to 5 cm) are dry,

💧 Spring (March–May)

Perennials that you've just planted or transplanted benefit from watering once or twice a week if rain is lacking, while established plants (those that have been in place for a year or more) generally need supplemental watering only every week or two during hot, dry spells. If the long-range weather forecast for your area predicts a dry summer, try to wait the full two weeks (or even a bit longer) between thorough waterings of established perennials during spring; that schedule will help your plants toughen up a bit and help reduce the amount of water they'll need later on.

⚙ Summer (June–August)

Spring plantings and transplants still benefit from weekly watering when summer rainfall is scarce. Perennials that you plant or move during the summer months need extra-careful watering: figure every day for the first few days (especially if the weather is hot, dry, or windy, or any combination of those factors), then every 2 to 3 days for the next few weeks. As a very general rule, established plantings of most perennials look best if they get about 1 inch (2.5 cm) of rainfall or irrigation each week through the summer. However, most can get by (even if they don't look lovely) if you water them only once every 2 to 3 weeks. Many can survive for a month or more if you simply can't supply supplemental water.

🍁 ❄ Fall & Winter (September–February)

Rainfall tends to be more dependable in fall than in summer, but if it's lacking, remember to water new plantings and transplants regularly (roughly every 2 to 4 days), at least for the first month or so. If late-season rainfall is undependable, keep watering once every week in sandy-soil gardens or every 2 to 4 weeks in more clayey soil, right up until the ground freezes or is covered by snow (or all through the winter in mild areas). The same guidelines for summer-watering established perennials apply here as well, at least into midfall.

don't water yet; replace the soil and mulch and plan to check again in 2 or 3 days if no rain is due. Remember, these guidelines apply only to *established* perennials. Those you've planted or moved recently have much more limited root systems, so they need watering far more often. (See the Watering Calendar above.)

As for the time of day, the right time to water is basically whenever your schedule allows. If you're using some kind of overhead watering (a sprinkler, for instance, or a hand-held watering wand), early morning is ideal; you won't lose so much moisture to evaporation, and the leaves won't stay wet for long, reducing the chance for some disease problems. But if you're using a watering can for spot watering, or an irrigation system that wets the soil but not the plants, any time of day is fine.

Ways to Water Perennials

Spending a few minutes sprinkling your perennials with a hose every evening may be relaxing for you, but it doesn't do much good for your plants. The secret to irrigating established perennials effectively is to water *deeply*, not *often*. The general rule is to apply the equivalent of 1 inch (2.5 cm) of rainfall, which should be enough to thoroughly soak the top 4 to 5 inches (10 to 12.5 cm)

of soil. Applying this much water at one time can be a slow process, because you want to make sure the water is being absorbed instead of running off. Loose, sandy soil may absorb the water as fast as you can supply it, while hard, clayey soil may need short spells of watering over the period of a few hours for all the water to soak in. (Keep in mind that sandy soil will also dry out again much more quickly than the clayey soil.)

Here's an overview of the various ways to supply water to your perennials. Most gardeners use a combination of two or more techniques, depending on the size of their yard and their usual watering patterns.

LEFT Some watering cans come with a "rose": an attachment that fits onto the spout, with many tiny holes to soften the flow of the water.

RIGHT A watering wand with a breaker at the tip (to soften the flow of the water) extends your reach and lets you deliver water right where you need it.

❧ Watering can. For spot-watering individual plants, a watering can is a must-have. Figure on applying one-half to 1 gallon (1.9 to 3.8 l) of water per plant. A 2-gallon (7.6 l) can is a good size to choose; larger ones are very heavy when filled, though they can save you steps if you have several

Avoiding Hose Woes

DRAGGING HOSES AROUND isn't just a hassle — it can be a real heartbreak, too. Even if you're being very careful, it's easy for the hose to flip or shift right into the garden, breaking or crushing your plants in the process. An easy way to prevent this is by installing hose guides along the edges and at the corners of your beds and borders. These simple barriers extend several inches (cm) above and below the soil, protecting your plants as you pull the hoses around.

You can buy commercial hose guides (they're functional but often not very attractive) or create your own from more decorative items such as rocks or sections of copper tubing.

plants to water. If you don't use a rose on your watering can, tip it very slowly to let the water out gently, or the force of the flow may wash soil away from the crown and roots.

Pros: Watering cans are generally inexpensive, readily available, and easy to use.

Cons: They can be heavy and hard to carry, and they hold enough water for only a few plants.

❖ **Hand-held hoses and hose-end tools.** You can find a wide variety of plastic and metal watering attachments to fit on the end of your garden hose. Experiment with a few different ones to find out which work best for your watering needs. (Some produce a strong spray that's fine for filling watering cans but too powerful to use directly on garden plants or bare soil.) Regardless of which spray attachment you select, it's worth investing in a hose-end shut-off attachment, too; that way, you can temporarily stop the water flow as needed without traipsing all the way back to the spigot.

Pros: Hoses and hand-held attachments are relatively inexpensive, and they let you apply as much water as you have patience for.

Cons: Someone needs to be there to hold and drag the hose around for however long it takes to supply enough water to soak the soil thoroughly. You can reach only as far as the hose extends. Trigger-type spray attachments can be too forceful and are tiring to hold.

❖ **Overhead sprinklers.** Some sprinklers spray water in a constant pattern, while others twist or spin to vary where the water falls. Overhead sprinklers can be useful for watering newly planted gardens. They're less effective where the dense foliage of established plants blocks some of the moisture from reaching the root zone.

Pros: Sprinklers don't need to be constantly supervised, but you should check them often to make sure the water is falling where you need it to, and that it's soaking in rather than running off.

Cons: Sprinklers wet the foliage as well as the soil, possibly encouraging some disease problems. Some water is lost to evaporation before it reaches the soil. And you need to move the sprinkler at intervals to make sure the area is evenly watered.

TOP To install a soaker hose, lay it along the front of the border, about 18 inches (45 cm) in from the edge. When you get near the other side, bend the hose and run it back the other way, so it's parallel to and about 2 feet (60 cm) apart from the first pass. Continue as needed to cover the whole planting area. If needed, hold the hose in place with metal pins.

BOTTOM If water tends to run off instead of soak in when you use a watering can or sprinkler, create individual "water collars" for your perennials by cutting empty plastic pots into rings about 4 inches (10 cm) high. Slip a ring around each clump and push it about halfway into the soil. The ring will trap rain or irrigation water long enough to let it soak down to the root zone. Remove the rings in late fall.

❁ Drip irrigation systems. Watering systems that stay in your garden for the entire growing season are the ultimate in convenience. Your most basic option here is called a soaker hose; it resembles a heavy black garden hose but has many tiny pores in its surface and a cap at one end. When you attach the free end to a regular garden hose, the water slowly seeps out of the soaker hose, moistening the soil along its whole length. Cover all but the connection end of the hose with mulch, and you won't even see it — but it will be there when you need it. Fancier drip systems include lengths of solid-sided pipe with many smaller side pipes tipped by special "drip emitters." You can place these emitters right where you want them for individual plants.

Pros: Drip irrigation systems make watering as easy as turning on a faucet (or even easier, if you have them on an automatic timer). They save time and deliver water directly to the soil, without getting the foliage and flowers wet, and the flow rate is adjustable. Once installed, they can stay in place for months or years.

Cons: The initial cost of drip systems can be pricey. They need to be installed at planting time, or at least early in the growing season. You also need to check them regularly to make sure the water is coming out evenly, that it's going where you want it, and that it's not coming out faster than the soil can absorb it.

FERTILIZING AND SOIL-BUILDING

Ask a dozen gardeners how they fertilize their perennials, and you're likely to get a dozen different answers. It's also likely that each one will swear that their way is best, and they'll show you a beautiful, bloom-filled garden to prove it. So, what can you learn from that? Basically, that perennials are very adaptable plants, and that there simply isn't one "right" way to fertilize or one "right" material to choose.

Building Soil Fertility the Natural Way

You might be surprised to know that many successful gardeners never bother buying commercial fertilizers for their perennials. Instead, they rely on

soil amendments: primarily organic materials such as compost, mushroom soil, and animal manures.

While the purpose of a fertilizer is to supply specific amounts of nitrogen, phosphorus, potassium, or other nutrients, an amendment actually changes your soil in various ways. In A Place for Design on page 5, you learned how valuable organic matter is for loosening up tight clay soil and for improving the ability of sandy soil to hold moisture. By physically changing the soil, amendments make it easier for roots to spread throughout the soil, and the more roots a plant has, the more surface area it has to absorb nutrients.

Just as importantly, amendments can boost the biological health of your soil. Many kinds of beneficial soil organisms survive by feeding on organic matter, eventually releasing the nutrients they ingest in a form that roots can absorb. So, when you apply compost, leaf mold, manures, or some other organic material to your garden, you're feeding the soil organisms, which in turn feed your plants. It's part of a long-term process of building healthy soil, not simply a quick-fix shot of nutrients.

All this may seem like a rather roundabout way to make sure your perennials have the nutrients they need, but it's really not at all complicated. It's simply a matter of adding organic matter to your soil while you're doing other routine gardening tasks. Use materials you already have around your yard — such as homemade compost, grass clippings, chopped leaves — or buy bags or get bulk deliveries of mushroom soil, commercial compost, livestock manure, or whatever else is locally available. You don't need to stick with just one material; feel free to mix them up, or to use different materials as you get them. Below are some ways to add all of this good stuff to your soil.

SOIL-BUILDING ON THE SPOT Moving or dividing established perennials gives you a great opportunity to add organic matter to your soil. Each time you remove a plant, toss a shovelful or two of compost into the hole that's left before you replace the soil or set another plant in there.

Fertilizing Calendar

⬤ Spring (March–May)

If you prefer to use a synthetic fertilizer, sprinkle it around your perennials as new growth starts in spring, according to the directions on the packaging. (Rake off any existing mulch first, or apply it right on top and scratch it into the mulch a little with a rake or narrow-bladed hoe.) To give new plantings a boost, you may want to use a liquid starter fertilizer; follow the application instructions on the package.

⬤ Summer (June–August)

If you used a dry synthetic fertilizer on your established perennials in spring, you may want to make another application in midsummer. Or, apply a liquid fertilizer every few weeks in early and midsummer, if you wish. (Either way, follow the application instructions on the package.) The general rule is to stop fertilizing by the end of July; as fall approaches, you want your plants' growth to slow down in preparation for winter. Hold off on fertilizing anything you plant or transplant during the summer until fall or next spring. If you're a hands-off type of gardener, don't bother with any kind of fertilizing during the summer months.

⬤ ⬤ Fall & Winter (September–February)

If you use commercial dry or liquid fertilizers, check out the end-of-the-season sales for bargains, then store them in a dry place for later use. Late fall to late winter is a good time to apply a general-purpose organic fertilizer, compost, or manure around your perennials every 1 to 3 years, depending on the needs of individual plants.

❖ Building fertility before planting. Adding organic matter *before* you plant is your best opportunity to improve the soil below the surface, down where plant roots will benefit most from it. After you remove the grass and weeds, but before you loosen the soil, spread a layer of organic matter 1 to 3 inches (2.5 to 7.5 cm) thick over the area; then, dig or till it into the top 6 to 8 inches (15 to 30 cm) of ground. Or, spread layers of organic matter on top of the soil, then plant directly into them. (See Mulch Now, Plant Later on page 47.) This one step gets young plants off to a super start and meets their nutrient needs for at least the first year or two.

❖ Improving soil after planting. Spreading organic matter on top of your soil is a good way to keep beds and borders in good shape once your perennials are in place. In addition to all of the other benefits well-chosen mulches can give your garden, shredded bark, compost, chopped leaves, and other organic mulch materials supply a surface layer of organic matter as they break down. Then, earthworms and other soil-dwelling creatures help to mix the organic matter into the top layer of soil. Depending on the material you select, you may apply it several times a year, once a year, or once every 2 to 3 years. To learn more about applying and managing mulches, see Choosing and Using Mulches on page 41.)

TOP IT OFF Late fall is a great time to add a 2-inch-deep (5 cm) layer of chunky garden compost or composted livestock manure around your perennials. It will decompose during the winter, leaving your soil in great shape for spring.

Using Commercial Fertilizers

Sometimes, you may decide to take the extra steps of buying fertilizer materials and adding them to your garden. Which ones you choose, and how much of them you apply, depends on why you want to fertilize in the first place, and on what results you expect to get.

❧ **To correct specific deficiencies.** If you're a particularly detail-oriented person, if you suspect a particular plant is nutrient deficient, or if you're starting a perennial garden for the very first time, you might decide to have the nutrient levels in your soil tested. Inexpensive home-test kits can be fine

for checking pH, but in this case, it's worth investing a few more dollars to get a complete and accurate report of your soil's fertility status through your state's Cooperative Extension Service or a private soil-testing laboratory. If your test results indicate any nutrient imbalances, the report should tell you what to add to correct them.

Adjusting the levels of specific soil nutrients is easiest to do as you prepare the soil before planting. That way, you can mix the fertilizer throughout the root zone. Here, you'll use a dry material (usually in a granular or powder form), spreading the quantity recommended on your soil test report evenly over the area — along with whatever organic matter you are adding for long-term soil building — and digging or tilling it into the top 6 to 8 inches (15 to 20 cm) of soil.

If you need to make adjustments to the soil in established plantings, scatter the required amount of dry fertilizer over the soil in spring,

The pH Factor

SOME THINGS you can tell about your soil just by looking at or feeling it — how gritty (sandy) or smooth (clayey) it is, for instance. One thing you can't tell so easily is how acidic or alkaline it is. This numeric rating, commonly referred to as pH, can range from 0 (most acidic) to 14 (most alkaline), with 7 being neutral. Nutrients tend to be most readily available to plants when the soil pH is around 6.5 to 7.2. In some areas, the soil naturally falls into this range. Not all of us are so lucky, though; depending on where you live, your soil may be more acidic or alkaline than that.

Do you need to know your soil's exact pH? Not necessarily. If you have an established garden and the plants basically look okay, you don't need to worry much about it. But if you're having trouble growing particular plants successfully, or if you're curious to know exactly where your soil pH stands, it may be worth having a sample tested to see how it rates. A simple kit from your local garden center can give you a rough idea of the pH. For more accurate results, spend a few dollars more to get a complete soil test report through your state's Cooperative Extension Service. (You can find your local office by visiting the Web site listed on page 355.)

It's possible to raise the pH of an acidic soil by adding garden lime, or to lower the pH of an alkaline soil with sulfur or other materials. A much easier approach, though, is to match the plants you want to grow with the natural pH of your soil. Fortunately, most popular perennials are quite adaptable to a range of pH levels. If you really want to grow acid-loving plants in an alkaline-soil area, or those that prefer alkaline conditions in acidic soil, your best bet is to create one special area just for them, instead of trying to mix them with your other perennials.

LONG-TERM PROJECT The process of changing soil pH starts before you plant, as you get the soil ready for a new garden. Don't expect to make drastic changes; adjusting the pH even one point may take anywhere from several months to several years.

DON'T OVERDO IT! If you're planning to use a dry or liquid fertilizer to provide a general nutrient boost, please remember that more is not better, especially if you're using synthetic materials. Applying too much can damage your perennials, discoloring the leaves and possibly killing the roots, and it's not a problem you can easily fix.

then use a hand fork or metal rake to lightly scratch it into the soil surface. The nutrients in most synthetic (also called chemical) fertilizers are available soon after they come in contact with soil moisture, so you'll probably notice their effect within a week or two. "Organic" or "natural" fertilizers may take several months to a year or more to make a noticeable difference. In the meantime, you may want to treat your plants to a dose of a liquid fertilizer applied to the leaves or watered into the soil, so they can absorb the nutrients they need right away.

❖ To give plants or plantings a general boost. Some gardeners choose to scatter a general-purpose, dry organic fertilizer around their perennials every 1 to 3 years in late fall to late winter to help maintain balanced growth and the overall fertility of their garden soil. Bagged organic fertilizers are convenient to use, and they

can be a good option if you can't make enough compost to top-dress your perennial gardens every year. You should apply them according to the package directions, of course, but if you happen to use a little too much here and there, it shouldn't do much harm to your perennials:

– **Think before you fertilize.** If you choose to use synthetic fertilizers instead, you need to be very careful to apply them according to the directions on the label, because the nutrients they supply become available to plants much more quickly. Applying regular doses of synthetic fertilizer can speedily produce a lush-looking, flower-filled garden that's the envy of all your neighbors, but that beauty comes at a price, in the form of more maintenance work for you. Be prepared to stake your plants, for instance, because stems that grow fast and tall are also more likely to sprawl than their shorter, stockier counterparts. The tender tissue of lush leaves and stems can also be more enticing to animal and insect pests, and more susceptible to some disease problems as well, so be alert for signs of damage and be prepared to take control measures. Fast-growing perennials also may need to be dug up and divided every 2 or 3 years instead of every 3 to 5 years — a significant chore in even a medium-sized garden.

– **When to hold back.** Whether you choose organic or synthetic materials, there are some situations where you may want to fertilize only every second or third year, or even not at all. Fertilizing plants that naturally tend to spread a bit, for instance, can super-charge them into thugs that creep far and wide, crowding out their bedmates and creating large patches that can be a real hassle to get rid of. Other perennials are naturally adapted to soil that isn't especially fertile — lavenders (*Lavandula*) and butterfly weed (*Asclepias tuberosa*) are just two that come to mind. Fertilizing them may give them a boost in the short run, but over time, even organic fertilizers may cause them to be more prone to sprawling and other problems.

CHOOSING AND USING MULCHES

As with fertilizing, mulching is one of those garden tasks that some gardeners swear by and others don't bother with. There are plenty of good reasons to consider using mulches on your perennials — most obviously, because a uniform carpet of mulch provides a great-looking background for emerging flowers and foliage, making your whole yard look neat and cared-for in spring and early summer. Mulching can also cut down on the time you spend on other garden chores by stopping weeds before they sprout, and by shielding soil from hot sun and drying winds. Some mulches also contribute significantly to the health of your soil by adding organic matter and to the health and good looks of your plants by keeping them from being splashed by mud.

If you can't or don't want to deal with mulch, don't despair; you can still have a fine-looking perennial garden. If you really want the best from your beds and borders, it's worth learning how to make the most of mulch.

MULCHING WITH PLANTS Spaced so their foliage mingles just a bit, your plants themselves can provide some of the benefits of a mulch. Their leaves shade the soil, reducing temperature extremes, and protect it from baking sun, drying wind, and pounding rain. What a great excuse to add more plants to your gardens!

Mulching Calendar

◉ Spring (March–May)

If you applied mulch to your garden in late fall or early winter to protect your perennials, start taking it off in early spring. It's best not to remove it altogether, because spring freeze-and-thaw cycles can still damage delicate roots; just make sure the crowns aren't covered so the leaves can emerge when they're ready. If the remaining mulch is thicker than about 2 inches, remove some of the excess to give the soil a chance to warm up and dry out a bit. (Rake it into a pile on one side of the garden so you can easily put it back later, or add it to your compost pile.)

Once you see new growth on established perennials, or when you get new plants settled into their new homes, it's time to think about applying fresh mulch. Some gardeners like to mulch right away, thinking that it's easier to spread the mulch without lots of leaves getting in the way. Early to midspring mulching is fine when the weather is mild and on the dry side and where the soil tends to be sandy. Waiting until late spring (or even early summer) is a better option when the spring has been cold and rainy, or if your soil tends to be on the clayey side. It also takes less mulch to cover the same area if you wait, because the leaves of your perennials will have already filled in some of the space between the plants.

◉ Summer (June–August)

If a busy schedule or dreary spring weather kept you from mulching sooner, early summer is the time to get the job done. Wait until just after a soaking rain, or water thoroughly, then pull or dig out any weeds before spreading the mulch. If you use an organic mulch, you may need to apply more during the summer to keep the layer about 2 inches (5 cm) deep.

◉◉ Fall & Winter (September–February)

There are two reasons you might mulch in fall or winter: to protect plants during the winter or to maintain soil fertility. Many mulch materials, of course, serve both purposes. (For details on using mulches specifically for winter protection, see Choosing and Using Winter Mulches on page 55.) To maintain soil fertility, spread about 2 inches (5 cm) of compost or livestock manure or up to 6 inches (15 cm) of shredded leaves between your plants in late fall to late winter. It's okay to cover plants if they've died completely back to the ground, but try not to pile mulch directly on plants that still have visible foliage. Many gardeners like to wait until the ground is frozen to apply a winter mulch, hoping to discourage mice and voles from making their homes under the cozy mulch layer. But if snows come early in your area, you may need to mulch sooner and hope for the best.

What Makes a Good Mulch?

You have lots of choices when it comes to mulch materials. Those derived from plants, such as leaves, grass clippings, shredded bark, wood chips, and compost, are usually ideal because they're the ones that will help improve your soil. But there really is no one best mulch: it mostly depends on what you can afford and what you can physically handle.

If you can make plenty of compost or have access to lots of leaves in the fall, that will save you lots of money and hassle. When homemade supplies aren't available or aren't enough to meet your mulching needs, then your budget can play a big role in what you choose. Bagged mulches are generally the most expensive option, and it takes a lot of energy to lug all those bags around, too. (Figure that a 2-cubic-foot bag will cover 12 square feet 2 inches deep or 8 square feet 3 inches deep [a 56.5-liter bag will cover 1 sq. m 5 cm deep, or 0.75 sq. m 7.5 cm deep].)

Despite their higher price, bagged mulches may be a good option if you don't have a large garden to cover, or if it's not practical to have mulch delivered. Mulches sold in bulk (usually by the cubic yard, which covers about 160 square feet of garden about 2 inches [5 cm] deep) tend to be less expensive, but if you don't have access to a pickup truck, you'll need to pay for delivery as well. You'll also need a place to dump all that mulch until you are ready to use it. But on the plus side, you aren't left with a whole pile of plastic bags to dispose of.

If you really want to mulch your garden but simply don't have the time or physical ability to deal with the hauling and spreading work, consider hiring a landscaper to do it for you. It's not a cheap way to go, but the peace of mind of having the job over and done with can be priceless.

Exploring Your Options

Here's an overview of some popular and widely available mulches for flower gardens, along with their good and bad points. Other materials — such as buckwheat hulls, peanut shells, cocoa shells, and spent hops — are available in different regions, depending on local crops and industries. These are often less expensive than commercial mulches that have been hauled in, so if you like the look of them, give them a try instead.

❖ Compost. Compost is basically a mixture of partially to mostly decomposed organic materials: usually grass clippings, leaves, plant trimmings, kitchen scraps, and the like. Make as much compost as you can at home. To supplement your supply, buy commercially made compost, or see if your community offers free or low-cost compost to residents.

Tips: To keep your soil in good shape, apply a 2-inch (5 cm) layer every year or two, or use a 1-inch (2.5 cm) layer and top it with a longer-lasting mulch, such as shredded bark.

Pros: Compost is superb for enriching your soil. Homemade compost is free, and it gives you a way to recycle garden debris, as well.

Cons: Used alone as a mulch, compost can provide ideal growing conditions for weeds as well as desirable plants. For weed control, top compost with 1 to 2 inches (2.5 to 5 cm) of another mulch.

❖ Leaves. If there are trees growing in or around your neighborhood, you have a marvelous mulch and ideal soil-improver right at hand. Don't have enough in your own yard? Ask your neighbors for their leaves as well, or scavenge bagged leaves set out for the trash. Have more than you can use right away? Make leaf mold out of them for use as a summer mulch or soil amendment.

Tips: Dump or rake whole leaves into your gardens in fall, or shred them first with your lawn mower or a leaf shredder. A layer applied about 6 inches (15 cm) deep will settle to about 4 inches (10 cm) in a few weeks and be an ideal 2 to 3 inches (5 to 7.5 cm) thick by spring.

Pros: Leaves are free for the raking (or taking), and they're invaluable for your garden. Leaf mulches have a natural appearance in any form but look particularly good when shredded or when applied as leaf mold.

Cons: Large, tough leaves, such as those of some oaks, may form dense mats if you don't shred them before using as mulch. Fall-applied leaf mulches may completely decompose by midsummer, so plan on topping them with another mulch in spring or summer. Whole-leaf mulches

MAKE THE MOST OF COMPOST Use finished (dark and crumbly) compost for spring and summer mulching, either alone or under another mulch. "Chunky" (not-quite-finished) compost works great when applied in late fall to late winter. It will finish decomposing over the winter and look nice by spring.

may blow away if you've cut all of your perennials to the ground before mulching.

❧ Bark and chip mulches. Available in bags or in bulk, shredded bark, wood chips, and other wood-based mulches can make durable and attractive choices for perennial plantings. In some areas, you can find wood mulches that are

dyed black, red, or other colors. These may have their uses in some situations, but they're not a great choice for flower gardens: here, the plants should be the stars, not the mulch!

Tips: Apply fine-textured wood mulches, such as shredded bark, in a 1- to 2-inch-deep (2.5 to 5 cm) layer; use 2 to 3 inches (5 to 7.5 cm) of coarser materials. Fresh wood chips can temporarily deplete some soil nutrients at the soil surface, so it's generally best to let them sit in a pile for a year or two before applying them, or else use them in a 1- to 2-inch (2.5 to 5 cm) layer over a 1-inch (2.5 cm) layer of grass clippings or compost.

Pros: Shredded bark looks great and breaks down at a moderate rate, so you need to add more

only once a year. Coarser wood-based mulches can last even longer. You may be able to get wood-chip mulches for free from tree-care companies working on your property or nearby.

Cons: Wood chips and bark chunks can be tough on your hands when you need to work around your plants, and they may look too chunky around small plants. Mulches that are more finely ground or shredded tend to be relatively expensive. Some gardeners find that wood-based mulches form a crust that can stop water from soaking in (fluff them up with a rake if this happens).

❖ Grass clippings. Unless you've already replaced all of your lawn with gardens, you probably have a free and unending source of grass clippings right in your own yard. It's generally best to let the clippings fall right back onto the lawn, but if you waited a little too long and the mower leaves piles of clippings behind, it's a good idea to rake them up. Also, keep an eye out for bagged grass clippings set out for the trash by other

LEFT Wood-based mulches can be more expensive than other mulch options, but they tend to last longer, too. It's a good idea to wear gloves while spreading or working around them, to protect your hands from splinters.

RIGHT Grass clippings are super for your soil but aren't particularly attractive as a mulch. Consider topping them with a 1-inch (2.5 cm) layer of a more-attractive material, such as shredded bark.

homeowners. Don't use clippings from lawns you know or suspect have been treated with weed killers, though, because any remaining herbicide reside can harm or kill your perennials.

Tips: Grass clippings work best in thin layers: roughly ½ to 1 inch (12 to 25 mm) at a time. Add more as needed to keep the soil covered. If you have more clippings than you can use for mulch at one time, add them to your compost pile.

Pros: Mulching with grass clippings is a great way to recycle what some consider yard waste,

ROCK ON! Mulching with gravel can be helpful around plants that appreciate extra drainage around their crown, such as lavenders and this dianthus. Spread a 6- to 12-inch-wide (15 to 30 cm) ring of gravel about 1 inch (2.5 cm) thick around the base of individual plants, or use gravel as the mulch for the entire planting area.

and you can't beat the price. The fine pieces break down quickly and supply a small but useful amount of nutrients as they decompose.

Cons: If applied thickly — especially in wet weather — grass clippings can create a slimy mat, so don't apply more than about 1 inch (2.5 cm) each time. The clippings usually decompose quickly, so you'll need to apply them several times during the growing season.

❖ Gravel. More and more gardeners are catching on to the idea of mulching their perennials with gravel, especially in hot climates where even thick organic mulches can disappear within a few weeks. Gravel can also be a good choice for mulching sloping sites where organic mulches quickly wash away.

Tips: It's possible to mix perennials that prefer gravel mulch with those that like organic mulch, but it's usually easiest to keep them separate. If you do want to use both kinds of mulches in one area, you could scatter a very thin layer of organic mulch over the gravel-mulched parts, too, to make the area look uniform in spring. By summer, though, the plants will have filled in, so you probably won't see either kind of mulch anyway.

Pros: Gravel mulches are great for keeping leaves and stems away from moist soil, reducing the chance of rot — a big plus for plants with silvery foliage and for those that prefer dry conditions. They're essentially permanent, so you don't need to apply them more than once unless you dig up the plants.

Cons: Gravel is heavy to handle and not as readily available as many organic mulches. It can also look out of place in some settings, especially if you use the bright white stone mulch that's often sold in bags. (If possible, use gravel from rock that's native to your area, so the color looks more natural.) Gravel mulches don't improve soil fertility.

Think Twice

Not all of the mulches sold at your local garden center or home-improvement store are a good option for perennials. Here are two you'll probably want to avoid, or at least consider carefully before using.

❖ Peat moss. This widely available material may be fine for adding organic matter if you dig or till it into your soil, but don't use it as a mulch. Dry peat moss blows around at first, then forms a water-repelling crust that can prevent rainfall from soaking into the soil.

MULCH NOW, PLANT LATER Sometimes, you may choose to mulch your garden *before* planting. This can work well if you've gotten the soil ready but can't put in the perennials for a few weeks, or if you're starting a new garden with many small plants. Simply apply the mulch over the prepared soil, then push it aside in each spot where you want to put a plant.

❖ Landscape fabric. Also known as geotextiles, these thin and flexible sheets are meant to be laid over the soil to prevent weeds from coming up. Usually, they're spread out before planting, then holes are cut for individual plants, but sometimes they're fitted around existing plants.

While they seem good in theory, landscape fabrics aren't a practical option for most perennial plantings, where you need to be able to dig up the plants every few years for division. Plus, weed seeds can still blow in and take root on top of the fabric. Landscape fabrics break down

Hold the Mulch

IN SOME CASES, the best mulch is no mulch at all. While mulches usually do great things for gardens, they can also cause problems if you don't use them wisely. Here are a few circumstances where mulch *isn't* the answer:

❀ Very wet weather. If weather forecasts predict frequent rains in spring, hold off until the weather dries out a bit to apply mulch.

❀ Constantly wet soil. Mulch will keep a naturally soggy site even wetter — possibly too wet even for plants that thrive with ample moisture.

❀ Where pests are a problem. The evenly moist soil conditions that are good for many beneficial soil organisms are also ideal for slugs and earwigs. Mulches also provide good cover for voles and mice, giving them easy access to your perennials.

❀ Where you want plants to self-sow. Mulches can prevent desirable seeds from sprouting just as easily as weed seeds. If you want to direct-sow annual or perennial seeds, or if you're hoping your established perennials will self-sow, leave some soil bare so the seeds can get warmth and light.

If slugs are a serious problem in your garden, consider waiting until early or even midsummer to mulch. That will give the soil a chance to dry out a bit and make conditions somewhat less welcoming to these pests.

when exposed to light, and they're ugly too, so you need to top them with another mulch anyway. Save yourself the expense and long-term hassle by using newspaper as a weed barrier, if needed; it will last most of one growing season. (Spread layers of wet newspaper 5 to 10 sheets thick over the soil, then top them with an organic mulch.)

Mulch Management

Mostly, mulches go on your garden after your perennials are in place. If the plants are up and growing, try to keep the mulch 1 to 2 inches (2.5 to 5 cm) away from the base of the stems. (It's fine if the mulch touches the leaves and stems a bit — just don't pile the mulch on or against them.) To make spring mulching of new or established perennials go more quickly and keep your plants cleaner, too, cover each clump with an overturned pot or bucket, then spread your chosen mulch over the whole area. Lift off the coverings, and voilà — a perfectly mulched planting!

Always weed any area carefully before applying mulch. (While mulch *can* prevent some weed seeds in your soil from sprouting, spreading it over already sprouted weeds will simply give them the same benefits as your perennials, and they'll probably pop up through the mulch to grow even more vigorously than before.) It's also smart to mulch right after a soaking rain or to water thoroughly first. Most mulches will absorb some amount of water themselves, so if you apply them to dry soil, you'll need to water that much more to soak the mulch and then soak the soil.

PERENNIAL CARE FROM FALL TO SPRING

To the uninitiated, gardening is something that people do mostly in spring and summer. But real gardeners know that the "off-season" months — roughly September through March — can be busy, too, with tasks such as cleaning up frost-killed stems and protecting plants from wild winter weather. Exactly what you need to do to get ready for winter, and then to get ready for spring, depends on a number of factors, including which perennials you grow, where you live, and what your general approach is to garden maintenance.

To Cut, or Not to Cut?

Deciding whether to do your main garden cleanup in fall or spring is really a matter of personal choice. There are some advantages to getting it over with early, but also many benefits to waiting for spring.

❖ The "let's get it over with" approach. If you think you want to do at least some cleanup before winter, don't be too quick to get started. It's fine to snip off the seed heads of any plants that you don't want to reseed as soon as their flowers fade. Go ahead and pull out any annual companions that got nipped by the first frost, too. Other than that, though, give your perennials a chance to die back naturally. You'll know it's time when their leaves and stems turn brown and dry — usually in early to mid-November.

One thing in favor of late fall cleanup is that you'll save yourself a lot of time in spring, when there are always so many other things that need to be done. You'll also eliminate some places where insect and animal pests and disease-causing

A CUT ABOVE Snip off dead stems and leaves roughly 2 to 4 inches (5 to 10 cm) above the soil. Leaving these short stubs prevents you from accidentally cutting into emerging buds and makes it easy to see where each clump will emerge.

A SPRING TRIM Most perennials don't care much whether you cut them back in fall or spring. Those that are on the shrubby side, however — such as lavenders, caryopteris, Russian sage (*Perovskia*), and woody-stemmed wormwoods (*Artemisia*) — generally respond better if you wait until their new growth appears in spring to trim them.

Spring (March–May)

As the days get noticeably longer and temperatures get milder, the urge to get busy in the garden is practically irresistible. If you can count on your spring weather being relatively mild, it's fine to start a thorough garden cleanup in early to mid-March. Remove winter plant coverings and excess mulch, cut off any remaining dead or winter-damaged growth, and generally make things tidy.

Where spring weather tends to be more fickle, hitting you with below-freezing weather after a few days of glorious sun and warmth, it's better to approach your cleanup in stages. Starting in mid- to late March, make one pass through your plantings to trim off whatever dead growth remains, then another a week or two later to start lifting off some of the protective winter mulch, if you used any. Once you're pretty sure that nighttime temperatures won't go much below freezing, you can finish removing any excess mulch and snipping off any remaining dead or damaged foliage to get your perennials in prime form for the upcoming season.

Summer (June–August)

Don't worry about winter right now — enjoy your beautiful garden!

Fall (September–November)

Once a few frosts have zapped your gardens, the show is pretty much over for the year. You may simply retreat indoors, leaving your plants to fend for themselves and delaying any cleanup chores until spring. Or, you may choose to do a complete cleanup, cutting off the tops of your perennials just above the ground, followed by a thorough mulching once the ground has started to freeze.

Most gardeners end up taking an approach somewhere in the middle, such as cutting down some of their perennials but applying no protective mulch, or leaving all the top growth on their plants and mulching around them. For the most part, perennials are surprisingly tough, so they'll probably survive the winter just fine regardless of what you do or don't do.

Winter (December–February)

Where snow doesn't cover the ground, take a quick walk around your yard once a week to make sure your plants look okay, paying special attention to perennials you planted in fall. If you see any of them pushed out of the soil, try to gently push them back in, if you can; otherwise, mound some compost or mulch over the exposed roots to protect them from drying out.

Don't be fooled by those few mild days that often happen in February; it's practically inevitable that they'll be followed by another cold snap, so you don't want to do any major cleanup then unless you know that the weather is most likely to stay mild in your area. It's fine to putter around a bit outdoors, but in most areas, you're better off using this time to plan your strategy for when spring really does arrive, and to make sure all of your tools are in prime shape for the busy season to come.

organisms can survive through the winter, possibly reducing problems when spring returns. If certain perennials frequently produce seedlings in your garden, getting rid of their seed heads can save you a lot of weeding next year. Removing debris right away means that you won't have to worry about leaves matting down and smothering perennial crowns or emerging bulbs in early spring. And if you're of the mindset that dead stems and seed heads simply look messy, then a late fall cleanup will give you a tidy blank slate to look at through the winter.

❖ The "I'll do it later" strategy. Procrastinators, rejoice: There are just as many good reasons to put off garden cleanup until spring. For one, you get to enjoy an abundance of striking seed heads and fascinating plant forms through the winter months. It's a somewhat stark beauty compared to the color and lushness of summer, but to many gardeners, it's better than looking at bare soil all winter! The remaining stems and foliage have practical benefits, too: they provide natural protection for ground-level buds and roots, and they trap and hold other leaves that blow into the garden,

WORTH WAITING FOR If you're too quick to cut everything down in fall, you'll miss out on the subtle but seductive beauty of interesting stems and seed heads.

essentially making their own mulch. While all this "leaf litter" can shelter some problem pests, it also provides winter homes for lady beetles, ground beetles, and many other beneficial insects. Plus, delaying cleanup gives the dead stems and leaves time to decompose right in place, so you'll have a whole lot less debris to deal with — a big bonus if you don't have much room for composting, or if you have lots of gardens to deal with.

❖ The "now and later" compromise. Most gardeners fall somewhere in between the all-fall and all-spring cleanup strategies, so they get the benefits of both approaches. Spread your cutting-back chores throughout late fall and winter, for instance, starting with perennials that have lost their good looks after the first few frosts. If you've had problems with fungal diseases on your peonies, summer-blooming phlox, or other perennials, put them on your early cleanup list as well.

Epimedium

What about Winter Greens?

NOT ALL PERENNIALS turn dry and stick-like during the winter months. Some hold the same basic foliage and form all year long, or at least keep their foliage well into winter before turning brown. Others die back to a low rosette or mat of fresh-looking leaves for the winter months. And then there are a few oddballs that turn the seasons upside down, dying back to the ground in summer and sending up a flush of lovely new leaves in fall. On any of these, feel free to snip off any dead or damaged growth as needed, but otherwise, leave their leaves alone. Here's quick rundown of some perennials that hold green (or yellow, purple, silver, or blue) foliage for most or all of the winter months:

Achillea (yarrows)
Agastache (agastaches)
Aquilegia (columbines)
Arabis (rock cresses)
Arum (Italian arum)
Aurinia (basket-of-gold)
Bergenia (bergenias)
Carex (sedges)
Chrysanthemum (mums)
Cyclamen (cyclamen)

Dianthus (dianthus)
Epimedium (epimediums)
Festuca (fescues)
Gaillardia (blanket flowers)
Helictotrichon (blue oat grass)
Helleborus (hellebores)
Heuchera (heuchera, coral bells)
Heucherella (foamy bells)
Iberis (perennial candytuft)
Iris (irises, some)

Lamium (dead nettles)
Leucanthemum (Shasta daisies)
Penstemon (penstemons)
Phlox (phlox, some)
Rudbeckia (rudbeckias)
Salvia (salvias, sages)
Sedum (sedums, stonecrops)
Stachys (lamb's ears, betonies)
Tiarella (foamflowers)
Yucca (yuccas)

Helleborus

Lamium

Heuchera

Sedum

Yucca

Salvia

Protecting Plants from Cold

If you're a plant-it-and-forget-it sort of gardener, worrying about protecting your perennials over the winter simply isn't on your agenda. Selecting only perennials that have proven to be cold hardy in your area, planting them early in the growing season, and accepting that any winter deaths are an opportunity to try something else free you up to think about lots of other gardening projects.

The reality, though, is that some of us simply aren't that hands-off in our gardens. We want to experiment with plants that are better suited to other climates, so we're willing to put extra effort into winter protection. We can't resist the lure of end-of-the-season sales, so we need to give those late plantings a little TLC to help them settle in for the cold months. And we feel guilty if any of our cherished perennials disappear, so we feel obliged to lavish them with all the special care we can provide. For those inclined to go the extra mile for their garden, applying a protective winter mulch is something worth considering.

❖ New plantings. Winter mulching can be a big help for those of you who like to take advantage of fall weather for planting and transplanting. Normally, if you get your perennials in their new homes at least 6 weeks or so before the ground freezes, they'll have enough time to produce a sturdy new root system. If you end up planting later than that, though, or if cold temperatures arrive sooner than expected, the roots may not have time to get well anchored. Then, the movement of the soil as it freezes and thaws can push the plants right out of the ground, a phenomenon known as "frost heaving." So the goal of mulching new plantings and transplants is two-fold: to keep the soil warm for as long as possible, which promotes new root growth, and to insulate the ground from the rapid temperature changes that lead to frost heaving. This sort of protective mulch is usually applied within a week or so of planting.

❖ Established plantings. Perennials that have been in place for at least one growing season — especially in areas south of Zone 6, or in colder areas where a blanket of snow covers the ground

THE GREAT COVER-UP The problem with waiting until your soil freezes to mulch is that your mulch may be frozen solid, too! Keeping the pile covered with a tarp will protect it from fall rains and increase the odds that you'll be able to use it when you need it.

By spring, all you'll have left to cut down are those plants with really long-lasting structure, such as warm-season ornamental grasses and fall-flowering asters. Waiting until spring seems to be a good approach with agastaches, salvias, and other hollow-stemmed plants, too, the theory being that fall-cut stems provide a conduit for water to enter their crown and possibly cause winter damage. Spreading out your cleanup chores over several sessions also eliminates the big buildup of garden debris that you need to deal with all at once.

all winter — usually do just fine without a protective winter mulch. Those of you gardening in the in-between areas, where the soil mostly stays bare and winter temperatures can be arctic one week and almost balmy the next, may want to consider at least a light winter mulch, particularly for plants that seem to be prone to frost-heaving, such as heucheras.

If you choose to mulch established perennials for the winter, the common timing is just after the top few inches (cm) of ground are frozen. The idea here is to keep the cold soil cold, thereby preventing the rapid thawing-and-freezing cycles that can happen on mild winter days followed by subfreezing nights. Waiting until the soil is frozen has another benefit: possibly encouraging voles, mice, and other critters to make their winter homes elsewhere.

❖ Choosing and using winter mulches. In areas where there are lots of trees, leaves are usually the mulch of choice for winter protection. It's fine to use small, slender, or thin leaves whole; that goes for pine needles, as well. Leaves that are large and leathery, such as those of some oaks and maples, usually work better if they're at least par-

tially shredded; otherwise, they can form dense mats. A lawn mower with a bag makes collecting and chopping leaves a breeze: simply mow as usual, then use the chopped-up leaves you gather for mulch. If you don't have a bag on your mower, rake your leaves into rows on your lawn or driveway and run over them with the chute pointing toward a wall or fence to create a pile, or shoot the chopped leaves directly into your garden. You can also buy a machine designed specifically for leaf shredding. The resulting finely chopped leaves make a great-looking mulch, but this approach takes a lot more time and energy: you need to rake up the leaves, haul them to another spot, shred them, and then haul them back to your gardens. Apply whole or partially shredded leaves in a layer up to 6 inches (15 cm) thick; 3 to 4 inches (7.5 to 10 cm) is fine for leaves chopped into small pieces.

SAVE THOSE TREES! Discarded Christmas trees and holiday greens are a great source of mulching material for winter gardens. Evergreens with soft needles, such as hemlocks and pines, are great if you can get them. Spruces and others with sharp, stiff needles can be really tough on your hands unless you wear gloves.

WATCH FOR WINTER DAMAGE Alternating cold and warm temperatures during the winter can push some unmulched plants right out of the ground. If you see frost-heaved clumps, replant them immediately if you can; otherwise, mound soil or mulch over the roots and replant them in spring.

Other organic mulches — compost, shredded bark, and the like — can also work well for winter mulching. Apply them in a layer roughly 2 to 3 inches (5 to 7.5 cm) thick. With any of these mulches (including leaves), it's fine to spread them directly over fully dormant clumps, especially if you're trying to overwinter plants that aren't fully cold hardy in your area. On perennials that hold some or all of their leaves through the winter, you could either leave them totally uncovered, tucking the mulch under the outermost leaves, or just cover them lightly with mulch. If you choose to mulch directly over your perennials, remember that you'll probably need to pull back at least some of the mulch in spring, when they're starting to sprout.

Evergreen boughs (usually cut from discarded Christmas trees and other holiday decorations) are an ideal option for mulching perennial gardens, because you can lay them directly over any plants without worrying about smothering what's underneath. And come spring, it's a simple matter to lift them off during warm days and replace them if frost threatens. Best of all, they're usually plentiful in late December and early January, just when you need them.

Believe it or not, a thick blanket of snow is one of the best mulches you can get for your perennials. If the covering on your borders gets a little thin, shovel on some extra from your lawn, paths, or other areas. Avoid using snow from paving that has been treated with de-icing salt, though.

PROPAGATING PERENNIALS

It's entirely possible to grow and enjoy perennials without ever dealing with propagating them. After all, it's easy to go to the garden center and buy new plants whenever you need them, right? But what if you want to create a new garden and don't have the money to spend buying enough new perennials to fill it? Or, what if you have a particularly nice perennial that you'd like to share with someone? Learning a few simple propagation techniques can save you a bundle and make you very popular with gardening friends and family. Plus, you can take your extra plants to swaps and trade them with other gardeners to further expand your own collection.

Multiplying by Dividing

Division is by far the easiest propagation technique, and it's something you need to do regularly anyway to keep many perennials healthy and vigorous. Propagating your perennials by division gives you exact copies of the original plant, and if you make just a few divisions from each clump, the "new" plants usually settle in quickly and fill out in just a year or two. Want to give it a try? You can find detailed information on the when and how of this technique in Dividing Your Perennials on page 84.

CUTTINGS UNDER COVER Stem cuttings can wilt quickly until they have some roots, so it's critical to keep the humidity high, but you don't want them to sit in water either. Remove their cover for an hour or two a few times a week to allow for some air circulation, and water only when the condensation disappears. Remove any dropped leaves or obviously dead cuttings immediately.

Taking Cuttings

Given the right conditions, pieces of stem may form new roots, and sections of roots may form new shoots, almost always giving you identical copies of the plants they came from. A single perennial can provide a dozen or more cuttings — typically far more new plants than you could get at one time from dividing it. Cuttings do, however, take a bit more care to get off to a good start, and they may take a year or two longer than good-sized divisions to fill out and flower well.

❧ Stem cuttings. As you can probably guess, stem cuttings are sections of leafy stems snipped off of a perennial for propagation. Midsummer is a great time to try stem cuttings of many perennials, because their growth has usually slowed down a bit by then and the slightly tougher leaves and stems won't be as quick to lose moisture. Some perennials take root more quickly from spring or early summer growth, though, so if you don't have good luck with midsummer cuttings, you may want to try taking them a few weeks earlier next year. Late summer to early fall can be fine for taking stem cuttings of perennials that aren't winter hardy in your area (you can keep them indoors as houseplants for the winter), but it's not an ideal time for hardy perennials because they probably won't have time to establish an adequate root system before winter arrives.

Before you gather perennial cuttings from your garden, get everything ready that you need to plant them, so you can "stick" the cuttings as soon as possible. Clean plastic pots that are about 4 inches (10 cm) across are ideal for cuttings of most perennials: they're large enough that they don't dry out quickly, but they don't hold so much mix as to end up staying soggy and leading to rot. Fill the pots almost to the rim with some kind of growing medium: a commercially

prepared potting mix, or a home blend of equal parts perlite and peat moss or vermiculite, or even plain vermiculite. (You can find all of these materials at your local garden center.) Whichever medium you choose, makes sure it's evenly moist before you fill the pots.

Morning is usually an ideal time to gather cuttings, because the stems are full of moisture and are not heat stressed. (If the weather has been dry, it's a good idea to water thoroughly the day before you plan to gather cuttings, so they aren't drought stressed either.) Using a clean, sharp pair of pruning or garden shears, snip off shoot tips 4 to 6 inches (10 to 15 cm) long, each with at least two nodes (the joints where the leaves or leaf pairs join the stem). If possible, take cuttings from nonflowering stems. Place cuttings in a plastic bag, keep them away from direct sun, and take them indoors as quickly as you can, before they wilt.

To prepare your cuttings for planting, first trim off the flowers or flower buds, if there are any. Next, make the bottom cut just below the lowest node, and pinch or cut off any leaves on the lower half of the cutting. Gently insert the prepared cutting about halfway into the moistened growing medium. Repeat with the remaining cuttings, inserting them roughly 2 to 4 inches (5 to 10 cm) apart. Press down gently with your fingertips to firm the growing mix around the stems, then water thoroughly.

At this point, your cuttings need light (but not direct sun), warmth, and humidity. Indoors, you can use plant lights; outdoors, try to find a site that's lightly shaded all day — at the base of a north-facing wall, for instance, or near a somewhat open shrub. Adequate warmth — around 70°F (21°C) — is seldom an issue with summer cuttings outdoors, but indoors, you could use a heated propagation mat to keep the growing mix evenly warm, if needed. To keep the humidity high around your cuttings, set the pots in some sort of enclosure, such as a shallow tray (called a flat) covered with a clear plastic dome, or cover them with a homemade wooden or PVC-pipe frame that's draped with clear plastic. Within a day or so, some condensation should form inside the cover; if it doesn't, water the pots again.

Most perennial cuttings start rooting in 2 to 5 weeks. A few days after you see new growth

CUTTING REMARKS Ready-to-plant cuttings generally have two or three leaves or leaf pairs above one or two leafless nodes. Insert the cuttings about halfway into the growing medium, to just below the lowest leaf or leaf pair. You can easily fit three to five cuttings of most perennials in one 4-inch (10 cm) pot.

Propagation Calendar

FOR CUTTINGS AND SEEDS

For details on when to divide perennials, turn to the Division Calendar on page 85.

Spring (March–May)

Finish collecting and planting root cuttings in early spring, before they start producing top growth. If your perennials are already up and growing vigorously, try stem cuttings in mid- to late spring. Sow seed of perennials indoors or outdoors throughout spring. After all danger of frost has passed, start moving pots of indoor-grown seedlings and cuttings outdoors. (See Handling Hardening Off on page 64.)

Summer (June–August)

Early to midsummer is the ideal time to take stem cuttings or sow seeds of many perennials. In mid- to late summer, try root cuttings of early bloomers that have gone dormant (died back to the ground), or sow their seed outdoors as soon as it ripens.

Fall (September–November)

In early fall, take stem cuttings of tender perennials to keep indoors for the winter. In mid- to late fall, sow seed outdoors or take root cuttings.

Winter (December–February)

Collect and plant root cuttings any time the ground isn't frozen. Sow seed that requires chilling outdoors through the winter, or sow it indoors and refrigerate it to provide the cold period. Late winter is a fine time to indoor-sow seed that needs warmth to sprout. (You may even want to sow in midwinter if you're trying for first-year blooms on fast-growing perennials.)

appear, tug gently at the base of the stem; if you feel some resistance, you know roots have formed. Gradually start opening the cover for longer periods over the period of several days to help the new growth toughen up. Move the rooted cuttings to individual pots for a few weeks, then transplant them to your garden or to a holding bed. One trick you can use to get a fuller-looking clump more quickly is to plant out several rooted cuttings close together.

✤ Root cuttings. For some perennials, you have a slightly different propagation option — taking pieces of their roots and putting them in the right conditions to form new shoots. Sometimes, you may do this unintentionally: you dig up a perennial such as Oriental poppy (*Papaver orientale*) or yucca to move it, and within a few weeks or months, you see new plants sprouting up in the original spot from root pieces left behind in the soil. Or, you can try this technique intentionally, usually in midfall to early spring, whenever the plants are dormant and the ground isn't frozen. Don't bother trying root cuttings with variegated plants, however, because the shoots they produce will be solid green; stem cuttings are a better choice for propagating most variegates.

To gather root cuttings from perennials, dig carefully on one side of the plant to expose some of the roots, then use a sharp knife or shears to snip off some healthy looking roots and cut them into sections 2 to 4 inches (5 to 10 cm) long. On some perennials, such as garden phlox (*Phlox paniculata*), purple coneflower (*Echinacea*), and fall anemones (*Anemone*), the roots are fairly thin; lay them horizontally on moist growing medium. Space the root pieces about 1 inch (2.5 cm) apart and cover them with about ½ inch (12 mm) of more growing mix. On root cuttings of perennials that tend to produce thicker roots, such as bear's breeches (*Acanthus*) and Oriental poppy (*Papaver orientale*), make a straight cut on the end that was closest to the center of the plant and a sloping cut on the other end, so you can remember which is which. Insert the pieces right-side (straight end) up into a pot of moist growing medium, with the tops of the cuttings just below the surface of the medium.

Unlike stem cuttings, root cuttings don't

have to be kept warm or in high humidity, but they do need to stay somewhat moist. A cool, bright room can be a great site for them. New top growth may sprout up before new roots form, so wait until you see roots peeking out of the bottom of the pot before moving the plantlets to individual pots or to a holding bed.

Growing from Seed

It's a common joke among gardeners that you really don't know a plant until you've killed it three times. But I propose an addition to that rule: ". . . or until you've grown it from seed." There's simply nothing like the experience of sowing a seed, watching it sprout, and then nurturing it into a beautiful, full-grown flowering or foliage plant to grace your own garden. There's also a completely mercenary reason to learn about seed-starting: it's a terrific way to grow large quantities of great perennials for just a few dollars — or even for free, if you collect

ROOTING FOR THE PERENNIAL TEAM Lay thin root cuttings horizontally on moist growing medium; they may send up several shoots along their length. Insert thicker root cuttings vertically into the pot.

the seed from your own garden.

Before you decide to grow an entire perennial garden from seed, it's important to keep some practical considerations in mind. First, be aware that it can take some perennials 3 to 5 years to reach flowering size when started from seed. Also, seed-grown plants won't be exactly identical to the plants that produced the seed. These differences may be so minor that you don't even notice them, or they may be obvious variations in height, form, flower and foliage color, disease resistance, and other important traits. If you're planting perennials in groups where uniformity is critical, or if you really want a particular flower or foliage effect, division or cuttings may be a

WORTH THE WAIT Most seed-grown perennials will send up at least a few flowers during their second summer, and a few may take an additional year or more before they begin blooming. But if you prefer more immediate results, seek out those that can flower the very same year you sow them, such as blanket flower (*Gaillardia*).

better choice. But if you're open to some variety, seeds can provide some fun surprises!

❁ Seed-sowing basics. In most cases, you'll be sowing perennial seeds in pots, rather than directly in the ground. Plastic pots that are 2 to 4 inches (5 to 10 cm) across are a handy size and reusable, but you can use other clean containers of about the same size, as long as they have drainage holes. You don't want to use garden soil to fill the pots, because it can be laden with weed seeds, and it tends to pack down tightly in containers with regular watering. Instead, try a commercial peat- or coir-based seed-starting medium, or blend your own with equal parts of

peat moss or coir, perlite, and vermiculite. Add water and knead the medium with your hands until it is evenly moist but not dripping wet. Fill your chosen pots to the rim, level the surface with the side of your hand, then firmly tap the base of the pot on your worktable a few times to settle the medium a bit. Now, you're ready to sow!

Scatter your chosen seeds — one kind per pot — as evenly as possible over the surface of the growing medium. Try to leave about ½ inch (1 cm) between them, if you can, to make later transplanting a bit easier. (If you have lots of seed, it's far better to sow it in two or three pots than to cram it all into one pot.) Tiny seeds, and those that require light to germinate, don't need to be covered; press them gently into the surface of the medium. Medium-sized seeds are usually fine if just barely covered, while large seeds can be covered with about ¼ inch (6 mm) of seed-starting medium. Add a label with the plant name and sowing date. Set the sown pots in a tray of warm water until the top looks moist, and then move

them to a spot where the excess water can drain away. Repeat this bottom-watering technique as often as needed to keep the soil evenly moist until the seeds sprout. Once the seedlings are large enough to handle, transplant them to individual pots or to an outdoor holding bed.

❖ Sowing seed indoors. Starting seed indoors in mid- or late winter to early spring is a great way to get a jump on the growing season. Besides giving you something fun to do even if

LET THERE BE LIGHT A simple shop light fixture can provide ample light for a dozen or more pots of perennial seedlings. Hang it 4 to 6 inches (10 to 15 cm) above the pots, using chains and S-hooks so you can easily raise the lights as the seedlings sprout and grow. Leave the lights on for 14 to 16 hours a day.

it's too early to garden outdoors, it provides the greatest amount of control over the temperature, moisture, light levels, and other environmental factors your seeds are exposed to. This is especially helpful when you're sowing seed that is very tiny or very expensive, if you have very limited quantities of seed, or if you want to try to get first-year bloom from the fastest-growing perennials.

Plant as explained in Seed-Sowing Basics on page 62, then set the pots in a shallow tray (flat) and cover it with a clear plastic dome or drape

EASY SOWING Large-seeded perennials are a snap to sow, but smaller ones can be a challenge to scatter evenly. Instead of trying to shake them out of the seed packet, crease a piece of stiff paper, carefully pour the seed into the crease, then tap the side of the paper gently with your index finger to shake off just a few seeds at a time.

Handling Hardening Off

THERE ARE A NUMBER of advantages to starting seeds and cuttings indoors: you can easily control the temperature, moisture, humidity, and light levels, and the young plants aren't exposed to pests or wind. Eventually, though, they need to adjust to the great outdoors, and it's up to you to help them make the transition. This process is called hardening off.

You can set out indoor-grown seedlings or rooted cuttings pretty much any time during the frost-free season. Start by setting the pots in a shady, sheltered spot. It's ideal to leave them out for just an hour or two the first day, then gradually extend the time an hour or two each day. However, if you're away from home during the day on weekdays, you could try speeding up the process with an hour or two on Saturday, a half-day on Sunday, and then all day starting on Monday. Once the seedlings are used to being outside all day, move those that prefer full sun to progressively brighter spots over the period of a few days. Throughout the process, check on your young perennials at least once a day, and water as needed to make sure they don't dry out. Figure on them being ready for planting 7 to 10 days after you first set them outside.

clear plastic over the pots to keep the humidity high around the seed. Many summer- and fall-blooming perennials sprout most quickly in warm soil, around 65°F to 70°F (18°C to 21°C), and it's relatively easy to provide that warmth in the average home. If you prefer to keep your rooms cooler, it's worth buying a heated propagation mat and setting your seed pots on it to speed up their sprouting.

Some perennials — particularly those that bloom early in the growing season — need to be exposed to a period of cool temperatures before they're ready to sprout. That's easier than it sounds: simply place each pot in a plastic bag, close the bag, and set it in your refrigerator for at least three weeks before moving it to a warm, bright place.

Unless you have ample window space or access to a greenhouse, you'll need to set up some artificial light source so the developing seedlings will have ample light. You can buy special plant light setups, but you can get equally good results with an inexpensive shop light fixture fitted with two 4-foot (1.2 m) fluorescent bulbs from your local home-improvement center.

❖ Sowing seed outdoors. Don't want to bother with heating mats and plant lights? Sowing seed outside can also produce good results. Fall to early spring is a good time for seeds that benefit from at least a short period of cold, or from alternating freezing and thawing, while midspring to midsummer is a good time for most others. Outdoor sowing is also ideal for bleeding hearts (*Dicentra*), hellebores, and other spring-bloomers whose seeds sprout poorly if they dry out, as they would if you stored them in paper envelopes for months. Sow them outdoors as soon as you collect them (or as soon as you can buy them) in summer, and they will likely sprout next spring.

You may choose to sow in pots, as you would indoors, or you can sow directly into the soil of a holding bed or other out-of-the-way spot. Either way, try spreading a layer of aquarium gravel or other fine grit about ¼ inch (6 mm) deep over the sown seed after planting. This mini-mulch helps to keep the seed-starting medium or soil from drying out quickly or crusting over, so the seeds will have an easier time sprouting. Regular rainfall will keep the sown seed evenly moist, but if it's lacking, you'll need to water by hand or with a very gentle spray from your hose through the seed and seedling stages.

A SEEDY SOLUTION Biennials like money plant (*Lunaria annua*) can be beautiful additions to perennial gardens, but what do you do with them when they start to look ugly after flowering? If you grow one or a few of each kind in a holding bed, you can pull out the garden plants as soon as they fade and still have a source for seed for future plantings.

Building a Holding Bed

THE ACTUAL PROCESS of building a holding bed is basically the same as for an ornamental bed or border: getting rid of whatever's already there (weeds, grass, and debris), then loosening the soil. (For a far more detailed explanation, turn to Getting Ready to Plant on page 23.) Ground-level holding beds are fine, but raised beds can be even better, because you can easily blend a loose, well-drained soil mix that's perfect for the tender roots of young perennials.

SIZING IT UP You can make your holding bed as long as you like, but don't make it much wider than 3 feet (90 cm) if you can access it from only one side, or about 5 feet (1.5 m) if you can access it from both sides. Otherwise, it'll be difficult to reach the plants in the middle of the bed.

(A blend of equal parts screened topsoil, compost, and sand works great for a wide variety of perennials.) Raised beds dry out more quickly than ground-level plots, which is a plus if your soil is naturally a bit soggy, especially in winter. But you don't want to raise the soil level too much, because then you'll have to water more frequently. Beds that are 6 to 8 inches (15 to 20 cm) deep are usually ideal for pampering young perennials.

If you choose the raised-bed route, you'll want to build some sort of frame to hold the soil mix in place. There are lots of options, including natural or composite lumber, cement blocks, rocks, and bricks — whatever you have easy access to. Fill the frame with the soil-compost-sand blend, and you're ready to plant!

MAKING THE MOST OF HOLDING BEDS

A word of warning: Propagation can be addictive. It starts with a single packet of seed, or a "slip" (cutting) shared by a friend, and before you know it, you can easily end up with dozens or even hundreds of tiny plants that need a safe place to live while they're growing up. Sure, you could keep them in pots, but that takes up a lot of space, and trying to keep them all watered can be a job in itself. Fortunately, the solution is relatively simple: create a special place specifically for nurturing young plants until they're large enough to move into the garden-at-large.

Whether you call them holding beds or nursery beds, these spaces are an invaluable tool for all perennial gardeners. Besides providing a safe haven for small divisions, rooted cuttings, and seedlings, they're an ideal place to stick those impulse purchases in the ground until you can find a permanent place for them — far better than letting them sit around in their pots for months or years. And if you've ever had trouble trying to manage forget-me-nots (*Myosotis*), money plant (*Lunaria annua*), or other biennials in your garden, holding beds can be a big help. Start the seedlings in these short-term spaces in spring to early summer, then move them to your garden in fall of their first year or early spring of their second season.

Holding beds also serve an important function for gardens on the move. Sooner or later, most gardeners are faced with the challenge of moving to a new location, and it's a rare one who can stand to leave *all* of her plants behind. Whether you're moving a few pots or a few hundred, the challenge of keeping them all safe and watered while dealing with other aspects of unpacking can be daunting. Instead of rushing to plant them in the ground, take a few hours to get some holding beds in place. You'll avoid making bad design decisions that need undoing later, and the plants can keep growing happily while you get the rest of your life in order. The same benefits apply if you need to relocate plants on your existing property due to house repairs, construction, or garden renovation. Move the keepers to a holding bed, and they'll be safe from falling debris and trampling feet until you're ready to move them to their new home.

Choosing the Right Site

Selecting a place for a holding bed is a relatively simple matter. If your space is limited, you may have to settle for any empty spot you can find, or even a section of an existing bed in a not-very-visible part of your yard. If you have a little more space to work with, you have more options, but it's still smart to keep the bed relatively near an outdoor faucet for easy watering. You might choose to give your holding bed a gardenlike look by shaping it like an ornamental border and perhaps putting some of the larger, showier plants on the most visible side. Or, site it in an out-of-the-way spot, so you can freely move plants in and out without having to worry about appearances.

Chapter Three

KEEPING UP APPEARANCES

HERE COMES THE GROOM

Sure, you could plant your perennials, meet their basic needs, and then stand back and let them do their thing. But if you enjoy puttering around with your plants, or if you like experimenting with different gardening techniques, then trying out one or more of the various grooming techniques can be fun and rewarding. All of these techniques have one basic premise: you're removing part of the plant's top growth. It's the *when*, *where*, and *how much* you cut that create the variety of effects on your perennials, changing their size and shape, delaying their bloom time, and improving their overall appearance, among other things.

Pruning for Shape and Size

When you're planning your perennial garden, it's generally best to stick with plants that naturally grow the height and shape that you want, so you don't have to fuss with them. But sometimes, you really want a particular flower or foliage effect in a given spot, and the only way you can get it is by using pruning techniques to get the right plant size and shape. Other times, certain plants may grow larger than you expected, and you need to do *something* to keep them from overwhelming their companions — at least temporarily.

Pruning perennials in spring to midsummer, before bloom, has a double benefit: besides reducing their overall height, it also gives them a bushier form. That's because removing shoot tips encourages buds lower down on the stem to develop; instead of a few tall, unbranched

SHAPING UP Proper pruning can make a drastic difference in the appearance of many perennials, turning tall, sprawling masses into dense, bushy, flower-filled clumps that stand up just fine without staking.

THE LAYERED LOOK It's fine to pinch or cut so all of the stems are the same height. But if you take the time to taper the sides down a bit from the middle, the clump will have a better-looking, somewhat rounded form.

stems, you end up with a much sturdier, denser-looking plant. Plus, each of the shoot tips on the branched stems will produce one or more flower buds, so trimmed plants have more blooms (although usually somewhat smaller ones) than untrimmed plants. Just as importantly, shorter, well-branched stems are less likely to sprawl than tall, top-heavy ones, reducing or eliminating the need for staking.

Frequent, light trimming — removing 1 to 2 inches (2.5 to 5 cm) from each shoot tip every few weeks starting in mid- to late spring — produces the densest, bushiest plants. Just remember that you're removing any flower buds, too, so give early to midsummer-bloomers only one or two pinches before stopping to let them flower. On

late summer- and fall-bloomers, you could continue the light trimming through midsummer. Stop pruning by the end of July, unless your first fall frost doesn't come until late October or later; otherwise, your perennials may not have time to set new buds and bloom before they get zapped by subfreezing weather.

If all this light trimming seems like too much work, you could simplify matters on fall-bloomers by pruning whole clumps just once or twice. Simply shear the entire plants back by roughly one-half (really, anywhere from one-third to two-thirds) in early summer. If desired, you could shear them again around early July; remember, though, that the plants will need time to regrow so they can bloom before frost.

For light trimming, you can literally pinch off tender shoot tips with the nails on your thumb and index finger, or else snip with a sharp pair of pruning shears or scissors. Pinching or snipping slightly above a leaf produces the neatest appearance. If you prefer to do the job more quickly, you

Grooming Calendar

⬤ Spring (March–May)

In mid- to late spring, pinch or snip off the shoot tips of asters, chrysanthemums, catmints (*Nepeta*), and other summer- and fall-blooming perennials that you want to be shorter and bushier. Taking off just 1 to 2 inches (2.5 to 5 cm) when the plants are about 6 inches tall (15 cm) encourages the stems to branch but has no effect on the bloom time of those that flower in late summer or fall; it may delay early summer and midsummer-bloomers a few days to a week or so.

⬤ Summer (June–August)

In early to midsummer, repeat the light pinch or snip on late summer- and fall-bloomers, if desired, to again encourage the stems to branch. Or, if you didn't trim them in spring, shear them back by about one-half in early summer. The earlier in the summer you pinch or shear, the less you will delay the bloom time. Pinching or shearing late-bloomers by one-third to one-half in midsummer produces plants that are somewhat shorter than usual, though not as short as they would have been if you had cut them back earlier. It will also likely delay their bloom time for several weeks; the more top growth you remove, the longer the delay. In most areas, it's best to stop pinching or shearing by late July; otherwise, the plants may form buds so late that they don't flower before frost.

Summer is also a busy time for deadheading (removing faded flowers), either by pinching or snipping off individual blooms or shearing off all the spent blooms at once. Some early-blooming perennials, such as pulmonaria and columbines (*Aquilegia*), benefit from being cut right to the ground after bloom; this promotes a flush of fresh new leaves for interest in late summer and fall.

During the summer months, feel free to snip off faded or damaged leaves as needed and to remove flowers from perennials you're growing for foliage interest. This is also the time to experiment with disbudding (removing side buds) on chrysanthemums and dahlias if you want to produce extra-large blooms.

⬤ ⬤ Fall & Winter (September–February)

By fall, most of your detailed perennial pruning is complete. Continue removing damaged leaves and faded flowers, if you wish, or let the seed heads ripen for winter interest. (For details on cutting back perennials for garden cleanup in fall and winter, see To Cut, or Not to Cut? on page 49.)

could gather all of the stems in one hand and cut them with pruning shears in your other hand, or use hand-held or electric hedge shears for even quicker results.

Pruning for shape works well on a wide variety of perennials, including artemisias, asters, balloon flowers (*Platycodon*), boltonia, catmints (*Nepeta*), chrysanthemums, ironweeds (*Vernonia*), Joe-Pye weeds (*Eupatorium*), upright sedums, and sunflowers (*Helianthus*), to name just a few. Don't try it on plants with leafless or naturally unbranched stems, such as daylilies (*Hemerocallis*) or true lilies (*Lilium*); you'll be removing this year's flowers from those stems!

Just Testing

ONCE YOU'VE BEEN GARDENING for any length of time, you learn that there are no absolutes with plants. You may find a perennial that supposedly demands full sun growing just fine in your shady site, or one that shouldn't be winterhardy in your area coming back year after year. So, it's no surprise that pruning perennials works the same way: you can pinch or cut the same plant at the same time and by the same amount every year and end up with somewhat different results each time, depending on the amount of rainfall, how much you fertilize, and other factors.

Keeping detailed records of your pruning experiments — how much you cut off, when you made the cuts, how tall the plant ended up, when it flowered, the average flower size, and so on — is invaluable if you want to fine-tune your timing and techniques. You can't be positive that a given plant will turn out exactly 25 percent shorter or bloom exactly 10 days later than usual, but after a few years of experimenting, you can have a good general idea of how a certain plant will respond in your particular conditions.

Thinning to Relieve Crowding

On bee balms (*Monarda*), summer phlox, and other upright perennials that produce many tightly packed stems, pinching or clipping out some shoots at ground level to leave some space between the stems — a technique known as thinning — can improve the plant's overall appearance. The remaining stems will be sturdier, and the improved spacing allows air to circulate more easily around the leaves and stems, decreasing the development of some disease problems.

Thinning out whole stems is usually done in spring, but you can certainly remove them later on instead, if you think it would make a particular plant look better. Also feel free to pinch or cut out some of the leaves on tightly packed foliage clumps, such as those of pulmonarias and lamb's ears (*Stachys byzantina*). As with the stems, this can improve the overall appearance and reduce the chance of rots, mildews, and other diseases.

If you find yourself doing a lot of leaf or stem thinning, think about dividing those plants next fall or spring, as a longer-term solution to overcrowding. (For more details, see Dividing Your Perennials on page 84.)

SPACING OUT Thinning to leave 2 to 4 inches (5 to 10 cm) between the stems can make a big difference in established clumps of spreading perennials, such as Tatarian aster (*Aster tataricus*). The remaining stems are taller and stronger, with larger flowers, and they're less likely to be bothered by powdery mildew.

Pruning to Extend or Delay Bloom

Besides changing a plant's size and shape, pruning your perennials has an influence on when and how they flower. Mostly, gardeners use this trick on late summer- and fall-blooming perennials to delay their display for a few weeks. Many garden mums, for instance, begin flowering in July or August if left untrimmed — not a problem if you want them to bloom then, but a disappointment if you want the mums to flower for fall color.

The same basic principles of pruning for size and shape control apply here: either pinch off just the shoot tips every few weeks starting in mid- to late spring, or shear the whole clump by about half in early to midsummer. Most perennials start blooming 3 to 4 weeks after you stop

MAKE IT LAST Many late-blooming plants like sneezeweed (*Helenium*) can be pinched back in early to midsummer to delay their bloom.

giving them a light pinch. If you give them a more drastic shearing in early summer only, you may delay their normal bloom time by just a week or two; midsummer shearing may delay bloom by a month or more.

If you want to get really sophisticated, you can use these pruning techniques to extend the bloom display of your perennials. You might pinch or shear only the front half of a clump or grouping, for instance: the untouched back half will bloom at the usual time, then the front half will produce a new flush of flowers a bit later.

Leave These Seeds

I N THE QUEST to get the most flowers possible and keep your garden neat and tidy, it's easy to get carried away with deadheading. But if you can spare the shears for a bit, you may find that you actually like the look of the seed heads that form after the flowers. Late summer- and fall-bloomers tend to have particularly long-lasting seed heads, extending their interest well into the winter months, but even those that hang around only a short time can offer an unexpected touch of beauty if you take the time to look closely.

Allowing seeds to form has some practical benefits, as well. "Volunteer" seedlings, for instance, can be handy for sharing with friends, taking to plant swaps, or filling empty spaces in your gardens. Self-sown seedlings are also a great source of replacements for biennials and short-lived perennials; the original plants last only two or three years, but their seedlings take their place, so you always have some around.

There are no rules about which plants you must deadhead and which you shouldn't; it's a matter of what looks best to you and what works best in your own garden. If you know from personal experience or from nearby gardening friends that a certain plant can self-sow too abundantly in your area, don't hesitate to snip off those spent blooms, no matter how pretty the seed heads may be. But if you're open to the beauty of plants beyond just their flowers, then why not leave some seed heads and see what you think?

SEEDY CHARACTERS Leaving seeds on your perennials can do more than add seasonal interest to your plantings: it will also attract a wide variety of wild birds to your yard.

Disbudding for Bigger Blooms

Usually, the point of pinching and shearing is to encourage stems to produce lots of side shoots. Since each of these side shoots can produce blooms, it's easy to see that more shoots means more flowers. The trade-off is that each flower will likely be somewhat smaller than it could be. If your goal is to produce huge, show-stopping blooms, you might try the opposite technique: disbudding. Instead of removing the shoot tips, pinch off any side branches that form on the main stem, as well as any flower buds except for one at the very top. That stem will put all of its energy into that one bud, so the resulting bloom can be quite a bit larger than usual. (It'll be extra heavy, too, so you'll probably need to stake the stem to support that added weight.) Classic candidates for disbudding include dahlias and chrysanthemums, but you could try it on other perennials with branching stems, too, if you're up for experimenting!

Removing Faded Flowers

Pinching or clipping off flowers that are finished blooming — a technique usually referred to as deadheading — is one of the most commonly used forms of grooming. Remember, plants don't bloom simply to look pretty; they're genetically programmed to reproduce themselves, and they do that mostly by producing flowers, which in turn produce seeds. When you remove the blooms before they set seed, many perennials respond by producing more flowers to complete the seed-to-flower-to-seed cycle. If you carefully remove individual blooms or clusters as soon as they fade, you can get many plants to keep producing more flowers for weeks or even months longer than they would if left alone. Or, you can clip off all of the faded flowers at one time, to possibly get a flush of all-new flowers a few weeks later. Deadheading to encourage repeat bloom seems to work best on perennials that flower from late spring through midsummer.

Not all perennials will send up more flowers if you deadhead them, but it can be worth the time anyway. Removing the flowers as they fade prevents the plant from putting energy into seed production, so the foliage may stay lush and good looking for longer, and you don't have to deal

SNIP IT Pinching or snipping just above a flower bud that's lower down on the stem keeps your perennials looking as fresh and flower-filled for as long as possible.

GETTING SNIPPY If you don't see any obvious flower buds below the faded bloom, cut or pinch just above a leaf or leaf pair. Often, a new shoot will soon appear, if there isn't one there already. If there are no leaves on the flowering stems and all the blooms have opened, cut off the entire stem at its base.

LEFT On daylilies (*Hemerocallis*), it's easy to remove spent flowers by snapping them off with your fingers. Be sure to get the base of the bloom too, or a seedpod may still develop.

RIGHT Once you know that "deadheading" means removing dead flower heads, it's obvious that "deadleafing" also refers to pinching or clipping off any dead, discolored, or damaged foliage. This simple sort of grooming can make a big difference in the overall appearance of your perennial plantings.

with yellowing and browning stems and seedpods. Stopping seed production serves another purpose, as well: preventing a plant from producing masses of unwanted seedlings. Most of us enjoy finding one or two seedlings of our favorite perennials, but when dozens or hundreds of them start popping up all over the yard or the neighborhood, that delightful bonus turns into a major maintenance problem.

Even if you wouldn't mind an abundance of free new plants, be aware that when those seedlings grow up, they may or may not resemble the plants they came from. If you don't mind some variation in their heights and flower colors, that's not a problem. But if you're hoping to get a dozen identical offspring from that hybrid perennial, you're better off trying division or taking cuttings than depending on self-sown seedlings.

Most variegated plants don't "come true" from seed, either.

You have a couple of options for removing faded flowers, depending on the where the blooms appear on the plant and how much time you want to spend. Below are some general pointers. For more detailed tips, see the individual plant entries in Part Two, starting on page 121.

❧ Removing individual flowers. Pinching or snipping off blooms one by one as they fade is the most time-consuming technique, but it can be worth the effort if you want to keep your plants looking good for as long as possible. With medium-size to large blooms held on single stems, remove them just above a leaf or leaf pair — ideally where you can see a new bud emerging — or cut off the whole stem close to its base if there are no more flower buds. If they're held in groups, you could remove them individually or wait until the whole cluster or spike has faded.

❧ Removing bunches of blooms. Taking off individual flowers can be very tedious, so you may instead choose to shear off all of the blooms at one time. It's a great time saver, and it's often the only practical way to handle perennials with many small blossoms, such as threadleaf coreopsis (*Coreopsis verticillata*). The trade-off is that you'll either be removing some still-open blooms

TOP If trailing geraniums start looking stringy, trim the stems back to the new growth at the center of clump.

LEFT Shearing is a super time-saving option for deadheading large perennial clumps, mass plantings, and individual plants that produce many small flowers, like this dianthus.

along with the faded ones, or you'll have to wait until all of the flowers turn brown. Simply gather the stems in one hand and snip with pruning shears in your other, or shear the whole clump at once with hedge shears. If you have a large patch to deadhead, you might consider using a string trimmer. That gets the job done quickly, but it can leave your plants looking rather ragged for a few weeks and may even pull shallow-rooted perennials right out of the ground.

You can shear your plants just enough to remove the spent flowers, or cut lower down (usually by one-third to one-half) to encourage some fresh new leafy growth. Some perennials — such as hybrid columbines (*Aquilegia*), lady's mantle (*Alchemilla*), and masterworts (*Astrantia*) — respond well to a more drastic cut, down to just a few inches (cm) above the ground, to remove both the finished flower stems and the foliage. Within a few weeks, they'll produce a flush of fresh new leaves that look great through the rest of the growing season.

THE SUPPORTING CAST

The very mention of staking is enough to cause many gardeners to shudder. It can bring up visions of tedious hours spent inserting stakes and weaving string around them to support stems that won't be tall enough to cover them up for days or weeks, leaving borders filled with more framework than flowers. All this seems like a high price to pay to keep perennials growing upward instead of flopping over! Fortunately, there are plenty of ways to eliminate most or all of your perennials' staking needs. And if you do decide to provide some support, either before the plants need it or at bloom time to salvage a sprawling clump, there are many more practical — and even attractive — options to choose from.

Minimizing Staking Chores

Plenty of people grow gorgeous perennial gardens without ever bothering with a single stake. Part of the secret is to avoid being overly nice to your plants. Abundant water and fertilizer pushes plants to grow tall and fast, with soft stems that are prone to leaning and breaking. Moving those same plants into soil that's not so rich and somewhat on the dry side — or simply holding off on adding compost, fertilizer, and water — will result in stems that are naturally shorter and sturdier.

Ample sunshine is important, too, because sun-lovers growing in too much shade tend to lean toward whatever direction they get the most light from. If you can't give them more light where they are, then consider moving them to a brighter site.

Some perennials tend to sprawl when their clumps get old or overcrowded, so if a perennial that stood unsupported last year starts to sprawl this year, that's your cue to try dividing it. (See Dividing Your Perennials on page 84.) Techniques such as pinching and shearing also are useful on many perennials, producing stems that are shorter and bushier than usual. (See Pruning for Shape and Size on page 69.) Or, save yourself even that effort by choosing cultivars that have been selected for their naturally compact growth habit or shorter-than-usual stems. Remember, too, that bigger blooms are not always better: cultivars touted as producing larger-than-usual flowers are also more likely to need staking than their less highly hybridized cousins.

Now, even if you use all of these tricks, it's possible that a wind storm or rainy spell will cause some of your perennials to lean or sprawl. Instead of rushing to tie or prop them up, consider simply enjoying their new look. Often, letting plants mingle and lean on one another creates interesting combinations and effects that you might not thought of otherwise. If a plant flops badly, snip off the blooms and bring them indoors for bouquets, prune the remaining stems to shape up the clump a bit for the rest of the growing season, and plan to take steps to prevent the same problem next year.

Staking before Bloom

Still want to give staking a try? Putting supports in place *before* your plants need them is the traditional way to go. The theory is that the plants grow up through their supports and cover them with their foliage, creating the effect that the stems are standing straight on their own. Staking early in the season is easier on both you and your plants, because you don't have to fiddle with bending delicate stems; in fact, you don't have to touch the plants at all.

Whether commercial or homemade, most grow-through supports share the same basic structure: several evenly spaced metal, wood, or bamboo legs that are inserted into the soil around a clump and topped with some sort of ring or grid. The legs on commercial grow-through supports are usually somewhere between 18 and 30 inches tall (45 to 75 cm); if you're making your own, they can be any height you wish. Figure on inserting the legs at least 3 inches (7.5 cm) into the soil for supporting relatively low, lightweight

ABOVE Choosing a site that's somewhat protected from wind is one way to minimize staking needs, particularly for perennials that tend to produce tall, top-heavy flowering stems, such as delphiniums, lilies, and lupins.

LEFT Pairing thin- or floppy-stemmed perennials with shrubs or other sturdy-stemmed partners is a super way to minimize your staking chores and create beautiful combinations at the same time.

Staking Calendar

⬤ Spring (March–May)

The traditional time to get supports in place is mid- to late spring. Install hoop stakes, support rings, stakes-and-string supports, wire cages, and other sorts of grow-through supports after new growth appears but before it's more than 1 foot (30 cm) or so tall. Remember, the idea is to let the plants grow up through the supports so the metal or wood isn't visible. Trying to install these sorts of supports around clumps that are already getting large and bushy makes your job harder and increases the chance that you'll break the stems.

✸ Summer (June–August)

If spring-staked plants start to sprawl, gently raise their supports, if possible. On previously unsupported plants, use single stakes or small gathering rings to tie up individual stems (ideally before they start to sprawl). Linking stakes and Y-stakes are handy for propping up leaning stems on larger or bushier clumps.

🍁 ❄ Fall & Winter (September–February)

Support leaning fall-bloomers with tall gathering rings, Y-stakes, or linking stakes, or prop them up with bamboo tripods, trellis panels, or other sturdy decorative items. Once the gardening season is over, remove all stakes and supports, wipe off any clinging soil, and store them indoors for the winter. (Be sure to remove them before you do any other garden cleanup, because hitting hidden wooden or metal stakes with your shears or string trimmer can be dangerous to both you and your tools.)

plants; for those with heavy flowers (such as peonies) or tall stems, it's better to insert the legs 6 inches (15 cm) or more into the soil, especially if there are only three legs on the support, or if the soil is very loose.

The simplest grow-through supports have a single ring of metal, string, or twine linking the legs. Weaving string or twine back and forth over the clump, or setting a metal or bamboo grid on top of the legs, provides much more support for the stems and holds them at a more even spacing. Ideally, the ring or grid should be just below the top of the foliage: you want it to support the flower stems as high up as possible while still being hidden by the leaves.

Another option is some sort of homemade cage fashioned out of wire mesh. Chicken wire is easy to bend into a dome shape to fit over relatively low, thin-stemmed clumps, and it serves the added benefit of protecting clumps from bunnies and other critters (at least until the stems grow through the wire). Larger-mesh garden fencing bent into an arch or folded into a box shape works fine for larger perennials. And for the tallest perennials and grasses, consider using concrete reinforcing mesh or large-mesh livestock fencing.

For super-easy homemade supports, consider using brushy shrub prunings (what some gardeners call pea brush or pea stakes). Simply insert the cut end of several pieces of brush into the soil around an emerging clump, so the leaves and stems can grow up through the twigs. This works best with relatively low-growing perennials, such as catmints (*Nepeta*) and coreopsis.

TOP Those flimsy metal hoops sold for holding up tomato plants aren't much use in the vegetable garden, but they can be great for perennial supports. Cut off either the top or bottom ring, then lay chicken wire over the remaining upper ring and fold the edges over the metal ring. If desired, add a coat of black spray paint to make it practically invisible in the border.

LEFT AND BOTTOM Other options for keeping stems upright include bamboo stakes or cages (top left), grow-through hoop-type supports (left), and linking stakes (bottom).

Out-of-the-Ordinary Supports

WHO SAYS that stakes have to be ugly? When you use your imagination, you can find all kinds of fun and unusual ways to support your perennials and add a touch of whimsy to your gardens at the same time. Portable trellis panels are perfect for propping up larger perennials, while low sections of decorative garden edging are handy for holding up lower-growers that are sprawling into pathways. Flea markets, antique shops, and old farm junk piles can be a veritable gold mine of quirky supports, from old wooden chairs to rusty bits of machinery. Touch them up with a coat of colorful paint to draw attention to them, or let their weathered look help them blend in. Wire topiary forms in geometric or animal shapes are another option for a grow-through support that doubles as garden art.

A NEW LIFE With a coat of copper-toned paint, this frame for a broken table top got new life as a decorative and sturdy plant support.

Supporting Mature Plants

Maybe you simply don't have the time to deal with spring staking, or maybe you hate looking at a forest of stakes while you're waiting for plants to grow up and cover their supports. Single stakes are a traditional choice for holding up individual stems, and now garden-supply catalogs carry a wide variety of other supports you can install any time you need them. Single-stem supports that are topped with a smaller plastic or metal loop, or with two flexible arms that create a Y shape, eliminate the need for you to hand-tie each stem. Stakes topped with larger rings or a horizontal spiral, and those that link together to create any size or shape, can easily corral multiple stems.

With any of these staking systems, it's still best to put them in place before the plants actually sprawl. Propping or tying up stems that have already leaned severely or flopped entirely seldom produces attractive results.

UPSTANDING CITIZENS Staking individual stems can be tedious and time-consuming, but the elegant effect of spikes standing straight and tall can be worth every effort.

DIVIDING YOUR PERENNIALS

Considering the time, money, and love you put into getting your perennials off to a great start and keeping them looking their best, the idea of digging them up and chopping their clumps into pieces is understandably a bit daunting. Division is a handy skill to learn, though, because it serves a number of purposes. It rejuvenates tired, old plants, for instance, improving their bloom production, encouraging stronger stems, and decreasing disease problems. On plants that are too vigorous, frequent division slows down their spread. And as an added benefit, division gives you lots of extra plants, which you can use to fill new borders or share with friends.

THE DOUGHNUT SYNDROME If you see a perennial that has an empty center surrounded by a ring of vigorous growth, you know it's time to divide that clump. Replant the healthy-looking parts and discard the rest.

Deciding When to Divide

If your goal is simply to make more plants, you can divide most perennials as soon as they look large enough to separate into at least two parts. It's usually best to give them at least a full year after planting before you do this; otherwise, the pieces may be too small to survive. Give the replanted pieces at least the same amount of time before dividing again. Gardeners have a saying about perennials: "The first year, they sleep; the second year, they creep; and the third year, they leap." If you divide too often, your plants may never have a chance to really show you what they can do.

When your goal is mainly to keep your perennials healthy and attractive, let them tell you when they need to be divided. Generally speaking, most perennials take a few years to get established and really look their best, so don't worry much about dividing for the first 3 years after planting. Toward the end of the third growing season, and in the years after that, keep an eye out for clumps that aren't flowering as well as before, or that are starting to sprawl. You may even notice that the whole center of a clump looks weaker than the rest or has died out altogether. Bearded iris, coreopsis, daylilies (*Hemerocallis*), heucheras, and Shasta daisies (*Leucanthemum*) are a few perennials that tend to need division every 3 or 4 years. Other perennials can easily go 5 years or more before getting overcrowded,

Division Calendar

⬤ Spring (March–May)

Early to midspring — as soon as your soil has thawed out and dried up a bit — is a great time to divide many perennials, particularly those that flower from midsummer to fall and any that you grow primarily for their foliage. The earlier you get the job done, the longer they'll have to settle in before they really need to get growing. In late spring, you can start dividing early bloomers that have finished flowering for the year.

⬤ Summer (June–August)

In early summer, finish dividing spring-bloomers, as well as any fall-bloomers you didn't get to earlier. Midsummer isn't a good time to divide actively growing perennials, except for bearded irises once they're finished flowering. Start again toward the end of August with any spring and early summer-bloomers that you didn't get to earlier or that are now showing signs that they need dividing.

⬤ ⬤ Fall & Winter (September–February)

Finish up dividing spring- and summer-blooming perennials as soon as possible in early fall, so they'll have plenty of time to grow new roots before winter. This is also a good time to scout fall sales for full pots of easy-to-divide perennials, such as hostas and sedums. You can often separate one clump into several pieces, giving you two or more new plants for the price of just one. From late fall through winter, check on fall divisions once a week or so (unless they're covered with snow) to make sure that freezing-and-thawing cycles haven't pushed the crowns out of the soil. (If this does happen, cover the exposed crown and roots with some soil or mulch until you can replant the clump properly in spring.)

while some — such as peonies and large hostas — rarely, if ever, need to be divided.

There is one situation where dividing frequently can be a good idea: with plants that tend to spread vigorously by creeping roots. When you lift, divide, and replant them every other year, you stop them before they're able to "leap," so they don't get out of control. Yes, it's a bit of work, but it can be worth it if your gardening space is limited and you want to grow creepers without bothering with root barriers.

Perennial Division 101

Once you've decided which plants to divide and when you want to do the job, it's time to get busy. (See Division Calendar above.) First, you want to make sure the clumps you're going to divide aren't drought-stressed, so if the soil isn't already moist, water thoroughly the day before you plan to divide. Have some topsoil (or a blend of topsoil and compost) on hand to fill the hole where you dig up the clump. If you plan to replant some or all of the divisions elsewhere, get their new home ready before dividing, or have pots and growing mix ready to pot them up.

With plants that already have top growth, it's a good idea to cut them back by about one-half first before dividing them; it will be easier to see what you're doing, and the pieces will re-establish more quickly when replanted. (Cutting back isn't an issue in early to midspring, because the new leaves are just emerging.) Then, use a shovel to

BREAK IT UP If you can easily see or feel that a perennial's crown is rather loose, you'll probably be able to break it apart by hand. Make sure each new piece has some top growth (or at least ground-level buds) and some roots, too.

dig around and lift the clump. (See Digging and Moving the Plants on page 28.) Shake or brush off as much loose soil from the root ball as you can. If there's still a lot of earth clinging to the roots, you might want to wash it off, either by rinsing the roots with a gently running hose or by swishing the clump around in a bucket of water. Now, you're ready to divide.

Whether you cut or pull the clump apart, remember that each new piece will need some roots and some top growth or growth buds. You can divide down to single stems or buds, if your goal is to get as many new plants as possible. Keep in mind, though, that these small divisions will need careful attention from you for the first year, at least, and it will probably take them 2 or more years to make an impact again in your garden. Larger divisions give you fewer new pieces per clump, but they'll recover much more quickly and give you a good show during their first growing season. Most 3- to 5-year-old perennial clumps can yield three to five good-sized divisions.

Regardless of how many new pieces you make from one perennial, be sure to discard any dead or weak-looking portions from the center of the clump. Also, check the new pieces for signs of weeds or other plants that may have mingled with the original clump, and carefully remove the roots of the interlopers.

It's best to get your perennial divisions back in the ground quickly, so they don't have a chance to dry out. Replant good-sized pieces at the same depth the original clump was growing, then water thoroughly. If you divided down to single crowns, it's best to pot them up or plant them into a holding bed, and keep their soil evenly moist to help them get re-established.

Dividing Loose Clumps and Patches

On some perennials, such as heucheras and geraniums, you can easily see that the clumps are made up of many smaller plantlets grouped together. It's often possible to separate these plantlets simply by pulling them apart with your fingers.

Other perennials form a carpet of rosettes or shoots, rather than a distinct clump. On ajugas, creeping sedums, and some other low-spreaders, for instance, you can easily separate the dug-up plantlets by hand. Or, you could leave the main carpet in place, then simply dig out trowel-sized "plugs" 6 to 12 inches (15 to 30 cm) apart. Hand-dividing perennials that expand by runners, such as bee balms (*Monarda*) and obedient plant (*Physostegia*), can sometimes leave you with a stringy mess of roots and runners. Instead of trying to pull the pieces apart, use an old pair of garden shears to cut them. Make the new pieces about as big as the palm of your hand, and they'll re-establish quickly.

Dividing Tight Clumps

Some perennials — among them, astilbes, larger hostas, and woody-stemmed asters — produce such tightly packed crowns that there's no choice but to cut them apart. You can use a knife made especially for gardening, or else an old bread or steak knife. If you can see where the crown separates naturally into sections, use those lines to guide your cuts; otherwise, just slice down through the center of the clump. Try to make a clean, straight cut, with a minimum of chopping or sawing. Keep dividing the sections until they are the size you want them. Remember, each new piece must have its own roots and at least one bud or shoot.

Larger clumps may be too big or tough for a knife, at least for the first few cuts. A sharp-bladed garden spade can be a good tool to use for these, because the combination of your weight pressing down on the straight blade usually makes a quick, clean cut. If you happen to own two spading forks, you could try inserting them back to back in the middle of the clump and then pulling the handles to pry the pieces apart. Some gardeners faced with very tough clumps have resorted to cutting them up with an axe or even with a bow saw.

Handling Hard-to-Dig Clumps

Digging and then dividing is the usual order of business, but in some situations, you may want or need to divide a clump while it's still in the ground. For instance, if you'd just like to share a piece of a favorite perennial with a friend without disturbing the whole plant, you can use a trowel or spade to cut a bit from one side of the clump

LEFT A hori hori knife is a great tool to have on hand for dividing perennial clumps. Use the pointed tip to pry the crown apart, or cut with the straight side of the blade. The serrated side makes quick work of cutting tight or woody crowns.

RIGHT Digging out "plugs" with a trowel is an easy way to thin out or propagate carpet-forming perennials, such as creeping sedums. Fill the holes you leave with soil or a soil-compost mix.

(making sure to get some of the crown *and* some of the roots).

Perennials that tend to form huge clumps over the years — particularly large ornamental grasses, such as miscanthus — may defy all of your efforts to dig them up in one piece; in this case, you can resort to cutting them up right in place. Using a sharp spade, try first cutting across the center of the clump to divide it in half, then

DIVIDING IN PLACE Huge clumps of grasses and other large perennials can be daunting to dig up, let alone divide. Try cutting them into divisions while they're still in the ground; then it will be much easier to dig out the individual chunks.

keep cutting through the halves until the pieces are small enough to dig up separately. If the center is too tough to cut, then work around the perimeter of the clump, cutting off the outer parts in wedges. Once you're able to lift them out, you can divide those wedges into smaller sections, if needed. Don't forget to dig out and discard the dead or weak growth, too.

Perennials that spread by creeping roots can also be tough to dig up if they've been left undisturbed for a number of years. Their roots aren't all that deep, but the wide, shallow mat they form can be a challenge to divide in the usual way. It's usually easiest to work from the outer edge of the patch toward the center, cutting and digging out squares or wedges with a sharp spade or chopping them out with a mattock or grubbing hoe.

Love Those Leftovers!

PLANT SWAPS ARE A GREAT PLACE to trade your extra divisions and seedlings with other gardeners. Be sure to label each plant you take with you, and note on the label if the plant tends to spread quickly or self-sow abundantly, so the recipients know what to expect.

Once you've divided your perennials, you'll usually put only one piece back in the original spot (or maybe a few, if it's a large area). So, what are you going to do with all of the extras? Here are some ideas:

❧ Pot them up to share with friends, or to swap with fellow gardeners.

❧ Use them to fill gaps in other beds and borders and provide some repetition between your plantings at the same time.

❧ Create whole new gardens to house them.

❧ Grow them in attractive containers for mobile spots of color.

Still not sure what to do with all of the pieces? If you think you might use them later, tuck them into a holding bed or other out-of-the-way spot until you find a permanent home for them. As a last resort, you could compost the leftovers. Before doing this, though, you may want to leave them out in the sun for a few weeks to dry out thoroughly, so they don't take root in your compost pile.

DEALING WITH DEBRIS

When we plan and plant a new garden, our minds are filled with visions of abundant blooms and lush foliage, of rich color and the interplay of form and texture: all of the exciting aspects of design. One thing we seldom stop to consider is how we're going to deal with all of the debris — dead leaves, faded flowers, stiff stalks, and the like — that plants naturally produce as part of their life cycle.

Until you've actually gone through a few full gardening years, it's tough to imagine how much debris even a moderately sized border can produce each season, especially when the time comes for fall or spring cleanup. Then, the challenge becomes figuring out what to do with it all! The same "3 Rs" you use with your household waste — reduce, reuse, and recycle — are the secrets to turning garden debris from a problem to a valuable resource.

CHOP ON THE SPOT "Mulching in place" — snipping plant trimmings into small pieces and letting them fall back into the garden — takes a little extra time, but it's a good option if you don't have the space to pile up or compost debris elsewhere in your yard.

Minimizing Garden Debris

Debris isn't a factor that most people consider when planning their gardens, but it's worth thinking about, especially if your outdoor space is limited. Generally speaking, perennials that are prized for their winter form and seed heads — among them, sturdy-stemmed asters, Joe-Pye weeds (*Eupatorium*), ironweeds (*Vernonia*), and warm-season ornamental grasses — produce a large quantity of slow-to-decompose debris. Don't give up on growing these plants for that reason; just think ahead about how you're going to handle them during your fall or spring cleanup. Chopping them up a bit by hand, into pieces roughly 2 to 4 inches (5 to 10 cm) long, is a reasonable option if you have only a few plants; otherwise, it may be more practical to rent a shredder once a year. A brush mower, or a string trimmer with a blade attachment, can make quick work of cutting down mass plantings in fall or spring and chop up the debris right in place.

Another option for minimizing debris is adjusting your maintenance routine. Cramming all of your off-season garden cleanup into one weekend in fall or early spring leaves you with a big pile of debris to deal with all at once. That may be your only option where snow covers the ground through the winter, but elsewhere, consider spreading out your garden tidying through the late fall to early spring months, just a few hours here and there. It's a great excuse to get out in the garden for an hour or two if you have a mild day, and you'll have much less debris to deal with after each session.

◖ Spring (March–May)

Unless you cut all of your perennials to the ground in late fall, you'll have some cleanup to do in spring: mostly dried stems, perhaps with a few clinging dead leaves, and some lingering seed heads (which will likely have dropped their seeds by this time). Also remove any protective winter mulch. (See Perennial Care from Fall to Spring on page 49.) Evergreen perennial foliage that still looks good can stay on the plant, but feel free to snip off any winter-damaged leaves as part of the cleanup process. Pull out chickweed, dandelions, and any other cool-season weeds before they bloom, too. Most of this debris makes great fodder for your compost pile. Hand-chop or use a shredder to reduce the bulk of stiff perennial stems, as well as any evergreen boughs you used for winter protection.

◉ Summer (June–August)

There's lots of soft material to add to your compost pile during the summer: shoot tips from pinching and shearing, dead or discolored leaves, faded flowers, and weeds, too. Things to discard or otherwise keep separate include any diseased or insect-infested plant parts, weeds and perennial seed heads with seeds, spiny stems, and weeds with creeping roots.

◉ ◉ Fall & Winter (September–February)

This time of year is when garden debris can really pile up (literally)! Pull out any frost-killed annuals, and cut down any perennials that don't offer winter interest. This material can get pretty tough and "stalky," so hand-chop or shred it if you can before adding it to your compost pile, or create a separate debris pile where the stalks can start to break down over winter and then be added to your compost pile in spring. Let fall leaves from deciduous trees and shrubs blow into your borders for a no-fuss winter mulch, unless mice and voles are a common problem in your area; in that case, rake up the leaves and add them to your compost pile (either whole or shredded), or save them for mulching later in the fall (ideally shredded first).

Offbeat Uses for Perennial Trimmings

Before jumbling all of those browned leaves, twiggy stalks, and dead flowers into one pile, see if you can find a use for some of them. When you pinch or shear perennial clumps for shape and size in spring and summer, for instance, use some or all of those trimmings as cuttings to start new plants. (See Taking Cuttings on page 59.) Save interesting seed heads for use in holiday decorations, either indoors or outdoors, or gather the seeds themselves and use them to start new plants.

(See Growing from Seed on page 61.)

Clippings from perennials with fragrant flowers and foliage, such as bee balms (*Monarda*) and lavenders, can be worth drying for use in potpourri or for tossing into the fireplace in winter.

The stiff, twiggy stems of last year's tall asters can find new life when used as "pea staking" for supporting slender-stemmed annuals and perennials. In spring, insert the cut end of each stalk in the ground around the plants you want to support, then trim the dead stalks to whatever height you want.

Plan Your Strategy

DECIDING WHAT you're going to do with the debris before you start your garden cleanup will make the job go much more smoothly. Here's an overview of your options:

❖ **Leaves:** Add fresh or dried, whole or shredded leaves to your compost pile, or stockpile them in a bin (so they don't blow away) for use as mulch. Yellowed foliage is also fine for composting, but discard any obviously diseased or insect-infested leaves.

❖ **Stems:** Compost fresh or dried stems, ideally after hand-chopping them or running them through a shredder, or leave them in their own open pile. Discard any that are diseased, as well as those with sharp spines, especially if you can't shred them first.

❖ **Flowers:** From bud stage to full bloom to faded petals, flowers in just about any form are fine for adding to compost, because they're soft and will break down quickly. Discard any that are diseased or that have already formed seeds, though.

❖ **Roots:** It's fine to compost the roots of annual weeds and of most garden perennials (the bits left over from division, for example). It's smart to let them dry in the sun for a few weeks, though, so they don't start growing in your compost pile. Discard any roots from creeping weeds and fast-spreading creeping perennials.

Separating the various ingredients while doing your cleanup will make finishing up a snap. A 5-gallon bucket or large plastic tub is handy for gathering stuff you plan to discard, such as seed heads, diseased plant parts, and creeping weeds. Toss dead leaves, dried stalks, and other light-weight but bulky parts onto a tarp that you can drag around. Use a wheelbarrow to collect the heavier material, such as fresh leaves and stems, for easy transport to your compost pile.

By the way, you'll often see the advice (here and elsewhere) to discard material such as creeping roots, diseased leaves, thorny stems, and seed-laden weeds. Yes, this does usually mean to put it in your household trash. Adding more trash to landfills isn't the ideal solution, of course, and burning isn't an option in most areas. As an alternative, you may want to pile or bury this waste in an out-of-the-way spot on your property, or else keep a fully enclosed compost bin that's used only for holding this problem debris.

Roots from creeping perennials and weeds — especially serious thugs such as quack grass and Canada thistle — need to be disposed of carefully. *Don't* add them to your compost pile!

TARP IT! Piling light but bulky garden debris on a tarp makes for quick and easy cleanup. Just pull the four corners together and drag the tarp to your compost area when you're done!

The dead top growth of miscanthus, switch grass (*Panicum virgatum*), and other warm-season grasses is essentially just dried leaves and stalks, so you can use it as you would straw: as a mulch for fruits and vegetables, for instance, or on the paths of your veggie garden. (If you're concerned about the grasses self-sowing, you may want to cut off the seed heads first and discard them.)

Trash into Treasure

Now, what are you going to do with all of the remaining "trash" you've collected? It's time to make compost! No need to worry about getting the perfect mix of ingredients so the pile will heat up and break down quickly; just toss in whatever garden trimmings you have, and eventually, they'll break down into compost that you can add back to your garden soil. It's nice to have

a proper wooden, wire, or plastic bin to contain your garden debris while it decomposes, but a free-standing pile is fine, too.

Left in an open, uncovered area, a pile of "raw" debris from fall or spring garden cleanup may take a full year or two (or even longer) to completely break down. Can't wait that long? The quickest way to reduce the bulk of the debris and speed up the decomposition process is to run it through a shredder. Even a huge pile will be a fraction of its original size after shredding, and the finished product can go right back on your garden as a mulch. Or, if you let it sit in a pile, it can turn into dark, crumbly compost in just a few weeks: perfect for adding to planting holes, for working into the soil of new borders, or for mulching.

Chapter Four

TROUBLESHOOTING PERENNIAL GARDEN PROBLEMS

EVALUATING PERENNIAL PROBLEMS

It sounds a little depressing, but it's simply a fact of life in the garden: no matter how carefully you plan, plant, and nurture your perennials, it's almost inevitable that one or another of them is going to have some kind of problem. It's not worth getting stressed about, though; just try to figure out what the trouble is, choose an appropriate solution, and then do what you can to make sure the same problem doesn't happen again. Of these three steps, the most important one is correctly identifying the cause of the trouble. Simply grabbing a bottle of insecticide and hoping for the best is never the answer!

Consider the Possibilities

Sometimes, the problem you're confronted with is obvious: a plant is covered with pests, for instance, or you've found a herd of deer treating your perennial garden like an all-you-can-eat buffet. In other cases, the challenge is more subtle: a plant didn't behave as you expected it to, perhaps, or something just doesn't look right. Here are some potential causes to consider.

❃ **Insect pests** can produce a wide range of symptoms, from holes in leaves to distorted growth. For more diagnosis details, turn to Insects and Related Pests on page 96.

❃ **Rabbits, deer, and other critters** can quickly demolish a garden, eating entire plants in one night, so you need to identify the culprit quickly! See Animal Pests on page 106.

❃ **Spots, streaks, powdery patches, or generally poor growth** may be due to pathogens (disease-causing organisms) or to plant-care problems, such as overwatering. Perennial Diseases on page 110 has the scoop on some of the most common problems you're likely to encounter.

❃ **Weeds** can compete with "good" plants for light, water, and nutrients, weakening the growth of your prized perennials, so you'll want to keep these pesky plants from taking over. Turn to Perennial-Garden Weeds on page 115 for control tips.

❃ **Some problems seem to just happen with no obvious cause.** If your perennials aren't acting like you think they should, check out the Perennial Problem Gallery on page 98.

SHOW AND TELL When you're seeking help with a diagnosis, it's ideal if you can actually show someone the problem, either in your garden or with a sample of the affected plant part. A clear close-up photograph of the problem, and possibly of the whole plant as well, can be useful for getting an online diagnosis.

Getting Help

Having trouble figuring out what's wrong? Experienced gardeners in your area can be a great resource for diagnosis and control pointers: it's likely that they've had the same problem with their perennials at some point. Your local Cooperative Extension Service office can also be a good resource (check the "Government Offices" section of your phone book or visit the Web site listed on page 355 to find it.) Local nurseries and garden centers may or may not be able to help. Sometimes the employees there are very knowledgeable, and sometimes they'll just try to sell you whatever chemical they have on hand without really diagnosing the problem. Internet gardening forums are much the same, even though the folks there generally aren't interesting in selling you anything: the advice you get there may or may not be appropriate for your particular conditions.

Regardless of who you ask for help, remember that the more details you can give them, the better your chances of getting a quick and accurate answer. Make note of information about the site (sun or shade, wet or dry); your hardiness zone (see the USDA Hardiness Zone Map on page 355); how you've cared for the plant (when you fertilized it, how often you water it, and so on); and any unusual circumstances that may have caused the problem (soil disturbance near the affected plant, for instance, or house painting or deck staining). It's also useful to know *when* the problem happened — within a week or two after planting, during the first year, or after several years — as well as *where* it happened: on just one clump, on several plants in one area, or in an entire border. Recording details like this will help you with a diagnosis now and provide an invaluable resource to look back on in case you see similar symptoms in future years.

INSECTS AND RELATED PESTS

If you have a garden, you'll have insects: it's just that simple. It doesn't necessarily follow that you constantly have to worry about pest problems on your perennials, however. If you've chosen plants that are adapted to your climate and your soil and light conditions, their well-balanced, vigorous growth will enable them to shrug off minor pest damage on their own. It also helps if you can learn to see a few chewed leaves or imperfect petals without getting upset. Plant-eating insects are a natural part of a balanced ecosystem, so when you accept that there will be some of these "bad guys" around, you're also doing your part to help protect the other wild creatures that share your yard, neighborhood, and region.

Admittedly, it can be hard to stand back and watch your beloved perennials being chewed down to stubs. So sometimes, you may choose to try simple, homemade or commercially available organic controls to reduce the problem pests before they devastate your borders. Remember, though: There's no place for one-spray-kills-all chemical warfare in the flower garden. If some of your perennials are seriously damaged by hard-to-control pests every year, the sensible approach is to replace them with less problem-prone plants. You'll be a lot less stressed in the long run, and you'll enjoy your perennials all the more for it!

Perennial Pest Damage Signs

If your perennials get attacked by pests and you decide to take control measures, you first need to figure out which insects are at work. Sometimes, you can see the actual pests; other times, you'll only see the damage they cause. Here's an overview of some common types of plant damage that insects and related pests can cause.

❖ **Holes in leaves or flowers.** A wide variety of pesky pests can chew on your perennials, leaving holes in a variety of sizes and shapes. Some of the most common culprits include pest beetles, caterpillars, earwigs, grasshoppers, and slugs and snails. Soft flower petals often get eaten completely. Several of the pests that create this kind of damage are fairly large, so they can do a lot of damage quickly, and when there's an infestation, entire plants can be demolished in just a few days. Control options vary, depending on the specific pest. Once the pests are under control, most perennials can send out fresh foliage and flowers within a few weeks.

❖ **Discolored patches on leaves or petals.** Instead of chewing on foliage or flowers, some pests feed by sucking sap out of the plant, leaving yellowish, tan, or silvery spotting, speckling, or streaking behind. Spider mites and thrips are two possible causes; aphids and plant bugs (such as tarnished plant bug and four-lined plant bug) can cause similar damage. Generally, minor infestations of sap-sucking pests aren't serious, and the plants can outgrow the damage once the pests are taken care of. However, these pests can transmit some diseases from affected plants to healthy ones as they feed, which creates a more serious problem. Beneficial insects often take care of these pests before they get out of hand; simple soap-based sprays can work, too, if needed.

❖ **Distorted growth on leaves, shoots, or buds.** Left unchecked, infestations of aphids, spider mites, and other sap-sucking pests can produce curled or twisted growth on your perennials. One or two affected leaves are a minor problem, but when shoot tips are damaged, it can change the shape and size of the plant for that

BEETLE FEEDING Leaf-eating beetles tend to partly or entirely devour tender foliage. On older, tougher leaves, these pests may eat the softer tissue and leave the tougher veins behind, producing a lacy or "skeletonized" effect.

year: at best, it may simply be lower and bushier, but it's more likely to just look ugly for the rest of the growing season. If you notice this sort of damage starting, snipping off affected shoot tips immediately is a quick and effective way to stop further damage.

❖ **Sticky or black coating on leaves and buds.** The sticky coating is actually a material called honeydew, which aphids excrete as they feed. In some cases, a fungus grows on this sticky honeydew, producing a black coating known as sooty mold. Neither symptom directly harms plants, but their presence tells you to look for an infestation of aphids, either higher up on the same plant, or perhaps on a taller companion. Once the pests are under control, rain will wash the coating off of the leaves.

Perennial Problem Gallery

NO MATTER HOW CAREFULLY WE PLAN, our perennials sometimes don't act the way we expect them to. Here's a rundown of some common "behavioral" problems you might find in your beds and borders.

▶ No flowers

What's the problem: It could be that the plant is still too young to flower, or maybe it's too early in the season for it to bloom. The clump may not be getting enough sun, or it may be planted too deep. Transplanting or dividing can stress the plant and prevent flowering during the current year; so can insects or animals eating the flower buds.

What's the solution: Expect seed-grown plants to take 2 to 4 years to reach flowering size. Already-started plants may need a year or two to settle in and start blooming after planting or transplanting. Be patient: It could be that cool weather has delayed the flowering time. Make sure the plant is getting plenty of sun. If you think it might be planted too deep, dig it up in fall or spring and replant it slightly higher. If you have to transplant or divide an actively growing perennial before it blooms, expect that it may not flower until the following growing season. If you suspect insect or animal pests ate the buds, take preventive measures next year.

▶ Flowers aren't the color you expected

What's the problem: If newly planted perennials don't match their label or catalog picture when they bloom, it could be that they were mislabeled when you bought them, or it could be due to natural variation if they were grown from seed. Very cool or very warm weather can change the intensity of the bloom color, making it deeper or paler than you expected. If an established plant appears to completely change flower color, it could be that a seedling has grown up in the same spot and crowded out the original plant.

What's the solution: If you suspect that the plant you bought was mislabeled, discuss your concerns with the business you bought it from. Accept that seed-grown perennials can vary in flower color, and that weather conditions can cause color changes. There's not much you can do if an off-color seedling has completely crowded out the original clump, but if part of the original is still there, you may be able to separate the two by division.

Expect seed-grown perennials to vary in bloom color (and other traits too).

▸ Stems are weak

What's the problem: Some perennials naturally have somewhat weak stems. Ample water and fertilizer can encourage lush growth and soft, floppy stems; so can too much shade. Borers are insect pests that tunnel into stems and cause them to flop or break.

What's the solution: Support floppy perennials with stakes or sturdy companions, or pinch or shear them once or twice early in the growing season to encourage lower, bushier growth. Shelter plants from strong winds, make sure they get plenty of sun, and cut back on fertilizing and watering. There's not much you can do about borers, except to prune off affected stems.

Mums are notorious for flopping when in flower if not sheared or staked earlier in the growing season.

▸ Plant is smaller than expected

What's the problem: Most likely, the plant simply isn't mature yet. If it's been in place for more than 3 years and is still smaller than you thought it would be, it might have been mislabeled or it might not be getting the right amount of sunlight, water, or fertilizer. Or, soil-dwelling insects or animal pests (such as voles) may be feeding on the roots.

What's the solution: Expect perennials to take 2 to 4 years to settle in and start to fill out. If a particular plant is still small after that time, try watering and fertilizing it more often, or move the clump to a different spot (if it's been in partial shade, for instance, move it to a sunnier site). When you dig it up, take a look at the roots for signs of pest damage, such as chewed or damaged roots; removing any obvious pests and replanting in a different site may prevent further damage.

▸ Plant is larger than expected

What's the problem: When they're growing in ideal conditions, it's not unusual for established perennials to turn out somewhat taller or wider than their predicted size. If the plant is significantly larger than you thought it would be or if it spreads much faster than you expected, it may have been mislabeled when you acquired it.

What's the solution: There's not much you can do about mislabeled plants, except replace them with a smaller plant, if needed. If many of your perennials end up growing larger than expected, you may want to cut back on watering and fertilizing, or allow extra space between them at planting time. Other ways to control the size of your perennials include dividing them every year or two, pinching or shearing once or twice early in the growing season, and root pruning in early spring (cutting a circle around the clump with a shovel or spade, as if you were going to dig it up, to sever some of the roots).

In ideal growing conditions, some perennials (like *Petasites japonicus*) can spread far more quickly than you expected at planting time.

▶ Plant wilts

What's the problem: Lack of water is a common cause of wilting, but too much water can cause the same symptom. Recently moved or divided perennials may wilt on sunny days, even with regular watering, until the roots get re-established. Wilting may also be a symptom of root damage due to diseases or pests. If only one or two stems are affected, suspect stem borers.

What's the solution: Protect newly planted or divided, leafed-out perennials from strong sun for the first week or so, and water them regularly through the first growing season. Established perennials may need watering during extended dry spells. If you suspect the soil is staying too wet, try moving the plant to a spot with better drainage. It's tough to deal with root-attacking diseases, but you could try potting up the plant and watering it carefully to see if it recovers. If root-feeding pests are the cause, remove any that you can find and try replanting in a different site. Snip off and destroy borer-damaged shoots.

▶ Plant doesn't sprout in spring

What's the problem: Winter weather that's excessively cold or unusually wet and mild can kill perennials not adapted to those conditions. Mice or voles may have eaten the roots, and possibly the crown, too. Some perennials — such as blanket flowers (*Gaillardia*) — seem to be naturally short lived, thriving for a few years and then suddenly disappearing. Others sprout so late that you may think they are dead, but they will eventually emerge if you don't dig them up by mistake.

What's the solution: Don't assume a perennial is dead just because it's slow to sprout, unless it's a plant that's normally up and blooming in spring or early summer. If the plant really is dead, there's not much you can do except try to protect new plantings next winter — with mulch for protection against cold, for instance.

Rose mallow (*Hibiscus moscheutos*), balloon flowers (*Platycodon*), and a few other perennials may not send up new sprouts until May or June — several weeks after the plants growing around them have started to fill out.

Perennial Pest Gallery

▶ Aphids

What you see: Aphids are very small — about ¼ of the size of a grain of rice — and come in many colors, including red, gray, and black. They usually congregate on buds and shoot tips, causing yellowing, stickiness, and distorted growth. Some feed on the roots instead. Oxeyes (*Heliopsis*), chrysanthemums, and upright sedums are a few plants that seem especially attractive to aphids, but just about any perennial can be affected.

What to do: Rub infested shoots gently with your fingers to squash the pests, use a soap-based spray, or snip off and discard damaged shoot tips.

A variety of beneficial insects help keep aphids under control, but if these pests get out of hand, it's easy to control them by squashing them with your fingers or using a soap-based spray.

▶ Beetles

What you see: Beetles chew holes in foliage, sometimes eating whole leaves and sometimes leaving just the lacy veins behind; they chew buds and petals as well. Japanese beetles have roughly oblong, greenish black bodies and bronze-colored backs; they're especially fond of rose mallow (*Hibiscus moscheutos*), hollyhocks (*Alcea*), and persicarias. Blister beetles are elongated and usually black or brown; they can quickly defoliate anemones, clematis, and bugbanes (*Actaea*). Lily leaf beetles are bright red and are quickly becoming serious pests on true lilies (*Lilium*) and other plants, particularly in the Northeast.

What to do: If there are just a few beetles, pick them off by hand (wear gloves when handling blister beetles, which can irritate your skin) and drop them into soapy water. Neem or pyrethrin sprays may help for short-term control. Applying milky disease spores to your lawn can kill the larvae (grubs) of Japanese beetles and some other species for longer-term results.

Each kind of beetle seems to have its favorite food, but Japanese beetles seem to affect a number of different plants.

Perennial Pest Gallery *(continued)*

▶ Caterpillars

What you see: These somewhat wormlike creatures come in a range of sizes, from less than 1 inch (2.5 cm) to several inches (cm) long, and in several colors. Various types feed on a wide variety of perennials, chewing holes in leaves, buds, and flowers. Sometimes, caterpillars are easy to see; other times, you may need to look closely (don't forget to check the undersides of the leaves).

What to do: Pick off the pests by hand and drop them into soapy water, or snip them with your garden shears. If there are many caterpillars, try spraying with Btk (*Bacillus thuringiensis* var. *kurstaki*), a microorganism that attacks only caterpillars. Keep in mind that some caterpillars develop into beautiful butterflies, such as swallowtails and monarchs, so it's worth learning which of them you might want to protect in your garden.

If you see parsleyworms on your perennials, leave them alone so they can develop into beautiful black swallowtail butterflies.

▶ Plant bugs

What you see: These ¼-inch-long (6 mm) bugs are often brown (tarnished plant bug) or yellowish with black stripes (four-lined plant bug). As they suck the sap out of leaves and shoots, they produce small, light brown spots and may also cause distorted growth. Bee balms (*Monarda*), catmints (*Nepeta*), and chrysanthemums are just a few of the many perennials that may be affected.

What to do: Hand-pick the bugs, if you can catch them, and squash them or drop them into soapy water. As a last resort, try a pyrethrin-based spray.

Usually, perennials will produce fresh new growth above the parts that have been damaged by plant bugs, but if the leaves are very discolored or twisted, you may choose to snip them back to undamaged growth.

▶ Leaf miners

What you see: The adult flies are so tiny that you'll probably never notice them, but you *will* notice when their larvae start to feed between the upper and lower surfaces of plant leaves, producing pale, winding tunnels. Columbines (*Aquilegia*) and chrysanthemums are two favorite targets of leaf miners.

What to do: If there are just a few affected leaves, pinch them off and destroy them. If most of the foliage is affected, cut off all of the top growth 1 to 2 inches (2.5 to 5 cm) above the ground and destroy it.

Once leaf miners are inside the leaves, there isn't much you can do to control them, other than cutting off and destroying the affected foliage.

▶ Earwigs

What you see: These slender, dark-colored insects are roughly ¾ inch (18 mm) long and carry distinctive straight or curved pincers on their posterior end. Usually, they're considered beneficial, because they eat other insects, but they can also attack leaves, shoots, and flowers, leaving behind chewed or lacy-looking foliage and flowers. Dahlias and hostas are two plants earwigs often feed on, but other perennials can be damaged, too.

What to do: You may be able to trap earwigs by laying loosely rolled, moistened newspapers near affected plants. The pests will hide in there during the day, and you can shake them into a bucket of soapy water. For a different type of trap, pour ½ inch (12 mm) or so of cooking oil into a small, shallow container, such as a tuna fish can, and set it on the ground near your plants. Spraying earwigs directly with a soap-and-water spray might help to control them.

Earwigs feed mostly at night, so if you suspect that they are causing damage, inspect your plants after dark with a flashlight.

▶ Slugs and snails

What you see: These soft-bodied, wormlike creatures can be anywhere from ⅛ inch (3 mm) to 8 inches (20 cm) long and are usually brownish, black, or yellow. Snails have a coiled shell; slugs lack a shell. As they feed, both types of pests rasp small to large holes in leaves and petals; sometimes, only the main leaf veins are left. Delphiniums, hostas, and lilies (*Lilium*) are particular favorites of slugs and snails, but just about any perennial is susceptible. Damage is often most severe in damp conditions.

What to do: Wait until early or even midsummer to apply your usual mulch, or try using pine straw (pine needles) as a mulch to possibly discourage slugs and snails. Trap or hand-pick these pests (wear gloves or use tongs if you're squeamish) and drop them into soapy water. When you can see that slugs are active, spray damage-prone plants with an ammonia solution (1 part household ammonia mixed with 9 parts water). This dilution should be safe for most perennials, but before you start spraying it everywhere, test it on a few leaves of each plant you want to treat and wait two or three days to make sure no damage is visible. Consider using a natural (iron phosphate-based) slug bait, such as Sluggo or Escar-go.

Slugs and snails feed mostly on low-growing plants, but when plants are wet or the weather is very humid, they may climb several feet above the ground.

THINK BEFORE YOU SPRAY Some biological controls like Bt kill the good guys, like monarch butterfly caterpillars, along with the bad guys.

Choosing Pest Controls

Plenty of gardeners grow great-looking perennials without bothering with sprays and dusts of any kind; others get by just fine with a few simple homemade or commercially available controls. If you find pests bugging your perennials, consider the various options below, listed in order of first choice to last resort.

❧ **Adjust the growing conditions.** If the same pests attack your plants every year, simply tweaking the care you give your garden can prevent or minimize damage from now on. Aphids, for instance, are particularly fond of soft, lush growth; cutting back on watering and fertilizing (particularly with synthetic fertilizers) can produce tougher, slower-growing shoots that aren't as attractive to these pests. If slugs are your nemesis, you may hold off on applying mulches until early or even midsummer, to minimize the moist soil conditions that these pests love.

❧ **Change your plant choices.** Some perennials are simply more prone to certain pests. If you live where Japanese beetles are a common problem every summer, for instance, you either have to accept the damage they'll cause on their favorite plants or forgo those plants in favor of less-enticing options. One compromise is to site pest-prone perennials in less-visible parts of your yard: in the back or side yard, for example, instead of by your front door. That way, you can more easily ignore them when pests attack and then enjoy them again once the pests go away and the plants produce clean, new leaves.

❧ **Take a hands-on approach.** The quickest way to deal with pests is to kill them right on the plant, by crushing them with your fingers. Or, knock or drop the pests into a container of soapy water, from which they can't escape.

❧ **Try biological controls.** If you want to supplement the native beneficial insects in your garden, you may choose to buy and release commercially raised beneficials, such as lady beetles and predatory mites. Some naturally occurring microorganisms can also be helpful in keeping troublesome pests under control. Strains of *Bacillus thuringiensis* (Bt), for example, are available under a number of brand names to control caterpillars and other pests.

❧ **Consider sprays and dusts.** If other approaches aren't working, you may choose to try a homemade or commercial pest-control remedy. A simple spray of 1 teaspoon to 1 tablespoon of liquid dish soap to 1 gallon of water (perhaps with a small dash of cooking oil) can help knock down populations of aphids, thrips, mites, earwigs, and some other pests. (Any soap spray can harm foliage, so try it on a few leaves and wait a day or two to make sure it doesn't cause spotting or other leaf damage before spraying the rest of the plant.) Some garden-supply catalogs and garden centers carry commercially produced soap sprays and other organic options to control a variety of perennial pests. Remember to use any spray sparingly and only on affected plants, to minimize harm to nearby beneficial insects, spiders, bees, and other good guys.

Protect the Good Guys

NOT OF ALL THE INSECTS you see in your garden are likely to harm your plants. In fact, the majority of them won't affect your perennials at all, and some will actually help your garden by feeding on the pests. Flower gardens naturally provide great habitat for many beneficial insects, supplying an abundance of pollen and nectar for beneficials to eat when pests are scarce.

You can buy commercially raised beneficials to release in your garden, but there's usually no need; they'll be there anyway, as long as you avoid using pest-control sprays and dusts. (That goes for most organic controls, as well as synthetic ones. Unless the label specifically states that it does not harm beneficial insects, you can guess that the material will kill the good guys as well as the bad ones.)

Keep in mind that it takes the population of beneficials anywhere from a few days to a few weeks to build up enough to control the pests. Whenever possible, just be patient and wait for them to show up. If there's a severe pest infestation, or if you're concerned that the pests will cause serious damage, then consider using a simple control, such as removing the pests by hand or snipping off infested shoots. If you really feel you need to use an organic spray, choose the mildest one possible and use it only on the affected plant parts, to knock down the pests until enough beneficials build up to do the job. Remember, beneficials won't *totally* wipe out pests; if they did, they'd eventually disappear themselves. But given a chance, they'll keep the bad guys down to levels that won't seriously affect your perennials.

Lady beetle larva

Mantis

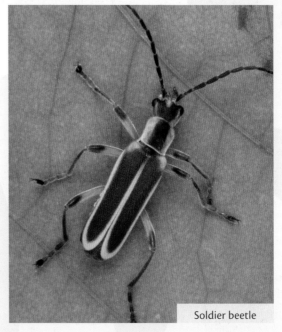

Soldier beetle

Lacewing

ANIMAL PESTS

It's one thing to see a few holes chewed in the leaves of your perennials; it's another to find entire plants eaten to the ground. Considering how much damage animal pests can do and how quickly they act, it's tough to take a "live and let live" approach with them. On the other hand, it's not practical for most of us to enclose our yard with extensive fencing simply because hungry wildlife might be a problem. Somewhere in between, there's the sensible compromise of watching out for potential animal pest problems, taking simple precautions where you can, and being prepared to jump into action if it looks like hungry critters have decided to turn your garden into their own all-you-can-eat buffet.

Signs of Animal Damage

When critters first appear, signs of their presence may be small and possible to mistake for insect pests or disease problems. A nibbled leaf or two may be the work of either beetles or bunnies; a couple of broken stems may indicate a few stem borers or one wandering deer. Missing shoot tips may be due to voracious caterpillars or to the initial foray of a hungry groundhog. Wilted plants may have root damage from fungal or bacterial diseases or from voles, or they may simply need watering.

One clue to the differences between insect and animal pests is the number of plants affected; another hint is how fast the damage appears. Unless you already have a severe insect infestation in action, it usually takes at least a few days for insects to build up enough to cause major damage. Animals, on the other hand, can eat whole leaves

MOUSE TRACKS Voles and mice can have a field day tunneling through the crowns of your perennials, especially if you apply mulch or if snow falls before the soil is frozen.

KEEP OUT Fencing deer out of your garden isn't an inexpensive option, but the investment is worth every penny where large numbers of deer make gardening practically impossible otherwise. Six feet (1.8 m) in height may be enough for a solid fence; with a see-though type of barrier, such as plastic netting, 8 feet (2.4 m) is better.

repellents to deter them from feeding, or use barriers to physically prevent them from reaching your plants.

❁ Repellents. Many animals have a strong sense of smell, so sprinkling or spraying plants with fish emulsion or other odiferous materials may encourage them to feed elsewhere. Some of these materials also have an unpleasant taste; animals may nibble a little but then don't want to eat any more. Homemade repellent sprays are usually based on eggs or hot pepper. Sprinkling blood-meal around plants is another popular barrier option. There are also a number of commercially produced repellents.

If you're facing animal damage on your perennials for the first time, applying some kind of repellent within a day or two may be enough to stop further damage. Where the same animals appear each year, it's smart to apply repellents before they start feeding. In some cases, a single treatment can be enough to chase troublesome critters away; in other years or other areas, you may need to reapply the repellent every week or

in seconds and multiple plants in minutes. Some animals have the infuriating habit of nipping off stem tips or whole stems and leaving them scattered next to the plant, which insect pests generally don't do. You may also see more distinct signs of animal pests, such as tracks or trails, dug-out holes in the ground, piles of droppings, or tufts of fur — or even the animals themselves.

Animal Pest Control Options

When you first see signs of animal pests, it's tempting to cross your fingers and hope that it's just a one-time problem. For some lucky gardeners, that approach works. In most cases, though, taking action as soon as animals appear is the better option. It's far easier to take simple measures to deter a few critters than to wage all-out war once they've made your garden their home. Sometimes, it's simply a matter of protecting your plants for a month or two in spring, until they have fully leafed out and are less enticing to animal pests. There are two main options: use

The Myth of Resistance

Garden books, nursery catalogs, and online gardening forums are chock-full of lists of perennials touted as being resistant to deer or other animal pests. They claim that plants with strong scents or spiny leaves are safe from four-footed menaces, and it's true that critters might pass by these plants when other food is plentiful. But in reality, when food is scarce — and sometimes even when it isn't — animal pests will feed on pretty much any perennial, no matter how many lists it appears on. So, go ahead and build your gardens around "animal-resistant" plants to possibly avoid some damage, if you wish, but don't be surprised if deer and rabbits eventually attack anyway!

Animal Pest Gallery

THE ANIMALS YOU MAY ENCOUNTER IN YOUR GARDEN vary depending on where you live. Here are a few of the most common problem critters, along with some control tips. For advice on identifying and coping with other perennial-garden animal pests, consult with your local Cooperative Extension Service or regional online gardening forums.

▸ Rabbits

What you see: Rabbit damage usually occurs within about 1 foot (30 cm) of the ground and may range from nibbled foliage and missing buds and blooms to neatly nipped-off stems or entirely eaten plants. These animals particularly like tender new growth. You may see the animals themselves hopping around your garden or see piles of their dark, pea-sized droppings. Sometimes, you may find one of their cupped, fur-lined nests right in the border, hidden under plant leaves.

What to do: Apply repellent sprays or granules such as Liquid Fence or Plantskydd, or sprinkle blood meal around your garden every week or so for a month or two. Protect individual plants from spring until midsummer (or permanently) with chicken-wire collars or cages. If you have an existing perimeter fence, line the bottom with 1-inch-square (2.5 cm) wire mesh, extending about 6 inches (15 cm) below the soil surface to prevent digging and 18 to 24 inches (45 to 60 cm) above the ground.

Rabbits are fun to watch, but there's nothing fun about the damage they can cause in the perennial garden.

two (follow label directions) through part or all of the growing season.

❁ Barriers. When repellents aren't doing the job, or where you want to make very sure a perennial doesn't get damaged (or damaged more than it is), physical barriers can be the answer. Sometimes, you can get away with draping groups of plants with plastic netting or surrounding individual clumps with commercial or homemade wire cages for a few weeks, at least.

A permanent fence extending both above and below the ground around all or part of your yard is a long-term solution for many animal pests, but it has some drawbacks, as well: perimeter fencing can be expensive and not especially attractive, it can block your view, it can make your yard feel smaller, and it can still allow in tiny pests, such as voles. Still, if rabbits and deer are troublesome enough to make gardening a misery instead of a delight, installing a fence can be worth every penny and every inconvenience.

▸ Voles and Mice

What you see: You won't often see these small, brownish to grayish pests at work, but they can cause serious damage. They feed very close to ground level or below it, sometimes chewing on new shoots but more commonly feeding on plant roots. During the growing season, you may notice that part or all of a clump is wilted even though the soil is moist, due to root damage. These pests feed on plant crowns and roots all through the winter, too. You may find that you can lift entire clumps right out of the ground by their stems because there's nothing anchoring them in the soil.

What to do: Minimize or eliminate the use of mulches, which provide great hiding places for these critters. You may have success with repellent sprays or granules, such as Repellex. It's not practical to try to exclude these pests from your yard with fences, but you may be able to protect plant roots and bulbs by lining their planting holes with sharp gravel or a similar commercial product, such as VoleBloc (also sold as PermaTill), or with 1-inch-square (2.5 cm) wire mesh.

Voles and mice feast on new shoots and plant roots.

▸ Deer

What you see: Deer may eat whole leaves and flowers or eat the tender parts and leave the tough stalks, usually causing jagged tears. You may also see their hoof prints in soft soil, or even see the animals themselves wandering around.

What to do: If there are only a few deer around, and if other food is plentiful, repellent sprays such as Deer Off, Liquid Fence, Plantskydd, or ordinary fish emulsion may be enough to encourage them to leave your garden alone. A single application might work, but usually, you'll want to reapply the repellent at regular intervals (according to label directions), particularly after a rain. Draping plastic netting over borders, or surrounding them with a netting barrier, can be a useful short-term solution to prevent damage, but it's not a practical or aesthetically pleasing permanent solution. For long-term protection, consider some sort of perimeter fencing, such as an 8-foot-tall (2.4 m) woven-wire or netting fence, or a combination of a 4-foot-tall (1.2 m) wire fence paired with a 3- to 4-foot-tall (90 to 120 cm) electric fence set 3 to 4 feet (90 to 120 cm) farther out.

Hungry deer can quickly demolish a perfect patch of hostas, leaving only the leafless stems behind.

PERENNIAL DISEASES

Insect and animal pests aren't the only challenges in your quest for a glorious perennial garden: diseases, too, can put a damper on some of the fun. Fortunately, most of the common perennial diseases aren't fatal. They can be unsightly, though, interfering with the good looks of your plants and reducing their vigor, so it's worth learning how to identify and control them — and how to prevent them from appearing in the first place.

Disease Signs and Symptoms

As with insects, the majority of the microorganisms that live in the garden are either harmless or even beneficial, but it's mostly the trouble-makers that grab our attention. Several common perennial diseases — including mildews and rusts — are caused by fungi, while bacteria mostly appear as leaf spots or root rots. Other pathogens (disease-causing organisms) include viruses, mycoplasma-like organisms, and tiny wormlike creatures called nematodes.

Different diseases cause different symptoms, but here are some general clues that pathogens may be plaguing your perennials:

- **Discolored patches, spots, or streaks on leaves, buds or flowers**
- **Curled or twisted leaves and shoots**
- **Stunted or wilted plants**
- **Blackened, mushy roots**

It's pretty easy to tell disease problems apart from the chewing damage done by many insects and animal pests. There is some overlap in other types of damage, though: both insects and diseases can cause symptoms such as distorted or wilted growth. To confuse matters further, there is also the matter of disorders: environmental or care problems that interfere with normal plant growth (just as diseases do) but that aren't caused by pathogens. Disorders can include a wide range of factors, including too much or not enough sun or water, excessive heat or cold, and nutrient imbalances. So, before you decide that a disease is at work in your garden, remember that the symptoms you see might be due to something as simple as over- or underwatering. (You can find information on dealing with some common disorders in the Perennial Problem Gallery on page 98.)

Disease Control Options

Diseases can be tough to deal with once they appear, so it's worth taking steps to discourage them in the first place. The most important thing to remember is that when plants are growing in their ideal light and soil conditions and they have the amount of moisture they prefer, they are naturally less susceptible to pathogens in the first place. That makes it worthwhile to do your research before you plant, so you can match the perennials you choose to the parts of your yard that best suit them and then give them the right care to keep them sturdy and vigorous.

WATCH THAT SPOT Powdery white spots on foliage can be an early sign of fungal disease. Fortunately, the corrective measure may be as simple as changing how frequently you water.

Also, keep in mind that not all plants are equally susceptible to diseases. So, if you want to grow a perennial that tends to be bothered by a certain disease — such as powdery mildew on phlox or bee balms (*Monarda*), or rust on hollyhocks (*Alcea*) — then it makes sense to seek out species and cultivars that have shown some resistance. *Resistant* does not mean *immune* — the plants may still be infected if conditions are ideal for disease development — but they will likely be among the last ones to show symptoms, and the symptoms will probably not be as severe as they would be otherwise.

When disease symptoms do appear, picking off and destroying infected leaves as soon as you notice them may slow or stop further damage. If symptoms keep appearing, you may apply an organic fungicide based on sulfur or copper, such as Soap-Shield, or on neem, such as Shield-All II.

DISPOSING OF DISEASES Don't add diseased plant parts to your compost pile. Throw them out with your household trash, or let them decompose in a separate, covered bin. (Don't add the compost from that bin back to your garden.)

Or, you might try a biofungicide — a foliar spray or soil drench that contains a solution of beneficial microorganisms; Root Guardian, Plant Guardian, and Serenade are a few names to look for. If certain plants in your garden are disfigured by diseases every year, though, the simplest approach is to replace them with other perennials that aren't affected. You may also want to do a thorough garden cleanup in fall, instead of waiting for spring, to remove debris that could harbor disease spores over the winter.

Perennial Disease Gallery

QUITE A NUMBER OF DISEASES can attack perennials, but you're likely to come across only a few of them. Here's an overview of some of the diseases you might see, along with suggestions for coping with them.

▶ Powdery mildew

What you see: This fungal disease produces white or grayish, dusty-looking patches on leaves, stems, and buds. Affected leaves may be distorted or shrivel up and drop off. Some common targets include asters, bee balms (*Monarda*), phlox, pulmonarias, veronicas, and yarrows (*Achillea*). Keep in mind that different types of mildew fungi affect different plants, so even if your phlox is affected, for instance, the disease won't spread to other nearby perennials (though they may develop another strain of mildew from spores that blow in from elsewhere).

What to do: Growing resistant cultivars is a good first line of defense. If you do notice symptoms, pick off and destroy infected leaves immediately; then, if you wish, follow up with some type of organic fungicide to reduce the chance of disease development on the rest of the plant.

Powdery mildew infections can appear any time during the growing season, but they're particularly common when days are warm, nights are cool, and the air is very humid.

▶ Botrytis blight (gray mold)

What you see: Symptoms include discolored to brownish patches on leaves and fluffy, grayish or brownish patches on buds and petals. Infected flowers usually turn brown and shrivel up, and their stems often droop. If the disease strikes at ground level, entire stems may turn black at the base, or just wilt and fall over. This fungal disease can affect a number of perennials, including chrysanthemums, true lilies (*Lilium*), and peonies.

What to do: Remove and destroy affected plant parts. Pull mulch a few inches away from plant crowns in spring to allow good air circulation around emerging shoots. Applying a biofungicide as soon as you notice the first symptoms appear might help to prevent further damage.

Drooping buds and shriveled-up blooms may be a sign that botrytis blight is at work.

▶ Leaf spots

What you see: Both fungi and bacteria can produce leaf spots in a variety of sizes, shapes, and colors. Severely affected leaves may turn yellow or brown and drop off. Leaf spots can affect a wide range of perennials.

What to do: Remove and destroy affected foliage right away. Sulfur-based sprays or dusts may help prevent further disease development if fungi are causing the problem; a bio-fungicide spray may stop or slow the spread of both fungi and bacteria.

Lots of different leaf spots can affect your perennials, but most of them aren't especially serious. Snipping off affected leaves when the first spots appear may prevent further damage.

▶ Rusts

What you see: Infections caused by rust fungi produce leaf streaks or spots that are usually yellowish to light brown on top, with a rusty-looking powder (the spores) on the underside of the leaf. Seriously affected leaves drop off early. Some perennials susceptible to rusts include asters, daylilies (*Hemerocallis*), hibiscus, hollyhocks (*Alcea*), lavatera, mallows (*Malva*), and yarrows (*Achillea*), as well as a number of ornamental grasses.

What to do: Choose resistant species and cultivars, when available. Try to avoid wetting the foliage when you water. If symptoms appear, pick off and destroy affected leaves. You may then follow up with an organic fungicide spray to protect the remaining leaves. Or, use the fungicide every 7 to 10 days starting before symptoms appear as a preventive measure on plants that have been affected in previous years.

As with mildew fungi, different rusts usually infect different types of perennials. So, if your hollyhocks (*Alcea*) show symptoms of rust, you don't need to worry about it spreading to your daylilies (*Hemerocallis*), or vice versa.

▶ Wilts

What you see: Leaves turn yellow and droop, then die. Symptoms may appear on just one or a few stems at first, but soon, the entire clump is affected. Fungal wilts can attack many kinds of perennials.

What to do: There is no cure once symptoms appear, so remove and destroy infected perennials. If you want to grow something else in that spot, consider treating the soil with a biofungicide drench before replanting with a different type of perennial.

When you see a perennial wilting, it's normal to assume that the soil is too dry. But if the soil is moist and the plant is still droopy, a fungal wilt disease may be at work.

▸ Root and crown rots

What you see: Affected plants may disappear during the winter, or the stems may emerge in spring and then turn black at the base and wilt. If the disease strikes later in the growing season, you may notice the foliage yellowing, as well as overall slower-than-usual growth. Infected roots turn black and die. Many perennials can be affected by rots.

What to do: Remove and destroy seriously affected plants. To prevent problems, avoid planting in soggy soil (unless you're growing perennials that prefer it), and try not to overwater. Also, keep mulches a few inches (cm) away from the base of your perennials; don't pile it right next to the stems. If you've had problems with root or crown rot in your garden in the past, you might try a bio-fungicide drench to treat the soil before planting something else there.

Rots are mostly a problem where the soil is too wet. If symptoms appear, you might be able to stop further damage by removing the mulch around the plant so the soil can dry out a bit.

▸ Aster yellows

What you see: The most common symptoms of aster yellows include twisted or stunted shoots and leaves. Flowers tend to be smaller than usual and distorted, and they often have a greenish color. Sucking pests, such as aphids and leafhoppers, can spread this disease as they feed. Many perennials can be affected, but this disease seems to most commonly attack daisy-family plants, such as chrysanthemums, coneflowers (*Echinacea* and *Rudbeckia*), and blanket flowers (*Gaillardia*), as well as asters, of course.

What to do: If you suspect aster yellows, it's best to remove and destroy the plant immediately. It's not an easy solution, but otherwise, you run the risk of insects spreading the disease to more of your perennials.

Aster yellows is sometimes referred to as a virus, but it's actually caused by a mycoplasma-like organism or phytoplasma. Once a plant is infected, you need to dig it out and destroy it.

EVALUATING PERENNIAL PROBLEMS

It sounds a little depressing, but it's simply a fact of life in the garden: no matter how carefully you plan, plant, and nurture your perennials, it's almost inevitable that one or another of them is going to have some kind of problem. It's not worth getting stressed about, though; just try to figure out what the trouble is, choose an appropriate solution, and then do what you can to make sure the same problem doesn't happen again. Of these three steps, the most important one is correctly identifying the cause of the trouble. Simply grabbing a bottle of insecticide and hoping for the best is never the answer!

Consider the Possibilities

Sometimes, the problem you're confronted with is obvious: a plant is covered with pests, for instance, or you've found a herd of deer treating your perennial garden like an all-you-can-eat buffet. In other cases, the challenge is more subtle: a plant didn't behave as you expected it to, perhaps, or something just doesn't look right. Here are some potential causes to consider.

❧ **Insect pests** can produce a wide range of symptoms, from holes in leaves to distorted growth. For more diagnosis details, turn to Insects and Related Pests on page 96.

❧ **Rabbits, deer, and other critters** can quickly demolish a garden, eating entire plants in one night, so you need to identify the culprit quickly! See Animal Pests on page 106.

❧ **Spots, streaks, powdery patches, or generally poor growth** may be due to pathogens (disease-causing organisms) or to plant-care problems, such as overwatering. Perennial Diseases on page 110 has the scoop on some of the most common problems you're likely to encounter.

❧ **Weeds** can compete with "good" plants for light, water, and nutrients, weakening the growth of your prized perennials, so you'll want to keep these pesky plants from taking over. Turn to Perennial-Garden Weeds on page 115 for control tips.

❧ **Some problems seem to just happen with no obvious cause.** If your perennials aren't acting like you think they should, check out the Perennial Problem Gallery on page 98.

SHOW AND TELL When you're seeking help with a diagnosis, it's ideal if you can actually show someone the problem, either in your garden or with a sample of the affected plant part. A clear close-up photograph of the problem, and possibly of the whole plant as well, can be useful for getting an online diagnosis.

Getting Help

Having trouble figuring out what's wrong? Experienced gardeners in your area can be a great resource for diagnosis and control pointers: it's likely that they've had the same problem with their perennials at some point. Your local Cooperative Extension Service office can also be a good resource (check the "Government Offices" section of your phone book or visit the Web site listed on page 355 to find it.) Local nurseries and garden centers may or may not be able to help. Sometimes the employees there are very knowledgeable, and sometimes they'll just try to sell you whatever chemical they have on hand without really diagnosing the problem. Internet gardening forums are much the same, even though the folks there generally aren't interesting in selling you anything: the advice you get there may or may not be appropriate for your particular conditions.

Regardless of who you ask for help, remember that the more details you can give them, the better your chances of getting a quick and accurate answer. Make note of information about the site (sun or shade, wet or dry); your hardiness zone (see the USDA Hardiness Zone Map on page 355); how you've cared for the plant (when you fertilized it, how often you water it, and so on); and any unusual circumstances that may have caused the problem (soil disturbance near the affected plant, for instance, or house painting or deck staining). It's also useful to know *when* the problem happened — within a week or two after planting, during the first year, or after several years — as well as *where* it happened: on just one clump, on several plants in one area, or in an entire border. Recording details like this will help you with a diagnosis now and provide an invaluable resource to look back on in case you see similar symptoms in future years.

INSECTS AND RELATED PESTS

If you have a garden, you'll have insects: it's just that simple. It doesn't necessarily follow that you constantly have to worry about pest problems on your perennials, however. If you've chosen plants that are adapted to your climate and your soil and light conditions, their well-balanced, vigorous growth will enable them to shrug off minor pest damage on their own. It also helps if you can learn to see a few chewed leaves or imperfect petals without getting upset. Plant-eating insects are a natural part of a balanced ecosystem, so when you accept that there will be some of these "bad guys" around, you're also doing your part to help protect the other wild creatures that share your yard, neighborhood, and region.

Admittedly, it can be hard to stand back and watch your beloved perennials being chewed down to stubs. So sometimes, you may choose to try simple, homemade or commercially available organic controls to reduce the problem pests before they devastate your borders. Remember, though: There's no place for one-spray-kills-all chemical warfare in the flower garden. If some of your perennials are seriously damaged by hard-to-control pests every year, the sensible approach is to replace them with less problem-prone plants. You'll be a lot less stressed in the long run, and you'll enjoy your perennials all the more for it!

PERENNIAL-GARDEN WEEDS

Unwanted and out of place, weedy plants can quickly spoil the good looks of a carefully planned perennial garden. But weeds are more than just an aesthetic problem: they also compete with more desirable plants for space, light, nutrients, and moisture, and they can harbor troublesome pests and diseases as well. It's easy to see that keeping these pesky plants in check is worth your while!

When it comes to dealing with weeds in your perennial garden, a little knowledge of their habits is your best weapon. First, just as with desirable flowers, weeds can be annual (sprouting, growing, setting seed, and dying within one growing season), biennial (producing foliage their first year, then setting seeds and dying the second year), or perennial (returning from their roots for 3 years or more). Because annuals and biennials spread by seed, your main goal is to get rid of them before their flowers mature. With perennials, it isn't enough to stop them from making seed; you need to remove their persistent roots as well, or they'll simply resprout.

Another thing to know about weeds is that they're not just a summer problem. It's true that a number of common annual and perennial weeds — including crab grass, and quack grass, and ragweed — thrive in warm weather, sprouting in spring or summer and flowering in summer or fall. But there are also quite a few weeds that prefer to grow in cooler weather, sprouting up in fall or early spring; some of these include chickweeds, dandelions, and wild garlic. It's easy to overlook cool-season weeds if you don't spend much time outdoors in winter, but you're sure to notice them in spring, when they're spoiling the display of your early blooming perennials.

Preventing Weed Problems

Of all the things that can interfere with your perennial-gardening pleasure, weeds are among the easiest to prevent. Here's a rundown of some simple but effective tricks for stopping these pesky plants before they even get started.

❧ **Don't bring weeds home.** When you're plant shopping, avoid buying perennials with weedy pots. Be careful with gifts or trades or plants and seeds, too: well-meaning but misinformed gardeners sometimes misidentify weeds as desirable perennials.

❧ **Watch out for weeds in topsoil, compost, and mulch.** Bulk topsoil usually looks clean and weed free when it's delivered, and so do municipal compost and mulch. All of these can come with a generous crop of weed seeds and roots, though. You may want to moisten the pile and let it sit for a week or two to see if anything troublesome sprouts (and, obviously, think twice about using any mulch or soil amendment that *does* sprout a large crop of weeds). You can be pretty sure homemade compost is "clean" if you're careful not to add roots of perennial weeds or seed-laden flower heads of any plants to your pile.

❧ **Get rid of weeds before planting.** Getting rid of weeds thoroughly before putting any perennials in a new garden will go a long way toward minimizing future problems. That includes turf grass as well as tough-to-control spreaders, such as Canada thistle. If you simply till or dig the grass or weeds into the soil, they'll pop right back up after you plant. Where this thorough removal isn't possible or practical, consider covering the site with cardboard and 4 to 6 inches (10 to 15 cm) of mulch and let it sit for at least one full growing season before planting.

❧ **Keep the soil covered.** Bare soil is an open invitation to weeds. While you're waiting for newly planted perennials to fill out their allotted space, you could tuck in annuals as fillers for a year or two. Or, simply cover the space between your plants with mulch. Do not be tempted to use landscape fabric! Yes, it will work fine for a

USE THE NEWS Any time you disturb the soil, you bring new weed seeds to the surface. But you can smother them before they get growing by laying strips of wet newspaper on the soil around newly planted perennials before adding mulch.

Controlling Garden Weeds

As important as it is to prevent weeds as much as possible, it's inevitable that some will eventually appear in your garden. Getting rid of them doesn't have to involve weekend-long weeding marathons, though. Here are some pointers to make the job much more manageable.

❖ Weed early, weed often. If you put off weeding, you give the weeds a chance to get their roots more firmly established, and they'll be that much harder to pull; plus, you run the risk of them dropping their seeds before you remove them. Instead, keep a bucket and some kind of sharp-bladed weeding tool in a handy spot, then try to spend 15 minutes or so weeding every day or two through the entire growing season. The job will be much more manageable that way. (Don't forget to include a few winter weeding sessions, as well, whenever the soil is unfrozen and not covered by snow, to control cool-season weeds.)

❖ Do a thorough job. Don't speed through your weeding sessions; take the time to remove each weed completely (roots and all). Otherwise, you'll have to deal with the weeds again if they resprout. If weeds are seriously intertwined with your perennials, dig up the clumps and wash the soil off the roots, then carefully pick out all of the weed parts before replanting. (For extra protection, plant the clumps in pots or a separate holding area for a few months to make sure the weeds are completely gone before returning the perennials to your garden.) If the entire border is seriously weed infested, you could cover the whole area with cardboard and 4 to 6 inches (10 to 15 cm) of mulch, then let it sit for at least one full year (ideally two) before replanting.

❖ Don't take shortcuts. It's tempting to toss a layer of mulch onto a weedy bed to improve its appearance, but in most cases, the weeds will still come through. It's far better to weed first, then mulch. One exception: If there are many tiny weeds, you could cover the soil between your plants with strips of wet newspaper (several sheets thick, to smother the seedlings) before you mulch.

year or two; eventually, though, weed seeds will blow into and sprout in the mulch layer on top, then root down through the fabric and be almost impossible to pull out. The fabric also makes continuing soil improvement practically impossible, and digging up perennials that need to be divided will be a nightmare.

❖ Say no to seeds. Growing perennials from seed is great fun, but don't sow them directly in your garden. Many of them are easy to confuse with weed seedlings, so you may either pull out the perennials or leave weeds that you would have otherwise removed. Also, watch out if you leave seed heads for your perennials for winter interest. Birds will eat many of the seeds, but at least some of the seeds may drop to the soil and sprout. A few self-sown seedlings may be welcome, but dozens or hundreds can qualify as a weed problem!

Perennial Weed Gallery

WEEDS VARY FROM ONE REGION of the country to another, not to mention from one end of the yard to the other. Here's an overview of some of the weeds you might find, along with information on how to deal with them.

▶ Ragweed

What you see: Common ragweed (*Ambrosia artemisii-folia*) is a warm-season annual weed with hairy, deeply lobed leaves on upright, branching stems that can reach to about 5 feet (1.5 m) tall. In late summer, narrow clusters of tiny, greenish flowers appear at the stem tips. The insignificant blooms release large amounts of wind-carried pollen that is a main cause of fall hayfever — a problem usually blamed on the showier perennial goldenrods (*Solidago*) that bloom around the same time.

What to do: Common ragweed readily blends into other plants, so you may not notice it until it's flowering (and then only if you are looking closely). Pull out the plants as soon as you can (wear gloves and long sleeves when you do it to prevent skin irritation) — ideally before you have to deal with the pollen-filled flowers.

Common ragweed

▶ Chickweed

What you see: These cool-season, annual weeds form low-growing clumps of small leaves and starry white flowers. Their slender stems root where they touch the soil, creating dense mats that can smother desirable plants. Common chickweed (*Stellaria media*) has mostly smooth, heart-shaped, bright green leaves; mouse-ear chickweed (*Cerastium vulgatum*) has oblong to lance-shaped, deep green, hairy leaves. Chickweeds tend to be most noticeable during the winter and early spring, when other plants are dormant.

What to do: Plan a few weeding sessions from late fall through early spring to catch chickweeds before they can set seed. Pull the entire plant. If you've had problems with chickweeds in past years, consider applying corn gluten meal (a natural herbicide) to the soil in fall and in early spring to discourage their seeds from sprouting.

Chickweed

▸ Plantains

Plantain

What you see: Plantains are rosette-forming, cool-season perennial weeds that are typically less than 1 foot (30 cm) tall. Broadleaf plantain (*Plantago major*) has broad, oval, somewhat leathery leaves and narrow spikes of tiny whitish flowers. Buckhorn plantain (*P. lanceolata*) has much narrower foliage and wiry flower stalks topped with conelike clusters of tiny white flowers. Plantains are distinctly clump forming, but their vigorous leafy growth can smother more delicate companions.

What to do: Dig out the clumps as soon as you spot them. If you try to pull plantains, the tops tend to snap off, and the plants will simply resprout.

▸ Dandelion

What you see: This cool-season perennial weed is a common problem in lawns, but it can also appear in garden beds. Dandelions (*Taraxacum officinale*) form low, dense rosettes of jagged-edged leaves that grow from a thick taproot. The distinctive, bright yellow blooms mature quickly into puffy globes of white-tufted seeds, which are carried by the wind. Besides ruining the look of your carefully planned borders, dandelions' broad foliage clumps can crowd out less vigorous perennials.

What to do: When the soil is moist, use a long-bladed weeding tool to pop the whole plant out of the soil. Try not to snap off the leafy tops; otherwise, the root left in the soil will resprout.

Dandelion

▸ Grasses

What you see: Many kinds of grasses can invade perennial plantings. They range in height from a few inches to a few feet tall, with slender leaf blades and small, greenish flowers. Annual grasses include crab grasses (*Digitaria*), foxtails (*Setaria*), and Japanese stilt grass (*Microstegium vimineum*); perennials include Bermuda grass (*Cynodon dactylon*), Johnson grass (*Sorghum halepense*), and quack grass (*Agropyron repens*).

Lawn grass

What to do: Keeping the soil covered with mulch can discourage annual grasses from sprouting; pull out any that do appear before they set seed. Weedy perennial grasses are very difficult to control, because they have aggressive and tenacious creeping roots. Use edging strips to prevent lawn grass from creeping into perennial beds. Remove all perennial grasses as completely as possible (including their roots) before planting; carefully dig out those that appear later. If they get out of hand, it's easiest to remove the desirable perennials and cover the whole bed with cardboard and mulch for 2 years before replanting.

► Woodsorrel

What you see: Usually growing less than 1 foot (30 cm) tall, these warm-season perennial weeds have small, three-part leaves with heart-shaped, green to purple leaflets that usually close up at night. Small, five-petaled, bright yellow flowers are followed by narrow, light green seedpods that pop open to fling the seeds far and wide. Yellow woodsorrel (*Oxalis stricta*) tends to be upright, and it has slender rhizomes that creep below the soil surface. Creeping woodsorrel (*O. corniculata*) is usually more ground-hugging, with surface-creeping stems that root where they touch the soil.

What to do: Woodsorrels are tough to control once they get established, so it's important to dig out the plants as thoroughly as possible (including the creeping roots and stems) as soon as you spot them — and definitely before they set seed!

Yellow woodsorrel

► Canada Thistle

What you see: Canada thistle (*Cirsium arvense*) is a warm-season perennial weed that grows about 4 feet (1.2 m) tall, with lobed, prickly leaves on equally prickly, upright stems. The purplish, tufted flowers appear in small clusters at the shoot tips in summer and fall. Besides spreading by wind-carried seed, Canada thistles produce vigorous underground stems that creep horizontally through the soil, sending up vertical shoots as they travel.

What to do: If a thistle seedling appears in your garden, remove it immediately, getting as much of the root as possible. (Do not add it to your compost.) Once Canada thistle has sent out creepers, control is much more difficult; unless your soil is very loose and sandy, the horizontal parts will stay in the soil when you dig out the vertical shoots. Removing shoots as thoroughly as possible as soon as they resprout (every few days for weeks or months) may work in a small area. Use the smothering technique (cardboard topped with 4 to 6 inches [10 to 15 cm] of mulch and left for at least 2 years) to deal with larger patches.

Canada thistle

PART TWO

PLANT-BY-PLANT PERENNIAL GUIDE

Whether you're looking for tips on caring for perennials you already grow or want to learn more about potential new additions to your garden, you've come to the right place. In this section, you'll find 125 entries covering hundreds of popular garden perennials arranged alphabetically by their genus name. (There are also three general entries: Bulbs, Ferns, and Grasses.) If you're not completely comfortable using scientific names, refer to the common-name index on page 122.

In each entry, you'll find brief descriptions of some of the most popular species and cultivars, followed by a season-by-season care calendar. Growing Tips includes details on the preferred light and soil conditions, information on common pests and diseases that may attack, and propagation tips. Some entries also include troubleshooting, which highlights specific problems and solutions. For more detailed information on any of the techniques mentioned in these plant-by-plant entries, turn to Part One: Perennial Care Basics, starting on page 3.

OPPOSITE Doing your homework before you buy your perennials can prevent many headaches later on. Obedient plant (*Physostegia virginiana*), for example, spreads freely by creeping roots, which can be a problem in the rich, loose soil of a well-prepared border but a blessing in a difficult site where daintier perennials don't thrive.

PLANT REFERENCE BY COMMON NAME

Bee balm (*Monarda*)   Catmint (*Nepeta*)   Butterfly weed (*Asclepias*)

THE PLANT-BY-PLANT GUIDE is organized by the plants' botanical names. But not all gardeners are familiar with the botanical names of their favorite perennials, so I've created an index of common names to
make it easier for you to find the plant you're looking for.

Adam's needle — see *Yucca*

Allium — see Bulbs

Alumroot — see *Heuchera*

Anise hyssop — see *Agastache*

Autumn fern — see Ferns

Avens — see *Geum*

Baby's breath — see *Gypsophila*

Balloon flower — see *Platycodon*

Baneberry — see *Actaea*

Barrenwort — see *Epimedium*

Basket-of-gold — see Relatively Speaking in
    Arabis

Bear's breeches — see *Acanthus*

Beardtongue — see *Penstemon*

Bee balm — see *Monarda*

Bellflower — see *Campanula*

Betony — see *Stachys*

Blackberry lily — see *Belamcanda*

Black-eyed Susan — see *Rudbeckia*

Blanket flower — see *Gaillardia*

Blazing star — see *Liatris*

Bleeding heart — see *Dicentra*

Blue fescue — see Grasses

Blue oat grass — see Grasses

Bluebeard, blue mist — see *Caryopteris*

Bluestar — see *Amsonia*

Bluestem — see Grasses

Bowman's root — see *Gillenia*

Bugbane — see *Actaea*

Bugle — see *Ajuga*

Bugloss — see *Anchusa*

Burnet — see *Sanguisorba*

Butterfly weed — see *Asclepias*

Calamint — see Relatively Speaking in *Nepeta*

Campion — see *Lychnis*

Candy lily — see Relatively Speaking in
    Belamcanda

Candytuft — see *Iberis*

Canna — see Bulbs

Cardinal flower — see *Lobelia*

Catchfly — see *Lychnis*

Catmint — see *Nepeta*

Checkerbloom — see Relatively Speaking in
    Alcea

Christmas fern — see Ferns

Christmas rose — see *Helleborus*

Globe thistle (*Echinops*)

Flax (*Linum*)

Coral bells (*Heuchera*)

Cinquefoil (*Potentilla*)

Feverfew (*Tanacetum*)

Foxglove (*Digitalis*)

Cinnamon fern — see Ferns

Cinquefoil — see *Potentilla*

Columbine — see *Aquilegia*

Comfrey — see *Symphytum*

Coneflower, orange — see *Rudbeckia*

Coneflower, prairie — see Relatively Speaking in *Rudbeckia*

Coneflower, purple — see *Echinacea*

Coral bells — see *Heuchera*

Cornflower — see *Centaurea*

Cranesbill — see *Geranium*

Crocus — see Bulbs

Culver's root — see *Veronicastrum*

Cupid's dart — see Relatively Speaking in *Centaurea*

Cyclamen — see Bulbs

Daffodil — see Bulbs

Dahlia — see Bulbs

Daylily — see *Hemerocallis*

Dead nettle — see *Lamium*

Deer grass — see Grasses

Dittany — see *Dictamnus*

Dropwort — see *Filipendula*

Evening primrose — see *Oenothera*

False aster — see Relatively Speaking in *Aster*

False indigo — see *Baptisia*

False lupine — see Relatively Speaking in *Baptisia*

Feather reed grass — see Grasses

Fennel — see *Foeniculum*

Fescue — see Grasses

Feverfew — see *Tanacetum*

Flag — see *Iris*

Flax — see *Linum*

Fleeceflower — see *Persicaria*

Flowering fern — see Ferns

Foamflower — see *Tiarella*

Foamy bells — see Relatively Speaking in *Tiarella*

Fountain grass — see Grasses

Foxglove — see *Digitalis*

Gardener's garters — see Grasses

Gas plant — see *Dictamnus*

Gayfeather — see *Liatris*

Ginger — see *Asarum*

Globe thistle — see *Echinops*

Globeflower — see *Trollius*

Gloriosa daisy — see *Rudbeckia*

Goat's beard — see *Aruncus*

Golden glow — see *Rudbeckia*

Golden lace — see *Patrinia*

Goldenrod — see *Solidago*

Grape hyacinth — see Bulbs

Hakone grass — see Grasses

Hardy ageratum — see *Eupatorium*

Hardy geranium — see *Geranium*

Hardy hibiscus — see *Hibiscus*

Hollyhock — see *Alcea*

Knapweed (*Centaurea*)

Meadowsweet (*Filipendula*)

Lamb's ears (*Stachys*)

Jerusalem sage (*Phlomis*)

Loosestrife (*Lysimachia*)

Peony (*Paeonia*)

(continued from previous page)

Hyacinth — see Bulbs

Iceland poppy — see *Papaver*

Ironweed — see *Vernonia*

Italian arum — see *Arum*

Jacob's ladder — see *Polemonium*

Japanese blood grass — see Grasses

Japanese silver grass — see Grasses

Jerusalem sage — see *Phlomis*

Joe-Pye weed — see *Eupatorium*

Jupiter's beard — see *Centranthus*

Knapweed — see *Centaurea*

Knautia — see Relatively Speaking in *Scabiosa*

Knotweed — see *Persicaria*

Lady fern — see Ferns

Lady's mantle — see *Alchemilla*

Ladybells — see Relatively Speaking in *Campanula*

Lamb's ears — see *Stachys*

Lenten rose — see *Helleborus*

Little bluestem — see Grasses

Loosestrife — see *Lysimachia*

Lungwort — see *Pulmonaria*

Lyme grass — see Grasses

Maiden grass — see Grasses

Maidenhair fern — see Ferns

Male fern — see Ferns

Mallow — see *Malva*

Maltese cross — see *Lychnis*

Meadow rue — see *Thalictrum*

Meadowsweet — see *Filipendula*

Milkweed — see *Asclepias*

Monkshood — see *Aconitum*

Montauk daisy — see Relatively Speaking in *Leucanthemum*

Montbretia — see *Crocosmia*

Moor grass — see Grasses

Mugwort — see *Artemisia*

Muhly — see Grasses

Mullein — see *Verbascum*

Mum — see *Chrysanthemum*

Nippon daisy — see Relatively Speaking in *Leucanthemum*

Obedient plant — see *Physostegia*

Oregano — see *Origanum*

Oriental poppy — see *Papaver*

Osmunda—see Ferns

Ostrich fern — see Ferns

Oxeye daisy — see *Leucanthemum*

Oxeye — see *Heliopsis*

Painted daisy — see *Tanacetum*

Painted fern — see Ferns

Pampas grass — see Grasses

Pasque flower — see Relatively Speaking in *Anemone*

Wormwood (*Artemisia*)

Sea holly (*Eryngium*)

Sneezeweed (*Helenium*)

Evening primrose (*Oenothera*)

Poppy (*Papaver*)

Russian sage (*Perovskia*)

Peony — see *Paeonia*
Perennial flax — see *Linum*
Perennial statice — see *Limonium*
Pincushion flower — see *Scabiosa*
Pink — see *Dianthus*
Plantain lily — see *Hosta*
Poppy — see *Papaver*
Primrose — see *Primula*
Primrose, evening — see *Oenothera*
Purple moor grass — see Grasses
Queen-of-the-meadow, queen-of-the-prairie — see
   Filipendula
Red valerian — see *Centranthus*
Red-hot poker — see *Kniphofia*
Regal fern — see Ferns
Ribbon grass — see Grasses
Rock cress — see *Arabis*
Rose campion — see *Lychnis*
Russian sage — see *Perovskia*
Sea holly — see *Eryngium*
Sea kale — see *Crambe*
Sea oats — see Grasses
Sedge — see *Carex*
Shasta daisy — see *Leucanthemum*
Siberian bugloss — see *Brunnera*
Snakeroot, black — see *Actaea*
Snakeroot, white — see *Eupatorium*
Sneezeweed — see *Helenium*

Snowdrops — see Bulbs
Soapwort — see *Saponaria*
Solomon's seal — see *Polygonatum*
Speedwell — see *Veronica*
Spiderwort — see *Tradescantia*
Spotted lamium — see *Lamium*
Spurge — see *Euphorbia*
Statice, perennial — see *Limonium*
Stonecrop — see *Sedum*
Sundrops — see *Oenothera*
Sunflower, false — see *Heliopsis*
Sunflower, perennial — see *Helianthus*
Switch grass — see Grasses
Thrift — see *Armeria*
Tickseed — see *Coreopsis*
Toad lily — see *Tricyrtis*
Torch lily — see *Kniphofia*
Tulip — see Bulbs
Turtlehead — see *Chelone*
Vervain — see *Verbena*
Wild ginger — see *Asarum*
Wild indigo — see *Baptisia*
Windflower — see *Anemone*
Wormwood — see *Artemisia*
Yarrow — see *Achillea*
Yellow archangel — see *Lamium*

Acanthus

BEAR'S BREECHES

Usually reaching about 3 feet (90 cm) tall and wide, bear's breeches produce mounds of leathery, lobed leaves that are invaluable for bold foliage interest through much of the growing season or even through most of the year in mild climates. In the warmer parts of their range, bear's breeches also produce dense spikes of white-and-purple or white-and-green flowers on stems 3 to 4 feet (90 to 120 cm) tall.

ONE OF THE BEST-KNOWN SPECIES is *Acanthus mollis*, usually rated for Zones 8 to 10. Spiny-leaved *A. spinosus* (pictured) is typically recommended for Zones 6 to 10 and reportedly performs better than the other species in humid climates. Note that bear's breeches can be remarkably hardy if you find an ideal site for them. *A. hungaricus*, in fact, can thrive as far north as Zone 3, while some gardeners in Zone 5 have been able to grow the other species.

Acanthus spinosus

❁ GROWING TIPS

▸ **Light & soil.** A site with morning sun and afternoon shade is usually ideal; in cooler areas, the plants can take full sun. Bear's breeches like rich, deeply dug soil that's also very well drained; soil that stays soggy (especially in winter) is usually fatal.

▸ **Division & propagation.** If you try to move established clumps, the roots you leave behind will send up lots of new sprouts, which you'll need to dig out completely before you plant something else there. To propagate, divide in spring, take root cuttings in spring or fall, or sow seed ¼ inch (6 mm) deep outdoors in spring or summer.

▸ **Potential problems.** Slugs and snails like to feed on the foliage, especially young leaves. Bear's breeches can spread by creeping roots. Minimize the chance of spreading by planting within a root barrier, such as a large, bottomless bucket.

❁ SEASONAL CARE

◗ Spring

▸ In early to midspring, set out new plants or move or divide existing clumps. Space them 3 to 4 feet (90 to 120 cm) apart. Trim dead or winter-damaged top growth to the ground. If rain is lacking, water new plantings regularly, and water established plantings, too, if they're already growing. If you used a winter mulch on established clumps, wait until mid- to late spring to remove it. In the cooler parts of their growing range, bear's breeches may not even come up before the end of the spring. In mild climates, bear's breeches may be in bloom by late spring. Apply an organic mulch around already-growing plants before summer.

◎ Summer

▸ In cool areas, your clumps may just be emerging now; apply an organic mulch around them. Elsewhere, the plants should be in full leaf and in flower, or else preparing to bloom. The flowers usually look good for about a month, and the seed heads

remain a few weeks after that. If the whole plant looks droopy after flowering, cut everything to the ground in midsummer; otherwise, just cut off the spent flowering stems. Wear gloves to protect your hands from the spiny flower bracts. Water both new and established plantings regularly during summer dry spells if they're still actively growing; after flowering, regular watering isn't so critical.

✪ ◉ Fall & Winter

▸ New foliage usually appears in fall and remains through at least part of the winter; leave it in place. Scatter a general-purpose organic fertilizer or a shovelful of compost around each clump in late fall to late winter. In Zones 3 to 6, you may want to protect the roots with a thick mulch for the winter. Avoid watering.

❁ TROUBLESHOOTING

▸ **Lots of leaves but no flowers.** In cool climates, the flower buds may be killed by cold snaps, in which case the plants won't bloom. Winter mulching may help; leave the covering on until mid- to late spring.

Achillea

YARROW

Yarrows are a classic choice for sunny summer gardens, producing abundant, flat-topped to slightly domed flower clusters that offer a distinctive form as well as a range of colors. Their aromatic foliage is usually deeply dissected, giving it a fernlike or lacy look that adds some year-round interest.

AMONG THE SEVERAL YELLOW-FLOWERED YARROWS is fernleaf yarrow (*Achillea filipendulina*), with light green leaves and golden yellow blooms on stems 4 to 5 feet (1.2 to 1.5 m) tall. Hybrid 'Coronation Gold' is similar in bloom color but tends to be more compact (to about 3 feet [90 cm]). The flowers of 'Moonshine' are clear yellow, while 'Anthea' is a softer yellow; both of these hybrids grow 24 to 30 inches (60 to 75 cm) tall and have grayish foliage. All of these usually perform well in Zones 3 to 8. Woolly yarrow (*A. tomentosa*) also has yellow flowers, but it's just 6 to 12 inches (15 to 30 cm) tall and recommended for Zones 3 to 7.

The white-flowered species *A. millefolium* is commonly considered a roadside weed, but many of its cultivars and hybrids are prized as garden plants, and they offer a much wider range of colors, including shades of pink, red, orange, yellow, and pinkish lavender as well as white. The species and its cultivars usually have lacy green foliage, while that of the hybrids may be green or grayish green. Height is usually 2 to 3 feet (60 to 90 cm). Sneezewort (*A. ptarmica*) is another species with white flowers and green foliage; unlike those of most yarrows, its leaves are only lightly toothed instead of lacy. Plants sold as 'The Pearl' should have pure white, double blooms to about 2 feet (60 cm) tall. All of these yarrows can grow in Zones 2 to 9.

Achillea millefolium 'Summer Pastels'

✿ GROWING TIPS

▶ **Light & soil.** Yarrows grow best in full-sun sites. They tolerate light shade but tend to be floppy and more disease prone there, and they won't bloom as freely. Loose, dryish soil is best, especially for most of the yellow yarrows; *A. millefolium* cultivars and hybrids usually tolerate a bit more moisture. It's common for yarrow flower stems to sprawl in the loose, compost-enriched soil that many other common perennials prefer.

▶ **Division & propagation.** *A. millefolium* cultivars and some of its hybrids, as well as *A. ptarmica*, can spread 1 foot (30 cm) or more each year by creeping roots. Divide the clumps every other year in spring or fall to slow their spread (keep only one quarter to one third of the divisions and give away or discard the rest), or plant them in a bottomless pot sunk into the soil or in a spot surrounded by paving as a root barrier. Division every 3 years is fine for maintaining yarrows that tend to stay in distinct clumps. It's also a simple way to propagate your favorite plants.

To grow yarrows from seed, sow outdoors or indoors in spring or summer; leave them uncovered. Note that seedlings can vary in height, color, and stem sturdiness.

▶ **Potential problems.** Other possible problems include aphids and several fungal diseases, including botrytis blight (gray mold), powdery mildew, root rot, and rust.

✿ **DEFINITELY DEADHEAD** All yarrows may self-sow, but *A. ptarmica* and cultivars and hybrids of *A. millefolium* can be especially prolific. Snipping or shearing off the flower heads as they fade prevents a major maintenance headache later on.

Achillea (continued)

✿ SEASONAL CARE

◐ Spring

▸ Set out new plants, or move or divide existing clumps, in early to midspring. Space them 18 to 24 inches (45 to 60 cm) apart. Water new plantings regularly if rain is lacking. Snip off any winter-damaged foliage in early to midspring to neaten plants for the growing season. Apply an organic or gravel mulch in early to midspring. If you've had problems with the flower stems sprawling in the past, consider installing grow-through supports over the clumps in early to midspring. Yarrows may begin blooming in late spring in mild areas.

☀ Summer

▸ In warm climates, yarrows are typically in full flower in early and midsummer; in cooler areas, they usually bloom through the summer. If the stems start to sprawl, prop them up with linking stakes. Cut off faded flower heads just above a lower bud, if there is one, or all the way down to the foliage. Water spring-planted yarrows during dry spells; established plants usually don't need it.

✿ ☉ Fall & Winter

▸ Set out new plants, or move or divide existing clumps, in early fall. Water new plantings occasionally for the first month if rain is lacking. You may get a few additional flowers in fall. It's tempting to leave the spent flower heads in the garden for winter interest, because they hold their form well and look great dusted with snow. Be aware, though, that yarrows can reseed prolifically, so it's usually best to snip off the faded bloom clusters. Leave the basal foliage; it often remains attractive through most or

Achillea 'Fireland'

all of the winter. Scatter a general-purpose organic fertilizer or a few handfuls of compost around each clump every other year in late fall to late winter.

✿ TROUBLESHOOTING

▸ **Flowers change colors.** It's not unusual for yarrow blooms to fade or discolor as they age. Newly opened blooms may vary somewhat in color due to weather conditions (they often bleach out a bit in hot weather), but if the color is very different than in previous years, it's possible that self-sown seedlings have mingled with or crowded out the original plant.

▸ **Whole plant dies.** Weather that's cold and damp or hot and humid can quickly kill yarrows. Make sure they have well-drained soil, or even a raised bed if your soil is on the clayey side. In humid climates, try 'Anthea' or 'Coronation Gold', or *A. millefolium* hybrids, which appear to be more tolerant of sultry summers.

✿ **SNIPPING TIPS** When the main flower clusters fade, look for side buds growing from the leaf joints slightly lower on the stem. If you see these side buds, snip off the main cluster just above the uppermost bud to get a second flush of bloom; otherwise, cut the whole flowering stem down to the basal leaves.

Aconitum

MONKSHOOD, ACONITE, HELMET FLOWER, WOLFSBANE

For gardeners who adore delphiniums, later-blooming monkshoods can be a great choice to continue the show of spiky blue flowers.

MONKSHOODS OFFER good-looking, lobed, deep green leaves, but it's their loose spikes of hooded blooms that make them worth the effort to grow. While there are many species and hybrids available, only a few are likely to show up at your local garden center. Common monkshood (*Aconitum napellus*) flowers in various shades of blue on stems 3 to 4 feet (90 to 120 cm) tall. Hybrid 'Spark's Variety' is purple-blue and reaches 3 to 5 feet (90 to 150 cm); two other hybrids in the same height range include blue-and-white 'Bicolor' and deep purple-blue 'Bressingham Spire'. Late-blooming plants sold as azure monkshood (*A. carmichaelii*) are variable, typically blooming in shades of medium to deep blue. They are usually 4 to 5 feet (1.2 to 1.5 m) tall, but some can reach 6 to 8 feet (1.8 to 2.4 m) in height (these are often sold as 'Wilsonii' or *A. wilsonii*). All of these monkshoods generally perform best in Zones 2 to 7.

✿ GROWING TIPS

▸ **Light & soil.** Ample light encourages the best flowering, but too much sun (particularly during the hottest noon to mid-afternoon hours) can stress monkshoods, especially in Zones 6 and 7. A site with sun only in the morning and late afternoon can be a good compromise. Compost-enriched soil that's neither soggy nor dry is ideal; the more sun the plants get, the more important it is to keep the soil moist. Avoid sites that are open to strong winds, which can topple the stems.

▸ **Division & propagation.** If you need to reduce the size of large clumps, or if you want to propagate your favorite monkshoods, divide them in early spring or after bloom. Handle the rather brittle, tuberous roots as carefully as possible to avoid breaking them. Expect monkshoods to take 2 to 3 years to settle in and bloom well after planting or division. Another propagation option is to grow them from seed. Collect seed in fall (very late fall or early winter for *A. carmichaelii*), sow in pots (do not cover), and leave outdoors for the winter to get sprouts in spring.

Aconitum carmichaelii

Aconitum (continued)

Don't be alarmed if the seedlings disappear during their first summer; they'll normally resprout the following spring. Seedlings may take 3 to 4 years to reach flowering size.

▸ **Potential problems.** Various fungal diseases, including southern blight and verticillium wilt, can cause monkshoods to wilt and die. (Also see Troubleshooting, below.) Note that all parts of monkshoods are poisonous if ingested or possibly even if the sap gets on your hands. For that reason, it's smart to wear waterproof gloves when handling the plants, especially when dividing them or cutting them back.

❃ SEASONAL CARE

◐ Spring

▸ Set out new plants, or move or divide existing clumps (if you must), in early spring, just as the new leaves appear. Space most monkshoods about 18 inches (45 cm) apart; allow 2 feet (60 cm) between the tallest types. Install grid-type hoop stakes over the clumps in early to midspring if your plants tend to sprawl by bloom time. Or, try cutting them back by one third to one half in late spring; the resulting stems will be shorter with more but smaller flower spikes that may be less prone to flopping. Water new plantings regularly if spring rains are lacking; established monkshoods also appreciate watering during dry spells. A generous layer of organic mulch will also help to keep the soil evenly moist.

◯ Summer

▸ If you didn't cut back lateflowering monkshoods in late spring to discourage sprawling, you could still try it in early summer. Common monkshood and 'Spark's Variety' usually bloom in mid- to late summer; 'Bicolor' and 'Bressingham Spire' typically begin in late summer. In late summer, snip off the faded main spikes of the midsummerbloomers down to a side shoot and they may rebloom into autumn. Keep watering during dry spells to keep the soil evenly moist.

✪ ☉ Fall & Winter

▸ Set out new plants in early to midfall. Keep watering both new and established plants during dry spells into midfall. Summer-blooming monkshoods may still have a few flowers into early fall; azure monkshood doesn't start blooming until early or midfall. If large clumps of any of your monkshoods didn't bloom as well as you expected this year, try dividing them when they're done flowering, or make a note to divide them in early spring. Cut down the stems of all monkshoods just above the ground when they're finished flowering in autumn, or at some point during the winter. Scatter a general-purpose organic fertilizer or a shovelful of compost around each clump in late fall to late winter.

❃ TROUBLESHOOTING

▸ **Flower buds turn black.** Cyclamen mite is a tiny pest that can cause the flower buds to turn black by midsummer. Your best bet is to destroy (not compost) affected plants.

▸ **Lower leaves turn yellow and drop off.** Botrytis is a fungal disease that can cause these symptoms. Affected plants usually still flower, so you may just want to combine them with companions that can cover up their bare stems.

Actaea

BANEBERRY, DOLL'S EYES, BUGBANE, BLACK COHOSH, BLACK SNAKEROOT

This genus includes a number of elegant options for shady borders and woodland gardens.

THESE CLUMP-FORMING PLANTS offer multipart foliage and upright stalks topped with wandlike or branching clusters of fuzzy-looking flowers. Those commonly known as baneberries typically produce white flowers followed by showy (but poisonous) berries atop stems 2 to 3 feet (60 to 90 cm) tall. On red baneberry (*Actaea rubra*), the berries are rounded and red. On doll's eyes (*A. pachypoda*), the berries are oval and held on a thickened stalk; they may be white or red. Both species are generally rated for Zones 4 to 8.

Formerly classified in the genus *Cimicifuga,* the several species of bugbanes tend to be taller — anywhere between 3 and 7 feet (90 to 210 cm) tall in flower — and bloom somewhat later than baneberries, with white or cream-colored flowers. Black cohosh (*A. racemosa*) produces odd-smelling flowers in mid-summer; Kamchatka bugbane (*A. simplex*) blooms later and has a much sweeter scent. *A. simplex* Atropurpurea Group includes seed-grown plants with varying amounts of purple in their leaves and stems. For dependably dark foliage, look for vegetatively propagated, named cultivars, such as 'Black Negligee'. 'James Compton' may grow almost as tall as some other dark-leaved cultivars in ideal conditions but is usually more compact: to about 3 feet (90 cm) in full bloom.

Actaea pachypoda

❋ GROWING TIPS

▸ **Light & soil.** Baneberries and bugbanes grow well in all-day dappled shade or morning sun and afternoon shade. They appreciate compost-enriched soil that stays evenly moist. If the soil does dry out, even once, the leaf edges are likely to turn brown and crispy, and fresh new leaves won't appear until next year — a big incentive to keep the plants well mulched and watered during dry spells.

▸ **Division & propagation.** These plants tend to grow slowly and seldom need division. Bugbanes, especially, can take several years to settle in and reach flowering size. If established plants don't bloom, they may need more light. To propagate, sow seed outdoors in fall; barely cover it with soil. It may take two years for seedlings to appear.

▸ **Potential problems.** Leaf spots and rust may cause leaf damage, too. (See Troubleshooting, page 132.)

❋ SEASONAL CARE

◐ Spring

▸ Set out purchased plants, or move or divide established clumps, if needed, in early spring. Space baneberries about 18 inches (45 cm) apart and bugbanes about 2 feet (60 cm) apart. Apply a generous layer of organic mulch to keep the soil cool. Water new plantings regularly if spring rains are lacking.

❋ **A BERRY GOOD IDEA** Don't deadhead baneberries. If you do, you won't get the showy fruits in mid- to late summer.

Actaea (continued)

◎ Summer

▸ Baneberries typically bloom in early to midsummer. Black cohosh usually starts flowering in midsummer; the other bugbanes usually don't start until late summer or later. Keep watering spring plantings regularly during dry spells. Established plantings also benefit from occasional watering if rain is lacking.

✿ ◉ Fall & Winter

▸ Set out new baneberries, or move or divide existing clumps, in early fall; water new plantings for the first month or so during dry spells. Most bugbanes are in full bloom by early fall. Unless they get nipped by early freezes, bugbanes produce long-lasting seed heads that are worth leaving for winter interest. (As a bonus, you may find a few self-sown seedlings.) Scatter a general-purpose organic fertilizer or a shovelful of compost around each baneberry and bugbane clump in late fall to late winter.

✧ TROUBLESHOOTING

▸ **Leaves eaten, with only stalks and main veins remaining.** Blister beetles can demolish plants in just a few days. You could try hand-picking the beetles (wear gloves) and dropping them into soapy water; usually, though, by the time you notice the damage, it is too late. New foliage will appear next year.

Actaea simplex 'Brunette'

Seedlings of purple-leaved bugbanes can vary widely in coloration; keep only the darkest ones. Or, buy named cultivars selected for dark foliage. Heavy shade may cause normally dark-leaved plants to turn greenish.

Agastache

AGASTACHE, ANISE HYSSOP

Agastaches aren't always the easiest perennials to grow successfully, but they can be worth putting up with their quirks.

THESE CLUMP-FORMING PERENNIALS are beloved by bees, butterflies, and birds, and they're pleasing to people, as well, thanks to their aromatic foliage and spikes of tiny but abundant blooms. Those with bluish to purple-blue (or sometimes white) flowers — including anise hyssop (*Agastache foeniculum*), Korean mint (*A. rugosum*), and hybrids such as 'Blue Fortune' — are typically dense, bushy plants reaching 3 to 5 feet (90 to 150 cm) tall, with roughly triangular leaves. Those that tend to be a bit shorter — roughly 2 to 4 feet (60 to 120 cm) tall with woodier stem bases, narrower leaves, and flowers in shades of peach, pink, and coral — are often referred to as the "western types." These include species such as *A. cana, A. mexicana,* and *A. rupestris,* and hybrids such as 'Apricot Sunrise', 'Pink Panther', and 'Tutti Frutti'. Both groups are generally rated for Zones 5 to 8, but their winter survival seems to depend a good deal on having very well-drained soil.

Agastache 'Black Adder'

GROWING TIPS

▸ **Light & soil.** Blue-flowered types can perform acceptably with just a half-day of sun, but for the most part, agastaches thrive in full sun. Good drainage is a must (especially in winter), and somewhat alkaline soil is a plus, although the plants can adapt to a range of conditions.

▸ **Division & propagation.** Agastaches can be slow to recover if you move or divide them, and they usually don't need to be divided anyway. To propagate, take stem cuttings in late spring to early summer, or sow seed indoors or outside in mid- to late winter (surface-sow, or just barely cover it).

SEASONAL CARE

Spring

▸ Set out new plants, or move or divide existing clumps (if really necessary), in early to midspring. Space them about 2 feet (60 cm) apart. Water new plantings if spring rains are lacking. Wait until mid- to late spring (ideally until new growth appears) to cut back the tops of established plants of western types. Before summer, apply a thin layer of organic mulch around the blue-flowered types; the western types often perform better with a gravel mulch.

Summer

▸ Agastaches generally start blooming in early to midsummer. Shear the plants back lightly (by about one quarter) in late summer, once the flowers have faded, to minimize self-sowing and promote possible rebloom. Water spring plantings during dry spells.

Fall & Winter

▸ In Zones 8 and 9, you could set out new plants in fall; elsewhere, spring planting is a better choice. On the blue-flowered types, the sturdy stems and spiky seed heads can

WAIT TO WATER Don't be surprised if your blue-flowered agastaches (*Agastache*) wilt during the hottest part of the day, even if the soil is moist. If they haven't perked up again by the next morning, though, try giving them a good soaking.

Agastache (continued)

provide great winter interest, but you may choose to remove them now, if you haven't already, to prevent self-sowing. Scatter a general-purpose organic fertilizer or a few handfuls of compost around each clump every year or two in late fall to late winter.

❖ TROUBLESHOOTING

▸ **Plants decline or die after a few years.** Agastaches seem to be naturally short lived, often performing admirably for a year or two and then fading away. Propagating new plants by seed or cuttings each year can help ensure you always have vigorous, young plants. Or, treat them like annuals and buy small starter plants each spring; they grow quickly.

▸ **Plants seed too abundantly.** One major drawback to the blue-flowered types is their propensity to produce hundreds of seedlings each year. Shearing off the blooms as soon as they start to fade can help prevent this. Or try 'Blue Fortune', which should not produce viable seed. (If you have a plant by this name that does self-sow, it is not the true 'Blue Fortune'.)

❖ **LEAN AND MEAN** Avoiding very rich soil and minimizing the use of mulch and fertilizer help to encourage strong stems on your agastaches. If the plants sprawl due to storm damage or over-quick growth, shear them back by one-third to one-half to improve their shape.

Agastache 'Blue Fortune'

Ajuga

AJUGA, BUGLE, BUGLEWEED

Although they're often touted as a low-maintenance groundcover, ajugas can end up making more problems than they solve.

THE INDIVIDUAL PLANTS ARE harmless enough: tidy rosettes of green, bronzy, purple, or variegated leaves accented with small, purple-blue, pink, or white flowers on spikes typically 6 to 8 inches (15 to 20 cm) tall. The drawback is their ability to spread by creeping roots, as well as by creeping aboveground stems, in the case of common ajuga (*Ajuga reptans*); they can self-sow, too. Their ability to form a dense, low carpet quickly is a plus where you need to fill space fast. But once that space is filled, the challenge is preventing them from spreading into the rest of your yard. (In fact, common ajuga is considered invasive in some areas.) Ajugas are generally hardy in Zones 4 to 9.

Ajuga reptans

🌣 GROWING TIPS

▸ **Light & soil.** Amazingly adaptable, ajugas can grow in anything from full sun (if the site is somewhat moist) to full shade, and they tolerate a wide range of soil conditions, except for constantly soggy spots.

▸ **Division & propagation.** Dig up and transplant rooted plantlets in spring or fall.

▸ **Potential problems.** Upright bugleweed (*A. pyramidalis*) and Geneva bugleweed (*A. genevensis*) spread somewhat more slowly but can still fill a good bit of space over time. Use some kind of edging strip to keep ajugas from creeping into adjacent lawn areas.

🌣 SEASONAL CARE

◐ Spring

▸ Set out new plants, or move or divide existing patches into individual rosettes, in early to midspring. Space ajugas about 6 inches (15 cm) apart for solid cover in about 2 years, or around 1 foot (30 cm) apart for coverage in roughly 3 to 4 years.

Water new plantings during dry spells. If you've used 1-foot (30 cm) spacings for new plantings, cover bare soil between them with organic mulch for weed control. Ajugas usually start flowering in late spring.

◎ Summer

▸ The bloom season usually finishes in early summer. It's not absolutely necessary to deadhead ajugas, but it makes them neater and helps prevent self-sowing. Clip them off by hand (for small areas) or use a string trimmer or a lawn mower set to cut at 3 to 4 inches (7.5 to 10 cm). Water spring plantings during dry spells.

✿ ◉ Fall & Winter

▸ Set out new plants, or move or divide existing plantings in early fall; water these new plantings for the first month or so if rain is lacking. In

mild areas, ajugas are evergreen; in cooler zones, they often turn brown and look dead at some point during the winter. It's not necessary to do anything to them; they'll sprout fresh leaves when the growing season starts. Scatter a general-purpose organic fertilizer or a shovelful of compost around them every other year in late fall to late winter, if desired.

🌣 TROUBLESHOOTING

▸ **Plantings die out in patches.** Crown rot, caused by a fungus, can spread quickly, particularly on ajugas growing in moist soil. Also known as southern blight, it's particularly a problem in hot, humid climates. Remove and destroy infected plants. It's best to avoid replanting there, but if you must, try drenching the soil with a biofungicide first.

❖ **FAR AND WIDE** Common ajuga (*A. reptans*) spreads vigorously and can quickly creep out of bounds, creating a maintenance headache in a perennial border. Save it for tough sites, such as dry shade or slopes, or for areas surrounded by paving, where it can spread freely.

Alcea

HOLLYHOCK

At their best, hollyhocks are stunning garden plants, lighting up summer gardens in Zones 2 to 8 with large, single or double blooms in a wide range of colors on spires anywhere from 3 to 10 feet (90 to 300 cm) tall.

SEEING AS HOW they're such common plants, you might assume that hollyhocks are easy to grow. But there's a big difference between simply growing hollyhocks and growing them *well*. The plants are subject to a number of pest and disease problems, and they seem to be a favorite with a number of animal pests as well. Plus, common hollyhocks (*Alcea rosea*) tend to be biennial, which means that they're inclined to die off after flowering anyway. Still, if you luck out and find just the right spot for your plants, it's possible to enjoy their spectacular bloom display year after year — and it's that magic that makes many of us overlook their flaws.

✿ GROWING TIPS

▸ **Light & soil.** Hollyhocks grow best in full sun and average, well-drained soil. Moist, compost-enriched soil encourages lush growth, but the fast-growing stems are likely to sprawl.

▸ **Division & propagation.** No division needed. Sow hollyhock seeds ⅛ inch (3 mm) deep indoors in late winter (they may bloom the same year from an early sowing) or outdoors during the growing season.

▸ **Potential problems.** Rust is a major problem (also see

Alcea rosea

A site that's sheltered from wind reduces the chances of your hollyhocks toppling over, but it also might increase the possibility of disease problems. If you don't want to bother with staking, try cutting the developing flower stalks back by about one-half in late spring or early summer. Or, stick with compact strains, such as 'Majorette Mix'.

Troubleshooting, below); other common problems include various caterpillars, Japanese beetles, leaf-miners, plant bugs, spider mites, and fungal leaf spots.

✿ SEASONAL CARE

◐ Spring

▸ Set out small purchased plants or transplant young seedlings in early to late spring, spacing them around 18 inches (45 cm) apart. Established hollyhocks usually don't like to be disturbed, but if you must move them, you could try in early spring, taking a large rootball to get as much of the root system as possible. Water new plantings during dry spells. Apply an organic mulch before summer.

◎ Summer

▸ Insert a couple of tall stakes (plastic-coated metal stakes about 6 feet [1.8 m] tall work great) next to each clump as the flower stalks form, so you can quickly attach the growing stalks as they need support. Hollyhocks tend to be in peak bloom around midsummer. Once the flowers fade, cut the entire plant just above the ground to get a good-looking clump of fresh foliage and improve the odds of the plant surviving for another year. Or, let the seeds form, with the idea that the seedlings will replace the parent clump if it doesn't return next year. Water spring-planted hollyhocks during dry spells through the summer.

✪ ◉ Fall & Winter

▸ Transplant summer-sown seedlings or set out purchased plants in early fall. Water new plantings for the first month or so if rain is lacking. If you allowed seeds to form on established plants, cut off the dried stalks and crumble the seedpods where you want the seedlings to grow. Hollyhock foliage may stay green

Hollyhock rust

through at least part of the winter; clip off damaged leaves in late winter (or early spring). In late fall to late winter, scatter a general-purpose organic fertilizer or a shovelful of compost around each clump.

✿ TROUBLESHOOTING

▸ **Leaves with small, yellow speckles; leaves turn brown and drop.** A rust fungus affects hollyhocks and their close relatives (including *Malva* and *Sidalcea*), mostly damaging the leaves but sometimes affecting the buds as well. Infected plants may still bloom but are weakened and look unattractive. Remove and destroy affected leaves as soon as you see them. To minimize further damage, treat the leaves (especially the undersides of the lower leaves) with sulfur dust or an organic fungicide.

Relatively Speaking

Checkerbloom (*Sidalcea*) — also known as checker mallow or prairie mallow — looks very much like a true hollyhock, with clumps of lobed leaves and loose spikes of summer flowers. The blooms are primarily in shades of pink or white, though, and the plants are shorter: usually 3 to 4 feet (90 to 120 cm) in height. Checkerblooms thrive in the same growing conditions as hollyhocks and are subject to the same problems, but they are less likely to need staking. They may rebloom if you cut off the whole stalk when the flowers fade; if you don't cut them back, the plants will likely self-sow. Zones 5 to 8.

Alchemilla

LADY'S MANTLE

Lady's mantles aren't likely to appear on any top-ten list of showiest perennials. But when you consider their adaptable, fuss-free nature and airy sprays of greenish yellow flowers, it's easy to see why their subtle beauty has won the hearts of so many gardeners.

Alchemilla mollis

THE MOST WIDELY AVAILABLE SPECIES is *Alchemilla mollis,* with velvety-looking, light green, scalloped leaves in mounds usually 1 foot (30 cm) tall and up to 2 feet (60 cm) across. For a smaller-scale clump, consider alpine lady's mantle (*A. alpina*), with shiny green leaves that are edged with silver, or red-stemmed lady's mantle (*A. erythropoda*), with bluish-green leaves on reddish stems; both grow 6 to 8 inches (15 to 20 cm) tall and about 1 foot (30 cm) wide. Lady's mantles tend to perform best in Zones 3 to 7.

GROWING TIPS

▸ **Light & soil.** Full sun and average, moist but well-drained soil are usually ideal for lady's mantles. In Zones 6 and 7, the plants often appreciate morning sun and afternoon shade, or light all-day shade, especially if the soil isn't dependably moist. They can survive in full shade but usually don't flower well there, if at all.

▸ **Division & propagation.** Lady's mantles don't need frequent division — usually just every 6 to 8 years or so. You can separate them a bit more frequently, either in spring or fall, for propagation. Or, sow seed indoors in late winter or outdoors in spring; barely cover it with seed-starting mix or soil.

SEASONAL CARE

Spring

▸ Divide overgrown clumps in early spring or set out new plants in early to midspring. Space *A. mollis* 18 to 24 inches (45 to 60 cm) apart and the smaller kinds about 1 foot (30 cm) apart. If desired, snip any remaining foliage off of established clumps in early spring. Flowers usually appear in late spring. Water new plantings during dry spells. Apply an organic mulch before summer.

Summer

▸ Snip off individual flower stems as they start to lose their "fresh" look, if you wish to discourage self-sowing and possibly promote rebloom. Or, simply leave the flowers on; they'll gradually be covered up by new foliage. Water spring plantings regularly during dry spells.

Fall & Winter

▸ Set out new plants or divide or move clumps in early fall; water them for the first month or so if rain is lacking. Established clumps occasionally send up a few new flowers until frost. Scatter a general-purpose organic fertilizer or a shovelful of compost around each clump in late fall to late winter.

TROUBLESHOOTING

▸ **Leaves are tattered, browned, or spotted.** It's not unusual for lady's mantle foliage to look a little "tired" by late summer, especially if it's getting too much sun, or if the soil is too dry. Fungal rots may also be a problem during rainy or very humid summer weather. Whatever the cause, the solution is usually as simple as cutting off all of the foliage about 2 inches (5 cm) above the crown in mid- to late summer. Fresh new foliage will emerge and look good into winter. Dividing overly large clumps can help prevent rotting problems next year.

DEFINITELY DEADHEAD In some conditions (particularly cool-climate gardens with moist soil), lady's mantles may self-sow freely. Many gardeners consider that a nice bonus, but if you get too many unwanted seedlings, then clip off the flower stems when they start turning dull yellow.

Amsonia

AMSONIA, BLUESTAR

Dependable, long-lived amsonias are invaluable for adding multiseason interest to beds, borders, and mass plantings.

IN SPRING, AMSONIAS ARE TOPPED with clusters of blooms in many shades of blue; in summer, their rich green foliage adds textural interest; and in fall, their leaves can turn to shades of glowing gold and orange. The growth habit tends to be very upright in spring, becoming more vase shaped to somewhat sprawling after flowering. Willow-leaved bluestar (*Amsonia tabernaemontana*) typically grows about 2 feet (60 cm) tall and wide, with lance-shaped leaves; it's usually recommended for Zones 3 to 9. Arkansas bluestar (*A. hubrichtii*), normally rated for Zones 4 to 9, has much narrower, almost threadlike leaves and grows in clumps that are 2 to 3 feet (60 to 90 cm) tall and 3 to 4 feet (90 to 120 cm) across. You can find hybrids between these, as well.

Amsonia hubrichtii

❁ GROWING TIPS

▸ **Light & soil.** Amsonias thrive in full sun but can perform well in partial shade, too, although their fall color may not be very showy there. Average, well-drained soil is fine.

▸ **Division & propagation.** Amsonias can stay in one place for many years, but if you want to propagate them, you can divide the clumps in fall, using a sturdy tool to cut through the tough crown. Or, take stem cuttings in early summer, or sow seed outdoors in fall or winter (barely cover it with soil).

▸ **Potential problems.** Pests and diseases are rarely a problem.

❁ SEASONAL CARE

◐ Spring

▸ Set out purchased plants or transplant seedlings in early to midspring. Space young plants 12 to 18 inches (30 to 45 cm) apart for a fuller look, then plan to move some of them in a few years. Or, set them at a permanent spacing of 2 to 3 feet (60 to 90 cm) apart — or 18 to 24 inches (45 to 60 cm) for compact cultivars — and fill the space between the clumps with spring-blooming bulbs or annuals for the first few years. Amsonias shoot up quickly in spring and are in bloom by mid- to late spring. Water new plantings regularly if rain is lacking. Apply an organic mulch before summer.

◎ Summer

▸ In early summer, after the flowers have faded, you may choose to shear established clumps back by about one-half. This will prevent self-sowing and produce more compact, bushier clumps. Water spring plantings occasionally during dry spells. Established clumps seldom need watering.

◑ ◉ Fall & Winter

▸ In early fall, set out new plants, or move or divide established clumps; water these new plantings for the first month or so if rain is lacking. After you've enjoyed their fall foliage display, cut down the frost-killed stems in late fall, or leave them until you do your garden cleanup in late winter or spring. Scatter a general-purpose organic fertilizer or a shovelful of compost around the clumps every year or two in late fall to late winter.

❁ TROUBLESHOOTING

▸ **Plants self-sow too freely.** If you start finding more seedlings than you can use or share, either snip off each spent flower cluster or shear back the whole plant as soon as the flowers fade to stop the seeds from forming.

❁ **SHEAR IT** Mature amsonias can take up a good bit of space and be a bit sprawling. Instead of staking them, shear them right after bloom to keep the clumps more compact and bushy. It's a good idea to wear gloves when trimming (or dividing) amsonias, because their cut or broken stems release a white sap that might irritate sensitive skin.

Anchusa

BUGLOSS, ALKANET

If you're one of those gardeners who simply can't get enough true blue flowers, it's worth finding a space for bugloss.

ITALIAN BUGLOSS (*Anchusa azurea*) has a fairly short season of interest compared to many perennials—mostly just late spring to early summer—so place plants where they can shine early in the season and fade into the background from midsummer on. Bugloss forms low clumps of large, deep green, hairy leaves, with loose clusters of bright to deep blue blooms on stems that usually reach 3 to 5 feet (90 to 150 cm) tall. It's recommended for Zones 3 to 8.

Anchusa azurea

❖ GROWING TIPS

▶ **Light & soil.** Italian bugloss grows best in full sun but also takes light shade. Average, well-drained soil is fine; the plants tend to rot in soggy soil but also don't like to dry out completely. They grow most quickly in rich, fertile soil but are also more likely to flop there.

▶ **Division & propagation.** Divide clumps every 2 or 3 years just after bloom; this can help to extend their life. Division is also one way to propagate the plants. Taking root cuttings in early spring is another propagation option. Or, sow seed outdoors in fall to early spring or indoors in mid- to late winter; barely cover it with soil or seed-starting mix.

❖ SEASONAL CARE

◔ Spring

▶ Set out purchased plants or home-grown seedlings in early spring, spaced 12 to 18 inches (30 to 45 cm) apart. If you've had problems with the flowers flopping in previous

❖ **VIVA BUGLOSS!** Italian bugloss (*Anchusa azurea*) tends to be short lived, but giving it a hard trim in midsummer and dividing it every 2 or 3 years may help extend its life. Or, pull out the plants after they drop their seeds (wear gloves to prevent skin irritation when handling the plants) and use the self-sown seedlings as replacements. Just be careful not to pull out the seedlings, because it's easy to mistake them for weeds!

years, install grow-through supports or individual stakes in midspring. If unsupported plants begin to sprawl as they begin full bloom in late spring, prop them up with linking stakes. Water new plantings regularly if rain is lacking. Apply an organic mulch in early to midspring.

◎ Summer

▶ When the blooms are finished by midsummer, you have several options. You could leave the plants alone, in which case they will produce seed and probably look somewhat ugly for the rest of the season; they may or may not return the next year, but you will likely have many replacement seedlings. Or, you could cut the flower stalks back by one-

half; this will prevent self-sowing and might encourage rebloom. Or, cut the entire clump to the ground to get a flush of fresh-looking foliage for the rest of the season; this may also help to extend the life of the plant. Both spring-planted and established clumps benefit from watering during summer dry spells.

◉ ◉ Fall & Winter

▶ Cut off any dead top growth whenever you do your usual garden cleanup. Keep watering through early fall if rain is lacking. Scatter a general-purpose organic fertilizer or a shovelful of compost around each clump in late fall to late winter.

Anemone

ANEMONE, WINDFLOWER

Anemones are quite a diverse group of plants, with a number of species and hybrids that can provide a succession of bloom through the growing season.

THOSE ANEMONES COMMONLY TREATED as perennials fall mainly into one of two groups: spring-bloomers and fall-bloomers. Among the early flowering types are wood anemone (*Anemone nemorosa*), with small, white, pink, or purple-blue flowers that are 6 to 10 inches (15 to 25 cm) tall, and snowdrop anemone (*A. sylvestris*), with pure white flowers that are followed by tufts of fluffy white seeds atop stems 12 to 18 inches (30 to 45 cm) tall. Both produce deeply cut, dark green leaves and are usually recommended for Zones 4 to 8.

Among the late-flowering anemones are a number of similar-looking species and hybrids with deep green leaves that are deeply cut or lobed and large flowers in shades of pink or white on slender, upright, branching stems. Chinese anemone (*A. hupehensis*) tends to be the most compact, at 2 to 3 feet (60 to 90 cm) in bloom. Japanese or hybrid anemones (*A. × hybrida*) can be anywhere from 2 to 5 feet (60 to 150 cm) in flower. Both of these are normally rated for Zones 5 to 8. Another plant commonly called Japanese anemone is sold under a variety of names, including *A. tomentosa* 'Robustissima' and *A. vitifolia*; it has pink flowers that reach 2 to 4 feet (60 to 120 cm) tall and is normally hardy in Zones 3 to 8.

From a maintenance standpoint, the most important trait shared by all of these anemones is their tendency to spread quickly — at least after their initial settling-in period. The fall-bloomers, in particular, can be aggressive creepers, forming large patches that can be difficult to eradicate. If you try to dig them out, small pieces of root left in the soil will resprout, so it can take a few years to eliminate them all. If you want to enjoy the beauty of anemones without worrying about them taking over, consider using them as groundcovers under or around trees and shrubs instead of expecting them to cohabitate peacefully with other perennials in a bed or border.

❖ GROWING TIPS

▸ **Light & soil.** Anemones generally grow well in a site with full sun to partial shade and average, well-drained soil. The more sun they get, the more moisture they need — however, they don't like constantly soggy soil, either. A spot with morning sun and afternoon shade and compost-enriched, well-drained soil is often ideal. A summer mulch of shredded leaves or some other

Fall-blooming anemones can be difficult to get established. Giving them a somewhat sheltered spot with good drainage, and mulching them and watering regularly during dry spells can help them settle in. Even in ideal conditions, it might take a few years before they begin to flower.

Anemone × hybrida

Anemone (continued)

organic material is also very helpful for keeping the roots cool and moist.

▸ **Division & propagation.** Divide spring-flowering species, in midsummer or early fall, or sow seed outdoors in summer and barely cover it with soil. Propagate late-bloomers by dividing them in early spring or taking root cuttings in late fall or late winter.

▸ **Potential problems.** A few problems can affect late-blooming anemones — among them, Japanese beetles, blister beetles, and various leaf spots — but established plants usually recover without treatment. (If leaf-eating pests severely damage the foliage, cut the plants to the ground to get fresh new leaves.)

❀ SEASONAL CARE

◐ Spring

▸ Set out new plants of early flowering species in early spring, spacing wood anemones about 10 inches (25 cm) apart and snowdrop anemones 1 to 2 feet (30 to 60 cm) apart. Wood anemones usually start blooming in midspring; snowdrop anemones normally start in late spring.

▸ Set out purchased plants of fall-blooming anemones in early to midspring, spacing them about 18 inches (45 cm) apart, or divide existing clumps in early spring. Don't be alarmed if their foliage is very slow to emerge; you may not see their leaves until late spring, especially on those growing in some shade.

▸ Water new plantings regularly if rain is lacking. Apply an organic mulch before summer.

Relatively Speaking

Pasque flower (*Pulsatilla vulgaris*) is sometimes listed as *Anemone pulsatilla*, and it shares some of the same traits with its close relatives. Pasque flower's deeply divided basal leaves are covered with fine, silky hairs, and the cupped flowers—usually in shades of purple but also in red or white—are followed by tufts of fluffy white seeds. The stems typically reach 12 to 18 inches (30 to 45 cm) in bloom. Pasque flower grows in full sun to light shade and average, very well-drained soil. Soggy soil is fatal. In most areas, pasque flower dies to the ground after flowering. It seldom requires division, but if you wish, you can divide it just after bloom or in early fall. Sow fresh seed outdoors in summer, or simply let the plants self-sow. Usually found in Zones 5 to 9, it may be even hardier with excellent drainage.

◉ Summer

▸ Wood anemones die back to the ground in early to midsummer; divide or move them then, if desired. This is also a good time of year to divide snowdrop anemone, if needed (it will still have leaves now). Watering isn't critical, since the plants aren't actively growing.

▸ Mulch fall-flowering anemones in early summer, if you didn't do it earlier, and water during dry spells (especially first-year plantings). In warm climates, the plants may begin blooming in late summer.

✤ ◉ Fall & Winter

▸ Late-flowering anemones usually begin blooming in early fall; in the coolest parts of their range, though, they may not start until midfall and

may get damaged by an early freeze. Water occasionally during dry spells in early to midfall. Trim off flowers when the petals drop to prevent self-sowing. In mild-winter areas, the foliage may be evergreen; elsewhere, it tends to die to the ground. North of Zone 6, the plants may benefit from a winter mulch.

▸ Early fall is a good time to divide or move snowdrop anemones, if you didn't do it earlier in the season, or to set out new plants. Plant or transplant dormant rhizomes of wood anemones in early fall.

▸ Anemones benefit from general-purpose organic fertilizer or a shovelful of compost scattered around the clumps in late fall to late winter.

Anthemis

MARGUERITE, CHAMOMILE

Marguerites produce mounds of ferny, often-aromatic leaves that are attractive in their own right, but you may not even notice the foliage due to the abundance of daisy-form flowers.

ONE OF THE MOST READILY AVAILABLE SPECIES is golden marguerite (*Anthemis tinctoria*), which grows 18 to 36 inches (45 to 90 cm) tall. It usually has green leaves and mostly blooms in shades of yellow. Hybrid 'Susanna Mitchell' stays mostly around 2 feet (60 cm) tall, with silvery gray leaves and creamy white, yellow-centered daisies. Dwarf marguerite (*A. marschalliana*; also sold as *A. biebersteiniana*) reaches about 1 foot (30 cm) tall, with silvery leaves and bright yellow blooms. Marguerites are generally rated as hardy in Zones 4 to 9, but they tend to perform poorly in areas with hot and humid summers, so they're not often used much south of Zone 7.

Anthemis tinctoria 'Kelways'

GROWING TIPS

▸ **Light & soil.** Marguerites can tolerate light shade, but they really prefer all-day sun. The ideal soil pH is near neutral to slightly alkaline, and good drainage is a must, especially in winter.

▸ **Division & propagation.** Divide the plants every 2 or 3 years in spring to keep them vigorous or to propagate. Taking stem cuttings in spring or early summer is another propagation option. It's also easy to grow marguerites from seed sown indoors in late winter or outdoors in early spring (just press it into the surface — don't cover it). It's not unusual for marguerite plants to die out after a few years, so it's smart to keep a few replacements coming along.

▸ **Potential problems.** Powdery mildew may discolor the foliage of green-leaved marguerites.

SEASONAL CARE

○ Spring

▸ Set out new plants or move or divide existing clumps in early spring. Space dwarf marguerites about 1 foot (30 cm) apart and the taller kinds about 2 feet (60 cm) apart. Water new plantings occasionally if rain is lacking. Trim off any dead growth on established clumps in early spring. The plants generally begin blooming by late spring. Apply a light layer of organic mulch, or a gravel mulch, before summer.

◎ Summer

▸ The first main flush of flowers usually slows down by midsummer. If you start deadheading individual blooms in early summer and continue through the summer, your plants are likely to continue producing new flowers. (This practice is also the best way to keep the plants from self-sowing enthusiastically, which can become a maintenance problem.) Or, you could cut the whole clump back by about one-half in midsummer; this encourages bushier regrowth, and new flowers will probably appear by late summer. Water spring plantings during dry spells; don't worry about watering established plantings.

◐ ◉ Fall & Winter

▸ Marguerites often continue to produce a few blooms into the fall months. Keep deadheading them to prevent self-sowing. The foliage may remain attractive through most or all of the winter. Every 2 or 3 years, scatter a bit of general-purpose organic fertilizer or a few handfuls of compost around the clumps in late fall to late winter.

TROUBLESHOOTING

▸ **Stems tend to flop.** This problem often occurs where you've worked to build "good" soil by adding lots of compost or where the soil tends to stay moist. If possible, move your plants to a site with less fertile, dryish soil; otherwise, support them with hoop stakes placed over the clumps in early spring or shear the clumps back by one-half in midsummer.

❖ HIGH AND DRY Marguerites generally aren't a good choice for the humus-rich, evenly moist soils that many traditional border perennials appreciate. They're much better suited to drier sites, such as raised beds or slopes.

Aquilegia

COLUMBINE, GRANNY'S BONNET

Columbines aren't the hardest-working perennials you can find: They bloom for only a few weeks in late spring to early summer, and their pest-prone foliage doesn't add much interest during the rest of the growing season. Their delicate-looking, spurred blooms are so elegant, though, that many gardeners wouldn't be without them.

COLUMBINES GROW from a thick taproot to form clumps of light green, multipart leaves with fan-shaped leaflets. There are hundreds of species, cultivars, and hybrids to choose from. Among the most readily available are common columbine (*Aquilegia vulgaris*) and hybrid columbines (often listed under *A.* × *hybrida*); these typically grow 2 to 3 feet (60 to 90 cm) tall in bloom and offer a variety of flower colors. Wild columbine (*A. canadensis*) can be anywhere from 1 to 3 feet (30 to 90 cm) tall and commonly has red-and-yellow blooms. Fan columbine (*A. flabellata*) tends to grow just 1 to 2 feet (30 to 60 cm) tall, with thicker, bluish green leaves and flowers in shades and combinations of blue, pink, red, and white. Columbines are typically recommended for Zones 3 to 8.

Aquilegia × *hybrida*

❀ GROWING TIPS

▸ **Light & soil.** In most parts of their range, columbines grow well in full sun, especially if the soil doesn't dry out completely. In warmer areas (roughly Zones 7 and 8), give them morning sun only or light all-day shade. Average, moist but well-drained, slightly acid soil is ideal.

▸ **Division & propagation.** The easiest way to propagate columbines is by seed. If you grow only one kind of columbine, or you grow different kinds in different parts of your yard, you could allow a few flowers to ripen and drop their seed for self-sown seedlings that look mostly like their parents. Where more than one kind is growing close together, it's not unusual for the plants to cross-pollinate and produce seedlings that vary in height and flower color. Another option is to grow new plants from purchased seed strains, which tend to produce fairly consistent-looking seedlings. Sow the seed (don't cover it) outdoors in summer or fall, or sow indoors in winter, then place the seed pots in a plastic bag and refrigerate them for about 3 weeks before putting them in a warm, bright place. Indoor-sown seedlings might bloom during their first summer.

▸ **Potential problems.** Common columbines and tall hybrids may fall over in bloom; provide temporary support with linking stakes, or pair them with shrubs or sturdy companions they can lean on. Columbine plants are susceptible to a variety of pests and disease problems: Aphids may feed on leaves, stems, and buds; borers may tunnel into stems and crowns, causing wilt; and root and crown rots may kill entire plants. (Other problems are covered in Troubleshooting, below.)

❁ SEASONAL CARE

◔ Spring

▸ Set out new plants in early spring, spacing them about 1 foot (30 cm) apart. Water new plantings regularly if rain is lacking. In early to mid-spring, cut off any remaining leaves that show winter damage on established plants, and apply an organic mulch. Columbines generally begin blooming in late spring.

◑ Summer

▸ Snip off individual columbine flowers as they fade, then cut off entire stalks at the base when all the flowers are done, to prevent self-sowing and possibly promote some rebloom. Water spring plantings during summer dry spells. Established clumps usually don't need watering, unless you've cut them back to promote new growth; then water if rain is lacking.

❂ ◉ Fall & Winter

▸ Set out new plants in early fall; water them during dry spells in early to midfall. Cut off individual leaves or shear entire clumps just above the ground if they are damaged by insects; otherwise, leave them

If the foliage of your columbines gets damaged by leaf miners or is tired looking in summer, cut it all off near the base of the plant. New growth usually appears before fall, but sometimes the plants may not resprout until next spring.

for some winter interest. Scatter a general-purpose organic fertilizer or a shovelful of compost around each clump in late fall to late winter.

❁ TROUBLESHOOTING

▸ **Leaves spotted, chewed, or marked with pale, winding tunnels.** Several fungal diseases may cause leaf spots; caterpillars can devour the foliage; and leaf miners chew squiggly tunnels as they feed within the leaves. The easiest solution is the same in all cases: cut off all of the foliage, and clean new leaves will appear in fall or next spring. It's smart to pair columbines with companions that will fill in by midsummer and cover up the cut-back clumps, such as ferns and hardy geraniums. Wild columbine and fan columbine tend to be less prone to leaf miner damage than other species and hybrids are.

❁ **LET IT SOW** Columbines are inclined to be short lived, dying out after 3 to 5 years (or even 1 to 2 years in hot climates or rich soil). They generally don't recover well after being divided, so it's best to plan for seed-grown replacements.

Arabis

ROCK CRESS

Rock cresses are true beauties during their spring bloom, but that's not the only reason to grow them: their evergreen foliage mounds add interest to your garden for the rest of the year, too.

WALL OR MOUNTAIN ROCK CRESS (*Arabis alpina* var. *caucasica*; also sold as *A. caucasica*) has toothed, hairy, grayish green leaves in mounds usually around 6 inches (15 cm) tall; its honey-scented, white or pink flowers are about 1 foot (30 cm) tall. Hybrid *A. × arendsii* looks similar but blooms in shades of pink.

White-flowered *A. ferdinandi-coburgii* is distinctly different in leaf, with rosettes of small, smooth, rich green leaves that typically reach only 2 inches (5 cm) tall. It's about 4 inches (10 cm) tall in bloom. *A. procurrens* is similar but somewhat larger — about 6 inches (15 cm) in leaf and to 1 foot (30 cm) in bloom — and it tends to spread a bit more vigorously.

All of these rock cresses grow in Zones 4 to 7 (even into Zone 3 with good winter snow cover); *A. ferdinandi-coburgii* and *A. procurrens* may perform well in Zone 8, too.

Arabis alpina var. *caucasica*

❈ GROWING TIPS

▶ **Light & soil.** While rock cresses can survive in shady sites (especially in warmer areas), they typically look much fuller and flower most abundantly in full-sun gardens. Average, dryish soil with a pH near neutral to slightly alkaline is ideal, and good drainage is a must. A site atop a retaining wall or on a slope often works better than a bed or border with rich, moist soil.

▶ **Division & propagation.** Sow seed indoors in late winter to early spring or outdoors in spring or summer; don't cover it. If the green-leaved types don't sprout within a few weeks indoors, try placing the pots in plastic bags and setting them in your refrigerator for about 3 weeks before moving them back to a warm, bright spot. Other ways to propagate rock cresses include stem cuttings in spring or summer or division just after bloom or in early fall.

▶ **Potential problems.** Aphids, as well as fungal diseases such as mildew, rots, and rust, may affect the plants — especially those growing in too much shade or too-moist soil. Mulching with gravel can help to prevent rotting.

⏾ Spring

▸ Set out new plants or move existing clumps in early spring. Space the grayish-leaved types and *A. procurrens* 12 to 18 inches (30 to 45 cm) apart and *A. ferdinandi-coburgii* 8 to 12 inches (20 to 30 cm) apart. Water new plantings occasionally if rain is lacking. In warm areas, rock cresses may begin blooming in early spring; in cooler areas, they may wait until mid- or even late spring to start. If desired, add a light layer of organic mulch — or better yet, a gravel mulch — around the plants before summer.

◎ Summer

▸ Once the flower petals drop, shear off at least the developing seed heads to prevent self-sowing. On the grayish-leaved types, it's a good idea to cut back a little harder, into the leafy parts: shear the mounds back by one-third to one-half so they stay dense and full looking. The clumps can grow fine for years without being divided, but if you do want to separate them, early summer is a good time to do it. Keep watering spring plantings occasionally during summer dry spells. Established plantings seldom require watering.

✛ ☉ Fall & Winter

▸ In warmer areas, early fall is another good time to set out rock cresses; you could also move or divide clumps now, if you didn't do it earlier. Rock cress foliage usually remains attractive all through the winter. Variegated cultivars of the green-leaved types often take on reddish tints during the colder months. Scatter a bit of general-purpose organic fertilizer or a handful or two of compost around the clumps every other year in late fall to late winter.

✿ **TIDY UP** Rock cresses can look a bit messy in summer if you don't shear off their developing seedpods. Consider leaving a few stems to ripen seed, though — especially on the gray-leaved types — so you have a few replacement plants in case the established ones die out.

✿ TROUBLESHOOTING

▸ **Plants flop open and drop most of their lower leaves.** The combination of heat and humidity can cause grayish-leaved rock cresses to decline in summer. If this is a common problem in your area and summer shearing doesn't help to prevent or fix the problem, consider growing rock cresses as annuals, sowing the seed in summer, planting the seedlings in your garden in fall, and pulling out the plants after bloom the following spring.

Relatively Speaking

At first glance, you might not guess that basket-of-gold (*Aurinia saxatilis*; also sometimes still sold as *Alyssum saxatile*) is related to the rock cresses. Basket-of-gold, after all, typically has bright yellow blooms, while rock cress is normally white or pink. But both genera belong to the cabbage family (Brassicaceae), and both have very similar growth and care needs. You can treat basket-of-gold just as you would the gray-leaved rock cresses. The same goes for another cabbage-family member: wall rock cresses (*Aubrieta*). Their leaves are tinier, and their flowers are commonly pink to purple, but they like the same growing conditions and care as gray-leaved rock cresses.

Aurinia saxatilis 'Compacta'

Armeria

THRIFT, SEA PINK

The spherical, slender-stemmed blooms of thrifts are a cute and quirky addition to the garden because they look so different from most other common perennials.

THRIFTS APPEAR IN WHITE or shades of rosy pink on stems usually 8 to 12 inches (20 to 30 cm) tall. The plants form dense mounds of narrow, grass-like leaves about 6 inches (15 cm) tall. The foliage is commonly deep green but may also be purplish (in *A. maritima* 'Rubrifolia') or variegated (in the cultivar 'Nifty Thrifty'). Thrifts are normally hardy in Zones 4 to 8.

Armeria maritima

❀ GROWING TIPS

▸ **Light & soil.** Full sun is ideal, but thrifts can also grow well in partial shade, especially in warmer areas.

Average, well-drained soil is fine. Thrifts tend to rot in the moist, humus-rich soil that many border perennials like, so keep them for sites that are dryish and not especially fertile: atop a low wall, for instance, or on a slope. They're also more salt tolerant than many perennials, so they're a good choice for planting along paths or paved areas that get treated with deicing salt in winter.

▸ **Division & propagation.** Thrifts usually prefer to be left undisturbed, so it's best to avoid dividing or moving them unless it's really necessary.

Fortunately, it's easy to grow thrifts from seed: sow indoors in late winter to early spring or outdoors in spring or summer (barely cover it).

▸ **Potential problems.** The plants are seldom bothered by pests or diseases. Remove any all-green shoots on 'Nifty Thrifty' as soon as you spot them.

❀ SEASONAL CARE

◐ Spring

▸ Set out new plants about 1 foot (30 cm) apart in early to midspring. You can also divide or move established clumps in early spring, but they may be somewhat slow to recover. Water new plantings occasionally if rain is lacking. Gravel is often a better choice than organic mulch for thrifts; apply it any time during the spring. The plants typically start flowering in mid- to late spring.

◑ Summer

▸ If you regularly pinch off the flowers as they fade, your thrifts may produce scattered rebloom well into summer. Or, wait until most or all of the flowers are done, then shear them all off just above the foliage. Don't be surprised if the leaves of 'Rubrifolia' turn greenish in the summer. Water both spring plantings and established thrifts occasionally during summer dry spells.

✚ ◉ Fall & Winter

▸ Thrifts normally keep their foliage through the winter, but their leaves may turn brown in open, windy sites; there, they can benefit from a loose winter mulch for protection. Fertilizing usually isn't necessary.

❀ **WEED MINDFULLY** It's easy to mistake thrift clumps for tufts of unwanted grass when they're not in bloom, so be alert when you're weeding and don't pull them out by accident!

Artemisia

While they do bloom — usually with small, yellowish to whitish flowers in mid- to late summer — artemisias are mostly treasured for their aromatic, grayish to silvery foliage.

MOST ARTEMISIAS FALL INTO one of three main types: the low-growers; the taller, upright-growers; or the shrubby, woody-based kinds.

Low. The low-growers mostly stay 12 to 18 inches (30 to 45 cm) tall — or rather lower if you cut them back during the growing season — forming spreading carpets or compact, feathery-leaved mounds. Among the low-growers are the well-known silvermound (*Artemisia schmidtiana*), which is usually recommended for Zones 3 to 7, and the similar-looking 'David's Choice' sandhill sage or coastal sandwort (*A. pycnocephala*), which is commonly rated for Zones 7 to 10, although some sources report it being hardier. *A. versicolor* 'Sea Foam', for Zones 4 to 10, also has finely cut, silvery foliage and is less prone to flopping than silvermound. 'Silver Brocade' beach wormwood, also known as dusty miller or old woman (*A. stelleriana*; also sold as 'Boughton Silver'), has somewhat wider leaves than the other low-growers; it's usually rated for Zones 3 to 7.

Upright. Among the taller, more upright artemisias are selections of white sage (*A. ludoviciana*) — also known as white wormwood, white sagebrush, and western mugwort. They produce slender stems clad in lance-shaped leaves that may be toothed or lobed. These plants have creeping roots and grow in ever-expanding patches that can be difficult to remove once established. The two best-known types are sold as 'Silver King' and 'Silver Queen'; they typically grow 3 to 5 feet (90 to 150 cm) tall. 'Valerie Finnis' is more compact — usually 2 to 3 feet (60 to 90 cm) tall—with wider leaves and more noticeable spike-like clusters of yellowish summer flowers. White sages are normally recommended for Zones 3 to 8.

Artemisia schmidtiana 'Silver Mound'

Artemisia (continued)

Shrubby. Shrubby artemisias grow in distinct mounds with woody stem bases. Common wormwood (*A. absinthium*) — usually grown as the cultivar 'Lambrook Silver' — grows 2 to 3 feet (60 to 90 cm) tall in Zones 3 to 9. Silvery hybrid 'Powys Castle', for Zones 5 to 10, and gray-green southernwood (*A. abrotanum*) — also known as old man and lad's love — for Zones 4 to 10, both usually reach 3 to 4 feet (90 to 120 cm) tall.

Not all artemisias fall neatly into one of these three categories. Mugwort (*A. vulgaris*), for instance, is an upright-grower for Zones 4 to 8, reaching anywhere from 3 to 8 feet (90 to 240 cm) tall. You normally wouldn't plant ordinary mugwort, because its plain green leaves and nonshowy flowers aren't very ornamental, but the foliage of Oriental Limelight ('Janlim') is heavily splashed with yellow, making it quite tempting. Like its parent, however, it's a rampant spreader, so don't be tempted to let it loose in a bed or border. (Be aware that mugwort is considered invasive in some regions, as is common wormwood.)

Ghost plant or white mugwort (*A. lactiflora*) is also an upright-grower, reaching 3 to 5 feet (90 to 150 cm) tall, forming clumps rather than spreading. Zones 4 to 9. Unlike other artemisias, this one is grown mostly for its airy plumes of creamy white flowers. While the deeply divided foliage is normally green, it can range from purplish green to deep purple in plants sold as 'Guizhou' or Guizhou Group.

❁ GROWING TIPS

▶ **Light & soil.** As a group, artemisias thrive in full sun; most can also tolerate partial shade, but their stems are more likely to sprawl there. Average, well-drained soil is generally fine. For the silvery to grayish kinds, near-neutral to slightly alkaline soil that's not especially fertile is ideal; they can grow in somewhat moist, rich soil but tend to be floppy and prone to rotting in those conditions. They prefer relatively dry climates but can tolerate humidity if their soil is very well drained. Ghost plant is somewhat different in that it looks best when grown in evenly moist, compost-enriched soil, but even it does not like soggy soil.

▶ **Division & propagation.** It's possible to grow some artemisias from seed sown (not covered) indoors in late winter or early spring or outdoors in spring or summer; however, the seedlings may vary somewhat in appearance. For quicker and more consistent results, take stem cuttings of any kind in late spring to early summer or divide the upright types in spring to early fall. Artemisias that grow mostly from a single point (such as silvermound), as well as those with a shrubby habit, may "layer" themselves (take root where their stems touch the soil); it's easy to cut these rooted stems from the main plant, then dig up and move the new plants during the growing season.

▶ **Potential problems.** Artemisias generally don't have many serious pest or disease problems. (See Troubleshooting, page 151.) Watch for all-green shoots on Oriental Limelight mugwort, and dig out and destroy the reverted shoots immediately; otherwise, they will quickly crowd out the variegated shoots.

❁ SEASONAL CARE

◐ Spring

▶ Set out new plants or move existing clumps any time in spring, spacing them about 2 feet (60 cm) apart (or about 3 feet [90 cm] for the shrubby types). You can also divide low-carpeting and taller, upright types in spring. Water new plantings regularly if rain is lacking. Ghost plant benefits from an organic mulch applied before summer; the other artemisias don't really need mulching. If you've had trouble with the mound-forming or upright kinds sprawling in previous years, shear them back by about one-third of their height in late spring. Wait until new growth starts to appear on shrubby types before cutting them back to 6 to 12 inches (15 to 30 cm); if the new growth is lower than that, it's all right to cut lower.

◑ Summer

▶ The main care the silvery to grayish artemisias need is cutting-back at some point. On the low-growers, you can simply shear them back by one-half to two-thirds in early or midsummer to remove the flowers. Silvermound, in particular, is prone to flopping open to leave a bare center; if this happens, cut it down to 1 to 2 inches (2.5 to 5 cm) above the ground, and it will quickly resprout. Upright types can be left alone, if desired, or you can cut them back to just above the ground in early or midsummer if they lose their bottom leaves or start to sprawl. Shear the shrubby types by one-third to one-half in early or midsummer if

Artemisia ludoviciana

If you really want to include creeping artemisias in a border, you could try surrounding them with a root barrier that's 18 to 24 inches (45 to 60 cm) deep. Check them regularly to make sure they don't creep out over the top. Or, dig up and divide them every year or two to reduce the chance that they'll start spreading.

you didn't do it earlier, if you want to further control their size or shape, if they start to sprawl, or if you want to remove their flowers. Ghost plant usually flowers in late summer. The only summer maintenance it needs is watering during dry spells. Spring plantings of other artemisias also benefit from occasional watering if rain is lacking.

✿ ☉ Fall & Winter

▸ Set out new plants or move existing clumps in early fall. You can also divide low-carpeting and taller, upright types in early fall. Water new plantings occasionally during dry spells in early to midfall. Silvery to grayish artemisias tend to hold their leaves into the winter, so don't cut them back. Cut mugwort stems to

the ground any time after frost. The frost-killed stems of ghost plant can add some winter interest, but it's fine to cut them off just above the basal leaves in late fall, if you wish. Scatter a general-purpose organic fertilizer or a few handfuls of compost around artemisias every 2 or 3 years in late fall to late winter, if desired (or every year for ghost plant).

✿ TROUBLESHOOTING

▸ **Leaves discolored or damaged.** Artemisia leaves can turn yellowish and drop due to fungal rust, or they may be chewed or disfigured by leaf miners and other moth and butterfly larvae. The simplest way to deal with any leaf problems is to cut the plants back as described in Summer (page 150) to encourage fresh new growth.

▸ **Creeping artemisias spread out of bounds.** When it comes to controlling creeping artemisias, prevention is definitely the wisest approach. Save them for difficult, dry sites where you have trouble growing anything else, or pair them with other "thugs" to fill space in out-of-the-way areas. Other options include keeping them in pots, dividing them frequently, planting them within a root barrier, or growing them in sites surrounded by paving or other hard surfaces so they can't escape. To get rid of an established patch, your best recourse is to cut it as close to the ground as possible, then cover the area with cardboard and a few inches of mulch for at least one year — ideally 2 or 3 years — to smother the roots.

Arum

ARUM, LORDS-AND-LADIES

With its long period of foliage interest — from fall through spring, and sometimes even into summer — Italian arum (*Arum italicum*) fills a place that few other perennials can match.

Arum italicum 'Pictum'

ARUM GROWS IN CLUMPS 12 to 18 inches (30 to 45 cm) tall, with arrow-shaped green leaves. The foliage is veined in creamy white to gray-green on plants sold as 'Pictum', 'Marmoratum', or *A. italicum* spp. *italicum* var. *marmoratum*. The hooded, greenish-white flowers are mostly hidden by the foliage, but they produce spikes of green berries that turn bright scarlet red in autumn, just as a new crop of leaves is emerging. Italian arum is usually rated for Zones 5 to 10 (sometimes into Zone 4); be aware, though, that it is considered invasive in some areas, particularly in the warmer parts of its range.

❖ GROWING TIPS

▸ **Light & soil.** Partial to full shade with average, evenly moist but well-drained soil is ideal. Italian arum also adapts to slightly drier conditions and looks great planted in groups or large masses under trees and shrubs.

▸ **Division & propagation.** Italian arum self-sows freely, sometimes to the point of becoming a pest in the garden as well as in surrounding natural areas. Remove the developing seed spikes before the berries turn color in fall if this is a concern in your area. Otherwise, let the berries ripen and drop in place, or toss them into other areas where you want them to grow. It may take the seedlings a few years to develop their leaf markings. For quicker results, dig up existing clumps as the leaves die back and separate the dormant tubers in summer.

▸ **Potential problems.** The plants are seldom bothered by pests or diseases. Wear gloves when working with Italian arum, as the plants and tubers can irritate sensitive skin; the berries are considered poisonous if ingested, as well.

❖ **BETTER TOGETHER** Italian arum (*Arum italicum* 'Pictum') is a beauty for adding interest to shady gardens in fall through spring. Plan on pairing it with a companion that can fill in when the arum goes dormant during the summer, such as a deciduous sedge (*Carex*).

❖ SEASONAL CARE

◐ Spring

▸ Set out new plants in early spring, spaced 6 to 12 inches (5 to 30 cm) apart. Water new plantings occasionally if rain is lacking. Established plants produce flowers in mid- to late spring. By late spring, the leaves may start to turn yellowish in preparation for dormancy. You can pick off the declining leaves to improve the appearance or just let them wither away.

◯ Summer

▸ In most areas, the leaves are mostly or completely gone by early summer, but they may stick around until midsummer in cooler climates. Remove the developing seed spikes if you want to prevent self-sowing, or leave them to ripen their showy berries. Plant new tubers, or move or divide existing clumps, if needed, while they are dormant in mid- to late summer; place individual tubers 4 to 6 inches (10 to 15 cm) deep and 3 inches (7.5 cm) apart.

◐ ◉ Fall & Winter

▸ New foliage emerges in early to midfall, usually a little after the berries have turned completely scarlet-red. This is a good time to set out new container-grown plants; water regularly during dry spells for the first month or so. Frost and freezes can cause the leaves to go limp, and they may not perk up, but fresh, new leaves may emerge during mild spells. Scatter a general-purpose organic fertilizer or a shovelful of compost around the clumps in late fall to late winter.

Aruncus

GOAT'S BEARD

Common goat's beard (*Aruncus dioicus*; also sold as *A. sylvester*) takes a few years to settle in and show off to full advantage, but it's worth waiting for.

EVENTUALLY REACHING 4 to 6 feet (1.2 to 1.8 m) tall when in full bloom, goat's beard is a beauty for the back of a border and a wonderful accent for a woodland garden. For a few weeks in late spring to early summer, the dense clumps of multipart, light to bright green leaves are topped with airy plumes of creamy white to greenish white flowers. If the shrublike size of common goat's beard doesn't quite work for your garden, then dwarf goat's beard (*A. aethusifolius*) may be more suitable. It flowers around the same time, and in the same colors, but it's usually no more than 1 foot (30 cm) tall in full bloom, with glossy, deep green leaves. Both species are usually recommended for Zones 3 to 7.

Aruncus aethusifolius

❁ GROWING TIPS

▸ **Light & soil.** In the cooler parts of their growing range (roughly Zones 3 to 5), goat's beards can perform well in full sun, especially if their soil doesn't dry out. Elsewhere, morning sun and afternoon shade or light, all-day shade is usually best, with evenly moist soil. The plants can also grow in fairly heavy shade but usually won't bloom there. It's ideal if the soil is rich in organic matter, so mix a shovelful or two of compost into the hole at planting time.

▸ **Division & propagation.** Goat's beards have a very dense crown that's difficult to cut apart, so division usually isn't practical for propagation. Instead, sow just-collected seed outdoors in late summer or fall and do not cover it. Or, sow indoors in winter, enclose the pots in a plastic bag, and refrigerate them for about a month before moving them to a warm, bright place.

▸ **Potential problems.** Sometimes goat's beards can be a little tricky to get established, and they tend to grow slowly. Aside from some fungal leaf spots, though, they're usually trouble free as long as you keep their soil moist.

❁ SEASONAL CARE

◗ Spring

▸ Set out new plants in early to midspring. Give common goat's beard a space roughly 5 feet (1.5 m) across to allow for its mature spread; space dwarf goat's beard clumps 12 to 18 inches (30 to 45 cm) apart. Both types grow relatively slowly and often take a season or two to recover from being disturbed, but if you must divide or move them, early spring is a good time. Water new

plantings regularly if rain is lacking. Apply a generous layer of organic mulch before summer. The plants are usually in bloom by late spring.

◔ Summer

▸ You can clip off the drying flower plumes of goat's beards after bloom or leave them in place. Water spring plantings regularly if rain is lacking. Established clumps also benefit from occasional soakings during dry spells.

◐ ◉ Fall & Winter

▸ It's not unusual for the leaves to take on reddish tints in fall. They usually die back and disappear on their own, so there's no need to cut them back. Scatter a general-purpose organic fertilizer or a shovelful or two of compost around the base of each clump in late fall to late winter.

❁ **SHOWY SEEDHEADS** If you leave the flower plumes of goat's beards in place when they're done blooming, they'll turn rusty brown by fall and remain into winter. As a bonus, you may find a few self-sown seedlings the following year.

Asarum

WILD GINGER

Even the most flower-focused gardeners can appreciate the alluring foliage of wild gingers.

EUROPEAN WILD GINGER (*Asarum europaeum*) is one of the best-known species, with glossy, rounded, evergreen to semievergreen leaves in slow-spreading carpets to about 6 inches (15 cm) tall. It usually grows best in Zones 4 to 7. Some other species with rounded to heart-shaped, evergreen leaves — often veined or mottled with gray or silver — growing roughly the same height include arrow-leaf ginger (*A. arifolium*), also known as little brown jugs, for Zones 4 or 5 to 8; Shuttleworth or mottled wild ginger (*A. shuttleworthii*), for Zones 5 to 9; and Chinese wild ginger or panda flower (*A. splendens*), for Zones 5 to 9. There is also a completely deciduous species: Canada wild ginger (*A. canadense*), with light to medium green foliage; Zones 2 to 8.

Asarum europaeum

✿ GROWING TIPS

▸ **Light & soil.** Gingers thrive in partial to full shade with evenly moist but well-drained soil. Dig some compost into the hole at planting time to enrich the soil.

▸ **Division & propagation.** They rarely require division, but they don't mind it, and it's an easy way to propagate them in spring or fall. If you can get seeds, sow them (lightly covered with soil) outdoors in summer or fall, or sow in pots indoors, put them in a plastic bag, and refrigerate them for about a month before moving them to a cool, bright spot.

✿ SEASONAL CARE

◐ Spring

▸ Set out new plants, or move or divide existing clumps, in early to midspring. Space them about 1 foot (30 cm) apart. Water new plantings regularly if rain is lacking. Snip off any damaged or discolored leaves on the evergreen types in early spring. Gingers usually appreciate an organic mulch, but if slugs or snails are a problem in your garden, you may want to hold off until summer to apply it.

◯ Summer

▸ Apply an organic mulch around gingers in early summer, if you didn't do it in spring. Water spring plantings regularly during dry spells. Established clumps usually don't need watering.

✿ ◉ Fall & Winter

▸ Set out new plants, or divide or move established clumps, in early fall. Water these new plantings in early to midfall if rain is lacking. Scatter a general-purpose organic fertilizer or a shovelful of compost around the plants in late fall to late winter.

✿ TROUBLESHOOTING

▸ **Leaves with holes or missing altogether.** While gingers generally aren't prone to problems, they're often a favorite with slugs and snails, especially in spring. If these pests are a serious problem in your garden, hold off until summer to mulch (or don't mulch at all); consider trying an organic slug bait.

✿ **FABULOUS FOLIAGE** Wild gingers are prized mostly for their lovely leaves. They produce flowers, too, but the blooms are typically brownish to maroon and hidden under the foliage, so you may not even notice them. If you're lucky, you may find a few self-sown seedlings.

Asclepias

MILKWEED, BUTTERFLY WEED

Milkweeds are a mainstay of butterfly gardens, providing an abundance of clustered, nectar-rich summer flowers that are irresistible to many types of butterflies. Plus, their slender, bright green leaves are a favored food for the larvae of monarch butterflies — reason enough to grow them even if their flowers weren't so pretty!

TWO OF THE MOST COMMONLY CHOSEN SPECIES for gardens are butterfly weed or pleurisy root (*Asclepias tuberosa*) and swamp milkweed (*A. incarnata*). Butterfly weed grows from 1 to 3 feet (30 to 90 cm) tall, with vibrant orange, red, or yellow flowers; it's recommended for Zones 4 to 9. Swamp milkweed blooms in shades of pink, or sometimes white, atop branching stems that are 3 to 5 feet (90 to 150 cm) tall. Zones 3 to 9. The flowers of both species are

Asclepias tuberosa

Asclepias (continued)

followed by elongated, green seedpods that turn brown and split to release silky-tufted seeds.

There are many other species of milkweed to choose from, and if you're after maximum butterfly action, it's worth doing your homework to find out which species are most common in your area, because those are most likely to draw in your local butterflies. The two species discussed here tend to form slowly expanding but distinct clumps, while others can spread vigorously by fast-creeping roots. You may want to keep the spreaders in a meadow garden or a spot by themselves instead of letting them loose in a high-visibility border.

❂ GROWING TIPS

▸ **Light & soil.** Milkweeds can tolerate light shade but generally grow best in full sun. Both butterfly weed and swamp milkweed will grow in average, well-drained soil, although butterfly weed really prefers loose, dryish, and not-especially-fertile conditions, while swamp milkweed appreciates more nutrient-rich, evenly moist to wet soil.

▸ **Division & propagation.** Milkweeds are usually slow to recover after being moved or divided. To propagate, take stem cuttings in late spring to early summer, or grow new plants from seed (ideally from seed collected the same year you plant it). Sow seed (and barely cover it with soil) outdoors in summer or fall. Or, sow indoors in winter, enclose the pots in plastic bags, then set them in your refrigerator for about a month before moving them to a warm, bright spot.

▸ **Potential problems.** Fungal rusts and various leaf spots can affect the foliage, but usually not seriously enough to need control. Mosaic virus causes discolored, distorted, and stunted growth; remove and destroy affected plants. Various types of insects feed on milkweeds (see Troubleshooting, page 157), which can be a problem if you want your plants to look perfect or a bonus if you appreciate their ecological value.

Consider planting milkweeds in a spot where you don't see them up close; that way, you can admire the flowers from some distance without looking at insect-chewed leaves.

❂ SEASONAL CARE

⊙ Spring

▸ Set out new plants any time in spring, spacing them 18 to 24 inches (45 to 60 cm) apart. Milkweeds

Asclepias incarnata

Although they attract butterflies, most milkweeds — including swamp milkweed (*A. incarnata*) — also release a milky sap that can irritate sensitive skin, so you may want to wear gloves when working around the plants.

generally don't need to be divided, but if you want to try it, early to midspring is a good time. The same goes for transplanting: if it's necessary, then do it early. It also helps to dig a deeper-than-usual rootball, so you disturb the roots as little as possible. Water new plantings regularly if rain is lacking. Keep in mind that even established milkweeds — and butterfly weed, in particular — can be very slow to send up their new growth, often waiting until mid- to late spring to sprout. Apply a light layer of organic mulch around butterfly weed, if desired. Swamp milkweed can also benefit from mulching if the soil isn't constantly moist.

◎ Summer

▸ Despite sprouting rather late in spring, milkweeds shoot up quickly and may be in bloom as soon as early summer. When most of their flowers have dropped, you might choose to snip off the developing pods to prevent self-sowing; this might also encourage the plants to produce a second flush of flowers later in the summer. Water spring plantings during dry spells. Established plants usually don't need watering, although swamp milkweed can benefit from an occasional soaking during summer droughts.

✚ ◉ Fall & Winter

▸ Set out new plants in early fall, and water them occasionally for the first few weeks if rain is lacking. Keep snipping off any developing milkweed seedpods through the autumn if you want to prevent self-sowing, or leave them for late-season interest. Scatter a general-purpose organic fertilizer or a shovelful of compost around swamp milkweed clumps in late fall to late winter, if desired. Butterfly weed seldom needs fertilizing.

✿ **DO NOT DISTURB** It's best to set out milkweeds as small plants, then avoid disturbing their roots as much as possible. They can start blooming during their first growing season, but usually take several years to form a sturdy, well-established clump.

✿ TROUBLESHOOTING

▸ **Leaves with holes.** You may see milkweed bugs or milkweed beetles (both of which are orange and black) on chewed plants. If they're causing serious damage, you may choose to pick them off and drop them into a bucket of soapy water. Monarch butterfly larvae — caterpillars with white, yellow, and black bands — are also common leaf feeders. If there are several of them, the entire plant may be stripped of foliage. The plants are adapted to this feeding and usually recover just fine, sprouting new foliage that season or else the next spring, so control isn't necessary.

▸ **Leaves distorted; clusters of tiny insects visible.** Aphids (especially orange ones) are very common pests on milkweeds, but they usually don't cause serious damage. If you are concerned about them, rub the leaves with your fingers to squash the pests. A soap spray can also help to control aphids, if you feel it's absolutely necessary.

If you grow milkweeds, it's almost inevitable that you'll see aphids on them at some point. Rubbing off or squashing the pests with your fingers, or snipping off infested shoot tips, is normally the only control needed.

Aster

ASTER, MICHAELMAS DAISY

Asters are considered classics for flower color in the fall garden, but some start blooming much earlier in the season.

THE MANY SPECIES AND CULTIVARS OF ASTERS also vary in height, habit, leaf shape, and flower color, as well as in their preferred growing conditions. Frikart's aster (*Aster × frikartii*) is one of the first to flower in summer, with purple-blue blooms on mounded plants that are 2 to 3 feet (60 to 90 cm) tall. It's usually recommended for Zones 6 to 9 but may be hardy into Zone 5 with very well-drained soil and a loose winter mulch.

One of the best-known later-bloomers is New England aster (*A. novae-angliae*), which usually flowers in shades of purple or pink from late summer well into fall. The upright clumps can be anywhere from 18 inches (45 cm) to 6 feet (1.8 m) tall, depending on the cultivar. Zones 4 to 8. New York aster (*A. novi-belgii*) usually starts a bit later and continues through autumn with white, pink, purple, or blue flowers on mounded plants anywhere from 1 to 4 feet (30 to 120 cm) tall. Zones 3 or 4 to 8. Low-growing hybrids (which are sometimes listed under *A. dumosus* or *A. × dumosus*) look similar but are commonly just 8 to 16 inches (20 to 40 cm) tall with purple, blue, or pink flowers from late summer into fall. Zones 4 to 8.

One of the lesser-known options for late color is aromatic aster (*A. oblongifolius*), which grows in dense mounds usually 18 to 36 inches (45 to 90 cm) tall. It is practically smothered with hundreds of blooms in shades of purple-blue. They typically don't start flowering until midfall but sometimes start as early as late summer. Zones 3 to 8. Calico aster (*A. lateriflorus*) grows in slightly more open clumps, commonly 2 to 4 feet (60 to 120 cm) tall, with an abundance of tiny white flowers through autumn. While the blooms of most asters are distinctly yellow in the center, those of calico aster quickly turn reddish pink in the middle. Also, instead of being solid green, the leaves of calico aster may be purple-tinted green to near black. Zones 4 to 8. Smooth aster (*A. laevis*) grows in narrowly upright to vase-shaped clumps typically 3 to 5 feet (90 to 150 cm) tall with purple-blue flowers through fall. Zones 4 to 8. One of the latest-to-bloom species is Tatarian aster (*A. tataricus*); its purple flowers open atop stiff, 5- to 8-foot-tall (1.5 to 2.4 m) stems in mid- to late fall. Zones 3 to 8.

All of these asters, and most other species and hybrids, are definitely sun-lovers, but there are a few species that naturally grow in woodland conditions. Two of these include white wood aster (*A. divaricatus*), with white flowers from late summer to early fall on clumps that are 12 to 18 inches (30 to 45 cm) tall, and heart-leaf aster (*A. cordifolius*), with white to pale lavender blooms atop stems anywhere from 1 to 3 feet (30 to 90 cm) tall. Zones 4 to 8 for both.

Aster tataricus with *Viburnum setigerum*

Aster novae-angliae 'Alma Potschke'

GROWING TIPS

▶ **Light & soil.** Full sun is ideal for nearly all asters. The exceptions are woodland species — including white wood aster and heart-leaf aster — which can grow in just about any amount of shade, although they, too, bloom best with a fair amount of light (morning sun and afternoon shade, for instance, or light all-day shade). Average, well-drained soil is generally fine. Fertile, compost-enriched soil encourages the most vigorous growth, but asters growing in very rich soil are more likely to sprawl if not sheared or staked. Frikart's aster needs better drainage than most asters; it especially dislikes soil that stays soggy in winter. The woodland species, too, can tolerate dry spells fairly well, but like most asters, they grow best when the soil stays evenly moist (though not waterlogged).

▶ **Division & propagation.** Asters form steadily expanding clumps that benefit from being divided every 2 or 3 years (or even as often as every year or two for New England and New York asters). Spring is a good time for most; Frikart's aster can be divided in spring or when the flowers finish in early fall. Division is also an easy way to propagate asters. Another is to take stem cuttings in late spring or early summer. If you don't need the new plants to be identical, growing from seed is yet another way to propagate asters. Sow fresh seed (barely cover it with soil) outdoors in fall to early winter, or sow indoors in winter, enclose the pots in a plastic bag, and refrigerate them for about 4 weeks before moving them to a warm, bright spot to sprout.

▶ **Potential problems.** Asters are susceptible to a number of pests, particularly aphids and Japanese beetles, as well as leaf miners, lace bugs, and various caterpillars. Usually, the plants can recover from even serious infestations, so you may just want to site asters where you don't see the foliage at close range and then not worry about controlling the pests. Several diseases can affect the plants, too. (Also see Troubleshooting, page 160.) The roots of aromatic aster seem to be a favorite winter food of voles, and the new growth of just about any aster appears to be irresistible to rabbits.

If your asters tend to lose their lower leaves every year, pair them with lower-growing companions that will cover up the asters' bare stems. Or, cut the outer stems shorter than the inner ones when you shear the clumps in early summer, to get lower branching around the edges.

SEASONAL CARE

Spring

▶ Cut down any remaining top growth in early spring. Set out new plants, or move or divide existing clumps, any time during spring. Space plants of compact hybrid asters or smooth asters about 1 foot (30 cm) apart; set the woodland species about 18 inches (45 cm) apart; and allow about 2 feet (60 cm) between the rest. Water new plantings regularly through spring if rain is lacking. Apply an organic mulch before summer arrives. Cut Frikart's aster back by about one-half in late spring, or else set some kind of grow-through support over it in mid- to late spring to prevent flopping in summer.

Summer

▶ Frikart's aster is usually in bloom by early summer, but if you cut it back in spring, it probably won't begin blooming until midsummer. You could snip off the faded flowers individually, which may extend the bloom period a bit, but the plants will likely bloom into autumn anyway. Early summer is a good time to cut tall, late-blooming types, such as New England, New York, and Tatarian asters, down to about one-half their current height; this will reduce their ultimate height a bit and help to reduce the chance of

Aster (continued)

the stems sprawling. Or, you could cut them back by about one-third in early summer and one-third in midsummer for even denser, sturdier clumps. Aromatic aster naturally forms well-branched, nicely shaped mounds, but if you'd like to keep it more compact, you could shear it back by about one-half in early summer. Keep watering spring plantings weekly if rain is lacking. Established plantings also benefit from watering once every 10 to 14 days during dry spells. Many asters start flowering by late summer, especially if they weren't cut back earlier.

✪ ☉ Fall & Winter

▸ Set out new plants, or move or divide existing plantings in early fall; water these new plantings for the first month or so if rain is lacking. In mild areas, ajugas are evergreen; in cooler zones, they often turn brown and look dead at some point during the winter. It's not necessary to do anything to them; they'll sprout fresh leaves when the growing season starts. Scatter a general-purpose organic fertilizer or a shovelful of compost around your ajugas every other year in late fall to late winter, if desired.

✿ TROUBLESHOOTING

▸ **Leaves are discolored or drop.** Downy mildew, powdery mildew, and various leaf spot diseases can attack aster foliage. Most aren't damaging enough to need control, although they can make the plants look unsightly and repeated, serious infections can weaken the clumps, so you may choose to use an organic fungicide. Or, replace New England and New York asters with other species and hybrids, which may not be quite as susceptible. Leaf drop can also be a sign of drought stress; applying an organic mulch before summer and watering regularly during dry spells can help to prevent this.

▸ **Plants wilt and die.** Asters growing where the soil is constantly wet can be more susceptible to various wilt diseases. You could try applying a biofungicide to the soil as soon as you notice symptoms. If the plants still succumb, remove and destroy them (both the tops and as many roots as you can), and choose a spot with better drainage if you plant new asters.

Relatively Speaking

Boltonia (*Boltonia asteroides* var. *latisquama*) — also known as Bolton's aster, doll's daisy, false aster, false chamomile, or thousand flower — is another beauty for late-season gardens, with an abundance of bright white or pale pink blooms from late summer or early fall into midfall. The clumps of upright stems clad in slender, blue-green leaves can reach as much as 7 feet (2.1 m) tall, although the commonly grown cultivar 'Snowbank' is often a more compact 3 to 5 feet (90 to 150 cm). 'Nana', with pinkish purple flowers, is even shorter: usually 2 to 3 feet (60 to 90 cm). Zones 4 to 9.

Boltonias perform well in the same growing conditions as most asters (full sun and average, well-drained soil) and need the same seasonal care. They'll thrive in rich soil with extra moisture, and they'll tolerate light shade, but in both conditions, they'll be prone to sprawling unless you stake them in spring or cut them back by about one-half in early summer. Keep in mind that the clumps can expand at a moderately fast rate. Leave about 3 feet (90 cm) between the clumps at planting time, or plan to divide them every 3 years or so to keep them from crowding out less-vigorous companions.

False aster is a common name that's also used for another white-flowered aster relative: *Kalimeris pinnatifida* (also sold as *K. mongolica*, *Asteromoea pinnatifida*, and *A. mongolica*). Other common names it's known by include Japanese aster, Mongolian aster, and orphanage plant. This moderate-creeper grows about 3 feet (90 cm) tall and generally blooms from midsummer well into fall. You'll most often see the selection called 'Hortensis', with small, semidouble, white daisies. *K. incisa* (also known as *A. incisa* or *Boltonia incisa*) is similar but grows about 2 feet (60 cm) tall and has single white to pale blue flowers through the summer. Both are usually hardy in Zones 4 to 8. They'll grow in full sun or partial shade with average, moist but well-drained soil. Space the clumps about 18 inches (45 cm) apart. Divide every few years in spring to control their spread, and trim the flowering stems back to the basal leaves once the flowers are finished; otherwise, they need little care.

Astilbe

ASTILBE, FALSE SPIREA

Astilbes are classics for summer color in shady gardens.

MOST ASTILBES GROWN in gardens are hybrids (often listed under *A.* × *arendsii*), but you may also find selections of a few species, such as Chinese astilbe (*A. chinensis*) and star astilbe (*A. simplicifolia*). Some traits they all share are toothed leaves that are also usually deeply cut, producing a lacy appearance, and an abundance of tiny flowers grouped into dense to airy plumes or sprays. Astilbes can be anywhere from 8 inches (20 cm) to 5 feet (1.5 m) tall, depending on the cultivar. They bloom in a range of colors, including white, cream, and many shades of pink, red, and lavender, and the foliage may be light to deep green and glossy or dull. It's also not unusual for the leaves to have a reddish to bronzy appearance, especially in spring. On 'Color Flash', the new leaves are bright green, while the older leaves turn bright red to deep purple. Astilbes are generally recommended for Zones 4 to 8, though they may survive a zone or two farther north with a deep winter mulch or dependable snow cover.

Astilbe 'Drum and Bass'

✿ GROWING TIPS

▸ **Light & soil.** Gardeners in cooler areas (generally north of Zone 5) may be able to grow astilbes in full sun, as long as the soil stays dependably moist. Elsewhere, a site with some morning sun and shade for the rest of the day, or else light all-day shade, is usually ideal. Too much shade leads to slow growth and few, if any, flowers. The ideal soil is rich in nutrients and organic matter, and it doesn't normally dry out below the top 2 inches (5 cm) or so, but it's not waterlogged either. Chinese astilbe and its cultivars are reportedly a bit more forgiving about drying out occasionally, but don't depend on that.

▸ **Division & propagation.** Astilbes benefit from being divided every 3 to 5 years. Early spring is usually the best time, but if necessary, you could divide them during late summer to early fall in cooler areas or during early to midfall in warmer zones. You'll need a sharp knife to cut through the tight crowns, especially on older clumps. While some astilbes occasionally self-sow, deliberately growing them from seed can be a little tricky, and the seedlings can be variable. Division is a more dependable way to propagate your plants.

▸ **Potential problems.** Japanese beetles can devour astilbe foliage, and powdery mildew may cause dusty patches on the leaves. For other possible problems, see Troubleshooting, page 162.

✿ SEASONAL CARE

◐ Spring
▸ Cut down any remaining top growth in early spring; set out new plants or move or divide existing clumps then, too. Space the low-growers (those to about 18 inches [45 cm] tall) roughly 1 foot apart; taller types can go 2 feet (60 cm) apart. If new growth gets nipped by frost, cut off the damaged parts. Water both new and established plantings regularly through spring if rain is lacking; add an organic mulch, too, to keep the soil from drying out. Some early blooming hybrids may be in flower by late spring.

◯ Summer
▸ Depending on which astilbes you have, they may not start blooming

Astilbe (continued)

Astilbe japonica 'Red Sentinel'

until early or midsummer. They usually stay colorful for 4 to 8 weeks, then the plumes turn golden to brown. Remove them if you don't like how they look, but don't expect the plants to produce more flowers. Keep watering both spring plantings and established clumps during dry spells.

✿ ☉ Fall & Winter

▸ In the warmer parts of their growing range (roughly Zones 7 and 8), you can set out, move, or divide astilbes in early to midautumn. If you must do this in cooler areas, complete the tasks as early as possible in fall. Water new plantings regularly if rain is lacking in early to midfall. Leave the top growth in place for the winter. Late fall to late winter is a good time to scatter a general-pur-

❖ **DON'T SKIMP ON SOIL PREP** Work a shovelful or two of compost into the hole at planting time and whenever you divide or move your astilbes. If you skimp on the soil preparation, the plants may survive, but they probably won't grow or bloom much.

pose organic fertilizer or a shovelful of compost (or both) around each clump.

❖ TROUBLESHOOTING

▸ **Leaf edges turn brown and crisp.** If the soil dries out at some point during the growing season, you'll know it by the leaf damage. Severely affected foliage looks unsightly for the rest of the season, so you may decide to cut it all off. If you do that early in the summer, new foliage may appear by late summer; if you cut it down later, the plants may wait until next spring to resprout. To prevent a recurrence, mulch generously and water regularly to keep the soil evenly moist if rain is lacking.

▸ **Plants wilt and die.** Fungal wilt may cause leaves and stems to droop, even if the soil is moist. You could try drenching the soil with a biofungicide at the first sign of damage; if that doesn't work, remove and destroy affected clumps. Black vine weevil larvae — curved, cream-colored, dark-headed grubs — may feed within the roots, causing similar symptoms. If the adults are also present, you may notice notches cut out of the leaf edges on your astilbes or on nearby susceptible plants, such as rhododendrons and heucheras. (This leaf damage usually starts earlier in the summer.) Once the plants are infested severely enough to wilt, it's best to remove and destroy them. If you've had problems with weevils in past years, you may be able to prevent further damage by applying beneficial nematodes (*Heterorhabditis*) to the soil around the plants in mid- to late summer — ideally about a month after you first notice the leaf-notching.

Baptisia

BAPTISIA, FALSE INDIGO, WILD INDIGO

Long lived and typically trouble free, false indigos are an ideal choice for easy-care color in sunny gardens.

BAPTISIA'S SHRUBBY CLUMPS of three-part, often bluish green leaves are topped with spiky bloom clusters for several weeks in late spring to early summer. Blue false indigo (*Baptisia australis*) blooms in shades of blue in clumps that are 3 to 5 feet (90 to 150 cm) tall and 4 to 6 feet (1.2 to 1.8 m) across. For white flowers, look for plants labeled as white wild indigo (*B. alba*), *B. alba* var. *alba* (also sold as *B. pendula*), or *B. alba* var. *macrophylla* (also known as *B. lactea* or *B. leucantha*). These normally all mature at about the same size as blue false indigo, though they may eventually reach to 6 or even 7 feet (1.8 to 2.1 m) in ideal conditions. It's not unusual for some of them to have purple-tinged to near-black stems. Both the blues and the whites are usually hardy in Zones 3 to 9. There are also species with bright yellow flowers, such as *B. sphaerocarpa*. It tends to be a bit more compact — roughly 2 to 3 feet (60 to 90 cm) tall and wide. Zones 5 to 9. There are also hybrids between the various species that produce plants with purplish to pale yellow blooms.

❇ GROWING TIPS

▸ **Light & soil.** Baptisias thrive in full sun but can perform well in even partial shade (they'll be more likely to sprawl there, though).

Average, well-drained soil is fine. Baptisias can grow in rich, moist conditions but adapt well to infertile soil, too, and they're quite drought tolerant once established.

▸ **Division & propagation.** Baptisias tend to recover very slowly if their roots are disturbed, so division generally isn't a good idea. To propagate, sow fresh seed about ¼ inch (6 mm) deep outdoors in late summer or fall, or indoors in mid- to late winter. Grow seedlings in deep pots for a year or two, or move them directly to their final spots during their first spring or summer. They may not flower until their second or third year, and it takes 5 to 6 years in one spot for them to really fill out. Another propagation technique worth trying is taking stem cuttings in midspring.

▸ **Potential problems.** Leaf spots, rust, and powdery mildew can all

Baptisia sphaerocarpa 'Screaming Yellow'

❇ **MOVE CAREFULLY** Baptisias can be slow to recover after being moved, especially after they've been growing in one spot for several years. But if you must transplant them, try in early spring and dig a deeper rootball than you normally would to get as much of the taproot as possible. Be prepared to wait at least a year or two for the plants to flower again.

affect the foliage, but these fungal diseases are rarely serious enough to need spraying; generally, the plants are problem free.

✿ SEASONAL CARE

☉ Spring

▶ Set out young plants in early to midspring. At this stage, they will be small, but keep in mind that the mature plants can be up to 6 feet (1.8 m) wide, so give them plenty of room: ideally a space at least 3 feet (90 cm) across, or more if you can. (Fill the empty space around them with low-growing annuals for the first few years.) Water new plantings regularly if rain is lacking. If your established plants tend to sprawl, set wire cages or hoop stakes over the clumps in early spring for later support, or plan to prune them in summer. Apply an organic mulch in early to midspring, if desired. In southern gardens, baptisias may be in full bloom by late spring; in the north, the first shoots may not even appear until mid- to late spring.

◎ Summer

▶ Even late-rising baptisias are usually in bloom in early summer. You may choose to shear established clumps back by one-third to one-half after flowering to encourage shorter, bushier regrowth that's less likely to flop (a big plus if you didn't stake them in spring, or where space is limited). This also removes the seed-pods, though, so if you find them attractive, then don't shear. Keep watering spring plantings during dry spells. Established baptisias rarely need watering.

✪ ☉ Fall & Winter

▶ Set out new plants in early fall, and water them for the first month or so if rain is lacking. Cut the top growth to the ground any time after the foliage turns black. Scatter a general-purpose organic fertilizer or a shovelful of compost around each clump every year or two in late fall to late winter.

Relatively Speaking

False lupines (*Thermopsis*) — also known as bush peas or golden banners — look very much like baptisias, but with light green leaves and yellow flower spikes. They, too, bloom in late spring or early summer and grow in dense clumps, usually reaching 3 to 5 feet (90 to 150 cm) tall and about as wide, and they adapt to the same range of growing conditions in Zones 3 to 9. The seasonal care advice for baptisias applies here, too.

Thermopsis caroliniana

Belamcanda

BLACKBERRY LILY, LEOPARD LILY

Despite the common names blackberry lily and leopard lily, *Belamcanda chinensis* is actually a member of the iris family (Iridaceae). In fact, some authorities have even reclassified it as *Iris domestica*. One look at the spiky fans of flat, straplike leaves, which grow from slow-creeping rhizomes, and the iris connection is rather obvious.

THE SUMMER FLOWERS OF BLACKBERRY LILY bloom mostly in shades of orange with reddish freckles atop upright stems that are typically 2 to 3 feet (60 to 90 cm) tall, occasionally to 4 feet (1.2 m). The selection 'Hello Yellow', which is sometimes sold as *B. flabellata*, has solid-yellow blooms and grows just 1 to 2 feet (30 to 60 cm) tall.

Each blackberry lily blossom lasts only one day, but the clustered buds open at different times to extend the flowering season. In warm climates, the show can extend for 2 months or more; in cool areas, it may last just a week or two. The blooms are followed by green seedpods that turn tan and split to reveal rounded, shiny, black seeds, which are held in clusters that resemble blackberries. The plants are commonly recommended for Zones 5 to 10, but gardeners in Zone 4 (and even some in Zone 3) have grown them successfully.

❖ GROWING TIPS

▸ **Light & soil.** Full sun is usually best, but blackberry lily can grow in light shade, too; in fact, afternoon shade can be very beneficial in southern gardens. As long as they have good drainage, the plants can adapt to a wide range of soil conditions, from nutrient rich to infertile and from dry to moist.

▸ **Division & propagation.** The plants may fade away after several years; divide them every 2 or 3 years to help maintain their vigor, or use self-sown seedlings as replacements. If you find too many seedlings, however, consider cutting off most of the seedpods before they mature. Divide clumps in spring or late summer to early fall for propagation. Or, sow the seed ¼-inch (6 mm) deep outdoors in fall to early spring, or indoors in winter. Fresh seed usually sprouts quickly, but if seedlings don't appear within a few weeks indoors, put the pots in plastic bags and refrigerate them for 4 to 6 weeks before moving them back to a warm, bright place. Winter-sown seedlings may bloom during their first growing season.

Belamcanda chinensis in flower

Belamcanda chinensis, post-bloom

❖ SEASONAL CARE

◐ Spring

▸ Set out new plants, or move or divide existing clumps, any time during the spring. Space them about 1 foot (30 cm) apart. Water new plantings regularly if rain is lacking. Apply an organic mulch before summer.

◎ Summer

▸ In southern gardens, blackberry lily often begins blooming in early summer; in mid-range zones, expect it to start in midsummer. In the coolest parts of its hardiness range, blackberry lily may not open until late summer, and the flowering season will be short; as soon as the show is done, move or divide clumps if needed, or set out new plants by the end of summer. In any climate, keep watering spring plantings regularly during summer dry spells.

✤ ◉ Fall & Winter

▸ Flowering can continue into fall in areas with long growing seasons. As soon as the flowers are done, move or divide clumps if necessary; water regularly for the first few weeks if rain is lacking. The seedpods may not have time to mature on plants that didn't bloom until late summer; in most areas though, the showy seed clusters are visible in early to midfall. The foliage may stay evergreen in frost-free areas, but elsewhere it will turn tan when cold weather arrives; clean up the dead leaves thoroughly but leave the seed stalks for winter interest (or remove them to prevent self-sowing). Scatter a general-purpose organic fertilizer or a shovelful of compost around the clumps every other year in late fall to late winter. North of Zone 5, a winter mulch can improve the odds of overwintering.

❖ **STOP THE SPRAWL** In moist, rich soil, blackberry lilies are likely to sprawl, and it's difficult to stake them effectively. Dividing them every year or two can help to prevent sprawling. Other options include setting grow-through grid supports over the emerging clumps in spring or propping up the flowering stems with linking stakes or Y-stakes.

▶ **Leaves chewed, streaky, or yellowed; plants die.** Iris borers attack blackberry lily, too, damaging the foliage in late spring to early summer. The pinkish, brown-headed larvae then tunnel into the rhizomes, providing an ideal entry for soft rot; affected fans turn yellow and fall over. If you suspect borers, dig up the clumps after bloom, and cut out and destroy any damaged rhizomes. Also, clean up all foliage thoroughly before spring to remove any overwintering eggs.

Relatively Speaking

Candy lily (currently known as × *Pardancanda norrisii*) is a cross between blackberry lily and vesper iris (*Pardanthopsis dichotoma*; also known as *Iris dichotoma*). It looks just like blackberry lily in leaf, but it blooms in a wider range of colors, including red, orange, yellow, pink, purple, and white, with or without spots. Give it the same growing conditions and care. One tip: If you grow candy lilies from seed, plant them in a holding bed until they bloom; then move those with the most interesting colors to your garden and compost or give away the rest.

Belamcanda chinensis seed heads

Bergenia

BERGENIA, PIGSQUEAK

It seems unlikely that bergenias will ever be considered trendy, but their sturdy nature and quiet beauty will always make them a valuable addition to gardens.

THERE ARE SEVERAL SPECIES — among them, heartleaf bergenia (*Bergenia cordifolia*), *B. crassifolia*, and *B. purpurascens* — along with a number of hybrids. They differ in small traits but are all fairly similar, with roughly oval to rounded, smooth, thick leaves that grow in rosettes typically 6 to 12 inches (15 to 30 cm) tall. The plants grow from thick rhizomes that creep right along the soil surface. Clustered flowers in white or shades of pink, red, or purple bloom atop stems that are 12 to 18 inches (30 to 45 cm) tall. Zones 3 to 8.

Bergenia cordifolia 'Perfecta'

❖ GROWING TIPS

▸ **Light & soil.** Bergenias can grow in light conditions from full sun (in northern gardens) to full shade (though they'll bloom poorly there, if at all). A site with morning sun and afternoon shade or light all-day shade is usually ideal. They adapt to a wide range of soil conditions: compost-enriched, moist but well-drained soil encourages lush growth, but bergenias can tolerate dryish, infertile conditions as well.

▸ **Division & propagation.** Bergenias grow slowly and can usually stay in one place for many years without getting overcrowded, but dividing them every 4 to 6 years in spring is a good way to propagate them. If you want to try growing them from seed, sow it uncovered outdoors in fall to spring, or sow indoors in winter, enclose the pots in plastic bags, and refrigerate them for about 3 weeks before mowing them to a warm, bright spot for germination.

▸ **Potential problems.** Slugs and snails may damage the foliage. Leaf spots may appear, as well, but they're usually not serious.

❖ SEASONAL CARE

◐ Spring

▸ In early spring, cut off any winter-damaged leaves. Set out new plants, or divide or move existing clumps, in early to midspring. Space them 1 to 2 feet (30 to 60 cm) apart. Water new plantings regularly if rain is lacking. Apply an organic mulch before summer. Flowers may appear any time during spring.

◯ Summer

▸ Snip off finished bergenia flower stems at their base, and any damaged leaves too, as needed through the summer. Keep watering spring plantings if rain is lacking.

✪ ◉ Fall & Winter

▸ Spring is generally a better time to set out, divide, or move bergenias, but if it's necessary to do it later, complete the tasks as early in fall as possible. Water new plantings for the first month or so if rain is lacking. Scatter a general-purpose organic fertilizer or a shovelful of compost around each clump in late fall to late winter.

▸ In areas without dependable snow cover, bergenias may be damaged by drying winds or rapid freeze-and-thaw cycles. Spread pine needles, chopped leaves, or another light mulch over the foliage, or just enjoy the leaves as long as they look good and then remove the damaged foliage in late winter or early spring.

❖ **THE SHOW GOES ON** Bergenias bloom mostly in spring, but established clumps can send up some flowers later on, too — even in winter in mild areas. It's common for the foliage to turn reddish or purplish in cold weather.

Brunnera

BRUNNERA, SIBERIAN BUGLOSS, FALSE FORGET-ME-NOT

Finding great-looking perennials for shade is often a challenge, especially if you want flowers as well as foliage.

BRUNNERA (*BRUNNERA MACROPHYLLA*) OFFERS BOTH, starting with clusters of small, sky blue blooms in spring atop stems typically 12 to 18 inches (30 to 45 cm) tall. As the flowers fade, larger, heart-shaped leaves emerge from the crown to form broad, mounded foliage clumps about 1 foot (30 cm) tall. The foliage is commonly dark green, but there are also selections with silvery spots or nearly all-silver leaves, as well as some with variegated leaves. Brunnera is usually recommended for Zones 3 to 8, although some gardeners in Zones 9 and even 10 have grown it successfully.

Brunnera macrophylla

☘ GROWING TIPS

▸ **Light & soil.** Partial shade and evenly moist but well-drained, compost-enriched soil is ideal for most brunneras. Those with solid-green or silver-marked leaves tend to be the most adaptable, tolerating morning sun (especially if the soil always stays moist) as well as dry shade. They can grow in full shade as well but may not flower well there. Variegated selections tend to scorch in too much sun or in dry soil, but they languish in too much shade, so you may need to experiment to find the perfect combination of light and moisture for them. You'll also need to watch for and remove any all-green growth on the variegates.

▸ **Division & propagation.** If you notice that your brunnera clumps have died out in the center, that's your cue to divide them, either in early fall or in early spring. Division is also a fine way to propagate them. It's easy to transplant small self-sown seedlings; there are often many of them, although they may not show the same leaf markings as the plants they came from. Sow fresh seed (barely cover it) outdoors in late summer or fall, or sow indoors in winter, enclose the pots in a plastic bag, and refrigerate them for about a month before moving them to a cool, bright place for germination.

▸ **Potential problems.** Slugs, snails, and aphids may bother brunneras but shouldn't cause serious problems.

☘ SEASONAL CARE

○ Spring

▸ Divide or move existing clumps in very early spring, before or just as new growth begins, or set out new plants in early to midspring. Space them about 18 inches (45 cm) apart. In mild-winter areas, brunneras may begin blooming in early spring; farther north, they'll start a few weeks later. Water new plantings regularly if rain is lacking. Apply a generous layer of organic mulch in early to midspring.

◎ Summer

▸ By early summer, you'll notice the flowers dropping and new leaves coming up. Snip off the flowering stems at their base to prevent self-sowing or just let the new leaves cover them up. Keep watering spring plantings during dry spells.

Established brunneras also benefit from regular watering if rainfall is lacking, although they can be quite drought tolerant if they're not in too much sun.

✿ ☉ Fall & Winter

▸ Set out new plants, or divide or move existing clumps, in early fall. Water them regularly for the first month or so if rain is lacking. The leaves may continue to look good into winter in mild areas but darken when hit by frost; cut off the damaged leaves in late fall or winter. Scatter a general-purpose organic fertilizer or a shovelful of compost around each clump in late fall to late winter.

☘ TROUBLESHOOTING

▸ **Leaves look tattered or crispy.** If the soil dries out too much, the foliage may look ugly for the rest of the season, or the whole plant may die back to the ground. If only a few leaves are damaged, snip them off; if they all look bad, the best route is usually to cut them all to the ground. Keeping the soil moist may encourage some new foliage to appear by fall; usually, though, the plants will wait until next spring to resprout.

Bulbs

It's tough to imagine a garden without at least a few bulbs!

WHETHER YOU CHOOSE early bloomers to welcome spring, midseason bloomers to spruce up summer borders, or fall-flowering bulbs to add freshness to your late-season plantings, you really can't go wrong. Bulbs are incredibly adaptable and versatile, and they're generally very easy to care for, too.

❇ GROWING TIPS

▶ **Light & soil.** Most bulbs thrive in average, well-drained soil, with full sun to light shade while they are actively growing and blooming. (While they are dormant, it doesn't matter to most whether their site is sunny or shady.) If your soil is on the clayey side, try planting your hardy bulbs a bit shallower than recommended, or plant them on a slope or in a raised bed, to minimize the chance of them rotting.

▶ **Design Approaches.** When you're planting bulbs among perennials, you have two options: either try to keep the bulbs in distinct groups or areas, or scatter small clumps of them throughout the area. The "scattering" approach can have a more natural look, but it increases the chance of you damaging some of the bulbs when you need to dig up and divide the perennials, or when you add bulbs in the future.

If you prefer to keep your hardy bulbs in more distinct clumps, you can make the most of your garden space by layering several kinds of bulbs in each planting hole. Dig each hole about 8 inches (20 cm) deep, set large bulbs such as giant alliums (*Allium giganteum*) and lilies in the bottom, and barely cover them with soil. Set in a layer of medium-sized bulbs, such as tulips and hyacinths, add more soil, add a layer of crocus, grape hyacinths, or other small bulbs, and then finish filling the hole with soil.

Lilium 'Ariadne'

Lilium 'Coral Sunrise'

❇ **BRING ON THE MULCH** Spring-planted bulbs like lilies can benefit from organic mulch applied soon after planting. You may also want to mulch around the emerging shoots of established bulbs to prevent later spring rains from splashing soil onto the leaves and blooms.

Colchichum 'Waterlily"

Allium schubertii

Pairing spring-blooming bulbs with perennials that fill out later, such as asters, catmints (*Nepeta*), daylilies (*Hemerocallis*), and warm-season ornamental grasses, is an easy and effective way to mask the foliage of the bulbs as it turns yellow and then dies back the ground.

Bushy, medium-sized perennials, such as artemisias (*Artemisia*) and bluestars (*Amsonia*), can make great companions for tall-stemmed summer bulbs, giving the bulbs some support and covering up the bulbs' uninteresting lower stems. Fall-blooming bulbs tend to be on the short side, so they pair perfectly with front-of-the-border perennials, such as lamb's ears (*Stachys byzantina*) or low-growing sedums (*Sedum*) and veronicas (*Veronica*).

Tender bulbs, such as dahlias and cannas, are terrific for adding height and color to young perennial gardens. Pop them in among clumps of perennials in the middle or back of the border for the first few years, at least, to fill space until the larger perennials settle in and start flowering well. You could also use these bulbs to fill gaps left by early flowering perennials, but if you do, be careful that you don't dig into the crowns of the dormant perennials.

▶ **Division & propagation.** By far the easiest way to propagate most hardy bulbs is to divide them after flowering, when their foliage is turning from yellow to brown. Divide tender bulbs in spring before you plant them out again. Growing from seed can be a slow proposition, but if you want to try, sow the seeds outdoors in late summer to fall. Smaller bulbs often self-sow, and a few of them seed to the point of being considered weedy or invasive in some areas: among these vigorous spreaders are grape hyacinths, Spanish bluebells (*Hyacinthoides hispanica*; also sold as *Scilla campanulata*), spring starflower (*Ipheion uniflorum*), and star-of-Bethlehem (*Ornithogalum*).

▶ **Potential problems.** A number of pests and diseases can bother the various types of bulbs, but for the most part, these easy keepers aren't seriously troubled as long as you plant them in well-drained soil. (See Troubleshooting, page 174 for more information.)

❖ **BULB TIPS** However you plant your bulbs, it's smart to take a lot of pictures of them, so you'll know exactly where they are and minimize the chance of digging into them by accident later on. Also, it's a good idea to wear gloves when planting or dividing bulbs, because some of them may irritate sensitive skin.

Bulbs (continued)

◑ Spring

▸ Many of the so-called minor bulbs — spring crocus, grape hyacinths (*Muscari*), squills (*Scilla*), and the like — are in full bloom in early to midspring. Other, larger bulbs may begin blooming at various times during the spring months. Spring is also a fine time to plant summer bulbs, such as true lilies (*Lilium*), glads, and (after all danger of frost has passed) cannas and dahlias. Give new plantings a good soaking when you set them out and occasional watering after that if rain is lacking.

◎ Summer

▸ Spring bulbs are mostly finished flowering by early summer, but in cooler climates, some may continue into this season. Their leaves start to look ugly as they start turning yellow, but resist the urge to clip them off early; the bulbs need their leaves to make and store food for next year's display. Once the yellow leaves start turning brown, though, it's a fine time to dig up and divide the bulbs if they're overcrowded or if you want to move them.

▸ Lilies, gladiolus, cannas, dahlias, and other hardy and tender bulbs start blooming at various times during the summer. Removing the flowers as the petals drop prevents the bulbs from wasting energy on forming seeds and can promote rebloom on some. You may need to use linking stakes, Y-stakes, or some other support to prop up tall-stemmed bulbs if they start to lean.

▸ Late summer is an ideal time to plant fall-flowering bulbs, such as autumn crocus (*Colchicum*). Some bulbs — such as spider lilies (*Lycoris*) and naked ladies (*Amaryllis*

✿ All in the Family

Here's just a sampling of some beautiful bulbs for perennial gardens, along with tips for growing them successfully.

▸ *Allium* (ornamental onions): Be aware that some ornamental onions, such as drumstick chives (*A. sphaerocephalon*), have slender leaves that emerge in fall and look much like weedy wild onion or wild garlic; be sure you don't pull them out by accident! Broader-leaved species don't emerge until spring, but they can get frost damaged, so consider protecting them overnight if late frosts threaten. Remove ornamental onion seed heads by clipping off the stems at the base to prevent self-sowing, or leave the larger kinds to dry in place and enjoy their interesting forms.

▸ *Canna* (cannas): In Zones 8 and south, cannas can be left in the ground year-round; farther north, you'll need to dig up the thick rhizomes and store them in a cool but frost-free place for the winter. (In Zone 7, you may be able to leave them in the ground if you mulch them heavily.) Plant indoor-stored rhizomes in pots in early spring and keep them warm and slightly moist to give them a head start, or plant the rhizomes directly in the garden after all danger of frost has passed.

▸ *Crocus* (crocus): These low-growing spring- or fall-bloomers generally grow best in sites that are on the dry side in summer.

▸ *Cyclamen* (cyclamen): Growing from plump, rounded tubers, these beauties are prized for their lovely, deep green leaves often showily marked with silver, as well as for their dainty flowers, which may appear late summer to fall or late winter to early spring. The fall-blooming species go dormant in summer and send up new foliage in early fall, often slightly after the flowers.

▸ *Dahlia* (dahlias): South of Zone 7, dahlias can stay in the garden all year; north of that, you'll need to dig them up after frost and store them in a cool but frost-free place for the winter, or else treat them like annuals and buy new ones each spring. Plant the tuberous roots in pots in early to midspring and keep them warm and barely moist to give them a head start, or plant them directly in the garden after all danger of frost has passed. Pinching off the shoot tips every few weeks through early summer encourages lower, bushier growth, but tall-growing types may still need staking. Pinch or snip off the dead flowers to promote rebloom.

▸ *Galanthus* (snowdrops): These early risers may begin

belladonna) — flower in late summer, often before their leaves appear.

▸ Bulbs that are actively growing in summer usually benefit from occasional to regular watering if rain is lacking. Those that don't have any leafy growth generally don't require watering.

✤ ☉ Fall & Winter

▸ Fall is the ideal time to plant most hardy bulbs — usually mid-September to late October for most bulbs and November to early December for tulips. Their packaging usually gives the recommended planting depth and spacing. If specific information isn't available, try to plant small bulbs 3 to 4 inches (7.5 to 10 cm) deep, medium-sized bulbs 4 to 6 inches (10 to 15 cm) deep, and

Allium 'Globemaster'

blooming in winter in mild areas, or in early spring elsewhere. They thrive in partial shade and moist but well-drained, compost-enriched soil. If the bulbs push up to the surface, dig up and replant them about 3 inches (7.5 cm) deep.

▸ *Gladiolus* (glads): Large-flowered glad hybrids usually need to be dug up after frost for winter storage indoors north of Zone 8, but they may overwinter farther north with a thick winter mulch. There are also several species, including *G. communis* spp. *byzantinus*, that may overwinter just fine outdoors as far north as Zones 4 or 5 even without protection. Tall-growing glads usually need to be staked or propped up.

▸ *Hyacinthus* (hyacinths): It's normal for hyacinths to produce dense flower clusters their first year or two and much looser spikes after that. If you prefer the larger, fuller flower spikes, you'll need to replace the bulbs every year or two.

▸ *Lilium* (lilies): Evenly moist but well-drained, compost-enriched soil is ideal for most lilies. Plant the bulbs as soon as you get them in spring or fall, because they can dry out quickly. After bloom, clip off the seedpods as they start to swell, but leave the leafy stalk until it turns brown. Bright red lily-leaf beetles are becoming

a serious pest of lilies, especially in the northeastern states.

▸ *Muscari* (grape hyacinths): Some grape hyacinths send up new leaves in fall, and the foliage sticks around through the winter. It can look somewhat messy by spring, but leave it in place to die off naturally; the flowers will mostly cover it up during bloom. Grape hyacinths can seed around freely, so you may want to clip off the spent flower stems to prevent that.

▸ *Narcissus* (daffodils): Daffodils usually do best in sites that are on the dry side in summer. Compact cultivars, such as 'Baby Moon' and 'February Gold', often blend more easily into beds and borders than taller, large-flowered types.

▸ *Tulipa* (tulips): Tulips grow best in sites that are on the dry side in summer. Hybrid tulips make a splendid show in bloom, at least in their first spring, but they're not very attractive as they decline after flowering, and many kinds don't bloom nearly as well in following years. In high-visibility beds and borders, consider pulling them out as soon as the flowers drop and planting new ones each fall. Small species tulips and compact types, such as cultivars of *T. greigii* and *kaufmanniana*, tend to be more dependably perennial.

Bulbs (continued)

larger bulbs 6 to 8 inches (15 to 20 cm) deep. Spread them out a bit so they evenly fill the space. If you can easily tell which end is up (it's often somewhat pointed), try to set them right-side up; if you can't tell, don't worry — they'll usually straighten themselves out. If you end up planting later than the ideal time, consider covering the bulbs with a thick layer of mulch to keep the soil warm a bit longer and give them a better chance to send out some roots.

▸ Hardy bulbs that have been in the ground for a year or more can benefit from a scattering of compost or an organic, general-purpose or bulb fertilizer — or both — in late fall to late winter. Don't be alarmed if you see them producing new leaves in fall: it's perfectly normal for some kinds of grape hyacinths (*Muscari*) and ornamental onions (*Allium*), and it can happen with daffodils and other bulbs, too. You generally don't need to worry; even if the leaf tips get a little damaged, the flowers should appear at the normal time. Bulbs that flower in late summer often send up their leaves in fall (or they may wait until spring).

▸ Autumn crocus and fall-flowering species of crocus, ornamental onions, and other bulbs send up their blooms in early to midautumn. Their leaves may not appear for a few weeks, or even until spring.

❖ TROUBLESHOOTING

▸ **Flowers nipped off or completely missing; leaves nibbled; no sprouts appear.** Besides slugs and snails, which can chew large holes in the shoots and leaves of emerging bulbs, animals tend to be the most serious pests of bulbs. Deer and rabbits readily dine on the shoots and flowers of many bulbs, while voles and mice work underground, damaging or devouring the bulbs themselves. For tips on coping with these menaces, see Animal Pests on page 106. Squirrels often dig up new bulb plantings in fall but usually don't eat the bulbs; to discourage them, lay chicken wire over the planted areas for a few weeks, so the soil has a chance to settle; then the squirrels will be less likely to dig there.

❖ **TUCK IN!** If you didn't plan ahead and plant last fall, consider treating yourself to some already-started potted bulbs and tuck them into empty spaces in your beds and borders in early to midspring.

Narcissus with *Heuchera* 'Caramel' (background) and *Hyacinthus* 'Festival Blue' (foreground)

Campanula

BELLFLOWER, BLUEBELL, HAREBELL

Gardeners who treasure blue flowers have many gems to choose from in the bellflowers.

THIS DIVERSE GENUS OFFERS DOZENS of species and hybrids varying in height, habit, and bloom time, with flower colors ranging through all shades of blue to purple, along with white and sometimes pink. Mostly, though, the plants fall into one of two groups: the upright types and the ground-hugging types.

Upright types. One of the best-known upright bellflowers is clustered bellflower (*Campanula glomerata*), with — as you might guess — clustered, upward-facing, purple or white blooms from late spring to early summer or early to midsummer atop stems usually 1 to 2 feet (30 to 60 cm) tall. Peachleaf bellflower (*C. persicifolia*) is another popular choice, with spikes of upward-facing, cupped, blue or white blooms mostly in early to midsummer; it can be anywhere from 1 to 3 feet (30 to 90 cm) tall. Milky bellflower (*C. lactiflora*) is even taller — usually 3 to 5 feet (90 to 150 cm) — and flowers from early or midsummer into fall, with upward-facing, blue or white bells. Great bellflower or giant bellflower (*C. latifolia*) is another tall-grower at 4 to 5 feet (1.2 to 1.5 m) in full bloom, with upward-facing, blue or white bells in early to midsummer.

Upright bellflowers with nodding, bell-shaped blooms include spotted bellflower (*C. punctata*) and Korean bellflower (*C. takesimana*). Both typically reach about 2 feet (60 cm) tall. Instead of the usual blue or white blooms, these two usually bloom in shades of pink with deeper pink speckles from early or midsummer into fall. Hybrid 'Sarastro', commonly 18 to 24 inches (45 to 60 cm) tall, also has nodding bells, but they're distinctive for their extra-large size and rich purple-blue color.

Ground-hugging types. That's just a sampling of the upright bellflowers, and there are just as many low-growing options. Carpathian bellflower (*C. carpatica*) is one of the most popular, due to its long bloom period: Its upward-facing, purple-blue or white cups start in late spring or early summer and can keep going well into fall. The mounded plants usually reach about 1 foot (30 cm) tall. Dalmatian bellflower (*C. portenschlagiana*) grows in creeping carpets typically 6 to 8 inches (15 to 20 cm) tall, with upward-facing, purple-blue bells from late spring through most of the summer. Serbian bellflower (*C. poscharskyana*), growing 6 to 12 inches (15 to 30 cm) tall, is another creeping carpeter with summer bloom, but its thinner-petaled, upward-facing,

Campanula 'Sarastro'

Campanula (continued)

blue flowers have a starry appearance. Similar-looking Gargano bellflower (*C. garganica*), also known as Adriatic bellflower, also has starry blue flowers on ground-hugging plants just 4 to 6 inches (10 to 15 cm) tall.

Low-growing species with nodding, bell-shaped, blue flowers include light blue, summer-blooming spiral bell-flower (*C. cochlearifolia*), which grows in mats that are 4 to 6 inches (10 to 15 cm) tall, and bluebell-of-Scotland or Scottish harebell (*C. rotundifolia*), which blooms in varying shades of blue from early summer to late summer or early fall atop mounds typically 6 to 12 inches (15 to 30 cm) tall.

Bellflowers are generally recommended for Zones 4 to 8, although many can survive the winter in Zone 3 with snow cover or a protective mulch, and some can adapt to warmer climates if they get the ideal combination of shade and moist soil.

❁ GROWING TIPS

▸ **Light & soil.** Bellflowers normally thrive in full sun but usually don't mind light shade; in fact, they appreciate afternoon shade or light all-day shade in hot-summer areas (roughly Zone 6 and south). Clustered bellflower and Dalmatian bellflower tend to be the most shade-tolerant species. Compost-enriched soil that's evenly moist but not waterlogged is ideal. Established plants can usually tolerate short dry spells, especially if they're well mulched and not in full sun, but they'll suffer if their soil dries out completely.

▸ **Division & propagation.** Most bellflowers benefit from being divided in spring or fall every 3 to 5 years; if they look overcrowded or start invading their companions (see Troubleshooting, page 177) divide more frequently. Division is also a great way to propagate bellflowers. Taking stem cuttings in late spring to early summer is another option. Or, sow seed indoors in late winter or outdoors in early spring; don't cover it.

▸ **Potential problems.** A number of problems can affect bellflowers, including aphids, slugs and snails, aster yellows, crown and root rots, powdery mildew, and rust, but none is especially common.

❁ SEASONAL CARE

○ Spring

▸ Set out new plants, or move or divide existing plants, in early spring. Use 1-foot (30 cm) spacings for most bellflowers; set milky bellflower or great bellflower plants about 2 feet (60 cm) apart. Water new plantings regularly if rain is lacking. Apply an organic mulch before summer to keep the soil cool and moist. If the flower stems of your taller bellflowers sprawled last year, cut the plants back by one-third to one-half in mid- to late spring to encourage lower but bushier stems, or install grow-through supports over the clumps in early to midspring. Some bellflowers begin blooming in late spring.

◎ Summer

▸ Early to midsummer is peak bloom time for many bellflowers; some continue into late summer. On upright bellflowers, you may choose to carefully snip off individual blossoms as they wither or wait until most or all of the flowers on a stem are finished and then cut off that stem at its base. (The latter approach takes much less time, but there's a chance the earliest blooms could form and drop seed before the last ones are finished — a problem if you don't want lots of self-sown seedlings.) Low-growing bellflowers produce so many blooms that snipping off individual blossoms is seldom practical. Instead, wait until the first flush of flowers is pretty much done in midsummer, then shear the

Relatively Speaking

With their nodding, bell-shaped, blue or white blooms on 2- to 4-foot-tall (60 to 120 cm) stems in early to midsummer, ladybells (*Adenophora*) look very much like bellflowers (*Campanula*), and they thrive with the same seasonal care. Ladybells are tough and adaptable, growing in full sun or partial shade with average, well-drained soil. Usually rated for Zones 3 or 4 to 8, they seem to be a bit more heat tolerant than most bellflowers. Just be aware that ladybells can be a little *too* adaptable, as they tend to spread by creeping roots — and by self-sowing as well — to form large patches. Treat them as you would potentially aggressive bellflowers (see Troubleshooting on page 177).

clumps back by about one-half, or even two-thirds if they have lots of stringy-looking stems. This practice will encourage new leaves that look fresh for the rest of the year; some species, such as Carpathian bellflower, will also produce more flowers by late summer or early fall. Keep watering spring plantings regularly if rain is lacking. Established plants, too, benefit from watering during dry spells.

◐ ◉ Fall & Winter

▸ Set out new plants, or move or divide existing clumps, in early fall. Water them regularly for the first month or so if rain is lacking. Keep removing any remaining flower stems on the upright types. Scatter a general-purpose organic fertilizer or a shovelful of compost around each clump in late fall to late winter.

A winter mulch can be beneficial in cooler areas (particularly Zone 4 and north), especially where you can't depend on the ground to be covered by snow all winter.

✦ TROUBLESHOOTING

▸ **Plants spread aggressively.** Once bellflowers get out of hand, it can be tough to get rid of them, so prevention is definitely best. Think twice before letting those with creeping roots loose in rich, moist border soil; those that are potentially aggressive spreaders include the upright clustered bellflower, great bellflower, spotted bellflower, and Korean bellflower and the low-growing Serbian bellflower, Gargano bellflower, and bluebell-of-Scotland. If you do choose to plant them, plan on dividing them every other year to control their spread, or — ideally — give them a site where they won't crowd out less-vigorous companions. Self-sowing can also produce over-abundant seedlings, so remove the faded flowers regularly.

✤ **FABULOUS FOLIAGE** Most bellflowers hold their basal leaves well into winter (some are even evergreen), so limit your fall cleanup to any dead or damaged foliage and leave the rest alone. Remove any winter-damaged leaves in early spring.

Campanula glomerata

Carex

With their long, slender, arching or spiky leaves, sedges look much like true grasses, and they serve a similar purpose in the garden.

WHILE TRUE GRASSES typically need full sun to thrive, sedges often adapt quite well to partially shaded sites, making them a welcome addition to shady borders and woodland gardens. Their flowers are interesting up close but generally not showy; the real appeal of most sedges is their mounded to tufted clumps of foliage, which can range from solid green, yellow, or blue to variegated and even brown. There are many dozens of species and cultivars to choose from, and new ones appear each year. The fact that quite a few sedges are sold under two or more names further confuses matters.

Most of the commonly sold garden sedges are evergreen in mild areas and deciduous in colder zones. One of the best known is Japanese sedge (*Carex morrowii*); some common selections include 'Goldband' (with creamy yellow–striped green leaves), 'Ice Dance' (with white leaf edges), and 'Variegata' (a name that can apply to a range of variegated forms). Evergold sedge (*C. oshimensis* 'Evergold'; also sold as *C. hachijoensis* or *C. morrowii*) has yellow-centered green leaves; Kaga brocade sedge (*C. dolichostachya* 'Kaga-nishiki'; also sold as 'Gold Fountains') has reverse variegation with green centers and yellow edges on its leaves. All of these generally grow about 1 foot (30 cm) tall and form distinct mounds, except for 'Ice Dance', which can spread moderately quickly to form broad patches; Zones 5 to 8. Plantain-leaved sedge (*C. plantaginea*) — also known as seersucker sedge — has much wider, medium to light green, somewhat puckered foliage in mounds to about 1 foot tall (30 cm); Zones 3 to 8.

Some sedges are more definite about being evergreen or deciduous. 'Sparkler' sedge (*C. phyllocephala*), for instance, is commonly evergreen throughout its range, with stiff, green leaves broadly edged with cream to white in spiky-looking clumps that are 1 to 2 feet (30 to 60 cm) tall; Zones 7 or 8 to 10. *C. siderosticha*, on the other hand, almost always loses its relatively broad, bright green, yellow, or variegated leaves in winter. It grows in slowly to moderately spreading carpets about 8 inches (20 cm) tall; Zones 5 or 6 to 9.

There's another group of sedges that you probably won't confuse with the others: the New Zealand sedges (also known as hair sedges), which typically have coppery to rusty brown foliage all through the year. Leatherleaf sedge (*C. buchananii*) grows in upright, vase-shaped clumps with curly leaf tips; it's usually 18 to 24 inches (45 to 60 cm) tall. *C. flagellifera* also forms vase-shaped clumps, but it tends to be lower and broader — commonly 12 to 18 inches (30 to 45 cm) tall — with straight leaf tips. *C. comans* grows in distinct mounds to about 1 foot (30 cm) tall. Similar-looking but pale green 'Frosty Curls' or 'Frosted Curls' is sometimes sold as a selection of *C. comans*, but it's commonly listed under *C. albula*. New Zealand sedges are normally recommended only for Zones 6 or 7 to 10, but gardeners as far north as Zone 4 have reported some success overwintering them outdoors, so it may be worth experimenting with them.

❁ GROWING TIPS

▸ **Light & soil.** Most sedges prefer partial shade, but they can also grow in full sun in northern gardens, especially where the soil doesn't dry out. Evenly moist but well-drained soil that's been enriched with some compost is generally ideal. Sedges with brown foliage usually thrive in full sun with moist but well-drained soil. Good drainage is especially important in winter; otherwise, they can be prone to rot. Other than occasional problems with rust, sedges are typically trouble free.

▸ **Division & propagation.** Most sedges don't need to be divided until you notice the center of the clump thinning or dying out. If the spreaders are creeping more than you wish, divide them every 2 or 3 years. Division in spring or fall is also an easy way to propagate sedges, and it's the only practical way to reproduce the variegated cultivars.

❁ SEASONAL CARE

◐ Spring

▸ Set out new plants, or move or divide established sedges, any time during spring. Space them about 1 foot (30 cm) apart and water

Carex buchananii

regularly if rain is lacking. Apply an organic mulch before summer.

▶ Early to midspring — after the hard freezes are over but before new growth appears — is a good time to give sedges their once-a-year groom-ground.

▶ On the New Zealand sedges, it's normally enough to run your gloved fingers or a small hand rake from the base of the clump out to the tips, tugging lightly as you go, to remove the dead foliage. If really needed, the lower-growing brown sedges can be cut back to about 4 inches (10 cm); leatherleaf sedge seems to really dislike this, though, so avoid cutting if at all possible.

On the New Zealand sedges, which are brown year-round, it can be tough to tell what's actually dead. Usually, dead leaves are stiffer and paler brown, while live leaves are more flexible and reddish brown with a tinge of green at the base.

◎ Summer
▶ Shear off sedge flowers to prevent self-sowing, if you wish. Keep watering spring plantings through the summer during dry spells; established clumps usually don't require it, however.

✪ ☉ Fall & Winter
▶ Set out new plants, or move or divide existing clumps, in early fall. Most sedges hold their foliage through most or all of the winter, so don't cut them back in fall. Scatter a general-purpose organic fertilizer or a shovelful of compost around each clump every year or two in late fall to late winter. In mild areas, you may want to start cleaning up any damaged foliage in late winter.

Caryopteris

CARYOPTERIS, BLUEBEARD, BLUE MIST, BLUE SPIREA

Grow them for their fall flowers (usually in shades of purple to blue) or primarily for their foliage; either way, caryopteris are a great addition to the garden.

C. × CLANDONENSIS, THE MOST COMMON KIND, is technically a deciduous shrub, but it's generally sold and grown as a perennial. North of Zone 7, its woody stems tend to die back at least partly to the ground, but the plants resprout from the base and bloom on the new stems, usually from late summer or early fall until frost. The size varies, depending on the selection you're growing and how much you cut it back in spring; it's normally about 3 feet (90 cm) tall and wide but can reach 4 to 5 feet (1.2 to 1.5 m) tall. Depending on the cultivar, the narrow, aromatic leaves may be medium green, grayish green, yellow, or variegated. Zones 5 to 9. C. incana has shorter green or yellow leaves and somewhat showier flower clusters but otherwise looks similar.

Perennial C. divaricata dies back to the ground each winter, but it, too, forms sizeable clumps during the growing season: typically 4 to 5 feet (1.2 to 1.5 m) tall. It normally doesn't flower until early to midfall, so in short-season areas, it may get nipped by frost before the blooms open. You very seldom see the green-leaved species for sale, but you may find 'Snow Fairy', with cream- to white-edged leaves. It tends to be a bit more compact: usually 3 to 4 feet (90 to 120 cm) tall once established. Note that the leaves tend to have a rank scent when you brush or rub them, so this isn't a great choice to grow right next to a path. Zones 5 to 9.

❀ GROWING TIPS

▸ **Light & soil.** A site with full sun to light shade and average, well-drained soil is fine.

▸ **Division & propagation.** Since it's a woody plant, caryopteris doesn't need to be divided. Taking stem cuttings in late spring to early summer is an easy way to propagate your favorites. Or, sow fresh seed outdoors in fall or indoors in winter; don't cover it. Caryopteris can also self-sow lightly to moderately (sometimes heavily for C. divaricata).

▸ **Potential problems.** Apart from possible rot in too-wet soil and branch splitting on the shrubby types not pruned heavily in spring, caryopteris are normally problem free.

❀ SEASONAL CARE

◐ Spring

▸ Set out new plants or move existing clumps from early to late spring, spacing them about 3 feet (90 cm) apart. (Plant early blooming perennials and bulbs around them to take advantage of the empty space until the caryopteris fill in later on.) Water new plantings regularly if rain is lacking. Apply an organic mulch before summer.

▸ Remove any remaining top growth on C. divaricata in early spring. Wait until you see new leaves appearing on the stems of the shrubby types before pruning; then cut back far enough to at least remove the dead growth. If there is very little dieback, it's still worth cutting the clumps back by at least one-half, to promote lots of new flowering growth and control the shape and size. In Zones 5 and 6, you may have to cut back much lower — to about 1 foot (30 cm), or even just above the ground — if most or all of the top growth has been winter-killed.

◎ Summer

▸ In early summer, trim C. divaricata back by one-third to one-half, if desired, to encourage somewhat lower, bushier growth. Keep watering spring plantings during summer dry spells. Established plants usually don't need watering. The shrubby types of caryopteris usually begin blooming in late summer.

✿ ◉ Fall & Winter

▸ In Zone 7 and south, it's okay to plant or move caryopteris in early fall, though spring is usually a better time. The shrubby types are usually in full bloom in early fall, while C. divaricata may start in early or midfall; they all normally continue until frost. Don't do any cutting back in autumn, except to remove the seed heads if you want to prevent self-sowing. Scatter a general-purpose organic fertilizer or a shovelful of compost around the clumps in late fall to late winter. In Zone 5, you may want to use a winter mulch to protect the roots.

Caryopteris incana 'Jason'

Centaurea

KNAPWEED, CORNFLOWER

As you may guess from the common name knapweed, the genus *Centaurea* contains some species that can be problem plants, but it also includes several that have been appreciated as ornamentals.

ONE FEATURE ALL *CENTAUREA* SPECIES SHARE is hard, rounded flower buds that are covered with overlapping scales; another common trait is deeply cut petals, which give their flowers a shaggy look.

One of the most widely grown species, *C. montana,* is known by a variety of names, including mountain bluet, perennial cornflower, and perennial bachelor's buttons. Its main flush of flowers — typically deep blue, but sometimes white or pink — blooms atop stems that are 1 to 2 feet (30 to 60 cm) tall. Their lance-shaped leaves are silvery green when young, later turning medium green, in clumps that spread moderately to aggressively to form broad patches. Persian cornflowers (*C. dealbata* and *C. hypoleuca*) bloom about the same time, with fuller, fluffier-looking flowers

that are usually purplish pink to rosy pink with paler centers. The plants are 18 to 30 inches (45 to 75 cm) tall in bloom, with deeply lobed, medium green leaves.

Basket flower or globe centaurea (*C. macrocephala*) is distinctly different from the others, with bright yellow, thistlelike blooms. It grows in broad clumps of large, long, deep green leaves and reaches 3 to 4 feet (90 to 120 cm) tall in bloom. (Note that this species is considered invasive in a few areas.)

As a group, knapweeds are usually rated for Zones 3 to 9, but they tend to perform poorly in heat (especially when combined with humidity), so they normally grow best in Zones 3 to 7.

❊ GROWING TIPS

▸ **Light & soil.** Full sun to light shade (especially in the afternoon) is fine for knapweeds. They thrive in nutrient-rich, moist but well-drained soil, but they can also adapt to average, somewhat drier conditions.

▸ **Division & propagation.** It's a good idea to divide the clumps every 3 years or so; you could do it more often, if desired, to control their spread or for propagation. It's also easy to grow knapweeds from seed, and the seedlings can bloom during their first year. Sow indoors in late

winter or outdoors in spring; barely cover the seed.

▸ **Potential problems.** Possible problems include aphids, aster yellows, downy and powdery mildews, root and stem rots, rust, and wilt; generally, though, the plants aren't seriously affected.

Relatively Speaking

Cupid's dart (*Catananche caerulea*) is another member of the daisy family (Asteraceae) that offers light blue to purplish blue (or occasionally white) flowers all through the summer and even into fall. It grows in Zones 4 to 9, forming rosettes of narrow, grayish green leaves with wiry, open-branched flower stalks that usually grow 1 to 2 feet (30 to 60 cm) tall. Full sun is best, and loose, well-drained soil is a must; cupid's dart tends to die out quickly in clayey soil.

Set out the plants in spring, spaced 8 to 12 inches

(20 to 30 cm) apart. Cupid's dart is normally quite drought tolerant, but you may want to water it occasionally during extended dry spells. Don't worry about fertilizing or mulching. Cut off all of the flower stems at the base when they're done blooming. The main problem with cupid's dart is that it tends to be short lived, dying out after just a few years even in ideal sites. You might try dividing it every spring to keep it vigorous, or simply grow replacements from seed every year or two; they normally bloom the same year you sow them. (Sow indoors in late winter or outdoors in early spring, barely covering the seed.)

Centaurea montana

Mountain bluet (*Centaurea montana*) may spread quickly in ideal conditions. Giving it a less-than-perfect site — relatively dry, infertile soil, for instance — is one way to slow its creeping nature. Dividing the plants every other year is another option.

❄ SEASONAL CARE

◐ Spring

▸ Set out new plants, or move or divide established clumps, in early to midspring. Space them 18 to 24 inches (45 to 60 cm) apart. If you've had problems with your knapweeds flopping in past years, consider setting grow-through supports over them as they emerge. Water new plantings regularly if rain is lacking. Apply a light layer of organic mulch before summer. Mountain bluet and Persian cornflowers may be in bloom by late spring in Zones 6 and 7.

◎ Summer

▸ Most knapweeds are in their full glory in early summer. Snipping off individual blooms, and then cutting off entire stems at their base when all the blooms on each stem are finished, helps to prevent self-sowing (which can be prolific), and it may encourage rebloom on mountain bluet and Persian cornflowers. Mountain bluet, in particular, can look tired and floppy by midsummer; in that case, shear the entire clump to about 4 inches (10 cm) to get fresh new leaves and possible rebloom in late summer. Keep watering spring plantings through the summer if rain is lacking.

✚ ☼ Fall & Winter

▸ Set out new plants, or move or divide existing clumps, in early fall. Water new plantings regularly for the first month or so if rain is lacking. Leave the foliage in place for the winter as long as it looks good; otherwise, it's fine to cut the clumps down after frost. Scatter a general-purpose organic fertilizer or a shovelful of compost around the clumps in late fall to late winter.

❄ TROUBLESHOOTING

▸ **Ants on flower buds.** It's not unusual to see lots of ants crawling on the about-to-open flower buds, especially on mountain bluet. Look closely to make sure the buds aren't infested with aphids; if they are, rub the buds with your fingers to remove the aphids and discourage the ants (which often feed on the sticky "honeydew" excreted by aphids). If you have ants but no aphids, then don't worry; the ants themselves don't seem to do any harm.

Centranthus

RED VALERIAN, JUPITER'S BEARD,
KEYS OF HEAVEN, PRETTY BETSY

Long-blooming perennials are a treasure for flower lovers, so it's little wonder that red valerian (*Centranthus ruber*) is on many gardeners' must-try list.

THE BUSHY, WELL-BRANCHED PLANTS grow 2 to 3 feet (60 to 90 cm) tall, with light green to bluish green leaves and clusters of red, pink, or white flowers. The first flush of bloom in late spring or early summer is usually abundant and colorful; after that, you may get good rebloom through the rest of the growing season, or scattered rebloom, or no more flowers at all. If you're willing to meet its needs, though, it's usually a real beauty in the border. While red valerian can be hardy in Zones 4 to 10, it grows best in cooler, drier climates: generally Zones 4 to 7, maybe into Zone 8.

Centranthus ruber

❀ GROWING TIPS

▸ **Light & soil.** Full sun is best. Red valerian can tolerate light shade (especially where summers get hot) but tends to sprawl more and bloom less there. Average, dryish soil with a near-neutral to slightly alkaline pH is ideal. Being too nice to red valerian — by giving it the rich, moist soil that many perennials thrive in — can lead to less-than-abundant bloom.

▸ **Division & propagation.** It's easy to grow replacements from seed; sow indoors (barely cover the seed) in late winter for bloom the same year. Or, take stem cuttings in late spring to early summer.

▸ **Potential problems.** Aphids are occasionally a problem but usually not serious. Red valerian plants may die out after just a year or two, particularly if the plants flowered heavily toward the end of the growing season, or if they're in moist soil.

❀ SEASONAL CARE

◐ Spring

▸ Set out new plants, or move or divide existing clumps, in early to midspring. Space them about 18 inches (45 cm) apart. If the young plants look "leggy," with just a few long stems, cutting them back by about one-half at planting time can encourage bushier growth. Water new plantings regularly if rain is lacking. Early to midspring is also a good time to cut established plants back to about 4 inches (10 cm). If your red valerian plants sprawled last year, place grow-through supports over the clumps by midspring, or pinch off their shoot tips in midspring to promote sturdier, well-branched growth. Add a light layer of organic or gravel mulch before summer. The plants may begin blooming in late spring.

◎ Summer

▸ Red valerian is in its full glory in early summer. Cutting off the clusters once the flowers drop will help prevent self-sowing and encourage rebloom. If you see few or no new flowers in midsummer, or if the stems have started to sprawl, shear the whole clump back by about one-half for possible rebloom later. Water spring plantings during dry spells.

◉ ◉ Fall & Winter

▸ Set out new plants, or move or divide existing clumps, in early fall. Water the new plantings regularly for the first month or so if rain is lacking. Red valerian may produce at least a few flowers until frost. Some foliage usually remains for the winter, at least around the base; wait until spring to cut back the top growth. Scatter a general-purpose organic fertilizer or a shovelful of compost around the clumps every other year in late fall to late winter.

❀ **A SEEDY CHARACTER** Red valerian (*Centranthus ruber*) can seed around prolifically in ideal growing conditions, to the point of becoming weedy. (In fact, it's considered invasive in a few western states.) Cut off finished flower clusters frequently to prevent self-sowing, and pull out unwanted seedlings as soon as you spot them.

Chelone

TURTLEHEAD

Turtleheads may not have the most romantic-sounding common name, but gardeners who grow them love them for their late-season blooms.

THE TUBULAR FLOWERS OF TURTLEHEADS form in clusters at the tops of upright stems clad in deep green, lance-shaped leaves. Bloom color varies by species: white turtlehead (*Chelone glabra*) has pink- or green-tinged white flowers, pink turtlehead (*C. lyonii*) is usually bright pink, and rose turtlehead (*C. obliqua*) — also called red turtlehead or purple turtlehead — tends to be a deeper rose-pink to purplish pink. Turtleheads normally grow about 3 feet (90 cm) tall and wide but some can reach 4 to 5 feet (1.2 to 1.5 m) tall and wide in ideal growing conditions. They're commonly recommended for Zones 3 or 4 to 8.

Chelone 'Hot Lips'

❁ GROWING TIPS

▸ **Light & soil.** If the soil stays consistently moist to wet, full sun is ideal. In somewhat drier conditions, partial shade is better, although the plants can be somewhat more likely to sprawl there.

▸ **Division & propagation.** Normally, you need to divide turtleheads only every 4 to 5 years, but if they look like they are starting to spread more than you'd like, divide them every 2 or 3 years to slow them down (and make sure you remove the developing seed heads to prevent self-sowing). Division is also an easy way to propagate turtleheads. Other options include taking stem cuttings in late spring to early summer or sowing seed (left uncovered) outdoors in fall to early spring or indoors in winter. (If you don't see any seedlings after a month or so, enclose the pots in plastic bags and refrigerate them for about 6 weeks before moving them back to a warm, bright spot.)

▸ **Potential problems.** A few disease problems are possible, including mildew, rust, and leaf spots, but they're usually not serious.

❁ SEASONAL CARE

◐ Spring

▸ Set out new plants, or move or divide existing clumps, any time during spring. Space them 18 to 24 inches (45 to 60 cm) apart. Water new plantings regularly through spring if rain is lacking. Apply an organic mulch before summer. If the stems sprawled last year, set grow-through supports over the emerging shoots, or pinch off the shoot tips once in mid- to late spring to encourage lower, bushier growth.

◐ Summer

▸ Turtleheads normally begin blooming in late summer. Keep watering spring plantings during dry spells through the summer. Established plants also benefit from occasional watering during dry spells.

✪ ◉ Fall & Winter

▸ Set out new plants in early fall. Move or divide existing clumps, if needed, once they're done flowering (usually midfall). Water new plantings regularly for the first month or so if rain is lacking. Scatter a general-purpose organic fertilizer or a shovelful of compost around each clump in late fall to late winter.

❁ **SNIPPING TIPS** In some gardens, turtleheads are very well behaved, staying in tight clumps; in others, they spread freely to form broad patches. Leave their interesting seed heads for winter interest or remove them (or cut the entire plant to the ground) during fall cleanup to prevent self-sowing.

Chrysanthemum

CHRYSANTHEMUM, MUM

Chrysanthemums are among the most widely known garden plants, brightening mid- to late-season borders with tight mounds or gently expanding patches of aromatic, lobed leaves topped by single, semidouble, or double, daisy-form flowers in a wide range of colors.

THE KIND COMMONLY SOLD FOR FALL COLOR is *Chrysanthemum × morifolium* (*Dendranthema × grandiflorum*) and is informally divided into two groups. Garden mums (also called hardy mums) are meant to be planted and left outdoors in Zones 4 or 5 to 9. Florist mums are generally grown in greenhouses and sold in full bloom as potted gift plants; they're normally hardy in Zones 7 to 9 and treated as annuals elsewhere. Florist mums are mostly sold in spring, while garden mums are a common sight in fall garden-center displays. In Zones 8 and 9, though, both kinds can bloom in both spring and fall.

Be aware that the florist and garden mums you buy in bud or bloom may have been treated with growth regulators to produce low, dense, heavily branched plants that look great near the front of a border. After the first season, though, they want to grow to their normal height, which can be significantly taller — anywhere from about 18 inches (45 cm) tall to 4 feet (1.2 m) or more in height. There are ways you can keep them somewhat shorter: with frequent pinching or shearing, for instance. But if you prefer your mums to be low-maintenance, it's smart to check the pot tags for the mature height and keep that in mind when you place the clumps in your garden. You'll probably still want to pinch or shear them at least once to encourage better branching (and more flowers).

Another sort of chrysanthemum you may find for sale is *C. zawadskii* var. *latilobum* (also known as *Dendranthema zawadskii* or *C. × rubellum*). Two common cultivars are pink 'Clara Curtis' and yellow 'Mary Stoker'. You can leave these unpinched, in which case they'll generally grow 2 to 3 feet (60 to 90 cm) tall and bloom in mid- or late summer. Or, you may treat them like other mums and pinch or shear them in late spring to early summer to get shorter growth and later bloom. Bear in mind that these two can spread a fair bit from creeping roots after a few years. Zones 4 to 9.

Chrysanthemum 'Hillside Sheffield Pink'

▸ **Light & soil.** Mums thrive in full sun with loose, compost-enriched, evenly moist but well-drained soil. They'll also survive in partial shade but usually don't bloom as well there and are more prone to sprawling.

▸ **Division & propagation.** Mum clumps tend to die out in the center after a few years, so it's smart to divide them every 2 or 3 years in spring. They'll survive for a while even if you don't, but they'll gradually get weaker and not bloom as well. Besides maintaining their vigor (or slowing the spread of the creeping types), frequent division offers a simple way to propagate your favorite mums. Taking stem cuttings in mid- to late spring is another option for multiplying your plants. It's also possible to grow mums from seed — sow indoors in late winter or outdoors in early spring, and don't cover it — although the resulting seedlings may vary in height and color.

▸ **Potential problems.** A number of problems are possible on mums, including aphids, leaf miners, spider mites, stem borers, aster yellows, and leaf spots. *Handling chrysanthemum foliage may irritate sensitive skin, so you may want to wear gloves when working around your plants.*

☽ Spring

▸ Early to midspring is a good time to set out new plants, or to move or divide existing clumps that are just starting to put on new growth. (If you live where mums bloom in spring, too, or if you want to enjoy a second bloom from a potted florist mum, wait until after the flowers fade to cut them back to about 4 inches [10 cm] and then move or divide them if needed.) Mum clumps can easily reach 2 to 3 feet (60 to 90 cm) across,

so space them at least 18 inches (45 cm) apart. Water new plantings regularly if rain is lacking. Apply an organic mulch before summer.

▸ If you don't plan to prune your mums, you may want to install grow-through supports over the emerging clumps by late spring. If you do plan to prune, you can start as early as late spring if the shoots are at least 6 inches (15 cm) tall; then pinch, snip,

or shear off the top 1 inch (2.5 cm) or so.

☀ Summer

▸ Give late-rising garden mums their first 1-inch (2.5 cm) pinch or snip in early summer. For the bushiest mums, repeat this light pruning every 2 to 3 weeks until early to mid-July (or as late as early August in the South). If you prefer a simpler approach, then just shear the clumps

When shopping for potted mums to use as fall fillers, look for those with lots of buds and a few open blooms so you can be sure of the flower form and color. Getting them in the ground in late summer increases the chance that they might survive the winter, and you'll get to enjoy their flowers for as long as possible.

Chrysanthemum (continued)

once, cutting them back by about one-half their height, in early summer. Or, if you prefer a looser look and don't mind that the plants might sprawl by bloom time, then simply leave them alone. Yet another pruning option is a technique called disbudding: instead of pinching off the shoot tips, regularly remove the side shoots instead, so the plant directs its energy into producing one larger-than-normal bloom at the tip of each stem. The results can be impressive, but the tradeoff is that you have far fewer flowers overall, and it's quite likely that the individual stems will need staking to support the weight of the bigger blooms.

▸ Mums such as 'Clara Curtis' and 'Mary Stoker' may be in bloom by midsummer, while unpruned clumps of other mums may begin flowering by late summer. Late summer is also the time potted mums start appearing in sales displays.

▸ Keep watering spring-planted mums regularly if rain is lacking. Established clumps also benefit from regular watering during dry spells. For the best possible bloom later on, apply a granular or liquid, general-purpose organic fertilizer in early summer to midsummer.

✦ ☉ Fall & Winter

▸ You can still buy potted mums in early autumn and tuck them into empty spaces for few weeks of fall color, but don't depend on them to come back next spring. (They might, but it's likely that they won't unless you cut off the flowers to encourage root growth instead, and that defeats the purpose of buying them!) Keep watering new plantings regularly for the first month or so if rain is lacking. It's worth setting a box or a sheet over still-blooming mums for the first frosty night or two; you'll often get another week or more of color out of them if the weather gets mild again. Don't be surprised to see the leaves turn purplish, reddish, or bronzy as the days get cooler.

▸ Unless your mums have had problems with leaf-disfiguring pests, such as mites or leaf miners, it's a good idea to leave the top growth in place to protect the crown from winter damage, especially in Zones 4 and 5.

Where the flowers of chrysanthemums have time to mature before freezing weather arrives, they may drop some ripe seed. Self-sowing isn't a problem in most gardens, but if you want to prevent it completely, it's fine to snip off the spent flowers.

Relatively Speaking

Grow a mum for its *foliage* instead of its *flowers*? It may sound strange, but once you see the gray-green, silver-edged leaves of silver-and-gold chrysanthemum (*Ajania pacifica*; also known as *Chrysanthemum pacificum*), you'll know that it makes perfect sense. Hardy in Zones 5 to 9, it creeps gently to form tidy patches about 1 foot (30 cm) tall and 2 feet (60 cm) across, with no pinching required. The yellow, buttonlike blooms don't open until mid- to late fall in most areas, often getting damaged by early frosts unless you cover the plants. Really, though, the point is to enjoy this plant as a foliage accent. It grows well in either full sun or light shade with average, well-drained soil. The foliage often looks good through much or all of the winter; cut it down in spring. Divide every 3 years or so in spring.

(For extra protection, tuck dried fall leaves in among the dead stems or cover the clumps with a loose mulch, such as evergreen boughs, for the winter months.) Scatter a general-purpose organic fertilizer or a shovelful of compost (or both) around each clump in late fall to late winter.

❖ TROUBLESHOOTING

▸ **Lower leaves drop.** This may happen if the soil gets either too dry or too wet. Water during dry spells and use an organic mulch to help to keep the soil moist. If you think the soil got too wet due to excessive rain or overwatering, use your fingers to gently rake the mulch away so the soil can dry out for a few days, then replace it. If this problem happens every year, try moving your mums to a different site, or pair them with low companions that can cover their "bare ankles."

▸ **Plants die over winter.** Probably the most common cause of winter losses is setting out mums in full bloom in fall. The plants are putting energy into flowering instead of making roots, and they simply don't have time to settle in permanently before the ground freezes. If possible, set out mum plants in spring instead. Also, look for suppliers that give hardiness ranges for each cultivar

If you protected your mums with a winter mulch, remove it gradually (over a period of a week or two) in early spring. You'll usually see some green leaves at the base of clumps that have successfully overwintered; cut off any remaining dead stems just above this live growth in early to midspring.

they sell. (Often, though, you'll find plants labeled only by color, so you'll just have to take your chances.) And don't count on florist mums overwintering unless you live in a warm climate. A few other ways to improve the odds of winter survival include making sure the planting site is well drained (mums don't like soggy soil in winter) and leaving the dead tops in place until spring.

Clematis

CLEMATIS

Bush clematis aren't nearly as dramatic as their large-flowered climbing cousins, but they have an elegance all their own.

SOME BUSH CLEMATIS are completely herbaceous, meaning that they die back to the ground each winter. Ground clematis (*Clematis recta*) generally grows 3 to 4 feet (90 to 120 cm) tall and wide, with starry white flowers over light green to bluish green leaves. The foliage of 'Purpurea' usually emerges deep purple but often turns greenish by midsummer. Ground clematis is usually recommended for Zones 3 to 8. Solitary clematis (*C. integrifolia*) tends to be somewhat smaller — about 2 to 3 feet (60 to 90 cm) tall and wide — with blue or pink flowers that have slightly recurved petal tips. Zones 4 to 8.

Other bush clematis die back to the roots in cold-winter climates but keep a framework of woody stems (like a deciduous shrub) in milder areas. The best known in this group is commonly called tube clematis or Chinese clematis (*C. heracleifolia*). It has large leaves and generally grows about 3 to 4 feet (90 to 120 cm) tall and wide, bearing clusters of tubular blue to purple-blue blooms with curled-back petals. *C. tubulosa* (also sold as *C. heracleifolia* var. *davidiana*) is similar, but with tighter clusters of larger flowers. Zones 4 to 9.

Clematis integrifolia

❖ GROWING TIPS

▶ **Light & soil.** Full sun with evenly moist but well-drained soil is ideal, but bush clematis can also perform well in partial shade with average, well-drained soil. The plants grow best if the soil pH is near-neutral to slightly alkaline.

▶ **Division & propagation.** Bush clematis can be slow to fill in, so you usually won't want to disturb them, but you could divide them in early spring for propagation. Or, take stem cuttings in late spring. Sow seed outdoors in fall or indoors in winter, and barely cover it; if no sprouts appear after about a month, put the pots in a plastic bag and refrigerate them for about 6 weeks before moving them to a cool, bright place. Bush clematis may self-sow.

▶ **Potential problems.** Blister beetles can quickly devour the foliage; handpick them (wear gloves) if you catch them early or cut severely damaged plants to the ground.

❖ **SHORT-TERM SPACE FILLERS** Bush clematis can take several years to reach their full size and fill the space you've allowed for them. To avoid having a large gap in your border, tuck annual seeds or transplants around the clematis for the first two or three growing seasons.

❖ SEASONAL CARE

◐ Spring

▶ Set out new plants or move existing ones, if really necessary, in early spring. Work a shovelful or two of compost into the planting hole. If you plan to let them sprawl, give them a space as wide as their expected spread, as indicated in the descriptions above. Or, install grow-through supports or other staking to encourage more upright growth that will take up less ground space.

▸ On the clematis that develop woody stems, wait until new growth appears to prune. If new shoots are visible along the stems, cut back to a framework of 1 foot (30 cm) or so; if the stems look dead but new growth is coming up from the roots, then cut off all the stems at their base.

▸ Water new plantings regularly if rain is lacking. Apply a generous layer of organic mulch before summer. Ground and solitary clematis may begin blooming in late spring.

◎ Summer

▸ Once ground clematis is done blooming, you may shear it back by one-third to one-half, or even completely to the ground, to get a flush of new growth and possible rebloom later. On solitary clematis, trimming off the faded flowers can encourage repeat flowering. Or, leave the plants alone and enjoy the interesting, tufted seed heads. Tube clematis and *C. tubulosa* usually begin blooming in late summer. Keep watering spring plantings of all clematis during summer dry spells; established clumps benefit from occasional watering, too. (Leaf edges or whole leaves may turn brown if the soil dries out; snip off damaged foliage.)

✪ ◉ Fall & Winter

▸ Set out new plants in early fall; water regularly for the first month or so if rain is lacking. Tube clematis and *C. tubulosa* continue to bloom into early fall, and solitary clematis may produce scattered rebloom, too. Cut ground clematis and solitary clematis back to the ground after frost. Scatter a general-purpose organic fertilizer or a shovelful of compost around the base of each clump in late fall to late winter.

Clematis recta 'Lime Close'

❖ **SUPPORT SYSTEMS** If you don't want to deal with staking bush clematis, pair the plants with azaleas, roses, or other shrubs for support, or let them sprawl as groundcovers.

Coreopsis

COREOPSIS, TICKSEED

With a bloom season that's long enough to rival many annuals, coreopsis are a popular choice for sunny gardens in a wide range of climates. Their daisylike blooms most commonly come in shades of yellow to gold, but you can also find them in pink, peach, red, and white.

AMONG THE MOST WELL-KNOWN of these perennials are large-flowered coreopsis (*Coreopsis grandiflora*), lanceleaf coreopsis (*C. lanceolata*), and their hybrids, with single, semidouble, or double yellow flowers. The slender-leaved clumps can be anywhere from 1 to 3 feet (30 to 90 cm) tall in bloom. They're generally rated for Zones 3 to 9. Threadleaf coreopsis (*C. verticillata*) has the same hardiness range but much narrower, almost needlelike foliage in creeping patches usually 18 to 24 inches (45 to 60 cm) tall. 'Moonbeam', with pale yellow flowers, is one of the most popular cultivars, although it can be a little tricky to grow successfully.

Mouse-ear coreopsis (*C. auriculata*), with orange-yellow blooms over oval leaves, forms creeping clumps. The species reaches about 2 feet (60 cm) tall in bloom; 'Nana' is half that size. Zones 4 to 9. At the other height extreme is tall tickseed (*C. tripteris*), with slender foliage and dark-centered, clear yellow flowers atop stems anywhere from 4 to 8 feet (1.2 to 2.4 m) tall. Zones 3 to 8.

Pink coreopsis (*C. rosea*) and its hybrids add some variety to the range of colors. The species is a vigorous spreader that blooms in shades of pink or white over needlelike leaves. The stems are usually 12 to 18 inches (30 to 45 cm) tall, but they tend to sprawl, so the plants often appear much shorter. Pink coreopsis is normally hardy in Zones 3 to 9; however, some hybrids, such as 'Limerock Ruby', have proven much less cold tolerant (Zones 7 or 8 to 9).

Coreopsis 'Limerock Ruby'

❖ GROWING TIPS

▸ **Light & soil.** Full sun encourages the most vigorous growth on most coreopsis, but the plants can also tolerate partial shade. Average, well-drained soil is fine.

▸ **Division & propagation.** Coreopsis plants grow quickly and generally benefit from being divided every 2 or 3 years. Besides keeping the plants vigorous, division also offers an easy way to propagate your favorite coreopsis. Taking stem cuttings in early summer is another option. Or, sow seed indoors in late winter or outdoors in spring; don't cover it. Some cultivars, such as 'Early Sunrise', may bloom the same year you sow them.

▸ **Potential problems.** Among the possible problems are aphids, leafhoppers, plant bugs, slugs and snails, aster yellows, and powdery mildew; fortunately, most of them aren't serious enough to need control.

❖ **BRING OUT THE BEST** Coreopsis are often touted as being ideal for poor, dry soil, and most can survive there, but working a few handfuls of compost into the planting holes, keeping the soil mulched, and watering them during dry periods can bring out their best bloom.

⦿ Spring

▸ Cut any remaining top growth to the ground in early spring. Set out new plants, or move or divide existing clumps, in early to midspring. Space most kinds 12 to 18 inches (30 to 45 cm) apart; pink coreopsis and tall tickseed usually work better with 2-foot (60-cm) spacings. Water new plantings regularly if rain is lacking. Apply an organic mulch before summer. Mouse-ear chickweed is usually in bloom by midspring; threadleaf coreopsis may just be coming up then, while the others are generally filling out well. If your pink coreopsis tends to flop in summer, shear it back by about one-half in late spring to keep it a bit bushier.

◐ Summer

▸ Most coreopsis are in full bloom in early summer, although threadleaf coreopsis may not start until midsummer where it's slow to sprout in spring. (Midsummer is also the usual time for tall tickseed to begin blooming.) Mouse-ear coreopsis normally finishes flowering in early to midsummer. On any coreopsis, snipping off individual blooms as they fade keeps the plants looking tidy, prevents self-sowing, and can extend the bloom season, but it's also a tedious task. To save time, you could instead shear the clumps back by one-third to one-half when flower production starts to slow down in mid- to late summer. (If the foliage gets damaged by pests or diseases, or if the lower leaves drop, shear by one-half to two-thirds in late summer to get fresh new leaves.) Keep watering spring plantings during dry spells. Established clumps can tolerate some drought but tend to perform better with regular watering when rain is lacking.

Coreopsis 'Moonbeam'

If your coreopsis plants fail to return after the first winter, it may be because the site is too wet, or because the cultivar isn't hardy in your climate. Even the widely grown 'Moonbeam' can be difficult to get established in some gardens.

✿ ◐ Fall & Winter

▸ Set out new plants, or move or divide existing ones, in early fall. Water new plantings for the first month or so if rain is lacking. Coreopsis often keep blooming into fall, especially if you removed the finished flowers in summer. The seed heads add winter interest and are a favorite food with many birds, but you may choose to remove them to prevent self-sowing. The foliage may stay evergreen into winter, so leave it in place until spring cleanup. A lightweight mulch can aid in overwintering in colder zones where winter snow is lacking. Scatter a general-purpose organic fertilizer or a shovelful of compost around each clump every year or two in late fall to late winter.

▸ **Flowers change color.** It's not unusual for light-colored coreopsis blooms to bleach out in strong summer sun. Moving them to a site with some afternoon shade may help maintain their color in the future. Conversely, the colors may be deeper than usual at the beginning and end of the growing season, when temperatures are cooler. This is more noticeable in the pinks and reds than in the yellows.

▸ **Plants die out after just a year or two.** Leaving the tops in place for the winter may help improve winter survival on coreopsis; so can dividing the clumps as often as every other year to keep them vigorous. Sometimes, the plants flower so heavily that they simply wear themselves out. Cutting them back by one-half to two-thirds in late summer or early fall may improve the odds of them being able to survive the winter.

Corydalis

CORYDALIS, FUMEWORT

With dainty flowers and lacy foliage, corydalis are enticing to all levels of gardeners.

MOST OF THE COMMONLY SOLD kinds of corydalis are in the range of 6 to 12 inches (15 to 30 cm) tall. Among the most sought-after are the blue-flowered corydalis, including *Corydalis elata* and *C. flexuosa*, which form creeping clumps of ferny green foliage that may be tinged with purple to bronze. Normally, they're at their peak bloom in spring; they may continue through the rest of the growing season or die back to the ground for summer and produce new leaves in fall. Blue corydalis are generally recommended for cool-summer areas in Zones 5 to 8. A somewhat more adaptable species is yellow corydalis (*C. lutea*), which forms tidy mounds of blue-green to gray-green leaves speckled with bright yellow blooms through much of the growing season. White corydalis (*C. ochroleuca*) is similar but has creamy white flowers. Zones 4 to 8.

Corydalis lutea

❁ GROWING TIPS

▸ **Light & soil.** Morning sun and afternoon shade, or light all-day shade, with moist but well-drained soil is ideal. Yellow and white corydalis can also grow in full sun if their soil doesn't dry out.

▸ **Division & propagation.** Once you get them established, it's generally best to leave them alone, unless you really must move or divide them. To propagate, sow fresh seed outdoors in summer or fall; don't cover it.

▸ **Potential problems.** Slugs and snails may be a problem, and so may voles. It can be tricky to get these plants established, but it's worth trying a few times in different sites. Small plants often settle in more readily than large ones.

❁ SEASONAL CARE

◐ Spring

▸ Set out new plants, spaced about 1 foot (30 cm) apart. Water new and established plantings regularly if rain is lacking. Apply an organic mulch before summer. Most corydalis are in full bloom by midspring, though they may flower later in some areas.

◯ Summer

▸ Unless your summers stay cool, it's likely that your corydalis will slow down a bit during the warmest weather. If the plants look like they're dying back to the ground, that's the time to move or divide them, if needed, so they'll be in place and ready to grow again once

cooler temperatures return. If the top growth looks a bit tired but new growth is visible near the base of the plant, cut the stems off just above the fresh foliage. Keep watering actively growing plants during dry spells.

❂ ◉ Fall & Winter

▸ Set out new plants, or move or divide existing clumps, if needed, in early fall. Water regularly for the first month or so if rain is lacking. The blue-flowered kinds usually produce fresh foliage in the fall, and yellow and white corydalis tend to keep their leaves through at least the first part of the winter. Scatter a general-purpose organic fertilizer or a shovelful of compost around the clumps in late fall to late winter.

❁ **LET IT SOW** Yellow corydalis and white corydalis (*Corydalis lutea* and *C. ochroleuca*) may bloom so heavily that they wear themselves out after a few years, but they also produce an abundance (or excess) of self-sown seedlings for replacements.

Crambe

CRAMBE, COLEWORT, SEA KALE

Good foliage, showy flowers, and great fragrance, too — crambes have a lot going for them.

CRAMBES' MANY-BRANCHED CLUSTERS of small but abundant, sweetly scented, white flowers appear in summer. Colewort (*Crambe cordifolia*) forms a mound of deep green, heart-shaped leaves that are 2 to 3 feet (60 to 90 cm) tall; in full bloom, its total height is 4 to 6 feet (1.2 to 1.8 m). Sea kale (*C. maritima*) produces masses of wavy, powder-blue foliage that's about 2 feet (60 cm) tall, with a total height of about 3 feet (90 cm) in bloom. Both are recommended for Zones 4 to 8, performing best where summers are relatively cool.

Crambe cordifolia

❖ GROWING TIPS

▶ **Light & soil.** Crambes thrive in full sun but also grow well with morning sun and some afternoon shade. They grow best with a steady supply of moisture during the growing season, but they hate soggy soil, especially in winter. Colewort, in particular, needs plenty of water to keep its leaves looking good through the summer. Once the plants have been growing in the same place for a few years, though, they can tolerate a fair bit of drought. As a compromise, give them a site with loose, well-drained soil (or a raised bed) and plan on watering them regularly for the first three or four summers. A soil pH that's near-neutral to alkaline is a plus. Sea kale is also salt tolerant.

▶ **Division & propagation.** If you must divide or move established clumps, dig deeply in early spring to get as much of the root system as possible. Instead of trying to propagate crambes by division, take root cuttings in late fall or early spring, or sow seed about one-half inch (1 cm) deep outdoors in fall to spring or indoors in late winter.

❖ SEASONAL CARE

◐ Spring

▶ Set out new plants in early to mid-spring. Give colewort a space about 4 feet (1.2 m) across; allow sea kale a space about 3 feet (90 cm) across. Fill in around them with annuals for the first few seasons. Water new plantings regularly if rain is lacking. Apply an organic mulch before summer. (Sea kale also looks great with a gravel mulch.)

◯ Summer

▶ Crambe flowers appear in early to midsummer and last about 3 weeks. Prop up leaning stalks with Y-stakes. Once the flowers drop, they're usually followed by rounded seedpods. If you don't find them appealing, cut off the spent flower stalks at the base. Keep watering spring plantings if rain is lacking. Established plants also benefit from occasional watering during dry spells, especially for the first few years.

◑ ◉ Fall & Winter

▶ Set out new plants in early fall; water them for the first month or so if rain is lacking. Leave crambe foliage in place as long as it looks good, then remove it. Scatter a general-purpose organic fertilizer or a shovelful of compost around each clump in late fall to late winter.

❖ TROUBLESHOOTING

▶ **Leaves with holes.** Flea beetles chew tiny round holes in the leaves. The plants can usually withstand the damage without help, but if really necessary, try spraying with an appropriate organic control, such as Pyola (a product that combines canola oil and pyrethrins). Larger, irregularly chewed areas can be due to caterpillars (hand-pick or spray with *Bacillus thuringiensis* var. *kurstaki*) or slugs and snails (try an iron phosphate-based bait).

❖ **ROOTING AROUND** Crambes can be slow to recover if you try to divide or move them. But if you do transplant them, you may find new plantlets sprouting from bits of root that are left behind, a good clue that you can propagate these perennials by root cuttings.

Crocosmia

CROCOSMIA, MONTBRETIA

Crocosmias light up the summer-to-fall garden with arching sprays of funnel-shaped red, orange, or yellow flowers.

CROCOSMIA PLANTS can be anywhere from 2 to 5 feet (60 to 150 cm) tall, depending on the cultivar, with smooth or pleated, upright to arching, swordlike leaves. They grow from rounded corms that form along creeping rhizomes. Crocosmias are usually hardy in Zones 6 to 9 — sometimes in Zone 5. You can also grow them as tender bulbs in Zones 4 and 5, digging them up in fall and storing them dry in a cool but frost-free place indoors.

Crocosmia 'Lucifer'

❖ GROWING TIPS

▸ **Light & soil.** Crocosmias usually prefer full sun but can also grow in partial shade. The plants perform best with a steady supply of moisture, but they don't like to be waterlogged, either; good drainage in winter seems especially important.

▸ **Division & propagation.** Divide the plants every 2 or 3 years — or even every year, if needed — to control their spread or for propagation. If you don't mind a variety of colors, you can grow crocosmias from seed indoors in late winter or outdoors in early spring; barely cover it. The seedlings may take 3 years to reach flowering size.

❖ SEASONAL CARE

◐ Spring

▸ Set out new plants in early to late spring, or move or divide existing clumps in early to midspring. Set dormant corms 4 to 8 inches (10 to 20 cm) apart and 3 to 5 inches (8 to 13 cm) deep in most areas, or 4 to 6 inches (20 to 30 cm) deep in Zones 5 and 6. If you're starting with potted plants, space them 18 to 24 inches (45 to 60 cm) apart. Water new plantings regularly if rain is lacking. Apply an organic mulch before summer. If your crocosmias sprawled last year and you didn't divide them since then, install grow-through supports over the emerging clumps.

◎ Summer

▸ You may want to apply another handful of fertilizer around each clump in early to midsummer. The flowers usually begin blooming in midsummer. Leave the seed heads that develop once the blooms drop, or snip off the stalk just above the uppermost leaves to possibly encourage more flowers. Keep watering spring plantings if rain is lacking.

✪ ☉ Fall & Winter

▸ In Zones 7 and south, it's fine to set out new corms in early fall or to move or divide existing clumps once they're done blooming. Water new plantings regularly for the first month or so if rain is lacking. Cut the stalks down to the ground once they've turned completely brown. Scatter a general-purpose organic fertilizer or a shovelful of compost around the clumps in late fall to late winter. In Zone 5, protect the dormant clumps with a winter mulch.

❖ TROUBLESHOOTING

▸ **Leaves turn brown.** Gradual leaf browning could be due to the corms rotting (make sure you've chosen a well-drained site). Or, spider mites could be feeding on the foliage; they're particularly a problem in dry conditions. Removing affected foliage and spraying the remaining leaves with insecticidal soap may help control these pests.

❖ **DEFINITELY DEADHEAD** Where crocosmias thrive, they may actually grow *too* enthusiastically, to the point of being aggressive in the garden and even invasive in some regions. In mild areas, it's a good idea to snip off the seedpods to prevent self-sowing.

Delphinium

The elegant spires of well-grown delphiniums are a treat to the eye, but that beauty definitely isn't the easy-care kind — at least in most areas.

THESE PERSNICKETY PERENNIALS grow best in areas with relatively cool summers and low humidity; elsewhere, they may last just a year or two and never quite reach their full glory. Still, they can be so stunning that for many of us even a few weeks of bloom is worth any amount of effort. Species and selections that bloom in shades of blue are usually most enticing, but you can find whites, pinks, and other colors, too. The spikelike flower clusters bloom over lobed green leaves.

The Elatum Group (also known as Elatum hybrids) includes most of the classic border delphiniums, which can grow anywhere from 4 to 7 feet (1.2 to 2.1 m) tall. Selections in the Belladonna Group (also listed as *Delphinium × belladonna*) also produce large spikes, but on more compact plants — typically 3 to 5 feet (90 to 150 cm) — that also tend to be more vigorous and longer lived. Chinese delphiniums (*D. grandiflorum*), such as 'Blue Butterfly' and 'Blue Mirror', are even shorter — usually just 1 to 2 feet (30 to 60 cm) tall — with deeply cut foliage. They, too, tend to be more heat tolerant than the traditional tall hybrids, but they may last only 1 or 2 years. Delphiniums are generally recommended for Zones 3 or 4 to 7.

❀ GROWING TIPS

▶ **Light & soil.** Delphiniums tend to bloom best in full sun, but they can benefit from a site with morning sun and some afternoon shade or light all-day shade south of Zone 5. Evenly moist but well-drained soil that's enriched with compost and has a near-neutral to somewhat alkaline pH is ideal.

▶ **Division & propagation.** Where delphiniums thrive, divide them every 2 to 4 years in spring to keep them vigorous. In less ideal areas, the plants may simply die out after a few years (or even just one), so it's smart to plan ahead for replacements. Take stem cuttings in early to midspring, or grow new plants from seed; freshly collected seed gives the best results. Sow the seed outdoors any time from late summer to early spring, or indoors in mid- to late winter; barely cover it with soil or seed-starting mix. (If no sprouts appear after a few weeks indoors, enclose the pots in plastic bags, refrigerate them for about 2 weeks, and then move them back to a bright place for germination.)

▶ **Potential problems.** Delphiniums are prone to a wide variety of pests and diseases, including aphids, caterpillars, leaf miners, spider mites, leaf spots, and viruses. For details on a few of the most common problems, see Troubleshooting, page 198.

❀ SEASONAL CARE

◐ Spring

▶ Set out new plants, or move or divide existing clumps, in early spring. Space the compact types about 1 foot (30 cm) apart; allow about 2 feet (60 cm) between the tall hybrids. Work a shovelful or two of compost into each hole at planting time. Water both new and established plantings regularly if rain is lacking. Scatter a general-purpose organic fertilizer around each clump and apply a generous layer of organic mulch before summer.

▶ If you're growing the taller hybrids (those over 3 foot [90 cm] or so), install some sort of support for the emerging clumps. Established Belladonna Group plants may begin blooming in late spring.

◎ Summer

▶ Most established delphiniums are in full bloom in early to midsummer. Once the main spike finishes flowering, cut it off just above a lower side-spike (if there is one) or the uppermost leaf on the stem. New shoots may appear at the base of the plant; if they do, it's fine to cut off the old flowering stems. In ideal conditions, your delphiniums may bloom again later in the season. Winter- or spring-sown delphiniums may bloom in mid- to late summer during their first year. Water regularly through the summer during dry spells.

◑ ◎ Fall & Winter

▶ Set out new plants, or move existing clumps if needed, in early fall. Water them regularly for the first month or so if rain is lacking. It's fine to cut down the dead top

Delphinium (continued)

growth after frost, but leave any green growth at the base of the plant. Scatter a general-purpose organic fertilizer and a shovelful or two of compost around each clump in late fall to late winter.

❖ TROUBLESHOOTING

▸ **Leaves with large, ragged holes; seedlings eaten partially or entirely.** Delphiniums are like candy for slugs and snails, especially when the plants are young. Scattering an iron phosphate–based slug bait around the plants can help prevent further damage; hand-picking and trapping are other options.

▸ **Leaves and stems with dusty white or gray patches.** Powdery mildew is a common problem on delphiniums. Pinching off affected parts at the first sign of damage may stop the disease from spreading; spraying with an organic fungicide may help, too. To possibly minimize mildew problems, thin out crowded clumps in spring by cutting out all but three to five of the strongest stems in each clump. Chinese delphiniums tend to be more resistant than other types.

▸ **Stems wilt even when soil is moist.** If just one or two stems in a particular delphinium clump start wilting at the tips, borers may be at work. You might find a small entrance hole on the stem just below the wilted part. Cut off the affected stem just below the entrance hole, or just above the uppermost unwilted leaf. Fungal crown rot may be the cause if most or all of the stems wilt suddenly; yellowed lower leaves are another symptom. Remove and destroy affected plants, and avoid replanting delphiniums in that spot

Delphiniums can be effectively combined with other container plantings for a temporary spot of color and drama. After they're finishing blooming, they can be planted out into the garden.

for several years. You may also want to try drenching the soil around any remaining plants with a biofungicide. Setting the crown just above the soil surface at planting time may help to prevent the problem.

❖ **SUPPORT SYSTEMS** Long-legged grow-through supports can work for delphinium cultivars that can reach about 4 feet (1.2 m) tall. For even taller types, figure on one 6- to 8-foot-tall (1.8 to 2.4 m) bamboo stake for each stem. Tie the growing stems to their stakes at 1-foot (30 cm) intervals.

Delphinium Elatum Group

Dianthus

DIANTHUS, PINK

Edging a border, lining a path, or carpeting a slope — wherever they grow, dianthus add a touch of charm, and often fragrance as well.

YOU'LL ALSO HEAR THESE perennial favorites referred to as pinks, which refers to their fringed petal edges and not to their color. While some *are* actually pink, they may also be red, white, or other colors, often with contrasting rings or edgings. The plants themselves have slender leaves that may be distinctly blue, grayish, or green, and they may grow in tight "buns," upright mounds, or ground-hugging carpets.

One of the classic blue- to gray-leaved species is cheddar pink (*Dianthus gratianopolitanus*), which grows in low, spreading carpets that usually reach about 6 inches (15 cm) tall in leaf and 8 to 12 inches (20 to 30 cm) tall in bloom. It is a parent of the popular cultivar 'Bath's Pink', with single pink flowers, as well as the similar but white-flowered 'Greystone'. Two other well-known blue- to gray-leaved dianthus are Allwood pinks (*D. × allwoodii*), which can reach anywhere from 8 to 18 inches (20 to 45 cm) tall in bloom, and cottage pinks, which form looser, more-upright clumps usually 18 to 24 inches (45 to 60 cm) tall in bloom.

Among the green-leaved species, maiden pinks (*D. deltoides*) is a readily available option, with mat-forming plants that usually reach just 6 to 10 inches (15 to 20 cm) in bloom. China pinks (*D. chinensis*) grow in upright clumps that usually reach 8 to 12 inches (20 to 30 cm) tall. They're commonly sold as annuals, but they can often survive for several years in the garden. Sweet Williams (*D. barbatus*), with upright mounds of green to maroon-tinged leaves that may reach 12 to 18 inches (30 to 45 cm) tall in bloom, may act as annuals, biennials, or short-lived perennials.

Dianthus are generally recommended for Zones 3 to 8, although some can perform well even into Zone 9. China pinks can thrive and bloom nearly year-round in totally frost-free climates.

❁ GROWING TIPS

▸ **Light & soil.** Dianthus thrive in full sun but can tolerate light shade. Average, dryish soil is fine; a pH that's near-neutral to alkaline is a plus; and good drainage is a must.

▸ **Division & propagation.** Dividing every 2 to 3 years is a good idea for most dianthus. Division is also an easy way to propagate your favorites. Taking stem cuttings of nonflowering shoots in summer is another option. Or, sow seed indoors in winter or outdoors in spring or summer; barely cover it.

▸ **Potential problems.** The list of possible problems is long, including aphids, caterpillars, slugs and snails, spider mites, thrips, botrytis (gray mold), leaf spots, rust, root and stem rots, southern blight, viruses, and wilts. Luckily, most of them aren't especially common.

❁ SEASONAL CARE

◐ Spring

▸ Remove any winter-damaged foliage in early spring. Set out new plants, or move or divide existing ones, in early to midspring. Space those that form tight tufts or upright mounds about 1 foot (30 cm) apart; for the carpeting types, 18 to 24 inches (45 to 60 cm) is about right. Water new plantings through spring if rain is lacking. Apply a thin layer of organic mulch before summer. Or, for the blue- to gray-leaved kinds, you may want to try a gravel mulch instead, especially if your soil isn't naturally loose and sandy. Most dianthus are in full bloom by late spring.

◐ Summer

▸ The main dianthus display continues through early summer. As individual blooms fade, you may choose to snip them off carefully so you don't damage the remaining buds, or you might just wait until most or all of the flowers are done, then shear them off all at once. If the foliage clump below the blooms still looks clean and tight, snip off the flowering stems just at the tips of the leaves. If the foliage is spotted or tired looking, or if the plants are sprawling a bit, cut back a bit harder so you remove the top one-third of the leafy growth as well as the spent flower stems. Many dianthus take a

❁ **DIVIDE AND THRIVE** Even in ideal conditions, dianthus plants may be short lived. Dividing them often (every 2 or 3 years) helps to maintain their vigor. It may also help to look for cultivars touted as being tolerant of heat and humidity, such as 'Bath's Pink' and 'Greystone'.

Dianthus 'Bath's Pink'

break in midsummer, especially if they've been cut back a bit, but they often rebloom later in the summer. Water spring plantings occasionally during dry spells.

✿ ☉ Fall & Winter

▸ South of Zone 6, it's fine to set out new plants, or move or divide existing clumps, in early fall. Water new plantings regularly for the first month or so if rain is lacking. It's not unusual to see scattered rebloom from early fall to frost. Clip off any seed heads if you want to prevent self-sowing, but leave the foliage in place for the winter. Scatter a general-purpose organic fertilizer or handful or two of compost around the clumps every other year in late fall to late winter.

✿ TROUBLESHOOTING

▸ **Plants die.** If you're trying to grow dianthus in clayey soil or in the compost-enriched, moist soil that many other perennials enjoy, you may find the clumps dying out after just a year or two. Try working a shovelful of gravel into the planting area, or grow your dianthus in raised beds or on a slope.

Dicentra

Dicentra spectabilis

BLEEDING HEART

The dangling pink, red, or white blooms of bleeding hearts may look dainty, but the plants can be surprisingly sturdy.

COMMON BLEEDING HEART (*Dicentra spectabilis*) grows in clumps of upright stems typically 2 to 3 feet (60 to 90 cm) tall, with toothed, light green leaves and arching sprays of large, pink-and-white hearts.

Dwarf bleeding hearts are much more compact — usually between 8 and 18 inches (20 to 45 cm) tall — with smaller flowers that tend to bloom over a much longer period. Fringed bleeding heart (*D. eximia*) forms dense mounds of lacy, blue-green to gray-green leaves. Western bleeding heart (*D. formosa*) looks very similar, but it's more of a creeper than a clumper. There are also hybrids between these and other species, with varying traits. As a group, bleeding hearts are generally recommended for Zones 2 to 9.

✿ GROWING TIPS

▸ **Light & soil.** In cool climates (roughly Zone 5 and north), bleeding hearts can grow in full sun as long as the soil doesn't dry out; elsewhere, partial shade is usually best. Evenly moist but well-drained, compost-enriched soil is ideal; a pH that's near-neutral to slightly alkaline is a plus.

▸ **Division & propagation.** Bleeding hearts usually grow best when left undisturbed, but you may choose to divide the dwarf kinds (like the spreading western bleeding hearts) every 3 to 4 years in early spring, in summer (if the plants are dormant), or in early fall. To propagate, take root cuttings in early spring or mid- to late fall or divide. Or, sow just-collected seed outdoors in mid- to late summer; barely cover it with soil. Note that bleeding heart foliage can irritate sensitive skin, so you may want to wear gloves when working around the plants.

▸ **Potential problems.** The plants may have a few problems, including slugs and snails, rots, and wilt, but none of these is especially common.

✿ SEASONAL CARE

◐ Spring

▸ Set out new plants, or move or divide existing clumps, if you must, in early spring. Common bleeding heart can eventually fill a space that's about 4 feet (1.2 m) across; space the dwarf species and hybrids 12 to 18 inches (30 to 45 cm) apart. Water new plantings regularly if rain is lacking. Apply an organic mulch in early to midspring. Most bleeding hearts are in bloom, or at least in bud, by late spring.

◉ Summer

▸ Early summer is peak bloom time for bleeding hearts. Removing the flowers as they fade can help prevent overabundant self-sowing; it can also promote rebloom on the dwarf species and hybrids. Water all bleeding hearts regularly during dry spells while they're actively growing. If the soil dries out, common bleeding heart and fringed bleeding heart tend to look ragged (in this case, cut off the top growth), or they may die back to the ground. Western bleeding heart is somewhat more tolerant of dry soil, but it, too, may go dormant if the weather gets hot.

◐ ◉ Fall & Winter

▸ Dwarf bleeding hearts that went dormant in summer usually produce new leaves by early fall, and they may bloom until frost. Early fall is also the time to set out new plants or to move or divide existing clumps if needed. Water new plantings regularly for the first month or so if rain is lacking. Cut down the tops when they're killed by hard frost. Scatter a general-purpose organic fertilizer or a shovelful of compost around each clump in late fall to late winter.

✿ **DEALING WITH DORMANCY** Common bleeding heart (*Dicentra spectabilis*) looks spectacular in bloom, but in hot, dry conditions, it can turn yellow or start dying back to the ground in summer. Cutting down the damaged stems gets rid of the ugly foliage but leaves a large hole in the border; fill the space with fast-growing annual seeds or transplants, such as cosmos.

Dictamnus

DITTANY, GAS PLANT, BURNING BUSH

Even when it's not in flower, dittany (*Dictamnus albus*) is a good-looking addition to the border, forming dense clumps anywhere from 2 to 4 feet (60 to 120 cm) tall.

THE STURDY, UPRIGHT STEMS are clad in often-glossy, medium to deep green, multipart leaves and topped with spikes of white or purplish pink flowers. The blooms develop into attractive seedpods that add interest through fall and often well into winter. Dittany is mostly grown in Zones 3 to 8.

Dictamnus albus var. *purpureus*

✿ GROWING TIPS

▶ **Light & soil.** Dittany grows best in full sun but also takes light shade (especially in hot-summer areas). Average, compost-enriched, well-drained soil is fine; a pH that's near-neutral to alkaline is ideal.

▶ **Division & propagation.** Established clumps generally don't take kindly to being moved or divided, so choose their planting spot carefully and then let them alone. Seed is the best option for propagation: Sow outdoors in fall, barely cover it with soil, and then wait. Some seedlings will sprout the next spring; others will take 2 years or longer to appear.

▶ **Potential problems.** Slugs and snails can quickly demolish young plants; otherwise, the only real challenges in growing dittany are waiting years for it to reach flowering size and making sure it doesn't get crowded out by more vigorous companions in the meantime.

✿ SEASONAL CARE

◐ Spring

▶ Cut back any remaining top growth on established clumps in early spring. Set out small potted plants, or move first- or second-year seedlings if you must, in early to midspring. Figure that each clump will eventually fill a space 2 to 3 feet (60 to 90 cm) across. It may take 4 or more years for it to fill out, though, so plan to fill around it with annual companions that won't smother it. Work a shovelful of compost into the hole at planting time. Water new plantings regularly if rain is lacking. Apply an organic mulch before summer. In some areas, dittany may begin flowering in late spring.

◎ Summer

▶ Early summer is usually prime bloom time for dittany. As the flowers age, they drop off on their own, and the remaining seedpods add some interest, so there's no need to fuss with the plants. Keep watering spring plantings during dry spells; established clumps usually don't need supplemental water.

◐ ◉ Fall & Winter

▶ Scatter a general-purpose organic fertilizer or a shovelful of compost around each clump in late fall to late winter. Other than that, simply leave the plants alone until next spring.

✿ **A SCENT OF CITRUS** The leaves, flowers, and seedpods of dittany (*Dictamnus albus*) contain an oil that has a citrusy fragrance. The scent is usually noticeable only if you rub or brush against the plant, which generally isn't a good idea unless you're wearing gloves. (If you get the oil on your skin and then expose it to sunlight, it can create a nasty burnlike rash.)

Digitalis

FOXGLOVE

Long favored for their striking flower spires, foxgloves are a classic choice for summer beds and borders.

THERE ARE A NUMBER of species of *Digitalis* to choose from, in a range of heights and colors. One thing they all share is their basic growth habit: a dense, low rosette that shoots up into upright, leafy stems topped with nodding, tubular to bell-like blooms. Most foxgloves grow well in Zones 3 or 4 to 8.

The best-known species is common foxglove (*D. purpurea*), with white, cream, peach, or pink, solid-colored or spotted blooms atop stems anywhere from 2 feet (60 cm) to more than 5 feet (1.5 m) tall. Common foxglove normally grows as a biennial (producing only leafy growth its first year, flowering the second, and then dying after dropping seed), but it may survive an extra year or two to act as a short-lived perennial.

Most other foxgloves are much more reliably perennial. There's strawberry foxglove (*D. × mertonensis*), for instance, which usually blooms in shades of pink and reaches 3 to 4 feet (90 to 120 cm) tall. Yellow foxglove (*D. grandiflora*; also sold as *D. ambigua*) is another perennial species, with light yellow flowers atop stems that are 2 to 3 feet (60 to 90 cm) tall. Straw foxglove (*D. lutea*) is about the same size, but it's even paler yellow, with much tinier blossoms and smooth leaves instead of the typical hairy ones of other foxgloves.

Digitalis lutea

❁ GROWING TIPS

▸ **Light & soil.** Full sun usually brings out the most abundant bloom, but foxgloves can grow well in partial shade, too (especially in hot-summer areas), and the yellow-flowered species can perform respectably even in full shade. Average, evenly moist but well-drained soil is fine.

▸ **Division & propagation.** Most foxgloves benefit from being divided in spring or fall every 3 to 5 years (or every year after bloom for common foxglove). Division is also a good propagation method. Or, sow seed indoors in mid- to late winter or outdoors in spring to midsummer; don't cover it.

▸ **Potential problems.** If you don't remove the spent flower spikes, foxgloves can self-sow readily, which is a plus if you get a few new seedlings to move or share but a problem if they start popping up everywhere. (In fact, common foxglove is considered invasive in a few western states.) Possible problems include Japanese beetles, slugs and snails, leaf spots, powdery mildew, and viruses.

❁ **WHACK IT BACK** If pests or other problems damage the leaves of your foxgloves in summer, cut off all of the foliage at the base to get a flush of new leafy growth.

◐ Spring

▸ Set out new plants, or move or divide existing clumps, in early to midspring. Space them about 18 inches (45 cm) apart. Work a shovelful of compost into each planting hole. Water new plantings regularly if rain is lacking. Early to midspring is also a good time to remove any winter-damaged foliage to tidy up established clumps, and to apply an organic mulch. Most foxgloves will be in bud, if not already starting to bloom, in late spring.

◉ Summer

▸ Early to midsummer is generally prime bloom time for foxgloves. You may need to stake some of the tallest types to keep them from falling over. Once the main spike is done, snip it off just above a side shoot or remove the whole flowering stem right at the base. It's not unusual to see some new flowers form later in the season, though not as tall or as abundantly as earlier. Through the summer, keep watering new plantings regularly during dry spells. Established foxgloves also appreciate occasional watering if rain is lacking.

◎ ◉ Fall & Winter

▸ Set out new plants, or move or divide existing clumps, in early fall. Water new plantings regularly for the first month or so if rain is lacking. You may see some rebloom well into fall. Cut off stems that are done flowering right at their base, but leave the green foliage in place for the winter. Scatter a general-purpose organic fertilizer or a shovelful of compost around each clump in late fall to late winter.

▸ **Plants die.** As beautiful as they are, common foxgloves are naturally

Digitalis purpurea

quite short lived. One option is to cut off the flowering stems as soon as most of the blooms fade, so the plants put their energy into producing offsets instead of into forming seeds. Dividing the clumps soon after bloom gives the offsets a chance to settle in and fill out before winter. You may want to allow one plant to form and drop seed, so you'll have replacements if the others don't make it. Or, simply plan on sowing seed each summer for next summer's show. To get flowers the same year, try sowing seed of 'Foxy' in mid- to late winter; the seedlings will bloom in mid- to late summer, then you can pull them out at the end of the growing season.

Echinacea

PURPLE CONEFLOWER

Purple coneflowers have long been a favorite for summer gardens, brightening borders with large, daisy-form flowers that each have a prominent orange to bronze center "cone."

THE CLUMP-FORMING PLANTS grow in mounds or tufts of deep green leaves, then produce upright flowering stems. *Echinacea purpurea* is the most widely grown species, with relatively broad leaves and showy blooms in shades of pink or white atop stems typically 3 to 5 feet (90 to 150 cm) tall. Its petals tend to be rather large and may be horizontal or downward-facing. Narrow-leaved coneflower (*E. angustifolia*) — also known as western coneflower — has narrower leaves and slender, drooping petals on stems about 2 feet (60 cm) tall. Pale coneflower (*E. pallida*) is also narrow leaved, with very slender, distinctly drooping, light pink petals. *E. paradoxa* looks similar to *E. pallida* but has yellow petals instead of pink ones; both species tend to reach about 3 feet (90 cm) tall. There are also a number of hybrids among these species, expanding the range of colors to include many shades of orange and yellow. *E. purpurea* and *E. pallida* are usually rated for Zones 3 to 9, while the others are normally recommended for Zones 4 to 8.

Echinacea purpurea

❖ GROWING TIPS

▸ **Light & soil.** Full sun brings out the most abundant flowering, but the plants may also perform acceptably with either morning or afternoon sun only. Average, well-drained soil is usually fine. *E. purpurea* can tolerate drought once established but tends to look best with evenly moist soil. (It appreciates compost-enriched soil, too, but if the soil is too rich, the stems may tend to sprawl.) The other species are naturally adapted to hot, dry sites; hybrids between these species and *E. purpurea* can vary in their moisture needs. Well-drained soil is a must for all coneflowers, though; soggy soil is fatal. It's also important to dig a generous planting hole where the soil is clayey or compacted, so the roots can spread out and down.

▸ **Division & propagation.** These perennials generally don't need to be divided, but if the clumps look crowded or you want to propagate them, you could try separating them in early spring or early fall. Root cuttings taken in fall or early spring are another option for reproducing your favorites. Purple coneflowers are easy to grow from seed, although the resulting plants can vary widely in flower color. Sow seed indoors in late winter or outdoors from early fall to early spring; barely cover or leave uncovered.

▸ **Potential problems.** Purple coneflowers are often touted as being tough and trouble free, but they can be affected by a number of pests and diseases, including aphids, fleahoppers and leafhoppers, botrytis (gray mold), leaf spots, and powdery

❖ **SNIPPING TIPS** Leave purple coneflower seed heads to provide winter interest and to feed wild birds, or remove all of the top growth after frost to minimize self-sowing and possibly reduce pest and disease problems next year.

Echinacea 'Sundown'

mildew. (See Troubleshooting, page 208, for other common problems.)

❋ SEASONAL CARE

◐ Spring

▸ Set out new plants, or move or divide existing clumps, in early to midspring. Space most of them about 18 inches (45 cm) apart; 2 feet (60 cm) is better for *E. purpurea*. Water new plantings regularly if rain is lacking. In northern areas, purple coneflowers may be a little slow to emerge, but they should be apparent in midspring, and then they tend to leaf out quickly. In warm climates, coneflowers may begin flowering by midspring. If coneflowers have flopped in previous years, install grow-through hoop supports over the clumps in midspring or cut them back by about one-half toward the end of spring. Apply an organic mulch before summer.

◎ Summer

▸ If you didn't cut back your coneflowers earlier to reduce their bloom-time height, you can still do it in summer; this will also delay their bloom time a few weeks. (Shear the clumps back by about one-half in early summer or about one-third in midsummer.) In southern gardens, coneflowers are often in peak bloom by early summer and continue through midsummer, at least; they may take a break during the hottest weather. Farther north, the flowers usually begin coloring up in midsummer and keep going through late summer. Once the petals drop, leave the center cones to enjoy their interesting shape, or snip them off just above a developing flower bud lower down on the stem to make the plants look tidier and prevent self-sowing. Keep watering spring plantings regularly during dry spells. You may also want to water established clumps if they start to wilt when rain is lacking.

◐ ◎ Fall & Winter

▸ Set out new plants, or move or divide existing clumps, in early fall. Established coneflowers may produce additional blooms until frost (or even through most of the winter, in mild areas), especially if you removed the faded flowers in summer. Scatter a general-purpose organic fertilizer or a shovelful of compost around each clump in late fall to late winter.

Echinacea (continued)

❉ TROUBLESHOOTING

▶ **Leaves and flowers deformed, discolored.** It's not unusual for coneflower blooms to change color somewhat as they age, usually fading to pale pink or white. The petal colors also tend to be richer in cool weather and paler in hot weather, especially when growing in full sun. But if the flowers look distinctly greenish, exceptionally pale, or otherwise abnormal for the plant, you could have a problem, especially if the discoloration is paired with twisted or distorted leaves.

Feeding by aphids, fleahoppers, or leafhoppers can cause these symptoms temporarily (lasting only one year), or it may transmit serious disease problems, such as viruses or aster yellows, both of which can eventually be fatal. Herbicide drift is another possible cause of distorted growth.

If you see pests, take steps to control them (try insecticidal soap for aphids and neem-based sprays for the hoppers). If you suspect that herbicides may have caused the problem, wait a few weeks to see if normal-looking new growth appears (in which case it should be fine after that).

Removing and destroying plants is the only way to handle viruses and aster yellows. It seems to be okay to replant coneflowers in the same area, but keep in mind that insects can transfer the disease to the new plants, so you need to make sure you remove all of the possibly infected clumps and control the aphids, hoppers, and other sap-sucking pests as well.

Some hybrids may produce blooms with petals that are quilled (rolled into slender tubes) when they're not supposed to be; so far, there is no obvious cause or solution for this problem.

▶ **Flowers missing petals, or with damaged petals.** The central cones are a key feature of coneflowers, but when the petals get eaten, or when they never appear, it can be very disappointing. Be aware that the cones form before the petals appear, so it may be that the flowers just aren't mature yet; give them a few more weeks.

If the petals never appear, the problem may be aster yellows; see "Leaves and flowers deformed, discolored" above. If the petals form but then get eaten, take a close look at the flowers. Possible culprits you may see during the day include Japanese beetles, slugs and snails, caterpillars, and rabbits; those that feed mostly at night include Asiatic garden beetles and earwigs.

Control strategies include hand-picking, trapping, appropriate organic sprays, repellents (for rabbits), or iron phosphate–based baits (for slugs and snails). Birds may also damage the petals as they peck at the cones to get the developing seeds.

▶ **Stems wilt.** If your coneflowers wilt and watering doesn't perk them up in a few hours or overnight, look for other possible causes. It may be that the soil there stays *too* wet; if you think that's the problem, try moving the plant to a drier spot.

Aphid infestations can cause wilted stems, along with discolored or distorted growth; control with soap sprays. If stems wilt, dry out, turn black at the base, and fall over, especially when the soil is constantly moist, a fungal disease called

Aster yellows

sclerotinia wilt may be the problem; try drenching the soil with a biofungicide. If just one or a few stems are affected, with wilted tops and normal-looking lower parts, borers may have tunneled into the stem; cut off the affected tops.

▶ **Plants are taller or shorter than expected, or are the wrong color.** Dig deeply at planting time to make sure the roots can spread freely; otherwise, cramped roots may lead to stunted growth. Growth that's taller than expected may be due to too-rich soil (don't add any more fertilizer or compost, and try cutting the plants back by one-half in early summer). Or, the plants may be mislabeled.

Improper labeling may also explain why a certain plant isn't the color you expected. Buying plants that are already in bloom is a good way to ensure you get the color you want. Keep in mind that plants grown from seed collected from named selections can vary in height and flower color.

Echinops

GLOBE THISTLE

Echinops bannaticus 'Blue Glow'

Globe thistles aren't the most pleasant perennials to work around, but their distinctive blooms definitely earn them a place in sunny summer borders.

THE PLANTS GROW in dense clumps of deeply cut, deep green to grayish green leaves that have white undersides and spiny tips. The upright flowering stems carry globe-shaped, spiky-looking, steel-gray buds that open into small, gray-blue to purple-blue flowers. Height is usually in the range of 3 to 5 feet (90 to 150 cm). Species names you may see include *Echinops bannaticus, E. ritro,* and *E. sphaerocephalus;* while they have some differences, they share the same maintenance needs. Globe thistles grow in Zones 3 to 9.

❁ GROWING TIPS

▶ **Light & soil.** Full sun is usually best, but globe thistles tolerate light shade; in fact, some afternoon shade can be beneficial in southern gardens. Average, dryish, well-drained soil is fine. The plants can grow lush and tall in rich soil but then need staking.

▶ **Division & propagation.** Globe thistle plants are often slow to recover after being moved or divided; if you must disturb them, dig deeply to keep as much of the root system as possible. To propagate, carefully split off a few offsets at the base of an established clump in spring, or take root cuttings in late fall to early spring. Other options are to sow seed indoors in late winter or outdoors — barely cover it — from spring to fall.

▶ **Potential problems.** Possible problems include aphids, plant bugs, and crown rot, but none is especially common.

❁ SEASONAL CARE

○ Spring

▶ Set out new plants, or move or divide existing clumps if really necessary, in early to midspring. Space them 2 to 3 feet (60 to 90 cm) apart. Water new plantings occasionally if rain is lacking. Keep in mind that it's common for the lower leaves to turn crispy and drop off later in the growing season, so place some 1- to 2-foot-tall (30 to 60 cm) companions in front of them. Apply a thin layer of organic mulch before summer.

◎ Summer

▶ Most globe thistles produce their rounded gray buds in early summer (or even a bit earlier), several weeks before the actual flowers bloom in mid- to late summer. To prevent self-sowing and to possibly promote later rebloom, it's a good idea to snip off the spent flower heads by cutting just above a side bud lower down on the stem or by removing the entire stem at the base if all the side buds are done. Globe thistles are very drought tolerant once established, but first-year plantings still benefit from watering every few days if rain is lacking, and older clumps grow best with an occasional deep soaking during extended dry spells.

◐ ◑ Fall & Winter

▶ Globe thistles often keep flowering into fall, especially if you removed the spent blooms earlier; even if you didn't, the globe-shaped seed heads continue to add interest through fall into winter. Birds love the seeds, too. But if you leave the seed heads, you'll likely end up with many self-sown seedlings the following year, so you may instead choose cut down the stalks once all the flowers are finished. Scatter a general-purpose organic fertilizer or a shovelful of compost around the clumps every other year in late fall to late winter.

❁ **PRETTY PRICKLY** Make sure you wear gloves when working with globe thistles, because both the leaves and the seed heads are spiny.

Epimedium

EPIMEDIUM, BARRENWORT, BISHOP'S HAT, FAIRY WINGS

Epimediums aren't the showiest perennials in the garden, but they do have a lot to offer, including multi-season interest and an easy-care nature.

THERE ARE DOZENS OF SPECIES and cultivars to choose from, forming clumps or carpets of multipart leaves mostly in the range of 8 to 12 inches (20 to 30 cm) tall, with red, pink, white, purplish, yellow, orange, or bicolored flowers. Many species are evergreen, among them *Epimedium × perralchicum, E. perralderianum, E. pinnatum,* and *E. × rubrum*; these tend to produce their blooms slightly above the leaves. Those that are usually deciduous — among them, alpine barrenwort (*E. alpinum*), *E. grandiflorum* (also sold as *E. macranthum*), and Young's barrenwort (*E. × youngianum*) — commonly produce their flowers just before or just as new leaves emerge in spring. It's normal for the young leaves to be brown, bronzy, or reddish, and a few keep these colors through the growing season. Epimediums are commonly recommended for Zones 5 to 8, but some gardeners in Zone 4 have luck with them, too.

Epimedium rubrum 'Rose Queen'

❖ GROWING TIPS

▸ **Light & soil.** You'll often hear epimediums touted as thriving in heavy shade and dry, root-filled soil, and it's true that some can survive in those tough conditions. If you really want them to look their best, though, give them partial to full shade with compost-enriched, evenly moist (but not soggy) soil.

▸ **Division & propagation.** Divide in early spring or in late summer to early fall if you want to propagate them or control their spread. Growing epimediums from seed can take several years; sow outdoors as soon as you collect it in summer and barely cover it.

▸ **Potential problems.** Chewed leaves may be a sign of slugs and snails, black vine weevils, or leaf-cutter bees (there are no practical control options for the bees).

❖ SEASONAL CARE

◐ Spring

▸ Set out new plants, or move or divide existing clumps, in early spring. Space the clumps about 1 foot (30 cm) apart. Dig a shovelful of compost into the planting hole. Water new plantings regularly if rain is lacking. Early spring is also a good time to add a fresh layer of organic mulch. New flowers generally emerge in early to midspring and continue through late spring.

◉ Summer

▸ Epimediums normally don't need deadheading, but you may choose to snip off the spent flower stems if they stick up over the leaves. Keep watering spring-planted clumps every few days during dry spells. Established clumps can tolerate drought, but they, too, benefit from occasional watering when rain is lacking. If you need to divide or move them, late summer is a good time.

✚ ◉ Fall & Winter

▸ Set out new plants, or move or divide existing clumps if you didn't do it earlier, in early fall. Water new plantings regularly for the first month or so if rain is lacking. The leaves of some species and hybrids turn shades of yellow, bronze, or red in fall, while others stay green; many continue to look good into the winter, or even through the whole season. Scatter a general-purpose organic fertilizer or a shovelful of compost around each clump in late fall to late winter. First-year plantings benefit from a winter mulch. If the foliage has become tattered or turned brown during the winter, cut it all off at ground level in late winter.

Eryngium

SEA HOLLY, ERYNGO

The curiously shaped blooms of sea hollies add both color and texture to summer gardens.

AMONG THE BEST-KNOWN SPECIES are those with rounded to cone-shaped flowers that are ringed with a ruff of spiny-looking, petal- or leaflike bracts. The blooms can range from greenish or silvery blue to brilliant blue, and their color often extends down into the stems and the upper leaves. Alpine sea holly (*Eryngium alpinum*) has a particularly large, lacy ruff at the base of each bloom; it's typically 1 to 2 feet (30 to 60 cm) tall; Zones 4 to 8. A few species that are more common and more adaptable, although less showy and with smaller flowers, include amethyst sea holly (*E. amethystinum*) for Zones 3 to 8 and flat sea holly (*E. planum*) for Zones 4 to 9; both are 2 to 3 feet (60 to 90 cm) tall.

Instead of the heart-shaped to deeply lobed leaves of other species, rattlesnake master (*E. yuccifolium*) has gray-green, straplike foliage, plus branching clusters of spherical, greenish white blooms on stems usually 3 to 5 feet (90 to 150 cm) tall. Zones 3 or 4 to 9.

Eryngium 'Sapphire Blue'

❖ GROWING TIPS

▶ **Light & soil.** Sea hollies thrive in full sun and dryish, well-drained, not-especially-fertile soil. In moist, fertile soil, or in some shade, these plants will likely sprawl if not staked. Rattlesnake master tends to perform well in moist (though not soggy) soil, but it's also quite drought tolerant once established.

▶ **Division & propagation.** Split off a few offsets or try root cuttings in early spring. Sow seed (and leave it uncovered) outdoors in fall or sow it indoors in winter, enclose the pots in a plastic bag, and put them in your refrigerator for about 4 weeks before moving them to a warm, bright place.

▶ **Potential problems.** Sea hollies and rattlesnake master can be slow to recover after being disturbed, but if you must move them, dig deeply to get as much of the main root as possible.

❖ SEASONAL CARE

◐ Spring

▶ Set out new plants, or move existing clumps if you really need to, in early spring. Space them 18 inches (45 cm) apart. Water new plantings occasionally if rain is lacking. Add a thin layer of organic mulch or a gravel mulch before summer.

◉ Summer

▶ Sea hollies usually are in full bloom in mid- through late summer. You may need to prop up the flowering stems with linking stakes or Y-stakes. Cut off spent flowering stems at the base once most of the blooms are finished if you want to prevent self-sowing, or leave them for later interest. Water spring plantings occasionally during dry spells.

✿ ◉ Fall & Winter

▶ Set out new plants in early fall; water them occasionally for the first month or so if rain is lacking. Established clumps may continue blooming into early fall. The seed heads are terrific for winter interest, and birds love the seeds, but you may choose to remove most or all of them to prevent self-sowing. Don't cut back the basal foliage unless it turns brown. Scatter a general-purpose organic fertilizer or a shovelful of compost around the plants every 2 or 3 years in late fall to late winter, if desired.

❖ **DEFINITELY DEADHEAD** Self-sowing may be a problem on sea hollies if you don't remove the spent flower stems. In fact, some species (particularly *E. planum*) are considered invasive in some areas. If you want to enjoy the interesting seed heads without having to worry about unwanted seedlings, look for sterile hybrids such as 'Sapphire Blue'.

Eupatorium

EUPATORIUM, JOE-PYE WEED, SNAKEROOT

Eupatoriums bloom in a range of heights and colors and vary in their preferred growing conditions, but they also have a few traits in common, including toothed leaves; fuzzy-looking, flattened, or rounded clusters of many tiny flowers; and fluffy-looking seed heads.

THE NAME JOE-PYE WEED refers to several similar species, including *Eupatorium purpureum, E. maculatum (E. purpureum* subsp. *maculatum), E. fistulosum,* and *E. dubium.* These all form broad clumps of upright stems topped with clusters of pale pink, rosy pink, or white flowers. The foliage is green but may be tinged with red or purple. Their height is usually somewhere between 5 to 7 feet (1.5 to 2.1 m) tall, occasionally to 10 feet (3 m), or even higher. (Those touted as being compact, such as 'Gateway', 'Little Joe', and 'Purple Bush' still tend to reach 5 to 6 feet [1.5 to 1.8 m] tall once established.) Joe-Pye weeds are generally recommended for Zones 3 or 4 to 9.

White snakeroot (*E. rugosum;* also known as *Ageratina altissima*) is also a clump-former, but it tends to be much more compact — commonly 3 to 4 feet (90 to 120 cm) in height — with much smaller clusters of white flowers from late summer to early or midfall. 'Chocolate' has deep purple to purple-brown stems and new leaves, usually aging to deep green by bloom time. Zones 4 to 8.

Hardy ageratum or mist flower (*E. coelestinum;* also known as *Conoclinium coelestinum*) is quite different from its cousins. Normally growing 2 to 3 feet (60 to 90 cm) tall, it spreads vigorously to form broad patches topped with purple-blue blooms. Zones 5 to 10.

❈ GROWING TIPS

▸ **Light & soil.** Joe-Pye weeds and hardy ageratum generally grow best in full sun with evenly moist soil but can also perform well in partial shade with average, well-drained soil. White snakeroot may tolerate full sun if the soil stays moist but generally prefers partial shade with average, moist but well-drained soil. (It can tolerate rather dry shade once established.)

▸ **Division & propagation.** Eupatoriums benefit from division every 4 to 5 years (or every 2 to 3 years to control the spread of hardy ageratum). Division is also an easy way to propagate your favorites. You could also take stem cuttings in early summer. Sow seed outdoors in fall or indoors in mid- to late winter; barely cover it. If indoor-sown seed doesn't sprout within a month or so, enclose the pots in plastic bags and refrigerate them for about 6 weeks before moving them back to a bright spot.

▸ **Potential problems.** These perennials can be attacked by a variety of pests and diseases, including aphids, caterpillars, leaf miners, stem borers, leaf spots, powdery mildew, root and stem rots, and rust; normally, though, these aren't too serious.

❈ SEASONAL CARE

◐ Spring

▸ Set out new plants, or move or divide existing clumps, in early to late spring. Space Joe-Pye weeds about 3 feet (90 cm) apart and white snakeroots and hardy ageratums about 2 feet (60 cm) apart. Keep watering new plantings regularly if rain is lacking. Established eupatoriums can be slow to send up new growth, often not emerging until late spring. Apply an organic mulch before summer.

◉ Summer

▸ Joe-Pye weeds usually start flowering in mid- to late summer; white snakeroot and hardy ageratum begin in late summer. All eupatoriums can be prone to flopping by bloom time, especially in rich soil or some shade. You may be able to prop up white snakeroot and hardy ageratum with linking stakes; for Joe-Pye weeds, you may need to support individual stems with tall Y-stakes. Better yet, avoid the need for staking by cutting the plants back by about one-half in early summer or about one-third in midsummer. Keep watering

❈ **SNIPPING TIPS** The seed heads of eupatoriums look great in the winter garden, especially when dusted with frost or snow, but they can also self-sow prolifically. To prevent a potential weed problem, you may choose to cut your plants to the ground as soon as the flowers fade.

Eupatorium 'Little Joe'

Eupatorium coelestinum 'Cori'

first-year plantings if rain is lacking. Established clumps also appreciate occasional watering during extended dry spells.

✪ ◕ Fall & Winter

▸ Joe-Pye weeds may bloom into early fall, and white snakeroot and hardy ageratum may continue into midfall or even later. Set out new plants in early fall, or move or divide established clumps as soon as their flowers fade. Water new plantings for the first month or so if rain is lacking. Scatter a general-purpose organic fertilizer or a shovelful of compost around the clumps in late fall to late winter.

❋ TROUBLESHOOTING

▸ **Leaves, stems turn brown.** If you choose not to water Joe-Pye weeds during summer dry spells, the leaves may wilt and eventually discolor. They might recover but keep a bronzy cast, or they may turn brown to black and die, and the stems may die too. The dead stems and flower-heads hold their form, so you could leave them for fall interest, or else cut them to the ground. Fresh new growth should appear next spring.

Euphorbia

EUPHORBIA, SPURGE

The genus *Euphorbia* is a huge and diverse group of plants, including quite a few hardy perennials that are appreciated for their colorful blooms and attractive foliage.

ONE FEATURE ALL EUPHORBIAS SHARE is a complex flower structure, which is actually a combination of tiny true flowers and showier modified leaves known as bracts. Most gardeners, though, simply use the term "bloom" or "flower" to refer to the entire colorful cluster.

One of the most popular species for perennial gardens is cushion spurge (*E. polychroma*; also known as *E. epithymoides*). It grows in dense, domed mounds typically 12 to 18 inches (30 to 45 cm) tall — sometimes up to twice that size in ideal conditions — with light green leaves that are practically smothered by the bright yellow blooms through the spring. It's usually recommended for Zones 3 or 4 to 8. 'Chameleon' euphorbia (*E. dulcis*) is another option for the front of a border. Its small chartreuse flowers are pretty in late spring to early summer, but it's mostly grown for its deep purple new foliage in mounds that are 12 to 18 inches (30 to 45 cm) tall. Zones 4 to 9. Griffith's spurge (*E. griffithii*) is larger — usually 2 to 3 feet (60 to 90 cm) tall — with red stems, light green leaves that are often tinged with red or orange when young, and bright orange flowers in early to midsummer. This one spreads moderately to form loose clumps. Zones 4 to 8. The leaves of all of these deciduous euphorbias turn bright red to orange before dropping in fall.

There are also a number of euphorbias that hold their foliage all year long. Myrtle spurge (*E. myrsinites*) carries short, gray-blue leaves on thick, sprawling stems that create a low clump 6 to 10 inches (15 to 25 cm) tall. Zones 5 to 9. Wood spurge (*E. amygdaloides*) has upright stems reaching to about 1 foot (30 cm) tall in leaf and 2 to 3 feet (60 to 90 cm) tall in bloom. It grows in fast-creeping carpets of evergreen foliage that may be solid green or tinged with red. The leaves of Robb's spurge (*E. amygdaloides* var. *robbiae*; also known as *E. robbiae*) are very dark green. Zones 6 to 9. Mediterranean spurge (*E. characias*) is the biggest of this bunch, normally growing 3 to 4 feet (90 to 120 cm) but possibly reaching to 6 feet (1.8 m) or more in ideal conditions. It grows in shrubby clumps of upright to somewhat sprawling stems clad in slender green to blue-gray leaves and topped with extra-large flower clusters. Zones 7 to 9. All of these evergreen types have yellow flowers in spring.

Euphorbia griffithii 'Fireglow'

✿ GROWING TIPS

▸ **Light & soil.** Euphorbias typically grow well in full sun to light shade in northern gardens. In hot-summer areas (roughly Zones 7 and south), a site with morning sun and afternoon shade or light, all-day shade is often ideal. Average, well-drained soil is generally fine.

▸ **Division & propagation.** For the most part, euphorbias grow best when left undisturbed, but you could divide the spreading types (Griffith's spurge, Robb's spurge, and wood spurge) every 3 to 5 years in early to midspring to control their spread. To propagate, take cuttings in early to midsummer after bloom. Cushion spurge usually grows readily from seed sown indoors (and lightly covered) in mid- to late winter. Try sowing the others outdoors in late summer or fall, or simply dig up and move self-sown seedlings.

▸ **Potential problems.** Insect pests are seldom a problem. Euphorbias may be attacked by a soil-borne wilt, particularly during hot, humid spells; remove and destroy affected plants. Other possible problems include powdery mildew and rust on some species; try cutting affected plants back to the ground to get clean new leaves.

It's smart to wear gloves, long sleeves, and pants (and possibly eye protection as well) when working around euphorbias to make sure the irritating sap doesn't get on you.

✿ SEASONAL CARE

◐ Spring

▸ Set out new plants, or move or divide established clumps if you must, in early to midspring. Space cushion spurge, myrtle spurge, and 'Chameleon' plants about 1 foot (30 cm) apart; Griffith's spurge, wood spurge, and Robb's spurge 2 to 3 feet (60 to 90 cm) apart; and Mediterranean spurge 3 to 4 feet (90 to 120 cm) apart. Water new plantings regularly if rain is lacking. If the foliage of evergreen species is damaged or discolored from the winter, you may want to cut off those damaged stems at the base in early spring to make the plant look better, although you'll remove the flowers, too. Mid- to late spring is prime bloom time for most euphorbias.

◯ Summer

▸ Griffith's spurge tends to be at its best in early summer, while the others are about finished by then. It's tempting to leave the clusters in place, because they remain attractive even while producing seed, but this may lead to over-enthusiastic self-sowing, as well as sprawling stems. (Note that cushion spurge, myrtle spurge, and Mediterranean spurge, in particular, can reseed to the point of being considered invasive in some areas.) Usually, it's best to cut cushion spurge back by about one-half in early summer, 'Chameleon' back to the ground in early summer, and Griffith's spurge back by one-half to two-thirds in midsummer. The evergreen species produce their blooms at the tips of second-year stems, and these stems won't flower again, so cut off the spent flower stems right at the base in early summer. Water spring plantings regularly during dry spells.

✿ ◉ Fall & Winter

▸ In mild climates, you could set out new plants in early fall; water them regularly for the first month or so. Cut down the deciduous species once they've dropped their foliage in fall or leave them until late winter. Scatter a general-purpose organic fertilizer or a shovelful of compost around your euphorbia clumps every year or two in late fall to late winter. First-year plantings of evergreen species benefit from a mulch of chopped leaves for winter, especially in cooler regions. In mild areas, euphorbias may begin flowering in late winter.

Euphorbias release a milky sap when you break a stem or leaf. This sap can cause a serious skin rash and is very irritating if you get it in your mouth or eyes, so use caution when working around the plants.

✿ **TOUGH CUSTOMERS** Euphorbias generally grow best with some moisture when young but tend to be quite drought tolerant once they've been in place for a few years. Protection from drying winter winds is a plus for evergreen species.

Ferns

Their lacy leaves may look delicate, but for the most part, hardy ferns are sturdy, dependable perennials that need practically no care to thrive. They're terrific for their textural interest, but they have more to offer than simple green leafiness: fascinating unfurling shoots, often-intriguing spore cases, and sometimes even seasonal color changes!

❖ GROWING TIPS

▶ **Light & soil.** Partial to full shade is best for most ferns, but a few — including *Dryopteris,* flowering ferns (*Osmunda*), and *Polystichum* — can tolerate full sun if they have enough moisture. In any site, evenly moist but well-drained, compost-enriched soil is ideal, and a pH that's neutral to acid is usually a plus. Flowering ferns (*Osmunda*) and ostrich ferns (*Matteuccia*) can tolerate wet soil, while established *Dryopteris* and *Polystichum* are more tolerant of occasional dryness than many other ferns.

▶ **Division & propagation.** Ferns rarely need division. If you want to propagate ferns, it's easiest to divide them in spring or fall, once they are large enough to have two or more crowns. In ideal conditions, some ferns can self-sow.

▶ **Potential problems.** Apart from occasional problems with thrips, leaf spots, and rusts, hardy ferns are seldom bothered by pests or diseases.

❖ SEASONAL CARE

◑ Spring

▶ Set out new plants, or move or divide existing ferns, in early to midspring. Space the shorter types 1 to 2 feet (30 to 60 cm) apart and the tall-growing types 2 to 3 feet (60 to 90 cm) apart. Water new plantings regularly if rain is lacking. In early spring, clip off any remaining dead fronds on deciduous ferns and any winter-damaged fronds on the evergreen types. Apply a generous layer of organic mulch before summer. New fronds generally emerge in early to midspring (a few not until late spring) and are pinkish, reddish, or purplish in some species.

◎ Summer

▶ There's not much to do with ferns in summer, except to water them regularly (especially spring plantings) if rain is lacking and their soil isn't naturally moist. If the soil does dry out, the fronds may start turning brown or completely die back to the ground.

✪ ◉ Fall & Winter

▶ Set out new ferns, or move or divide existing ones, in early fall. Water them regularly for the first month or so if rain is lacking. On deciduous ferns, the fronds will die, but leaving them in place provides a natural mulch. Evergreen ferns look good through most or all of the winter. Scatter a general-purpose organic fertilizer or a shovelful of compost (or both) around each clump in late fall to late winter.

Ferns produce dustlike spores, rather than seeds. On some species, the spores form on separate stalks or on separate sections of the leaflike fronds. On others, the spore cases look like dots on the underside of the fronds, and it's easy to mistake them for scale insects or some sort of disease if you've never seen them before.

Adiantum pedatum

Ferns (continued)

❖ All in the Family

Here's a small sampling of a few terrific hardy ferns that can look lovely combined with other perennials in beds and borders.

▶ *Adiantum* (maidenhair ferns): Deciduous ferns that spread slowly to moderately by creeping rhizomes. One of the best-known species is northern maidenhair fern (*A. pedatum*), with thin, black stems and light green fronds held horizontally; yellow fall color.

▶ *Athyrium* (athyriums): Deciduous ferns that are slow to moderate spreaders. Lady fern (*A. filix-femina*) has upright, light green fronds, sometimes with reddish stems. Japanese painted fern (*A. niponicum* var. *pictum*; also known as *A. goeringianum*) has arching, silvery gray fronds and deep purple stems. There are also several hybrids between these species.

▶ *Dryopteris* (dryopteris): Deciduous or evergreen, clump-forming to slow-spreading ferns. Male fern (*D. filix-mas*) has deep green fronds in broad, vase-shaped clumps. Evergreen in many areas. Autumn fern (*D. erythrosora*) is usually evergreen, with orangey red new fronds that age to coppery pink and then shiny, deep green. Bright red spore cases appear on the undersides of the mature fronds.

▶ *Matteuccia struthiopteris* (ostrich fern): Deciduous, upright, bright green fronds and separate spore-bearing stems that rise in late summer and persist through the winter. This tall fern can be an aggressive spreader; it is too vigorous for most borders but great for filling larger areas.

▶ *Osmunda* (flowering ferns): Large, deciduous and usually slow-creeping ferns with thick rhizomes. Cinnamon fern (*O. cinnamomea*) has deep green mature fronds that often turn golden in fall, plus separate, rusty brown spikes of spore cases that rise in spring and die back in mid- to late summer. Royal or regal fern (*O. regalis*) is even larger — typically 4 to 6 feet (1.2 to 1.8 m) tall — with broad, medium green fronds that may turn yellow to orange-yellow in fall, with spiky clusters of golden brown spore cases held at the tips of the fronds in late spring to early summer.

▶ *Polystichum* (shield or holly ferns): Many species of usually evergreen ferns, commonly growing in distinct clumps. One of the best known is Christmas fern (*P. acrostichoides*), with deep green, evergreen, arching fronds in broad, vase-shaped clumps.

Matteuccia struthiopteris

Filipendula

FILIPENDULA, MEADOWSWEET

While soggy-soil sites are certain death for many popular perennials, most species of *Filipendula* can positively thrive there.

THERE ARE A NUMBER of summer-flowering species of *Filipendula* to choose from, all with deeply divided to multipart leaves and upright stalks topped with many tiny flowers grouped into fluffy-looking, plumelike clusters. Filipendulas are generally recommended for Zones 3 to 8.

Dropwort (*F. vulgaris;* also known as *F. hexapetala*) has particularly lacy foliage and creamy white flowers to about 2 feet (60 cm) tall. Meadowsweet (*F. ulmaria*) — also known as queen-of-the-meadow — has creamy white blooms that can reach anywhere from 3 to 6 feet (90 to 180 cm) tall.

There are also a number of pink-flowered species, and their botanical names are often confused in the trade. The tallest one is commonly known as queen-of-the-prairie and usually sold as *F. rubra*. It typically blooms atop stems from 4 to 8 feet (1.2 to 2.4 m) tall. Plants sold as *F. palmata* or *F. purpurea* tend to be more compact — usually 3 to 4 feet (90 to 120 cm) tall; 'Kahome' (also sold as 'Kakome') reaches to just 1 foot (30 cm) in bloom.

Filipendula ulmaria 'Aurea'

:: GROWING TIPS

▶ **Light & soil.** Generally, filipendulas can grow in full sun in the coolest parts of their range, but they do best with morning sun and afternoon shade. The more sun they get, the more important it is that their soil stays evenly moist to wet; in some shade, they can adapt to slightly drier conditions. (Dropwort is the most adaptable of the bunch, as far as moisture goes.)

▶ **Division & propagation.** Divide the plants in spring or fall as needed for propagation or to control their spread. To grow them from seed, sow outdoors in fall or in a cool spot indoors in mid- to late winter; barely cover the seed.

▶ **Potential problems.** Japanese beetles are fond of the foliage. Possible disease problems include leaf spots, powdery mildew, and rust.

:: SEASONAL CARE

○ Spring

▶ Set out new plants, or move or divide existing clumps, in early spring. Allow 1-foot (30 cm) spacings for 'Kahome'; 18 inches (45 cm) for dropwort and meadowsweet; and 2 to 3 feet for the taller pink-flowered kinds. Water new plantings regularly if rain is lacking. Apply an organic mulch before summer. In warmer areas, some species may begin blooming in late spring.

◎ Summer

▶ Early to midsummer is peak bloom time for most filipendulas. *F. purpurea* and 'Kahome' tend to bloom a bit later, in mid- to late summer. Leave the spent flower stems for

height and interest or remove them at the base to prevent self-sowing (removal is a good idea on dropwort, in particular). Keep watering spring plantings regularly if rain is lacking. Established clumps also benefit from occasional soakings during dry spells.

❂ ◉ Fall & Winter

▶ Set out new plants, or move or divide existing clumps, in early fall. Water them regularly for the first month or so if rain is lacking. Cut back the dead tops in fall or leave them for spring cleanup. Scatter a general-purpose organic fertilizer or a shovelful of compost (or both) around each clump in late fall to late winter.

:: **WHACK IT BACK** Filipendulas are beautiful in bloom, but if the soil dries out, their leaves may turn brown and ugly. Cut the damaged plants to the ground and water thoroughly to get a flush of fresh new growth.

Foeniculum

FENNEL

Fennel is best known for its use as an herb, due to its flavorful and aromatic leaves and seeds, but it can be an attractive ornamental, too.

FENNEL FORMS TIGHT CLUMPS of very finely cut green leaves, which shoot up into 4- to 6-foot-tall (1.2 to 1.8 m) flowering stems topped with flat clusters of tiny yellow flowers. You don't often see "regular" fennel (*Foeniculum vulgare*) grown in perennial borders, though; it's usually the kind with grayish purple to brown leaves, commonly called bronze or copper fennel and sold under various names, including 'Purpureum', 'Rubrum', and 'Smokey'. Fennel plants are generally hardy in Zones 4 to 9.

❀ GROWING TIPS

▶ **Light & soil.** Fennels grow best in full sun but can also take a few hours of morning or afternoon shade. Average, well-drained soil is fine.

▶ **Division & propagation.** It's not unusual for fennel plants to die out after a few years, so you may want to allow just one seed head to drop seed for replacement plants. Or, sow seed (and barely cover it) indoors in late winter or outdoors in early spring. Fennels produce deep taproots that make them tricky to move or divide successfully, so it's best to leave established clumps undisturbed and set out new plants while they're relatively small.

▶ **Potential problems.** Fennels may be bothered by a few problems, including aphids, slugs, and stem rot, but these aren't all that common. One "pest" you may see is color-fully banded caterpillars chewing on the leaves; these are the larvae of swallowtail butterflies, so you don't want to kill them. If you can, let them eat their fill, then cut down any remaining foliage to get a new batch of leaves. Or, grow a few fennel plants in an out-of-the-way spot, and gently move the caterpillars to them if the larvae appear on your border clumps.

❀ SEASONAL CARE

◗ Spring

▶ Set out new plants in early to midspring, spaced about 18 inches (45 cm) apart. Water new plantings regularly if rain is lacking. Apply an organic mulch before summer.

◎ Summer

▶ Fennel plants generally begin blooming in midsummer. Most gardeners choose to remove most or all of the flower stalks at the base as soon as the flowers finish, because fennels can self-sow freely, to the point of becoming weedy in the garden and even invasive in some regions. Cutting off the flower stems also encourages the plant to produce a flush of fresh new foliage. Keep watering spring plantings during dry spells.

✿ ◉ Fall & Winter

▶ Set out new plants in early fall; water them regularly for the first month or so if rain is lacking. Cut down established clumps after frost. Scatter a shovelful of compost around the clumps every other year in late fall to late winter, if desired.

Relatively Speaking

Cow parsley (*Anthriscus sylvestris*) is another lacy-leaved herb that's most often seen in borders in its dark-leaved form, usually sold as 'Ravenswing'. Hardy in Zones 6 to 9, it reaches anywhere from 2 to 5 feet (60 to 150 cm) tall in bloom, with white to pink-tinged flowers in late spring to early or midsummer. 'Ravenswing' usually emerges green and quickly turns deep purple-brown. Give it the same general care as described for fennel, making sure you remove most of the flowers to minimize self-sowing. The species is considered invasive in some areas.

Foeniculum vulgare 'Bronze' with chive blossoms

Gaillardia

BLANKET FLOWER

With its months-long bloom period, blanket flower (*Gaillardia* × *grandiflora*) rivals many annuals for pure flower power. It grows in mounding clumps of hairy, lance-shaped leaves, with slender stems topped by daisy-form flowers that are red-and-yellow, solid yellow, or peachy yellow. The bloom height can range from 1 to 3 feet (30 to 90 cm), depending on the cultivar. Blanket flower is commonly recommended for Zones 3 or 4 to 10.

❁ GROWING TIPS

▸ **Light & soil.** Full sun with average, well-drained soil is ideal. Blanket flowers can tolerate some shade, but the plants are more open and floppy there. A soil pH that's near-neutral to alkaline is a plus. The plants perform best in loose, sandy soil and suffer in tight, clayey conditions. Blanket flowers are generally salt-tolerant, and established clumps can be quite drought-tolerant.

▸ **Division & propagation.** Divide blanket flowers every two or three years in spring or early fall to keep them vigorous, or for propagation. Taking cuttings in spring or summer is another way to multiply your favorites. It's also easy to grow new plants from seed sown indoors in late winter or outdoors in spring or summer; don't cover it. Indoor-started seedlings often bloom the first year. Blanket flowers may also self-sow freely if not deadheaded, but the seedlings can vary in height and bloom color.

▸ **Potential problems.** They may be bothered by a number of pests and diseases, including aphids, beetles, leafhoppers, plant bugs, slugs and snails, stalk borer, aster yellows, leaf spots, mildews, root rots, rusts, and viruses.

❁ SEASONAL CARE

◐ Spring

▸ Move or divide existing clumps in early to midspring, or set out new plants any time. Space them about 18 inches (45 cm) apart — or about 1 foot (30 cm) apart for dwarf types. Water new plantings occasionally if rain is lacking. If established clumps look "stringy" after winter, cut them back to the base to encourage bushier new growth. Apply a light organic mulch or a gravel mulch before summer, if desired.

◎ Summer

▸ Blanket flowers begin blooming by early summer. By mid- to late summer, you may want to start snipping off the rounded seedheads individually to encourage rebloom and prevent self-sowing, or else shear the whole clump back to about 6 inches (15 cm) in late summer. Water spring plantings occasionally during dry spells.

✿ ☉ Fall & Winter

▸ Set out new plants, or move or divide existing clumps, in early fall; water them for the first month or so if rain is lacking. Established plants can continue to flower well into fall (or even through winter in mild climates), especially if you deadheaded them or cut them back in late summer. Keep trimming off the seedheads to prevent self-sowing. Scatter a general-purpose organic fertilizer or a few handfuls of compost around the clumps every other year in late fall to late winter.

❁ TROUBLESHOOTING

▸ **Plants die.** The clumps tend to be short lived, so plan to divide them every few years or take stem cuttings to keep them going. Shearing the clumps back to 6 inches (15 cm) in late summer can also improve their chances of surviving the winter.

❁ **HIGH AND DRY** Blanket flowers (*Gaillardia* × *grandiflora*) are one of those quirky plants that many gardeners grow with ease but others just don't have luck with. If they don't thrive for you, it may be because your soil is too heavy, too wet, or too rich. Make sure the plants get full sun and try them in a drier, less-fertile spot, on a slope, or in a raised bed.

Gaillardia grandiflora 'Goblin'

Gaura

GAURA, WAND FLOWER, BEE BLOSSOM, APPLEBLOSSOM GRASS

Gauras grow in airy clumps of slender stems that are upright when young and arching to somewhat sprawling on older plants, reaching anywhere from 2 to 5 feet (60 to 150 cm) tall.

THE SLENDER GREEN LEAVES are sometimes spotted with red and may be blushed with red in cool weather. The stems are tipped with long, slender bloom spikes. White gaura (*Gaura lindheimeri*) has white flowers that age to pink, while selections and hybrids bloom in various shades of pink. Gauras are commonly recommended for Zones 5 to 10, but they may be hardy in even colder zones where the soil is very well drained.

❈ GROWING TIPS

▸ **Light & soil.** Gaura generally grows best with full sun and average, well-drained soil. The plants can tolerate some shade (especially in the south), but shady sites — and those with moist, rich soil, too — can lead to sprawling stems.

▸ **Division & propagation.** Gauras produce deep taproots and may be slow to recover if you try to move or divide them. Removing small offsets in spring is a better option for propagating your favorites. Or, sow seed (barely cover it) indoors in late winter — the seedlings may bloom in the first year — or outdoors in spring to fall. Another option is to transplant self-sown seedlings while they are still small.

▸ **Potential problems.** Possible problems include aphids, leaf spots, mildews, root rot, and rusts, but none of these is particularly common.

❈ SEASONAL CARE

◐ Spring

▸ If you must move or divide your plants, try in early spring; dig deeply to get as much of the taproot as possible. Set out new plants in early to midspring, spacing them about 2 feet (60 cm) apart. Water new plantings regularly if rain is lacking. Wait until established plants start producing new growth (possibly as late as midspring in cool areas) to cut them back; then remove only the dead tips, or cut the plants back to the new shoots at the base. Add an organic or gravel mulch before summer. In the south, gaura may begin blooming in mid- to late spring.

◑ Summer

▸ In northern gardens, gaura usually begins blooming in early to midsummer and continues well into fall. In warmer zones, the plants may take a break in mid- to late summer; in this case, either snip off finished spikes individually or cut the whole plant back by about two-thirds to promote later rebloom and minimize self-sowing, too. Water spring plantings occasionally if rain is lacking. Established gauras are quite drought tolerant but benefit from watering during extended dry spells.

◑ ◉ Fall & Winter

▸ Early fall planting is fine in southern gardens. Water new plantings for the first month or so if rain is lacking.

Gaura usually keeps flowering until frost or even well into winter in mild climates. The foliage also looks good through part or all of the winter. North of Zone 6, you may want to protect the roots with a layer of chopped leaves or another winter mulch. Scatter a general-purpose organic fertilizer or a shovelful of compost around the clumps every other year in late fall to late winter, if desired.

❈ TROUBLESHOOTING

▸ **Plants die.** Gaura plants tend to die out after a few years, so plan to buy new plants every second or third spring or allow some self-sowing to have replacements on hand. Pink-flowered selections seem to be less hardy than those with white new blooms.

❈ **SURVIVING WINTER** Waiting to cut back the top growth of your gauras until new shoots appear in spring can increase their odds of winter survival. Ensuring that the plants have a well-drained site is important, too.

Gaura lindheimeri 'Siskiyou Pink'

Geranium

HARDY GERANIUM, CRANESBILL

Hardy geraniums are among the most popular perennials for beds and borders, and for good reasons: along with beautiful blooms and often extended flowering periods, many also offer attractive foliage all through the growing season or even year-round.

THERE ARE MANY DOZENS of species, cultivars, and hybrids to choose from. A few species with upright to somewhat trailing stems include meadow cranesbill (*Geranium pratense*), with blue, purple, or white flowers mostly from late spring into summer on plants 2 to 4 feet (60 to 120 cm) tall; Clarke's geranium (*G. clarkei*), with purple or white flowers mostly in early to midsummer on 2-foot (60 cm) plants; Endress's geranium (*G. endressii*), with pink flowers from early summer to early fall on plants 12 to 18 inches (30 to 45 cm) tall; mourning widow (*G. phaeum*), with deep purple blooms from late spring to early summer on plants 18 to 36 inches (45 to 90 cm) tall; and wild geranium (*G. maculatum*), usually with purplish pink flowers in late spring to early summer on 2-foot-tall (60 cm) plants.

A few 1- to 2-foot-tall (30 to 60 cm) hybrids with purple-blue flowers and an upright or trailing growth habit include the old favorite 'Johnson's Blue', which blooms from midspring to midsummer, as well as the more recent introductions 'Brookside', an upright cultivar that blooms from late spring to early or midsummer, and the rambling 'Gerwat' (Rozanne), which flowers from early summer well into fall.

Other hardy geraniums grow more like ground covers, creating spreading cushions or creeping carpets. Bloody cranesbill (*G. sanguineum*) is one of them, growing anywhere from 6 to 18 inches (15 to 45 cm) tall and blooming in white or shades of pink to magenta, from late spring well into summer, over small, deeply lobed leaves. Bigroot geranium (*G. macrorrhizum*) is a 12- to 18-inch-tall (30 to 45 cm) creeper with magenta-pink blooms in late spring to midsummer over sticky, aromatic leaves. It is a parent of Cambridge geranium (*G.* × *cantabrigiense*), which has midspring to late-summer blooms in a similar color range over semievergreen, scented leaves on carpets 6 to 12 inches (15 to 30 cm) tall. Grayleaf geranium (*G. cinereum*) usually forms a tidy mound 6 to 10 inches (15 to 25 cm) tall, with flowers mostly in shades of pink from midspring to late summer or early fall over gray-green leaves.

As a group, geraniums generally perform well in Zones 4 to 8, and some are hardy even into Zone 3. Grayleaf geranium, though, is best in Zones 5 or 6 to 8.

Geranium sanguineum 'New Hampshire Purple'

❖ **TOUGH CUSTOMERS** If summer dry spells are common in your area and you don't want to water frequently, consider growing some of the more drought-tolerant hardy geraniums, such as bigroot geranium (*G. macrorrhizum*), bloody cranesbill (*G. sanguineum*), and Cambridge geranium (*G.* × *cantabrigiense*).

▸ **Light & soil.** In northern gardens, hardy geraniums generally grow well in full sun to light shade; in Zones 6 to 8, a site with morning sun and afternoon shade is ideal. Some geraniums that tend to be more shade tolerant than others include bigroot geranium, bloody cranesbill, mourning widow, and wild geranium. Compost-enriched soil that stays evenly moist but not soggy is ideal for most. Excellent drainage is especially critical for geraniums with grayish leaves.

▸ **Division & propagation.** Hardy geraniums can grow in one place for many years, so you don't really need to divide them unless they've gotten too big for their spot or if you want to slow the spread of creepers (such as bigroot geranium and Clark's geranium). Division in spring or fall is a great way to propagate your favorites. Seed-grown plants can vary in height and flower color, but if you want to try raising hardy geraniums from seed, sow indoors in late winter to early spring or outdoors in summer or fall; barely cover the seed.

▸ **Potential problems.** Some possible problems include aphids, plant bugs, slugs, leaf spots, mildews, rust, and root rots, but for the most part, geraniums are typically trouble free.

❀ SEASONAL CARE

◐ Spring

▸ Set out new plants, or move or divide existing clumps, in early spring. Space the low-growers about 1 foot (30 cm) apart; for those that have trailing stems or are taller than about 18 inches (45 cm), space the plants 18 to 24 inches (45 to 60 cm) apart. Water new plantings regularly if rain is lacking. On established clumps, remove any winter-damaged or dead growth in early to midspring.

Apply an organic mulch before summer arrives. Several species begin blooming in late spring.

◎ Summer

▸ Early summer is peak bloom time for most hardy geraniums. Some keep flowering through mid- to late summer even without deadheading, so if your plants look good, you can leave them alone. But if they stop blooming, outgrow their allotted space, develop leaf spots, or simply look straggly, snip off all of the spent flowering stems at the base or shear the tops back to the new growth emerging at the base. On the low-carpeters that keep good-looking leaves through the summer, simply shear off the very tops of the plants to remove the seed heads if you want to prevent self-sowing. Some geraniums rebloom lightly later on. Keep watering new plantings regularly through the summer if rain is lacking.

Established clumps also benefit from occasional watering during dry spells.

✿ ◑ Fall & Winter

▸ Set out new plants, or move or divide existing clumps, in early fall; water them regularly for the first month or so if rain is lacking. It's not unusual for established geraniums to produce additional blooms in autumn, especially if you had cut them back during the summer. The foliage of several hardy geraniums — among them, bigroot geranium, bloody cranesbill, Cambridge geranium, 'Brookside', and 'Gerwat' (Rozanne) — turns shades of red to orange in fall. If the foliage gets damaged or winter-killed, it's fine to snip it off at any point or leave it until spring cleanup. Scatter a general-purpose organic fertilizer or a shovelful of compost (or both) around each clump in late fall to late winter.

By the time upright or trailing geraniums start looking tired and sprawly in summer, fresh foliage is usually coming up at the base of the plants. Trim the leggy old stems back to these new leaves to make the whole clump appear bushy and neat.

Geum

GEUM, AVENS, GRECIAN ROSE

Geums aren't the easiest perennials to please, but where they're happy, they're beautiful border plants.

THE BEST-KNOWN GEUMS are those with single, semidouble, or double flowers in shades of red, orange, or yellow. Species names you may see associated with these include *Geum chiloense* (*G. quellyon*), *G. × borisii*, and *G. coccineum;* for the most part, though, the plants grown in gardens are hybrids. They form dense clumps of divided, velvety green, often-evergreen leaves, with slender, branching, flowering stems. Hybrid geums are generally recommended for Zones 5 to 7, though gardeners in colder or warmer zones may have luck with them, too.

Geum 'Georgenberg'

❊ GROWING TIPS

▸ **Light & soil.** Full sun is fine in cool-summer climates, but in most areas, a site with morning sun and afternoon shade is ideal. Geums appreciate evenly moist, compost-enriched soil, but they also require good drainage; soggy soil is fatal, especially in winter.

▸ **Division & propagation.** Hybrid geums may be short lived where the growing conditions are less than ideal, so it's a good idea to divide them every 2 or 3 years in early spring or early fall to keep them vigorous. Division is also a good way to propagate your favorites. It's easy to grow geums from seed, too; sow indoors in late winter to early spring or outdoors in spring or summer, and barely cover it. Indoor-started plants may bloom in their first year.

▸ **Potential problems.** Possible problems include spider mites, leaf spots, mildews, and root rots, but they usually aren't common.

❊ SEASONAL CARE

◐ Spring

▸ Set out new plants, or move or divide existing clumps, in early spring. Space the plants about 1 foot (30 cm) apart. Water new plantings regularly if rain is lacking. Snip off any winter-damaged or dead leaves on established plants in early spring. Apply an organic mulch before summer. Hybrid geums typically begin blooming in late spring.

◎ Summer

▸ Early summer is peak bloom time for hybrid geums. Snipping off individual blooms when the petals drop, and cutting off totally finished flower stems at their base, may extend the bloom season through most of the summer. Keep watering spring plantings regularly if rain is lacking. Established geums also benefit from watering during dry spells.

✪ ◉ Fall & Winter

▸ Set out new plants, or move or divide existing clumps, in early fall; water for the first month or so if rain is lacking. Geums occasionally produce a few flowers during the autumn season, and they tend to stay evergreen through the winter in all but the coldest zones. North of Zone 7, a light winter mulch can be helpful, especially for first-year plantings. Scatter a general-purpose organic fertilizer or a shovelful of compost around each clump in late fall to late winter.

❊ TROUBLESHOOTING

▸ **Flowers are an unexpected color.** Hybrid geums have a reputation of coming true from seed, but that's often not the case. If you're purchasing plants, buy them in bloom to make sure you get the colors you want, instead of just relying on the pot label. If you're raising your own geums from seed, consider growing them in a nursery bed until they bloom; then save those that are the height and color you want and give away the rest.

❊ **WHACK IT BACK** If the foliage of your geums gets damaged, spotted, or discolored during the summer, cut the plants to the ground to get a flush of new growth in a few weeks.

Gillenia

BOWMAN'S ROOT, INDIAN PHYSIC, AMERICAN IPECAC

Bowman's roots (*Gillenia*; also known as *Porteranthus*) aren't the longest-blooming perennials around, but they have many other great features to offer, including reddish new shoots, handsome summer foliage, attractive fall color, and an adaptable, trouble-free nature.

G. TRIFOLIATA GROWS IN SHRUBBY CLUMPS typically 2 to 3 feet (60 to 90 cm) tall, with thin but sturdy maroon stems clad in toothed, three-part, deep green leaves. *G. stipulata* is similar but has somewhat lacier-looking foliage. Both species produce an abundance of small, starry, white to pink-tinged blooms, followed by small, deep red seed heads. Zones 4 to 8.

Gillenia trifoliata

❖ GROWING TIPS

▶ **Light & soil.** The ideal site for Bowman's roots has morning sun and afternoon shade or light all-day shade, with evenly moist but well-drained, compost-enriched soil. These dependable perennials can adapt to just about any site with average, well-drained soil, though, from full sun to full shade. Established clumps can be quite drought tolerant.

▶ **Division & propagation.** It can take the clumps a few years to fill out, but once they're settled in, Bowman's roots seldom need to be divided. You *can* divide them in early spring for propagation, but you'll need a sturdy tool to cut through the woody crown. Other propagation options include taking stem cuttings in spring or sowing seed about ¼ inch (6 mm) deep outdoors in fall.

▶ **Potential problems.** Apart from occasional problems with slugs or spider mites, the plants are normally trouble free.

❖ SEASONAL CARE

◐ Spring

▶ Set out new plants, or move or divide existing clumps if needed, in early to midspring. Space them about 2 feet apart. Water new plantings regularly if rain is lacking. Apply an organic mulch before summer. Bowman's roots may begin blooming in late spring.

◯ Summer

▶ Early summer is peak bloom time for Bowman's roots; in some areas, flowering continues into midsummer. The small, deep red seed heads add some interest, and self-sowing is usually minimal, so there's no need to remove them. Keep watering spring plantings regularly during dry spells.

✚ ◉ Fall & Winter

▶ Set out new plants, or move or divide existing clumps, in early fall; water them for the first month or so if rain is lacking. The foliage of Bowman's roots typically turns shades of deep red to orange in autumn. Once the leaves drop, you could leave the stems for off-season interest or cut them down at any point during the winter. Scatter a general-purpose organic fertilizer or a shovelful of compost around each clump every year or two in late fall to late winter.

❖ **SUPPORT SYSTEMS** Bowman's roots are typically sturdy and fuss free, but they may sprawl a bit if the soil is very fertile. If that's the case in your garden, consider setting grow-through supports over the emerging clumps in early to midspring.

Grasses

Terrific texture, showy seed heads, seasonal color changes, and soft sounds — ornamental grasses offer all of these features and more without demanding much fussing from you in return.

FROM A MAINTENANCE STANDPOINT, the most important thing to know about these sturdy, adaptable plants is that perennial grasses mostly fall into one of two groups: cool-season grasses and warm-season grasses. Cool-season grasses usually start growing actively early in the growing season and flower in spring to early summer. They grow slowly — if at all — through the hottest months but may produce fresh new foliage when the weather cools again in fall. Warm-season grasses tend to start growing slowly in spring, but they speed up when the days get warmer, and they're usually in bloom by late summer or in fall and in seed by the end of fall. Their leafy stalks and seed heads, which dry to various shades of tan, golden brown, and copper, often stick around through most or all of the winter months.

Another important thing to know about grasses *before* you plant them is whether they're "clumpers" or "creepers." Clumpers, as you may guess, tend to stay in distinct clumps: those clumps can get quite large over time, but they basically stay in one place. Creeping grasses spread by horizontal stems called stolons (just above ground) or by rhizomes (below ground). These grasses may spread at a slow to moderate rate, forming broad but distinct patches, or they may spread aggressively, crowding out more-restrained companions and popping up all over the place. Also, be aware that many grasses produce large amounts of seed, and in some cases, those seeds may sprout freely and turn into a weed problem if you're not careful to remove them.

All that said, ornamental grasses truly are quite easy to care for, and if you choose them wisely, they're invaluable additions to the garden. In All in the Family on page 232, you'll find a rundown of some of the most popular perennial grasses with information on their growth cycles and clumping or spreading tendencies.

One more thing: The term "ornamental grasses" is often used a broad sense to include true grasses as well as other plants that closely resemble them, such as sedges (mostly *Carex* species). This entry covers caring for true grasses. Sedges have their own entry, because they have rather different growing and preferences. (See *Carex* on page 178.)

❀ GROWING TIPS

▶ **Light & soil.** Most ornamental grasses thrive in full sun but can tolerate light shade; in fact, some afternoon shade in summer can be beneficial for cool-season grasses. Average, well-drained soil is generally fine. Many grasses can adapt to both dry and moist conditions, staying relatively compact in drier sites and growing significantly taller in moist soil.

▶ **Division & propagation.** The ideal time to divide any grass is just before it starts to grow actively. For warm-season grasses, that's usually early to midspring (even into late spring in cool climates); for cool-season grasses, early spring is usually ideal, but early fall can work, too. (In cold-winter areas, you may want to protect fall divisions with mulch for the first winter.)

How often you need to divide depends on the grasses you're growing. With clump-formers, you can wait until they start to die out in the center or become more prone to sprawling, or you can divide them more often if you want to propagate them. (Just remember that the tall-growing grasses especially can take several years to start filling out, so you don't want to divide them too frequently.) With the creepers, you could try dividing them every year or every other year to slow their spread. Better yet, plant them within a root barrier, such as a bottomless bucket sunk into the soil almost to the rim, or in a site where they can spread freely without crowding out other companions.

If you want to grow grasses from seed, you can usually get good results from sowing them indoors in late winter to early spring or outdoors in

❀ **MIND THE GAPS** Tall-growing grasses can take several years to fill out and may look sparse at wide spacings, so you may want to plant them a little closer at first and plan to move some of them in 3 or 4 years; otherwise, use tall-growing annuals to fill around them for the first few years.

Pennisetum 'Karley Rose'

midspring to early summer; barely cover the seed, or leave it uncovered.

▸ **Potential problems.** Before planting ornamental grasses, make sure you've completely removed any weedy grasses from the bed or border. Having to weed "bad" grasses out of "good" ones is a maintenance nightmare! Apart from occasional problems with aphids, mealybugs, and rusts, grasses are seldom bothered by pests or diseases.

❖ SEASONAL CARE

◐ Spring

▸ Early spring is a good time to set out new plants of cool-season grasses, or to move existing clumps if necessary. Early to midspring is fine for planting, moving, or divid-

ing warm-season grasses. Space them about as far apart as the mature height of their foliage — roughly 1 to 2 feet (30 to 60 cm) for the lower-growers and 4 to 5 feet (1.2 to 1.5 m) for the tallest ones. Water new plantings regularly if rain is lacking. Apply an organic mulch before summer.

▸ Cool-season grasses generally jump into growth in early spring, if they haven't already. If their old foliage looks unattractive, you could try to rake or pull out the damaged or dead leaves with your fingers, or shear the whole plant to about 2 inches (5 cm) above the crown for a more complete cleanup. New leaves appear quickly on cool-season grasses, and they may even be blooming by late spring.

▸ If you didn't cut down the remaining top growth on warm-season grasses in late winter, try to get it done in early spring, so you don't nip off the tips of the new leaves too. (That's not a big problem, but it may cause a bit of browning at the cut tips.) Warm-season grasses can be slow to sprout, especially in cold, wet springs, but they're generally up and growing by mid- to late spring.

◎ Summer

▸ In most areas, cool-season grasses finish flowering in early summer and are in seed by midsummer. Shear the stems back to the foliage, or leave the seed heads for later interest. Cool-season grasses generally produce

continued on page 234

Grasses (continued)

❋ All in the Family

Here's an overview of some gorgeous ornamental grasses well suited to perennial gardens, with a few tips to help you get the best from them in your garden.

▶ *Calamagrostis* (feather reed grass): Medium-sized, clump-forming, cool-season grasses. 'Karl Foerster' feather reed grass (*C. × acutiflora*; also sold as 'Stricta') doesn't self-sow, so you can leave the dried flower plumes in place. Korean feather reed grass (*C. brachytricha*) blooms in late summer and fall, later than most cool-season grasses, and it tolerates partial shade.

▶ *Chasmanthium latifolium* (sea oats): A medium-sized, clump-forming, cool-season grass with fascinating, flattened seed heads that dangle from the branch tips. It can self-sow freely, though, so you may want to clip the seed heads off before they turn brown. Can tolerate partial shade.

▶ *Cortaderia selloana* (pampas grass): A tall-growing, warm-season grass that forms broad clumps of arching, sharp-edged foliage and dramatic flower plumes. May self-sow in warmer areas (and is considered invasive in some regions) unless you cut off the flower plumes, which basically defeats the purpose of growing it.

▶ *Festuca* (fescue): Compact, clump-forming cool-season grasses grown mostly for their tufted, blue-green to gray-blue foliage. Clip off the flower heads before they turn brown to prevent self-sowing, which otherwise may be abundant. Divide frequently — every 2 to 3 years — to keep the plants vigorous.

▶ *Hakonechloa macra* (Hakone grass): Compact warm-season grasses that spread gently to eventually form broad clumps. Grown mostly for its gracefully arching foliage, which is yellow-and-green on 'Aureola' and green-tinged yellow on 'All Gold'. Best in partial shade and evenly moist soil.

▶ *Helictotrichon sempervirens* (blue oat grass): Compact to medium-sized, clump-forming, cool-season grass. Prone to rust in hot, humid weather. Remove the flow-

ering stems after bloom (or even before); they decline quickly and don't add much interest.

▶ *Imperata cylindrica* var. *koenigii* 'Rubra' (Japanese blood grass): Also sold as 'Red Baron'. Compact warm-season grass that spreads slowly to form patches of red-tipped green leaves that turn solid red by fall. Usually produces flowers only in hot climates. While the species is considered seriously invasive, this selection so far appears safe to grow in gardens.

▶ *Leymus arenarius* (Lyme grass, dune grass): Also known as *Elymus racemosus*. Medium-sized cool-season grass with gray-blue leaves that turn tan in winter. Clip off the nonshowy flower spikes to tidy the plants and prevent sowing. Plant this vigorous spreader within some sort of root barrier to corral its rampant rhizomes or give it a site by itself; don't let it loose in a perennial border! Drought tolerant and salt tolerant.

▶ *Miscanthus sinensis* (Japanese silver grass, maiden grass, eulalia): Tall-growing warm-season grass that forms broad clumps. It may self-sow (especially in the case of early flowering cultivars) and is considered invasive in several regions; clip off the developing seed heads, if you can bear it, to prevent seeds from forming, or grow purple moor grass (*Molinia caerulea*) or switch grasses (*Panicum*) instead.

▶ *Molinia caerulea* (purple moor grass): This medium-sized to tall clump-former is usually treated like a cool-season grass, although it doesn't flower until mid- to

Molinia caerulea 'Variegata'

late summer. The foliage turns bright yellow and stays around into the winter but eventually breaks off on its own; new growth doesn't appear until early spring. Prefers evenly moist soil; tolerates partial shade.

▶ *Muhlenbergia* (muhly): Medium-sized, clump-forming warm-season grasses. Deer grass (*M. rigens*) is prized mostly for its handsome, gray-green foliage and very slender, silvery flower spikes. Pink muhly (*M. capillaris*), also known as gulf muhly, explodes into clouds of rosy pink flowerheads in mid- to late fall.

▶ *Panicum virgatum* (switch grass): Tall-growing warm-season grass that forms broad clumps. The foliage of some selections is tinged or tipped with deep red by late summer; others range from olive green to powder blue in leaf, and many have splendid fall color. They may self-sow lightly but usually aren't a big problem, so you can leave their long-lasting plumes for winter interest. Switch grasses are very adaptable, growing in sun or partial shade with soils ranging from dry to moist.

▶ *Pennisetum* (fountain grass): Medium-sized, clump-forming warm-season grasses. Some cultivars of *P. alopecuroides* — particularly 'Moudry' — self-sow freely; on these, you may want to clip off the flower spikes. The brushy seed heads of this species usually shatter by late fall, but the dried foliage holds up through the winter. *P. orientale*, on the other hand, loses its form by early winter.

▶ *Phalaris arundinacea* var. *picta* (gardener's garters, ribbon grass): Compact to medium-sized, vigorously creeping cool-season grass grown for its white-striped foliage (sometimes blushed with pink in cool weather). The flowers are not showy, and the foliage browns in hot weather, so cut the plants to the ground in mid- to late summer to get new leaves later on. Dig out and destroy any all-green shoots as soon as you see them, because *P. arundinacea* is considered invasive in many areas. Ribbon grass can tolerate partial shade.

▶ *Schizachyrium scoparium* (little bluestem): Medium-sized, clump-forming warm-season grass. Grown mostly for its slender, upright foliage, which is powder blue in the popular cultivar 'The Blues'. The silvery, tufted seed heads are also attractive, but they may self-sow. Little bluestem is prone to flopping in average to rich, moist soil; relatively dry, not-especially-fertile sites suit it best.

Panicum virgatum 'Dallas Blues'

Clockwise from top right: *Calamagrostis, Schizachyrium,* and *Muhlenbergia*

Grasses (continued)

continued from page 231

little or no new growth in mid- to late summer, or until cooler weather returns. Other than removing any dead or ugly foliage, if you wish, there's not much you need to do for them during this period.

▸ Once the sun-baked days of summer arrive, warm-season grasses grow rapidly and may be in bloom by late summer.

▸ Keep watering spring plantings of ornamental grasses regularly if rain is lacking. Established clumps of most can tolerate some drought.

◐ ◉ Fall & Winter

▸ Set out new plants of cool-season grasses, or move or divide existing clumps, in early fall. Water them regularly for the first month or so during dry spells. When the days are cooler and rains more frequent, new leaves normally appear, and they usually look good through the winter. In mild areas, these grasses may start growing actively again by late winter.

▸ Autumn generally isn't a good time to disturb warm-season grasses, because they're typically at their peak beauty then. The foliage of several kinds takes on bright to pastel colors in fall, then gradually bleaches to brown for the winter. Flowers usually appear in early to midfall, if they haven't already, followed by the seed heads. Clip off the developing seed heads if you want to prevent self-sowing, or leave them for their interesting form. Late winter to early spring is a good time to remove the remaining top growth on warm-season grasses. If the stems are fairly thin, you can use hand shears or hedge shears to snip or shear them

off. For hard-stemmed grasses, you may need loppers, electric hedge clippers, a bow saw, or a string trimmer with a blade attachment to make the cut. Either way, cut off the old stems 4 to 6 inches (10 to 15 cm) above the base of the plant.

And a word of caution: The leaves of some grasses have very sharp edges, so it's wise to wear gloves, long sleeves, and long pants when you're handling them (during cleanup, for example).

▸ Most grasses benefit from a general-purpose organic fertilizer or a shovelful of compost scattered around each clump every year or two in late fall to late winter.

❖ TROUBLESHOOTING

▸ **Leaves and stems sprawl.** Floppy grasses aren't very attractive, and

they can quickly smother nearby companions. It's difficult to stake them effectively, though — especially the tall-growing types — so it may be easier to try other options first. One reason that grasses may sprawl is too-rich soil, so hold off on additional fertilizing unless your soil is especially sandy. Abundant moisture or too much shade can have the same effect, so you could try moving the grasses to a somewhat drier or sunnier spot to reduce the chance of flopping. Sprawling grasses may also benefit from being divided. Another trick you could try is cutting warm-season grasses down to about 6 inches (15 cm) in early summer to get shorter regrowth.

To make cleanup easier with tall or broad clumps of grasses, wrap a bungee cord or a piece of twice snugly around the top growth before you cut, so the stems come off in one tidy bundle.

Gypsophila

BABY'S BREATH

The tiny flowers of baby's breath make great fillers in flower arrangements, and they serve the same purpose in summer beds and borders.

Gypsophila paniculata

BABY'S BREATH GROWS IN CLUMPS of mostly basal, slender, gray-green leaves and many-branched, wiry stems tipped with small but abundant, white or pink, single or double flowers. Common baby's breath (*G. paniculata*) typically grows in airy mounds 2 to 4 feet (60 to 120 cm) tall, while creeping baby's breath (*G. repens*) forms low, spreading carpets between 4 and 8 inches (10 and 20 cm) tall. Both species are usually recommended for Zones 4 to 8 but may also grow in slightly cooler or warmer areas. Be aware that common baby's breath is considered invasive in some areas.

❉ GROWING TIPS

▸ **Light & soil.** The ideal site for baby's breaths has full sun and average, well-drained soil with a pH that's near-neutral to slightly alkaline. The plants can take a few hours of shade but may be more prone to flopping. Sprawling can be a problem on common baby's breath even in sunny sites, so consider growing compact cultivars, such as 'Bristol Fairy' or 'Viette's Dwarf'.

▸ **Division & propagation.** Baby's breath plants tend to die out after a few years, so be prepared to replace them. The clumps generally don't like to be disturbed, but if you must move or divide them, you could try in early spring. (Dig deeply to get as much of the root system as possible.) Seed is another option for propagation: sow seed indoors in late winter or outdoors in fall to early spring; barely cover it with seed-starting mix or soil.

▸ **Potential problems.** Possible pests and diseases include leafhoppers and aster yellows, but they aren't very common.

❉ SEASONAL CARE

◖ Spring

▸ Set out new plants in early to midspring. Space common baby's breath plants 2 to 3 feet (60 to 90 cm) apart and creeping baby's breath about 18 inches (45 cm) apart. Water new plantings occasionally if rain is lacking. Apply a light organic mulch or a gravel mulch before summer. Common baby's breath is prone to sprawling in summer, so consider setting a wire cage or a grow-through support over the emerging clumps. In warm climates, baby's breath may begin blooming in late spring.

◯ Summer

▸ Prime bloom time for baby's breath is commonly early to mid- or late summer. Prop up sprawling stems on common baby's breath with twiggy branches or short

Y-stakes, if needed. Snip off the flowering stems at the base when most of the blossoms are finished to minimize self-sowing and possibly encourage rebloom. Another pruning option is to shear the whole plant lightly (by one-quarter to one-third) to remove the spent blooms and control the size. Keep watering spring plantings during dry spells.

✿ ◉ Fall & Winter

▸ Set out new plants in early fall; water them for the first month or so if rain is lacking. Some flowering may continue into autumn. Once cold weather has killed the top growth, cut the stems to the ground. The basal leaves often look good well into winter. Scatter a general-purpose organic fertilizer or a few handfuls of compost around the clumps every year or two in late fall to late winter.

❉ **DOUBLE TIME** Double-flowered cultivars of baby's breath tend to bloom all summer without deadheading, and they're not prone to self-sowing, either — a plus if you don't want to bother with trimming off the dead flowers to prevent unwanted seedlings.

Helenium

HELENIUM, SNEEZEWEED, HELEN'S FLOWER, DOGTOOTH DAISY

For late-season height and color, heleniums are tough to beat. These clump-forming perennials have upright, branching stems with slender, bright green, toothed leaves.

DAISY-FORM FLOWERS WITH PROMINENT, rounded centers bloom in shades of red, orange, or yellow. Common sneezeweed (*Helenium autumnale*) commonly grows 4 to 5 feet (1.2 to 1.5 m) tall — occasionally to 6 feet (1.8 m).

Hybrid heleniums are often a bit more compact: usually closer to 4 feet (1.2 m) tall. The recommended hardiness range is Zones 3 or 4 to 8.

❁ GROWING TIPS

▶ **Light & soil.** Full sun is best; a site with some morning shade and afternoon sun can be acceptable. Heleniums tolerate average, well-drained soil but perform best where the soil stays dependably moist.

▶ **Division & propagation.** Divide the clumps every 3 to 5 years, preferably in spring, to keep them flowering freely. In ideal growing conditions, helenium clumps can expand quickly; if your plants outgrow their space, divide them more often or replant them about 3 feet (90 cm) apart. Division is also a simple way to propagate your favorite heleniums; spring stem cuttings are another option. It's also easy to start new plants from seed; sow indoors in late winter or outdoors in early spring or fall, and barely cover it.

▶ **Potential problems.** Possible problems include plant bugs, slugs and snails, aster yellows, leaf spots, root rot, and rust; fortunately, these usually aren't common. Powdery mildew may discolor foliage and cause lower leaves to drop, especially if the soil dries out.

❁ SEASONAL CARE

◐ Spring

▶ Set out new plants, or move or divide existing clumps, in early to midspring. Space them about 2 feet (60 cm) apart. Dig a shovelful of compost into each planting hole. Water new plantings regularly if rain is lacking. Apply an organic mulch before summer. If you don't plan to shear your heleniums in summer, consider setting a grow-through support over each emerging clump to prevent the stems from sprawling by bloom time.

◯ Summer

▶ Shear unsupported clumps by about one-half in early to midsummer to encourage bushier growth that's less prone to sprawling. Some hybrids may begin flowering in midsummer, but most start in late summer. Snipping off the spent flowers can extend the bloom period. Keep watering spring plantings regularly if rain is lacking. Established heleniums also benefit from watering during dry spells.

❂ ◉ Fall & Winter

▶ Set out new plants in early fall; water for the first month or so if rain is lacking. Keep deadheading blooming heleniums through early fall. Cut the plants to the ground once all of the flowers are finished. Scatter a general-purpose organic fertilizer or a shovelful of compost around each clump in late fall to late winter.

❁ **STOP THE SPRAWL** Heleniums can be prone to sprawling by bloom time, so it's a good idea to cut them back earlier in the season. If you shear them in early summer, it won't have much effect on their bloom time. Shearing in midsummer may delay flowering for a few weeks.

Helenium 'Flammenspiel'

Helianthus

PERENNIAL SUNFLOWER

Perennial sunflowers may not have the huge blooms of their annual cousins, but they carry their flowers in such abundance that they can provide just as much garden impact.

THE UPRIGHT, BRANCHING STEMS of *Helianthus* carry deep green, heart-shaped or lance-shaped leaves and are topped with bright yellow single, semidouble, or double blooms in summer and fall. There are quite a few species and even more cultivars to choose from.

Among the relatively shorter options are thin-leaved sunflower (*H. decapetalus*) and many-flowered sunflower (*H. × multiflorus*), which generally form expanding clumps in the range of 3 to 6 feet (90 to 180 cm) tall, with flowers from mid- or late summer to early or midfall. These two are generally recommended for Zones 4 to 8. Hybrid 'Lemon Queen' shares the same bloom period but is taller — usually in the range of 6 to 8 feet (1.8 to 2.4 m). Other tall-growing species that bloom slightly later include swamp sunflower (*H. angustifolius*) for Zones 6 to 9; Maximilian or prairie sunflower (*H. maximiliani*) for Zones 4 to 9; and willow-leaved or narrow-leaved sunflower (*H. salicifolius*) for Zones 5 to 9. These three can reach anywhere from 4 to 9 feet (1.2 to 2.7 m) or possibly even taller, depending on the growing conditions.

❀ GROWING TIPS

▸ **Light & soil.** Perennial sunflowers tend to grow and bloom best in full sun; thin-leaved sunflower, however, usually prefers light shade. Average, well-drained soil is generally fine. Established clumps can be quite drought-tolerant, but they also adapt well to ample moisture.

▸ **Division & propagation.** Perennial sunflower clumps get large quickly and need to be divided in spring every 3 or 4 years (or sooner, if they aren't blooming well) to control their size and stay vigorous and healthy. Division is also a simple way to propagate the plants. Or, take stem cuttings in late spring or early summer. Sow seed outdoors in fall or early spring or indoors in late winter; barely cover it. Some species (particularly swamp sunflower) can self-sow prolifically.

▸ **Potential problems.** Possible problems include aphids, caterpillars, plant bugs, slugs and snails, powdery mildew, and rust; these usually aren't serious enough to need control, though.

❀ SEASONAL CARE

◑ Spring
▸ Set out new plants, or move or divide existing clumps, any time during the spring. Perennial sunflower clumps can expand quite a bit, so space them about 3 feet (90 cm) apart to avoid overcrowding. Or, set them about 18 inches (45 cm) apart, then divide them every year or two. Water new plantings regularly if rain is lacking. Apply an organic mulch before summer.

◔ Summer
▸ Perennial sunflowers — especially the very tall kinds — can be prone to sprawling as the summer progresses, but staking such big plants can be challenging. Pruning to control their size is a much more practical option. You could cut them back by about one-half in early summer, and again by about one-third in midsummer if desired. On the latest-blooming kinds — swamp sunflower, Maximilian sunflower, and willow-leaved sunflower — you can cut again in late summer. (If you want these giants to be significantly shorter at bloom time, you can cut them by as much as two-thirds in late summer and usually still get blooms before frost, at least in warmer zones.) It's generally best to stop pruning once the flower buds form. Flowering may begin as early as midsummer for some species; others start in late summer or even later. Keep watering spring plantings regularly if rain is lacking. Established plantings benefit from an occasional soaking during extended dry spells.

✪ ◉ Fall & Winter
▸ Set out new plants in early fall; water them regularly for the first

❀ **FEED THE BIRDS** Perennial sunflowers are dependable choices for colorful summer-to-fall flowers, but that's not all they have to offer! Their seed heads hold up well long after the growing season ends, and their seeds are a favored food for many wild birds, so you may want to leave them standing through the winter.

Helianthus angustifolius

month or so if rain is lacking. Perennial sunflowers that started blooming in midsummer are usually finishing by early fall, while others are just coming into flower then. Where the growing season is very short, swamp sunflower and willow-leaved sunflower may not have time to bloom before frost; in mild climates, they may continue flowering through late fall. If you notice more than a few perennial sunflower seedlings appearing after a few years, you may want to cut the plants down after frost to prevent self-sowing; otherwise, you can wait until late winter or early spring for cleanup. Scatter a general-purpose organic fertilizer or a shovelful of compost around each clump in late fall to late winter.

Heliopsis

OXEYE, FALSE SUNFLOWER

Heliopsis helianthoides 'Helhan'

If you're looking for lots of summer color without a lot of work, oxeye (*Heliopsis helianthoides*) is definitely worth considering.

THE UPRIGHT, BRANCHING STEMS grow in dense, bushy clumps anywhere from 3 to 6 feet (90 to 180 cm) tall, with bright golden yellow single, semidouble, or double flowers through the summer. Oxeye is recommended for Zones 3 to 8 or 9.

❖ GROWING TIPS

▸ **Light & soil.** Oxeyes can grow in full sun or partial shade. They thrive in evenly moist, compost-enriched soil but also adapt well to average, well-drained soil.

▸ **Division & propagation.** Divide the clumps every 3 to 4 years in spring or fall for propagation or to keep them vigorous and flowering freely. You can also take stem cuttings in late spring to early summer, or sow seed (and barely cover it) indoors in late winter or outdoors in early spring or early fall.

▸ **Potential problems.** Slugs and snails, leaf spots, powdery mildew, and rusts may bother the plants but usually aren't serious enough to require control measures.

❖ SEASONAL CARE

◑ Spring

▸ Set out new plants, or move or divide existing clumps, in early to midspring. Space them about 2 feet (60 cm) apart. Water new plantings regularly if rain is lacking. Apply an organic mulch before summer. Oxeyes normally don't need staking, but if your plants sprawled in previous years or if they're growing in some shade or in rich, moist soil, consider cutting them back by about one-half in late spring.

◎ Summer

▸ Oxeyes typically begin blooming in early summer and continue through midsummer, at least. (Those cut back in late spring generally start in midsummer and bloom into early fall.) If you keep the dead flowers snipped off, the plants often continue to bloom through late summer. Deadheading can also prevent over-abundant self-sowing. Keep watering spring plantings regularly if rain is lacking. Established clumps tolerate drought but benefit from an occasional soaking during extended dry spells.

◐ ◉ Fall & Winter

▸ Set out new plants, or move or divide existing clumps, in early fall. Water new plantings regularly for the first month or so if rain is lacking. Keep removing any remaining faded flowers to prevent self-sowing, then cut down the dead stems after frost; otherwise, leave them standing through the winter so birds can enjoy the seeds. Scatter a general-purpose organic fertilizer or a shovelful of compost around each clump in late fall to late winter.

❖ TROUBLESHOOTING

▸ **Stems and buds covered with small red insects.** If you grow oxeyes, it's almost inevitable that the plants will have red aphids. These pests generally appear in late spring or early summer and may cluster in large numbers on the stems. You may also see a sticky clear coating (excess sap, called honeydew, excreted by the aphids) or a black substance (sooty mold fungus that grows on the honeydew) on the foliage. Usually, rubbing the pests off the stems with your fingers a few times several days apart is enough to keep them from causing serious damage; if needed, you could try spraying with insecticidal soap. Or, simply shear infested plants back by about one-third to remove the pests; the plants will regrow and flower a bit later in the season.

❖ **WEED OUT THE GREENS** The variegated oxeye known as Loraine Sunshine (*Heliopsis helianthoides* 'Helhan') often produces variegated seedlings. Keep the ones that are heavily marked with white, if you wish, but pull out any that are solid green; otherwise, they may end up crowding out the variegated plants.

Helleborus

HELLEBORE, LENTEN ROSE, CHRISTMAS ROSE

When it comes to low-maintenance perennials, hellebores have to rank near the top of the list.

THESE CLUMP-FORMERS OFFER beautiful spring blooms and handsome, deeply divided, evergreen foliage on sturdy, adaptable plants that never need staking and are seldom bothered by pests or diseases. There are well over a dozen species and several hybrids, but only a few are commonly available, and they all fall into one of two main types.

The stemless, or acaulescent, hellebores send up their leaves and their flowering stems separately and directly from the ground. This group includes the Lenten roses (*Helleborus × hybridus*, also known as Orientalis Hybrids), with single, semidouble, or double flowers in white or many shades of pink, red, deep purple, and yellow, as well as bicolors. These beauties result from crosses between *H. orientalis* and various other species, so their height and hardiness can vary, but most are in the range of 12 to 18 inches (30 to 45 cm) tall and hardy in Zones 4 or 5 to 9. Christmas rose (*H. niger*) tends to be shorter — usually no more than 1 foot (30 cm) tall — and starts blooming several weeks earlier, with white flowers that may take on pink tinges as they age. Zones 4 to 8.

Stemmed, or caulescent, hellebores produce upright stems that carry both leaves and flowers. Individual stems die after flowering. Stinking hellebore (*H. foetidus*) has

Helleborus foetidus

narrowly divided leaves with many leaflets, while Corsican hellebore (*H. argutifolius*; also known as *H. corsicus*), *H. lividus,* and *H. × sternii* have three-part leaves. All four bear green flowers, sometimes rimmed with red on stinking hellebore or tinged with pink on *H. lividus* or *H. × sternii.* Stinking hellebore can reach 2 to 3 feet (60 to 90 cm) tall in full bloom. Corsican hellebore grows 2 to 3 feet (60 to 90 cm) tall, while *H. lividus* normally stays about 1 foot (30 cm) tall; *H. × sternii,* which is a cross between those two species, can be anywhere from 1 to 3 feet (30 to 90 cm) tall. Hardiness is usually Zones 4 or 5 to 9 for stinking hellebore and Zones 6 or 7 to 9 for the other stemmed types.

❖ GROWING TIPS

▸ **Light & soil.** Hellebores are typically touted as shade plants, and they do perform well in partial or even full shade with average, well-drained soil. Ample light encourages much faster growth and more abundant flowering, though, so don't hesitate to try them in a site with morning sun and afternoon shade, or — in cooler zones — even in full sun if the soil doesn't completely dry out. Avoid wet sites, though; hellebores hate soggy soil. A soil pH that's near-neutral to slightly alkaline is a plus.

▸ **Division & propagation.** Lenten roses, Christmas roses, and other stemless hellebores may take several years to fill out and bloom well; once settled in, though, they can live many years without needing division. (If you wish, you can divide them in late summer to early fall or early to midspring for propagation.) The stemmed hellebores grow more quickly but are also more likely to die out after several years. These types don't like to be divided, so it's a good idea to let them self-sow a bit to get replacement plants. To start any hellebores from seed, sow fresh seed about ¼ inch (6 mm) deep outdoors in late summer. Or, simply transplant self-sown seedlings.

▸ **Potential problems.** Slugs and snails, aphids, black vine weevils, and powdery mildew. (Also see Troubleshooting, page 242.) Many authorities claim that hellebores are deer-proof, but that's not always the case. Note that hellebore sap can irritate sensitive skin, so it's a good idea to wear gloves when working around the plants.

❋ SEASONAL CARE

◐ Spring

▸ Set out new plants in early to mid-spring. If you must divide Lenten roses, Christmas roses, or other stemless types, you could do it then, too. Space the plants 18 to 24 inches (45 to 60 cm) apart. Work a shovelful of compost into the planting hole. Water new plantings regularly if rain is lacking. Apply an organic mulch before summer.

▸ Most hellebores are in peak bloom in early to midspring, and they often hold some color well into late spring while their seedpods form. Cut off the finished flower stalks right at ground level if you want to prevent self-sowing. New foliage growth (either new leaves or new leafy stems) usually begins to appear in mid- to late spring.

◉ Summer

▸ If you didn't remove the spent flowers, they usually ripen and drop their seed in early to midsummer. By this time, the pods on stemless hellebores are usually hidden by the foliage; you can leave them or remove them. On stemmed hellebores, the stems that flowered in spring tend to sprawl as their seed forms; cutting them off at ground level isn't necessary but can make the clumps look tidier. Keep watering spring plantings occasionally during dry spells. Divide the stemless types, if needed, in late summer.

✜ ☉ Fall & Winter

▸ Set out new plants, or move existing clumps, in early fall. If you need to divide the stemless types and didn't get to it in late summer, do it as early in fall as possible. Water new plantings regularly for the first month or two if rain is lacking. Scatter a general-purpose organic fertilizer or a shovelful of compost around each clump in late fall to late winter. Adding 1 to 2 inches (2.5 to 5 cm) of organic mulch can improve the odds of winter survival in northern gardens, especially on first-year plantings.

▸ On the stemmed types, mature stems start producing flower buds as fall progresses. In mild climates or very protected sites in cooler zones, Christmas roses and the stemmed hellebores may begin flowering in mid- to late winter; Lenten roses may open some blooms by late winter. Hellebore leaves are usually evergreen, but if the foliage gets damaged during the winter weather, you can snip it off. If desired, cut off all of the old foliage on stemless types before the end of winter to make it easy for the new flowers to emerge.

❋ TROUBLESHOOTING

▸ **Leaves have dark spots or turn yellow; flowers fail to open.** Hellebore leaf spot, also known as hellebore black spot, causes irregular brown to black patches on the foliage; some leaves may turn yellow and die. Affected flower stems may wilt, and their buds may fail to open. Symptoms are especially noticeable in spring. Cut off and destroy affected leaves and flower stems immediately to prevent the spread of this disease. If your plants were affected in past years, cut off all the leaves of your stemless hellebores in late fall.

▸ **Flowers aren't the color you expect.** Seed-grown Lenten roses often don't exactly resemble the plants that produced them. If you want a specific color, buy blooming plants so you can check the flowers for yourself. Or, grow seedlings in a holding bed until they reach flowering size, then move them to your garden once you see what color they are. Sometimes seedlings sprout right next to established clumps, giving the appearance of two colors on the same plant.

If you don't want your hellebores to self-sow — which they can do prolifically in ideal growing conditions — remove the spent bloom stalks in late spring. Otherwise, let the seeds drop in summer, and as seedlings appear over the next few years, transplant them to a holding bed or to other parts of your garden.

Hemerocallis

DAYLILY

Daylilies are the darlings of the summer garden, adding an abundance of colorful flowers in a wide range of colors.

UNLIKE TRUE LILIES (*LILIUM*), which grow from a scaly bulb with a single leafy stem, daylilies produce clumps of tuberous roots. Each daylily plant is composed of a fan of long, slender basal leaves, along with one or more branching, leafless flower stems bearing single to double, trumpet-shaped flowers. Shades of yellow and orange are the most common, but you can find hybrids in just about any color but true blue.

The species and hybrids also come in a wide range of heights, from barely 1 foot (30 cm) to nearly 5 feet (1.5 m) tall in bloom. The upright to arching leaves may be evergreen, deciduous, or semievergreen (keeping their leaves in mild-winter areas and dying back to the ground in colder areas). Most daylilies grow in distinct clumps, but the common orange-flowered tawny daylily (*H. fulva*),

Hemerocallis 'Midnight Oil'

also called ditch lily or tiger lily, spreads by rhizomes to form large patches. The hardiness of the many daylily species and hybrids varies: most are fine in Zones 5 to 9 or 10, and some are winter hardy as far north as Zone 3. Note that both tawny daylily and lemon lily (*H. lilioasphodelus*) are considered invasive in some areas.

❁ GROWING TIPS

▸ **Light & soil.** Daylilies typically thrive in full sun, but where summers are hot, a site with morning shade and afternoon sun, or light all-day shade, is fine, too, especially for those plants with light-colored flowers. Moist but well-drained, compost-enriched soil is ideal, but the plants readily adapt to less-than-perfect conditions, as long as the soil doesn't stay soggy.

▸ **Division & propagation.** Divide daylily clumps (ideally in spring or early fall) every 4 to 5 years, or more often if you notice they're not blooming as well as in previous years. Division is also the quickest and easiest way to propagate your favorites. Hybrids won't come true from seed, but if you want to try raising your own plants, sow seed about ¼ inch (6 mm) deep outdoors in fall or spring. Or, sow indoors in mid- to

late winter, then place the pots in a plastic bag and refrigerate for 4 to 6 weeks before moving them to a warm, bright place.

▸ **Potential problems.** Aphids, earwigs, Japanese beetles, plant bugs, root-knot nematodes, slugs and snails, leaf streak (a fungal disease), and crown rot (also called bacterial soft rot). (Also see Troubleshooting, page 244.)

❁ SEASONAL CARE

◐ Spring

▸ Cut off any remaining top growth in early spring. Set out new plants, or move or divide existing clumps, any time during the spring. Space dwarf types about 1 foot (30 cm) apart and

others 18 to 24 inches (45 to 60 cm) apart. The crown (the buds, or the base of the leaves) should be just below the soil surface. Water new plantings regularly if rain is lacking. Add an organic mulch before summer. A few daylilies, such as lemon lily, begin flowering in mid- to late spring in warmer climates

◎ Summer

▸ Some daylily species and hybrids begin blooming in early summer; peak bloom time for most, though, is midsummer into late summer. Picking off the spent flowers frequently keeps the plants looking tidy — especially on the thick-petaled, tetraploid types, which look droopy

❁ **EPHEMERAL BEAUTY** Individual daylily blooms usually last only one day. Some open in the morning and close in early evening; others open in late afternoon and close the next morning.

Hemerocallis (continued)

and mushy as the petals shrivel — but it's not absolutely necessary, because the dead flowers eventually drop off on their own. If you do decide to remove the faded blooms, break or cut them off at the stem, making sure you get the base of the bloom, too. Once all of the blooms on a stalk have finished, cut that stalk off close to the base. Reblooming daylilies often send up new flowering stalks as the summer progresses.

▸ By late summer, the leaves of your daylilies may start to discolor and look ugly. On reblooming types, simply reach in and snap off any damaged leaves at their base so you don't damage the emerging flowering stems. On the others, it's easiest to cut off all the top growth just above the ground or back to any new leaves that have already emerged, then give the plants a good soaking if the ground is dry. They'll usually resprout by early fall and provide a clump of fresh-looking foliage for autumn.

▸ Keep watering spring plantings through the summer if rain is lacking. Established clumps can tolerate a fair bit of drought but flower best with occasional soakings during extended dry spells.

✪ ☉ Fall & Winter

▸ Set out new plants, or move or divide existing clumps, in early fall. Water new plantings regularly for the first month or so if rain is lacking. The leaves of deciduous daylilies usually wither away on their own after a few frosts. Others stay green through part or all of the winter; it's fine to cut off any leaves that get damaged by winter weather at any point. Scatter a general-purpose organic fertilizer or a shovelful of compost (or both) around each clump in late fall to late winter.

Deadheading a daylily

✿ TROUBLESHOOTING

▸ **Emerging leaves twisted and distorted, often with browned, chewed-looking edges or holes.** A phenomenon known as "spring sickness" occasionally affects daylilies early in the growing season. Sometimes, only part of a clump is affected, appearing distinctly stunted compared to the rest of the plant. The exact cause isn't currently known. The plants often outgrow the damage, but it's probably a good idea to cut off and destroy affected foliage.

▸ **Leaves with yellow to brown patches or streaks.** Daylily rust is a fungal disease that can cause discolored areas on the surface of the foliage and a powdery orange-yellow "dust" on the undersides. Seriously affected leaves may turn completely yellow and die. Cut off and destroy damaged leaves as soon as you notice them. Avoid buying or trading plants that show symptoms. If you've had problems with daylily rust in the past, look for cultivars described as being rust resistant. It is thought that the disease spores may overwinter on another perennial, known as *Patrinia*, so you may want to avoid planting patrinias if you're already growing many daylilies.

▸ **Leaves with pale streaking; flower buds distorted or fail to open.** Thrips are so tiny that you may not actually see them, but you can see the damage they cause to leaves and buds. You may also notice distorted new leaves or raised brown patches on the flower stems. Beneficial insects usually keep thrips in check, but if damage is serious, you could try spraying with insecticidal soap.

Heuchera

HEUCHERA, CORAL BELLS, ALUMROOT

For sun or shade, for foliage or flowers: You name the site or the use, and there's probably a heuchera to fill it.

THERE ARE SO MANY HEUCHERAS TO CHOOSE FROM that selecting the right kind for the conditions you have available can be a bit tricky, but once you have a good match, the plants typically don't take much care. As a group, heucheras share a number of basic traits: a clump-forming habit; evergreen leaves that are often lobed and rounded or heart-shaped; and relatively small blooms along the tops of separate, upright stems. The height in leaf is usually about 1 foot (30 cm), with the flower stems anywhere from 18 to 30 inches (45 to 75 cm) tall.

It used to be that the best-known heucheras were those grown primarily for their flowers. Coral bells (*Heuchera sanguinea*) produces rosettes of rich green to grayish green leaves with showy red, scarlet, pink, or white flowers. Hybrid coral bells (*H. × brizoides*) look basically similar but tend to be a bit more heat tolerant. These plants are normally hardy in Zones 3 to 8.

There are also a number of heucheras prized mostly for their foliage. As a group, they're often referred to as alumroots. American alumroot (*H. americana*) has silver- or gray-mottled green leaves, small-flowered alumroot (*H. micrantha*) has ruffled green leaves, and hairy alumroot (*H. villosa*) has larger-than-usual leaves; all three gener-

Heuchera americana 'Dale's Strain'

ally have small, greenish to white flowers. Zones 4 to 9.

Thanks to busy plant breeders, gardeners no longer have to settle for either showy flowers or exciting foliage: they can have both. Hybrid heucheras bloom in white or shades of red to pink, and their leaves come in a wide range of colors, including green, yellow, orange, maroon, purple, black, and silver. They're usually recommended for Zones 4 to 9.

❇ GROWING TIPS

▶ **Light & soil.** Generally, heucheras thrive in full sun (especially in cooler areas) to full shade. Ample sun encourages the best flowering, but intense sunlight can discolor the leaves, especially on those with peachy foliage. Shady sites can encourage lush leafy growth, but the plants won't bloom well. A site with morning sun and afternoon shade is often an ideal compromise. Somewhat moist but well-drained, compost-enriched, slightly acid soil is ideal. If your soil is on the soggy or clayey side, try growing heucheras in raised beds.

▶ **Division & propagation.** After a few years, the foliage rosettes may develop bare, woody bases. Topdressing the crowns with topsoil, mulch, or compost to cover the bare parts may help for a season or two, but it's usually best to dig up the whole clump in spring or fall, deepen the planting hole, and reset the clump so the base of the foliage is at ground level. Or, take the opportunity to divide the clump — ideally in spring — by breaking off the woody bases where they join, replanting the individual rosettes (don't worry if they have few or no roots), and discarding the remainder.

Division is also the best way to propagate your favorites. To grow

❇ **TOUGH CUSTOMERS** Hot, humid summers can be tough on many heucheras, but some kinds are better adapted than others to those challenges. So if you garden where summers are sultry, consider trying American alumroot (*H. americana*), hairy alumroot (*H. villosa*), and hybrids that have their "blood."

heucheras from seed, sow outdoors in fall to early spring or indoors in late winter; don't cover it.

▸ **Potential problems.** A few possible problems include leaf spots, rust, and powdery mildew (particularly on coral bells). (Also see Troubleshooting, below.)

❧ SEASONAL CARE

◐ Spring

▸ Pinch or cut off any winter-damaged foliage in early spring. Set out new plants, or move or divide existing clumps, in early to midspring. Space the clumps 12 to 18 inches (30 to 45 cm) apart. Water new plantings regularly if rain is lacking. Add an organic mulch before summer. Some coral bells begin blooming in late spring.

◎ Summer

▸ Early to midsummer is peak bloom time for most heucheras. Pinch or cut off the finished flower stems close to the base to promote rebloom (or remove them before the flowers open if you'd rather show off the foliage). Trim off older leaves that look damaged or discolored, if needed. Keep watering first-year plantings regularly if rain is lacking. Established plants also appreciate occasional watering during dry spells.

✪ ◉ Fall & Winter

▸ South of Zone 6, set out new plants, or move or divide existing clumps, in early fall. Water new plantings regularly for the first month or so. Hairy alumroot generally begins blooming in early fall; the others are normally done by then. Heuchera leaves usually look good through most or all of the winter. It's

Heuchera 'Dolce Key Lime Pie'

not unusual for green-leaved heucheras to take on reddish to purplish colors during the colder months. Scatter a general-purpose organic fertilizer or a shovelful of compost around each clump in late fall to late winter.

▸ Alternating freezing and thawing may push plants out of the ground, especially those planted in fall; prevent this frost heaving with a winter mulch. Spread mulch over the roots of unprotected clumps that get heaved until you can replant them in spring.

❧ TROUBLESHOOTING

▸ **Plants wilt and die.** One possible cause is a fungal disease called stem rot, particularly on coral bells. Remove and destroy affected plants. Prevent by choosing a site with excellent drainage. Crown damage caused by insect feeding is another possibility. The larvae of black vine weevils and strawberry root weevils are curved, white, brown-headed grubs that feed inside the crowns mostly in winter; adults cause chewed leaf edges in summer. Dig or cut out affected rosettes. To prevent further infestation, try drenching the soil around remaining clumps with parasitic nematodes (ideally *Heterorhabditis* genus) in summer to early fall.

❧ **OLDIES BUT GOODIES** Hybrid heucheras can vary widely in their sun tolerance, cold hardiness, disease resistance, and other traits. If you've had mixed luck with them, hold off on buying the latest-and-greatest introductions and instead look for slightly older cultivars that have grown well for other gardeners in your area.

Hibiscus

HARDY HIBISCUS, MALLOW

Hardy or perennial hibiscus can add a touch of the tropics to even distinctly nontropical climates.

THE KIND MOST COMMONLY GROWN in perennial gardens is known as common rose mallow or swamp rose mallow (*Hibiscus moscheutos*). It grows in bushy clumps of upright stems anywhere from 2 to 8 feet (60 to 240 cm) tall, with lobed, roughly heart-shaped leaves, plus extra-large, saucer-shaped red, pink, or white blooms from midsummer into fall. Zones 4 or 5 to 10.

Hibiscus moscheutos 'Luna Mix'

❖ GROWING TIPS

▸ **Light & soil.** Full sun is best. Light shade is acceptable, but the clumps won't bloom as freely and may be prone to flopping. Rose mallows thrive with a steady supply of moisture and perform well even in soggy sites. They can grow in average, well-drained soil, too, but then they may need regular watering during dry spells to look their best.

▸ **Division & propagation.** Rose mallow clumps seldom *need* to be divided, but if you *want* to divide them, spring is a good time. Take stem cuttings in summer to propagate your favorites. Or sow seed outdoors in fall or indoors in mid- to late winter after soaking it overnight in warm water; barely cover it with soil or seed-starting mix.

▸ **Potential problems.** Aphids, caterpillars, scale, whiteflies, leaf spots, and rust, but these usually aren't serious. Japanese beetles can quickly reduce the leaves to a lacework of veins; hand-pick and destroy these pests frequently (once or twice a day, if possible) to minimize the damage.

❖ SEASONAL CARE

◐ Spring

▸ Set out new plants, or move or divide existing clumps if absolutely necessary, any time in spring. Space them 3 to 4 feet (90 to 120 cm) apart. Dig a shovelful of compost into the hole at planting time. Water new plantings regularly if rain is lacking. Apply an organic mulch before summer. New shoots may not appear until late spring, or even later: a good reason to leave a bit of a stub as a marker when you cut down the dead stems in fall or winter.

◯ Summer

▸ If your rose mallow plants were taller than you liked last year, you can reduce their height by cutting them back by about one-half in early summer. Flowering usually starts in midsummer, with each flower lasting about a day. Frequent deadheading helps to keep the plants looking tidy,

minimizes self-sowing, and may extend the flowering period. Pinch or cut off damaged or dead leaves as needed. Keep watering spring plantings regularly if rain is lacking. Established clumps also benefit from watering during dry spells if their soil doesn't naturally stay moist.

✿ ◉ Fall & Winter

▸ Fall generally isn't a good time to plant or move rose mallows, except perhaps in the warmest parts of their hardiness range. Bloom often continues until frost. Stop deadheading by early fall to have some seed heads for later interest, or continue if you want to prevent self-sowing. If you want to tidy up the plants after frost, cut down the bare stems to about 6 inches (15 cm). Scatter a general-purpose organic fertilizer or a shovelful of compost (or both) around each clump in late fall to late winter. A winter mulch is helpful in northern zones.

❖ **BRING ON THE HEAT** The combination of heat and humidity, which is difficult for so many popular perennials to handle, is no problem for rose mallows (*Hibiscus moscheutos*). These sturdy plants normally don't require staking, but you may need to prop up the flower-filled stems in windy sites.

Hosta

HOSTA, PLANTAIN LILY

Hostas are the darlings of the shade garden, providing months of color and textural interest with a minimum of maintenance.

THERE ARE MANY hundreds of hosta species, hybrids, and cultivars to choose from to fit just about any site. Fortunately, it's not necessary to know exactly which species or hybrids you're growing, because they mostly have the same basic care needs.

Generally, hostas grow in dense clumps of lance- to heart-shaped leaves that may be green, yellow, or powder blue, often with stripes, margins, or other markings in white or shades of cream, green, or yellow. The white to purple flowers are produced above the foliage on upright stems in summer or fall and may be trumpet to funnel shaped. The leafy clumps can range in height from barely 6 inches (15 cm) to 3 feet (90 cm) or more, and the flowering stems can add another 4 to 12 inches (10 to 30 cm) to the total height. Hostas are generally recommended for Zones 3 to 8.

Hosta 'June'

❖ GROWING TIPS

▸ **Light & soil.** A site in light shade is generally ideal for hostas. They can perform well in full shade — especially those with all-green or mostly green leaves — but they may grow slower there. A site with morning sun and afternoon shade is usually fine, too. Even all-day sun can be acceptable in cool climates, although too much sun can cause the leaves of heavily variegated or yellow-leaved hostas to scorch (turn brown) if the soil dries out, and blue-leaved types may turn greenish. Evenly moist but well-drained, compost-enriched soil encourages the most vigorous growth.

▸ **Division & propagation.** It may take small starter plants 3 to 5 years (or even longer) to fill out and look their best. They can grow in one spot for many years without division, but if they start to look overcrowded or begin to flower poorly, you can divide them in either spring or fall.

Division is so easy that it's also the best way to propagate your favorites. If you feel adventurous, you could try growing hostas from seed; sow outdoors in fall or indoors in late winter and barely cover it with soil or seed-starting mix.

▸ **Potential problems.** Leaf spots, root rot, deer, and voles. Also see Troubleshooting, page 249.

❖ **FROST PROTECTION** Hostas tend to be slow to emerge in spring, which is a good thing, because the emerging shoots can be damaged by frost. If a late frost is predicted, it's worth covering your hostas with a box or bucket for the night to prevent leaf damage. If you forget and the shoots do get nipped, snip off the damaged foliage.

SEASONAL CARE

○ Spring

▶ Set out new plants, or move or divide existing clumps, in early to midspring. Hostas grow rather slowly, so it's fine to space them fairly closely — about 12 to 18 inches (30 to 45 cm) apart at first; then you can dig and divide them in later years if they start looking crowded. If you'd prefer to set the plants at their permanent spacings, check the recommendation on the pot tag or research your chosen hostas to find out their mature size. Water new plantings regularly if rain is lacking. Apply an organic mulch before summer.

◎ Summer

▶ Depending on the variety, your hostas may get flowers at any point during the summer. If you like the way they look, then wait until the blooms wither to clip off the flowering stems near the base. Or, if the blooms have set seed, you may choose to let the seedpods develop for later interest; self-sowing is seldom a problem. Don't care for the flowers? Then snip off the flowering stems near the base as they appear. Keep watering spring plantings regularly if rain is lacking. Established clumps also benefit from occasional watering during dry spells.

○ ◉ Fall & Winter

▶ Set out new plants, or move or divide existing clumps, in early fall. Water new plantings for the first month or so if rain is lacking. Remove frost-killed top growth in fall (especially if your plants have had insect or disease problems), or late winter. Scatter an organic fertilizer or a shovelful of compost (or both) around each clump in late fall to late winter. A winter mulch is beneficial for first-year plantings — particularly those set out in fall.

TROUBLESHOOTING

▶ **Leaves with irregular holes.** Hostas are a favorite food of slugs and snails. In large numbers, these pests can completely skeletonize entire clumps of foliage, leaving only the leaf veins. Hostas with thin, tender leaves are the most susceptible to slugs and snails, while those with thick, heavy-textured foliage — including 'Big Daddy', 'Blue Angel', 'Great Expectations', 'Halcyon', 'Krossa Regal', and 'Sum and Substance', to name just a few — are somewhat resistant (though

It's not unusual for the leaves of blue-leaved hostas to appear more greenish as the growing season progresses. Then there are some variegated hostas that emerge mostly green and develop their markings as the summer goes on ('Paul's Glory' is one), or that emerge with yellow markings that later turn cream to white.

not immune) to damage. Iron phosphate–based slug baits are also helpful. (For more control tips, see Slugs and Snails on page 103.)

▸ **Leaves with stripelike or angular patches that turn yellow, then brown.** Foliar nematodes are tiny, wormlike creatures that aren't readily visible to the unaided eye. They can attack a number of other perennials besides hostas, including anemones and phlox. Other symptoms include stunted or distorted growth; seriously affected plants die. Foliar nematodes spread readily when the leaves are wet. Control is very difficult, so it's usually best to dig up and destroy (don't compost) infested plants.

▸ **Leaves with yellow to brown edges, wilted.** Crown rot (also known as southern blight) can be a serious problem, particularly in the humid South and in the Midwest. The symptoms usually appear after a spell of warm, humid weather. The leaf bases also turn mushy and are easy to pull off. Crown rot can attack many other perennials, as well, and it spreads readily through soil clinging to tools and shoes. Remove and destroy infected plants, and thoroughly clean tools, shoes, and hands after handling infected perennials.

▸ **Leaves with greenish or yellowish mottling, in random patches or along leaf veins; foliage distorted or wrinkled.** A number of viruses can affect hostas, causing a variety of symptoms, but one of special concern is a relatively recent discovery called Hosta Virus X (HVX). In addition to discolored patches, other symptoms include puckering and brown spots. Infected plants might show symptoms in spring and appear normal later in the season, or show no symptoms at all. Sometimes, infected plants are quite attractive (or at least interesting), and some — including 'Breakdance' and 'Leopard Frog', to name just two — have actually been named. HVX isn't immediately fatal, and infected hostas (with or without symptoms) may live for many years with little reduction in vigor. Still, it spreads so readily and *can* produce so much leaf damage that it's not worth taking chances. If you suspect a hosta is infected, the safest route is to dig it up, roots and all, and destroy (don't compost) it. You can spread the virus between hostas on your hands and garden tools, so current recommendations include thoroughly washing your hands after handling any hostas and cleaning tools with rubbing alcohol (wipe and then let dry) or a bleach solution (1 part household bleach to 9 parts water) between handling each plant. To prevent problems, avoid buying or trading any suspect hostas, or any growing near possibly infected clumps.

Hosta 'Breakdance' with Hosta Virus X

Iberis

CANDYTUFT

The compact, shrubby form and handsome foliage of perennial candytuft (*Iberis sempervirens*) make it an excellent choice for lining walkways, edging borders, and covering slopes.

CANDYTUFT'S PLANTS TYPICALLY REACH about 1 foot (30 cm) tall when covered with clusters of bright white blooms, mostly in spring. The flowers may take on pinkish tints as they age. After bloom, the dense, slender, usually evergreen leaves provide interest through most or all of the winter in Zones 3 to 9.

Iberis sempervirens

✿ GROWING TIPS

▶ **Light & soil.** Full sun generally encourages the best flowering and bushiest growth, but perennial candytuft can perform respectably in light shade. Average, well-drained soil is fine; soggy soil is fatal.

▶ **Division & propagation.** Candytufts don't usually need division, but if you want to divide them, right after bloom is a good time; early fall is also fine in mild areas. Or, simply dig up rooted pieces around the outside of the clump. Summer stem cuttings are another way to propagate your favorites. To grow candytuft from seed, sow it about ¼ inch (6 mm) deep outdoors in fall to early spring or indoors in late winter to early spring.

▶ **Potential problems.** Candytufts are occasionally bothered by caterpillars, gray mold (botrytis), powdery mildew, and root-knot nematodes, but these problems aren't very common.

✿ SEASONAL CARE

◐ Spring

▶ Snip or shear off any winter-damaged shoots on established candytuft in very early spring. Set out new plants in early to midspring. Space them about 1 foot (30 cm) apart for a dense groundcover or about 18 inches (45 cm) apart in a border. Water new plantings occasionally if rain is lacking. Apply an organic or gravel mulch before summer. Flowering usually begins in early to midspring and lasts through late spring.

◯ Summer

▶ In cool climates, flowering may continue into early summer; in warm climates, the seedpods are forming by then. Once the flowers drop, regardless of timing, shear your candytuft plants back by about one-third to remove the seed heads and to promote compact, bushy new growth. If your plants are somewhat sprawling or open looking, feel free to cut them

back even harder (by one-half to two-thirds). This can also be a good time to move or divide clumps, if needed. An occasional bloom may appear during the summer months. Keep watering spring plantings and those moved or divided after bloom if rain is lacking. Established plants seldom need supplemental water.

✿◉ Fall & Winter

▶ In Zone 7 and south, it's fine to set out new plants or move or divide existing ones in early fall. Water new plantings for the first month or so if rain is lacking. The return of cool weather can bring out scattered flowers, particularly on plants sold as 'Autumn Beauty' or 'Autumn Snow'. Scatter a general-purpose organic fertilizer or a shovelful of compost around the clumps every other year in late fall to late winter. Candytufts growing in open, windy sites may develop browned leaves or shoots in winter, especially where there isn't a blanket of snow all winter. So, it's a good idea to protect first-year plantings, as well as established clumps that have had winter damage in the past, with a loose, lightweight mulch, such as evergreen branches.

✿ **WHACK IT BACK** If you cut back candytuft (*Iberis sempervirens*) clumps every year after their main flowering period in spring, they tend to stay in dense clumps that look great for the rest of the year.

Iris

IRIS, FLAG

It's hard to imagine a perennial garden without the cheerful blooms and strappy foliage of irises.

THERE ARE SO MANY IRIS SPECIES and selections to choose from, in such a dizzying array of heights and colors, that you're sure to find at least one to complement any combination. The challenge is choosing the right irises for the growing conditions your site has available, because they have such varying growth needs.

Some of the most popular types of perennial irises are the bearded hybrids, which brighten the late spring to early summer garden with large, bold blooms in a veritable rainbow of colors. Height in bloom can be anywhere from 4 inches (10 cm) to 3 feet (90 cm) or more. They grow in spreading clumps of thick, horizontal rhizomes with flattened fans of swordlike, light green to blue-green leaves. Zones 3 to 10. Sweet iris (*Iris pallida*) looks very much like a bearded hybrid, with grape-scented, purple-blue flowers in late spring to early summer on stems that grow 2 to 3 feet (60 to 90 cm) tall. You usually see this iris in one of its variegated forms: white striping on 'Variegata' and yellow striping on 'Aureovariegata'. Zones 4 to 8.

Another traditional favorite for perennial borders is Siberian iris (*I. sibirica*), which has thinner rhizomes and narrower foliage, producing an almost grassy appearance in leaf. In late spring to early summer, blue, purple, white, or yellow flowers bloom atop stems typically 2 to 3 feet (60 to 90 cm) tall.

A number of other irises find their way into perennial gardens. Japanese iris (*I. ensata*; also sold as *I. kaempferi*), for instance, grows 2 to 4 feet (60 to 120 cm) tall, with large, somewhat flattened single or double flowers in white or shades of blue, purple, or pink in early to midsummer. Zones 4 to 9. Louisiana hybrids come in a similar height range — typically 3 to 4 feet (90 to 120 cm) — and usually bloom in late spring (a little earlier in the warmest areas, a little later in cooler zones) in white or shades of yellow, blue, purple, rust, or red. Louisiana hybrids tend to perform better than many other irises in hot-summer areas. They're usually rated for Zones 6 or 7 to 10, but some selections can be hardy several zones farther north.

If you're looking for a more compact iris, consider roof iris (*I. tectorum*), with purple-blue or white flowers in late spring or early summer; it's usually just 12 to 18 inches (30

Iris cristata

to 45 cm) tall. Zones 4 to 9. Crested iris (*I. cristata*) is even smaller — usually about 6 inches (15 cm) in bloom and a little taller in leaf — with blue or white flowers in early to midspring. Zones 3 to 8.

Stinking iris (*I. foetidissima*), also called Gladwyn iris, is something of an oddity in the iris world, because it's grown more for its seeds than its flowers. The not-very-showy, purplish, earlysummer flowers are followed by puffy seedpods that split in fall to reveal showy scarlet seeds. It grows 18 to 24 inches (45 to 60 cm) tall and is usually recommended for Zones 6 to 9.

Another perennial species sometimes grown in gardens is yellow flag iris (*I. pseudacorus*), with yellow flowers in late spring to early summer. It can reach anywhere from 2 to 6 feet (60 to 180 cm) tall, depending on how much moisture it gets, and it can grow in Zones 2 to 9. Unfortunately, this vigorous, adaptable iris can also be invasive in many areas, so think twice before you plant it.

❖ **CAREFUL CLEANUP** It's a good idea to do a thorough cleanup around your irises after frost and again in late winter, removing any dead or damaged foliage; this care can go a long way toward preventing pest and disease problems.

▸ **Light and soil.** While irises vary in the specific conditions they prefer, you'll usually have good luck with them in a site with full sun and evenly moist but well-drained soil. Most can also grow respectably with a half-day of sun or light all-day shade — particularly crested iris, roof iris, and stinking iris — although they may not bloom as freely there. Siberian iris and yellow flag can also grow in wet soil. Japanese and Louisiana irises are good choices for sites that are wet in spring and summer but drier later. Irises that grow from thick rhizomes, such as the bearded hybrids and sweet iris, are a better choice for sites where the soil may dry out occasionally during the growing season. (They also perform well with some moisture, but soggy soil is fatal; raised beds are often an ideal solution where the soil is on the clayey side.) The bearded hybrids seem to prefer slightly alkaline soil, while Japanese and Louisiana irises grow best in acid conditions; the others can adapt to a range of pH levels.

▸ **Division & propagation.** Bearded irises tend to grow quickly and need division every 3 or 4 years in early spring, midsummer, or early fall. Break the rhizomes apart and replant the parts that have a fan of leaves; discard the leafless sections. Yellow flag and Louisiana hybrids can also spread quickly, so you may want to divide them every 3 to 4 years in early spring or early fall to control their spread. On other irises, you could divide every 4 to 6 years or wait until they look overcrowded or start to produce fewer flowers; early spring or early fall is fine for these, too. If the irises you're dividing have leafy growth, cutting the foliage back

Iris pallida 'Variegata'

by one-third to one-half makes the clumps easier to handle; this can also help reduce water loss from the divisions and prevent the wind from pushing them over after replanting.

Division is also an easy and dependable way to multiply your favorite irises. Growing irises from seed produces varying results but can be an interesting project. The different species have different germination preferences, but most respond well to sowing outdoors in fall. Some irises sprout best when their seeds are exposed to light, so it's usually best to leave them uncovered.

▸ **Potential problems.** Quite a number of pests can bother irises, among them aphids, caterpillars, thrips, slugs and snails, root-knot nematodes, botrytis (gray mold),

crown rot, bacterial and fungal leaf spots, mosaic virus, and rust. Fortunately, not all of these attack every iris, and you can prevent or minimize most of them by providing good growing conditions and cleaning up dead iris leaves regularly. (See Troubleshooting, page 255 for some more common problems.)

◐ Spring

▸ Set out new plants, or move or divide existing clumps, in early spring. Set bearded, crested, and sweet irises about 1 foot (30 cm) apart and the others 18 to 24 inches (45 to 60 cm) apart. If the irises you're planting grow from thick rhizomes, set them with the top of the rhizome right at or just below

Iris (continued)

ground level (in loose, sandy soil) or slightly above and left uncovered (in heavier soil). Water new plantings regularly if rain is lacking. Early spring is also a good time to clean up any remaining dead top growth. Apply an organic mulch before summer. (When mulching bearded and sweet irises, be careful not to pile mulch right on the top of the rhizomes; they should be left exposed.) Crested irises may begin flowering in early or midspring, and many others start in mid- or late spring, especially in warmer climates.

◎ Summer

▸ Prime bloom time for many irises continues into early summer. Tall-growing beardeds may need staking to prevent their bloom-laden stems from falling over, especially in windy sites. Iris flowers generally shrivel up and drop on their own, so you don't need to bother with removing the faded blooms, except perhaps on those with very large blossoms, such as bearded hybrids. (Deadheading doesn't extend the bloom period, but it does keep the plants looking tidy.) Once all of the flowers on the plant are done, cut off the bloom stalks at the base unless you want to keep the seed heads for fall and winter interest on Siberian and stinking iris. Remontant (also called repeat-flowering or reblooming) bearded irises, such as 'Immortality', occasionally send up new bloom stalks through the rest of the summer.

▸ Cut or snap off dead or discolored leaves as needed through the summer. If all of the foliage on a clump looks ugly (due to leaf spots, for instance), cut it back by about

You know it's time to divide a stand of irises when it starts to die out at the center of the clump.

two-thirds; it may take several weeks for new foliage to appear. If your bearded or sweet iris clumps need to be divided, you can do it in mid- to late summer.

▸ Keep watering spring plantings regularly during dry spells. Established clumps of bearded and sweet irises can tolerate dry spells once they're finished flowering, while the others appreciate regular watering if their soil doesn't naturally stay moist.

✪ ✪ Fall & Winter

▸ Set out new plants, or move or divide existing clumps, in early fall. Water new plantings for the first month or so if rain is lacking.

Remontant bearded irises may continue flowering well into fall, and the seedpods of stinking iris open in early to midfall to reveal their showy seeds. Louisiana irises usually send up fresh foliage in fall and keep green leaves through the winter; stinking iris also tends to be evergreen. Most other irises can hold good-looking foliage through at least the early part of winter. (Siberian irises also offer a pretty yellow fall foliage color.) Scatter a general-purpose organic fertilizer or a shovelful of compost (or both) around each clump in late fall to late winter. A winter mulch is beneficial for irises that you divided in midsummer or fall.

:: TROUBLESHOOTING

▶ **Leaves with dark green streaking or ragged edges and sometimes rotted at the base; rhizomes hollowed out or soft and foul-smelling.** Iris borer (an insect) and bacterial soft rot (a disease) are serious problems, particularly on bearded and sweet irises but also on other types. Adult borers lay eggs at the base of the plant or on nearby debris in late summer and fall. When the eggs hatch (generally midspring), the larvae tunnel through the leaves, then down into the rhizomes. Their feeding provides ideal entry points for the bacteria that cause the rhizomes to rot, so controlling the borers also helps to minimize this disease problem. If you notice the leaf tunnels in late spring, rubbing or pinching the leaves at that spot may kill the larvae and prevent further damage. Drenching the soil around the plants with parasitic nematodes in late spring to early summer may provide some control once the borers get down to the soil level. The borers usually leave the rhizomes in mid- to late summer, but you may still find the large, brownish to pinkish, dark-headed larvae in the rhizomes if you divide infested bearded iris clumps in midsummer. Cut out any rhizomes that show borer damage or that are soft or show obvious rot symptoms. Removing dead iris leaves and other debris around your iris plants from late summer through late winter can remove many of the eggs and minimize future borer damage. Rot is much more difficult to control and may occur even if borers aren't present. Dig up affected clumps and cut out affected parts. Try letting the remaining rhizomes air dry for a few days before replanting in a new site.

Iris 'Gerald Darby'

Kniphofia

TORCH LILY, RED-HOT POKER, POKER PLANT, TRITOMA

Whether you delight in bright colors or prefer softer pastels, the spiky flowers of torch lilies can add a distinctive touch to your beds and borders.

TORCH LILIES GROW in slowly expanding clumps of spiky, grasslike to swordlike, green to gray-green foliage, with separate, leafless stalks topped in tapering clusters of tubular blooms. There are several species to choose from, but most of the torch lilies commonly available are hybrids with varying traits. Height, for instance, can range from 1 to 5 feet (30 to 150 cm) or more in bloom. The flowers may be scarlet, glowing orange, or rich to pale yellow, or a combination of red, coral, or green buds aging to yellow as the blooms open. Torch lilies are usually recommended for Zones 5 or 6 to 10, though they may be hardy farther north with excellent winter drainage and a dependable snow cover for insulation.

❁ GROWING TIPS

▸ **Light & soil.** Torch lilies typically thrive in full sun but can also grow with morning sun and afternoon shade or light all-day shade (especially in hot climates). The plants perform best with evenly moist soil while blooming, but they prefer that the soil stays dryish in winter.

▸ **Division & propagation.** Torch lily clumps tend to be long lived in the right site, so it's best to leave them alone unless you really need to move or divide them; early spring is a good time to do this in most areas. Division is also an option for propagating your favorites. Another option is to dig up a few offsets from the outside of the clump. Or, sow seed outdoors in fall or early spring or indoors in late winter; barely cover it with soil or seed-starting mix. The seed strain 'Flamenco' may bloom the first year from a mid- to late winter sowing indoors.

▸ **Potential problems.** Other than rot in too-wet sites, torch lilies are seldom bothered by pests or diseases. If you're having trouble with torch lilies not being winter hardy or not blooming well, consider trying other species or hybrids; they can vary widely in their adaptability.

❁ SEASONAL CARE

◐ Spring

▸ Set out new plants, or move or divide existing clumps if necessary, in early spring. Space them about 2 feet (60 cm) apart. Water new plantings regularly if rain is lacking. On established clumps, cut off any remaining top growth 4 to 6 inches (10 to 15 cm) above the ground in early to midspring to make room for fresh new growth. Add an organic mulch before summer. Some hybrids begin to bloom by late spring.

◎ Summer

▸ Early flowering torch lilies continue blooming into summer; others may not start until early, mid-, or late summer. Once all the flowers on a stalk have finished, snip off the stalk close to the base to tidy the plant and possibly encourage rebloom on some selections. Water first-year plantings regularly if rain is lacking. Established clumps also benefit from occasional watering during dry spells, especially during their bloom period.

✪ ☉ Fall & Winter

▸ Some torch lilies continue to bloom into fall or don't even begin until then. The leaves of some types die after frost, while others stay evergreen. North of Zone 7, it's a good idea to gather all the leaves up and tie them together to create a built-in mulch for the crown. For extra protection, you could also mulch the clumps with evergreen boughs or another loose, lightweight mulch, such as straw or pine needles. Scatter a general-purpose organic fertilizer or a shovelful of compost around the clumps every year or two in late fall to late winter.

❁ **HIGH AND DRY** Torch lilies generally perform best with plenty of moisture while they're actively growing and drier conditions in winter. If your garden doesn't naturally provide those conditions but you still want to grow them, choose a site with excellent drainage (perhaps a raised bed, if necessary), then water regularly during the summer.

Kniphofia 'Royal Castle Hybrid'

Lamium

LAMIUM, DEAD NETTLE

If you have shady sites in your yard, or even an entirely shady garden, you know how hard it can be to find perennials that contribute color from both foliage and flowers without requiring much care in return.

LUCKILY, LAMIUMS CAN DO ALL OF THAT. Spotted lamium (*Lamium maculatum*), also known as spotted dead nettle, has trailing stems that root where they touch the soil, and it also produces creeping rhizomes, creating carpets of small, roughly triangular, green or yellow leaves that are usually marked with varying amounts of silver. The stems are 6 to 10 inches (15 to 25 cm) tall and tipped with clusters of purplish pink, light pink, or white flowers. It's usually recommended for Zones 3 to 9.

Yellow archangel (*L. galeobdolon*; also known as *Lamiastrum galeobdolon* or *Galeobdolon luteum*) is somewhat similar, with silver-marked green leaves on trailing, rooting stems. It is much larger, though, reaching to about 18 inches (45 cm), and it is a much more aggressive spreader — too vigorous for a mixed border. 'Herman's Pride' is a good compromise: it has the same pretty yellow flowers as the species and handsome foliage but on clump-forming plants. Zones 4 to 9.

Lamium maculatum

✿ GROWING TIPS

▶ **Light & soil.** Lamiums generally grow best in partial to full shade, though they can also perform well in full sun where summers aren't too hot. Evenly moist but well-drained, compost-enriched soil is ideal, but the plants can adapt well to less-than-perfect sites, too.

▶ **Division & propagation.** Divide the plants in early spring or early fall (south of Zone 6) for propagation or if they look overcrowded. It's also easy to root lamiums from stem cuttings in spring or summer. You'll probably find self-sown seedlings, but they likely won't be as silvery as the plants they came from.

▶ **Potential problems.** Crown rot can be a problem in hot, humid conditions, and slugs and leaf spots may damage the foliage.

✿ SEASONAL CARE

◑ Spring

▶ Set out new plants, or move or divide existing patches, in early spring. Set them 1 to 2 feet (30 to 60 cm) apart. Water new plantings regularly during dry spells. If the foliage on established lamiums looks damaged after the winter, shear the plants back by about one-third to one-half in early spring to get fresh new leaves. Apply an organic mulch in early to midspring. Lamiums usually begin blooming by late spring but may be earlier in warmer areas.

◎ Summer

▶ Lamiums typically continue flowering into early summer, at least. If your lamium patches look open or tired by midsummer, freshen them up by cutting them back — by about one-half on spotted lamium and two-thirds on yellow archangel.

This also removes the faded flowerheads, minimizing self-sowing. Keep watering spring plantings if rain is lacking. Established patches benefit from occasional watering during dry spells.

✦ ☉ Fall & Winter

▶ South of Zone 6, you can set out new plants, or move or divide existing lamiums, in early fall. Water new plantings regularly for the first month or so if rain is lacking. Spotted lamium occasionally blooms into autumn. In mild-winter areas, the plants are evergreen. In cooler areas without dependable snow cover, they may get a little tattered-looking, but they usually hold their color through the winter. Scatter a general-purpose organic fertilizer or a shovelful of compost around the plants every year or two in late fall to late winter.

Lavandula

With pretty flowers, handsome foliage, and unforgettable fragrance, lavenders hold a favored place in the hearts of many gardeners.

THESE SHRUBBY PERENNIALS GROW in woody-based clumps that can be anywhere from 1 to 3 feet (30 to 90 cm) tall, with slender, aromatic, gray-green to silvery gray leaves and dense, spikelike clusters of purple-blue, white, or pink flowers mostly in spring and summer.

English or common lavender (*L. angustifolia;* also sold as *L. officinalis, L. spica,* or *L. vera*) is usually recommended for Zones 5 to 9, but it can be hardy as far north as Zone 3 in areas with excellent soil drainage and a dependable winter snow cover. Lavandin is the common name for hybrids between English lavender and the slightly less hardy, more medicinal-smelling spike lavender (*L. latifolia*). These hybrids start blooming later, are taller, have somewhat larger leaves, and tend to be better adapted to humid conditions than English lavenders. Their suggested hardiness range is usually Zones 5 or 6 to 9.

Lavandula × intermedia 'Grosso'

❋ GROWING TIPS

▶ **Light & soil.** Lavenders love sunshine, so a full-sun site is best. Average, well-drained soil is fine; a pH that's near-neutral to slightly alkaline is a plus. Loose, sandy soil provides excellent drainage, which is critical for healthy growth.

▶ **Division & propagation.** These woody-based plants don't like to be divided, but sometimes their stems root where they touch the ground, and you could transplant these rooted stems in spring. (Established plants may sulk or die after being moved, but if you must do it, try in early spring, and dig a large circle around the clump to keep as many roots as possible.) Another propagation option is stem cuttings in spring or summer. Lavandins don't produce seed, and English lavenders can be slow to sprout and even slower-growing as seedlings. Still, if you want to try, sow seed (and barely cover it) outdoors in fall or early spring or indoors in mid- to late winter. Place the pots of indoor-sown seed in a plastic bag and refrigerate for 4 to 6 weeks before moving them to a bright spot to germinate. Seedlings of indoor-sown 'Lady' English lavender may flower in their first summer.

▶ **Potential problems.** Possible problems include caterpillars, plant

If your soil is on the clayey side, try planting your lavenders in a raised bed or on a slope. In cool areas, lavenders appreciate the extra warmth of a south-facing site close to a building foundation or the base of a wall. A gravel mulch is helpful, too.

It takes most lavenders about 3 years to fill out and bloom their best. Cutting them back every year before or just after bloom keeps them vigorous and flowering freely for many years.

bugs, root rot, and a disease called "shab," which causes black spots and browned stems (remove and destroy infected plants).

❖ SEASONAL CARE

◐ Spring

▶ Set out new plants, or move existing lavender clumps if really needed, in early spring. Water new plantings regularly if rain is lacking. Before summer, apply a thin layer of organic mulch or — better yet — spread a layer of crushed gravel 1 to 2 inches (2.5 to 5 cm) deep around each plant to help to keep the crown and foliage dry.

▶ English lavender may begin blooming in mid- to late spring in warm climates. In cooler zones, your lavender plants may not even begin producing new growth until late spring. If your plants start growing early and look good, leave them alone until after bloom. Otherwise, cut them back by one-third to one-half as soon as you see new foliage appear to remove any winter-damaged shoots and shape the clump. (Every second or third spring, consider cutting by one-half to two-thirds to keep the plants dense and vigorous.)

◎ Summer

▶ Lavandins tend to start blooming several weeks after English lavender, just about the time that the first flush of English lavender flowers is finished. Usually, that means that lavandins look their best in early to midsummer. However, if you trimmed your lavenders back before they flowered, then your English lavender plants may not start blooming until early summer, and the lavandins may be delayed until midsummer. Either way, the summer care mostly consists of snipping or shearing off the spent flower stems after the first flush of bloom on both types to tidy and shape the plants and possibly encourage rebloom. Keep watering spring plantings if rain is lacking. Established lavenders can tolerate drought, but they bloom best if you give them an occasional thorough soaking during dry spells.

✪ ☉ Fall & Winter

▶ It's generally best to leave lavender plants untrimmed in fall and winter, but if you don't like the dried flower stalks left from the later summer rebloom, it's fine to snip them off in autumn; don't cut into the leafy part of the stem, though. Scatter a general-purpose organic fertilizer or a thin layer of compost around each plant every other year in late fall to late winter. Lavenders usually hold their foliage through the winter but may drop their leaves in colder zones. For protection from winter wind and cold, cover them with evergreen boughs.

Leucanthemum

SHASTA DAISY, OXEYE DAISY

These classic yellow-centered, white-petaled daisies are a favorite for summer beds and borders.

SHASTA DAISIES (*Leucanthemum × superbum*; also known as *Chrysanthemum superbum*) grow in distinct clumps of toothed, rich green leaves with upright stems topped in single, semidouble, or double flowers. Height in bloom can be anywhere from 6 inches to 4 feet (15 to 120 cm) tall, depending on the cultivar. Shasta daisies are generally recommended for Zones 5 to 9, but they tend to suffer in hot, humid climates. They can, however, survive the winter a zone or two farther north, particularly if you have depend-able winter snow cover or provide winter protection.

Oxeye daisy (*Leucanthemum vulgare*; also known as *Chrysanthemum leucanthemum*) is a common roadside flower in many parts of the country. Usually growing 12 to 18 inches (30 to 45 cm) tall, it looks very similar to Shasta daisies but has an overall daintier appearance. This adaptable spreader can grow anywhere from Zones 2 to 10. Be aware, though, that it is considered invasive in a number of areas.

❈ GROWING TIPS

▸ **Light & soil.** Give the plants full sun to light shade; in too much shade, the plants tend to be floppy and bloom poorly, if at all. Average, somewhat moist but well-drained soil is fine. Sometimes, it can be a little tricky to get Shasta daisies through their first growing season, and it may take you a few tries to have success with them. Give them plenty of space, because they don't like to be crowded by their companions.

▸ **Division & propagation.** Dividing the plants every 2 to 3 years in spring or fall helps to keep them vigorous and blooming freely; it also slows the spread of oxeye daisies. Division is an easy way to propagate your favorite plants, too. You could also try stem cuttings in summer. Or, sow seed outdoors in fall or early spring or indoors in late winter to early spring; barely cover it. Some seed strains will bloom during their first summer.

▸ **Potential problems.** While the plants are generally healthy and vigorous, potential problems include aphids, caterpillars, earwigs, Japanese beetles, leaf miners, plant bugs, crown and root rots, and leaf spots.

❈ SEASONAL CARE

◐ Spring

▸ Set out new plants, or move or divide existing clumps, in early to midspring. Space dwarf Shasta daisies (such as 'Snowcap', 'Snow Lady', and 'Snow Princess') 12 to 18 inches (30 to 45 cm) apart; set the others 18 to 24 inches (45 to 60 cm) apart. Water new plantings regularly if rain is lacking. To minimize potential flopping in taller types, set grow-through supports over the emerging clumps in early to midspring, or cut back the clumps by about one-third in midspring or one-quarter to one-third in late spring. Apply an organic mulch before summer. Some Shasta daisies begin blooming in late spring.

◐ Summer

▸ Early to midsummer is peak bloom time for most leucanthemums. Removing the spent flowers keeps the bloom display looking fresh, prevents self-sowing (which can be prolific with oxeye daisy, in particular), and possibly extends the flowering season. Snip off dead flowers individually, snipping just above

Relatively Speaking

The crisp white flowers of Shasta daisies are a cheerful sight at the start of summer, and you can enjoy a similar effect at the end of the growing season with Nippon or Montauk daisy (*Nipponanthemum nipponicum*; also sold as *Chrysanthemum nipponicum* or *Leucanthemum nipponicum*). Its woody-based stems are clad in deep green leaves and form dense clumps from 1 to 3 feet (30 to 90 cm) tall. The single blooms open in late summer in the south and in mid- to late fall in cooler areas (if they don't get nipped by frost first). Choose a site with full sun and average, well-drained soil. Cut the stems back to about 6 inches (15 cm) in early spring, then pinch off the stem tips every few weeks through early summer to keep the plants bushy. Zones 5 to 9.

'Becky' Shasta daisy (*Leucanthemum × superbum*) is a popular cultivar that tends to start flowering a few weeks later than the others, with sturdier stems and more dependable rebloom than many other selections.

a bud forming lower down on the stem (if there *is* a developing bud) or cutting off the whole stem at the base. If your plants look floppy, leaf-spotted, or otherwise tattered by late summer, cut the whole clump to the ground for fresh leafy growth. Keep watering spring plantings regularly if rain is lacking. Established clumps also benefit from watering during dry spells. You'll know when they need it, because they're one of the first perennials to wilt if the soil dries out.

○ ☉ Fall & Winter

▸ Set out new plants, or move or divide existing clumps, in early fall. Water them regularly for the first month or so if rain is lacking. Keep removing the dead flowers and flowering stems through the fall. The basal leaves stay green and usually look good through the winter. Scatter a general-purpose organic fertilizer or a shovelful of compost around each clump in late fall to late winter. In gardens north of Zone 5 without a consistent blanket of snow, you may want to protect the clumps with evergreen boughs for the winter.

Liatris

LIATRIS, BLAZING STAR, GAYFEATHER

It's easy to find rounded and daisy-form flowers for the summer garden, but spikes aren't quite so abundant. One perennial that perfectly fits the bill as a vertical accent is liatris.

THIS ADAPTABLE PERENNIAL grows from corms, rhizomes, or tuberous roots to form tight clumps of upright stems with abundant, very slender green leaves. The tops of the stems are lined with fuzzy-looking clusters of blooms in white or shades of pinkish purple. The bloom time is typically mid- to late summer, but it can vary by climate, often starting a month or two earlier in the warmest zones. Height varies, too, depending on the species and the growing conditions, but it's most often in the range of 3 to 5 feet (90 to 150 cm).

Spike gayfeather (*Liatris spicata*), with long, dense flower spikes, is one of the best-known species; the popular compact cultivar 'Kobold', which usually reaches to about 30 inches (75 cm) tall, belongs here. Eastern blazing star (*L. scariosa*), also known as tall gayfeather, and Kansas gayfeather or prairie blazing star (*L. pycnostachya*) are two other similar-looking species. Small-headed blazing star (*L. microcephala*) is a much scaled-down version, reaching just 1 to 2 feet (30 to 60 cm) tall. On these four liatris, the bloom spikes generally open at the top of the spike first, then successively downward. On rough gayfeather (*L. aspera*) and button liatris (*L. ligulistylis*), the spikes are much looser, and the blooms all tend to open around the same time (or from the bottom to the top on rough blazingstar). The hardiness of liatris varies somewhat by species, but they generally perform well in Zones 3 to 9.

❊ GROWING TIPS

▸ **Light & soil.** Liatris thrive in full sun but can often perform well in partial shade, too. Average, well-drained soil is fine. Most liatris appreciate ample moisture in summer, but they're prone to rot in sites that stay soggy year-round. Fertile, compost-enriched soil encourages lush, tall growth, but the stems may be more prone to sprawling.

▸ **Division & propagation.** Liatris clumps can go many years without needing division, but if you want to reduce the size of a large clump, or if you want to propagate a favorite plant, divide it in spring or fall. To grow liatris from seed, sow it outdoors in fall to spring or indoors in late winter; barely cover it. Liatris may also self-sow.

▸ **Potential problems.** Root-knot nematodes, crown or stem rot, leaf spots, powdery mildew, and rust. The roots are often a favorite food of voles.

❊ SEASONAL CARE

◐ Spring

▸ Set out new plants, or move or divide existing clumps, in early spring. If you're starting with potted or existing clumps, space them about 1 foot (30 cm) apart. If you've bought bare-root liatris (they're often sold along with other bulbs), set the corms or roots about 2 inches (5 cm) deep and 4 inches (10 cm) apart. Water new plantings regularly if rain is lacking. Apply an organic mulch before summer. Unless you're growing a naturally compact species or cultivar, it's a good idea to set grow-through supports over the plants in mid- to late spring. In the deep South, liatris may begin blooming by late spring.

◎ Summer

▸ Liatris typically start flowering in early to midsummer in the warmer parts of their growing range; farther north, mid- to late summer is usually peak bloom time. You have several options for handling the stems once the flowers are finished: cut them off near the base to leave a tidy clump of foliage, cut them back by one-third to one-half to possibly get additional flowers, or leave them in place to enjoy the seed heads. Keep watering spring plantings regularly if rain is lacking. Established clumps also benefit from an occasional soaking during dry spells.

❊ **WEED CAREFULLY** Liatris are unmistakable in bloom, but when they sprout in spring, the emerging plants look very much like clumps of grass. Be sure to mark their spot at planting time so you don't accidentally weed them out!

Liatris spicata

✪ ◉ Fall & Winter

▸ Set out new plants in early fall, or move or divide existing clumps once they're done flowering. Water them for the first month or so if rain is lacking. Many liatris continue blooming into early fall, at least. Cut the spent stalks to the ground during fall cleanup or leave them until late winter or early spring so you can enjoy their winter form. Scatter a general-purpose organic fertilizer or a shovelful of compost around each clump in late fall to late winter.

Ligularia

LIGULARIA, GOLDENRAY, GROUNDSEL

The bold foliage of ligularias is so handsome that it's worth growing these perennials for their leaves alone.

Ligularia 'Britt-Marie Crawford'

BIGLEAF LIGULARIA (*LIGULARIA DENTATA*) forms dense mounds that reach 3 to 4 feet (90 to 120 cm) tall, with rounded leaves that range in color from green to purplish green to deep purple, depending on the cultivar. Their orange-yellow, daisy-form flowers are held in clusters. Bigleaf ligularia is recommended for Zones 3 to 9.

Two other species — Shavalski's ligularia (*L. przewalskii*) and narrow-spiked ligularia (*L. stenocephala*) — and their hybrid 'The Rocket' all produce roughly triangular, green leaves, near-black stems, and slender spikes of yellow flowers. They typically reach 4 to 6 feet (1.2 to 1.8 m) in bloom. The leaves of narrow-spiked ligularia are toothed, those of Shavalski's ligularia are deeply cut, and those of 'The Rocket' are jagged-edged. All three are hardy in Zones 4 to 8.

❀ GROWING TIPS

▶ **Light & soil.** If ligularias are growing in a shady site with little or no direct sunlight, they can tolerate average, well-drained soil, but they may wilt after a few dry days in the heat of summer. Where the soil stays constantly moist, they can take full sun; wilting is still a possibility in strong afternoon sun, but the plants will perk up overnight. The ideal site has compost-enriched soil that's moist to wet with light, all-day shade or just a few hours of morning sun.

▶ **Division & propagation.** The plants can stay in one place for many years without division. But if you want to reduce a huge clump or propagate a favorite plant, divide it in spring. To grow ligularias from seed, sow it outdoors in fall to early spring or indoors in late winter; don't cover it. The plants occasionally self-sow.

▶ **Potential problems.** Other than slugs and snails, ligularias are seldom bothered by problems.

❀ SEASONAL CARE

◑ Spring

▶ Set out new plants, or move or divide existing ones, in early spring. Space them about 3 feet (90 cm) apart. If rain is lacking, water new plantings regularly; water established clumps, too, if their soil isn't naturally moist. Apply a generous layer of organic mulch before summer.

◎ Summer

▶ Narrow-spiked ligularia, Shavalski's ligularia, and 'The Rocket' begin blooming in early summer; bigleaf ligularia generally starts in midsummer. When the flowers are finished, leave the stalks to enjoy the seed heads or cut them off to make the plants look tidy. Keep watering spring plantings regularly during dry spells; if rain is lacking, water established plants, too, so their soil stays evenly moist.

✿ ◉ Fall & Winter

▶ Bigleaf ligularia may keep blooming into early fall. Leave any remaining seed heads for winter interest, or cut the plants to the ground after frost. Keep watering first-year plantings through early to midfall if the weather is dry. Scatter a general-purpose organic fertilizer or a shovelful of compost (or both) around each clump in late fall to late winter.

❀ **MOIST, RICH SOIL** The secret to growing great-looking ligularias is simple: moisture, and lots of it! Digging a shovelful or two of compost into their planting hole can also help to get them off to a great start.

Limonium

PERENNIAL STATICE

Long a favorite filler for dried flower arrangements, perennial statice make great fillers in the garden, too.

Limonium latifolium

THEY GROW IN TIGHT ROSETTES of broad lance-shaped to oblong leaves, with slender, branching flower stalks carrying hundreds of tiny blooms. Sea lavender (*Limonium platyphyllum*; also sold as *L. latifolium*) bears light purple-blue flowers and grows about 3 feet (90 cm) tall. Zones 3 to 9. German or Tartarian statice (*L. tataricum*; also known as *L. dumosum, Goniolimon tataricum*, and *Statice dumosa*) appears pale pink when the blooms just open and you see it up close, but it mostly appears to be white; it reaches about 2 feet (60 cm) tall. Zones 4 to 9.

❖ GROWING TIPS

▶ **Light & soil.** Full sun is usually best, but a little afternoon shade can be helpful in hot climates. Average garden soil is fine as long as it's very well drained; loose, sandy, not-especially-fertile soil is ideal. Perennial statice can tolerate alkaline soil, as well as sites that are high in salt (such as in seaside gardens or along paved areas that are treated with de-icing salt in winter).

▶ **Division & propagation.** Perennial statice clumps grow in one spot for many years and produce deep taproots. They can be slow to recover if disturbed, but if you must move them, you could try in early spring, digging deeply to get as much of the root system as possible. Division isn't advisable either, but if your plant has offshoots around the crown, you could try splitting off one or two with a sharp trowel in early spring. Or, sow seed outdoors in fall to early spring or indoors in late winter or early spring; barely cover it.

❖ **LONG-LASTING GOOD LOOKS** It can take perennial statice (*Limonium*) clumps several years to settle in and begin their summer show of dainty blooms. Their tiny true flowers drop off after a few weeks, but they leave behind papery calyces that make the plants look like they're still in bloom into the fall months.

▶ **Potential problems.** Apart from occasional powdery mildew, or root rot in too-wet sites, these plants are generally trouble free.

❖ SEASONAL CARE

◐ Spring

▶ Set out new plants, or move existing clumps if you absolutely must, in early spring. Space sea lavender plants about 30 inches (75 cm) apart and German statice about 18 inches (45 cm) apart. Water new plantings occasionally if rain is lacking. In early to midspring, snip off any winter-damaged leaves. A gravel mulch can help to keep the crown and leaves dry.

◌ Summer

▶ Both sea lavender and German statice generally bloom from mid- to late summer. The flower stems may sprawl a bit. It's difficult to stake them effectively, but you could try propping them up with branching twigs or short linking stakes or Y-stakes. Or, clip off the sprawled stalks at the base, carefully pull them apart, and dry them for use in craft projects. Water spring plantings occasionally during dry spells.

◑ ◓ Fall & Winter

▶ Cut off any remaining flower stalks when they start to discolor, or else let them break down and blow away on their own. The foliage is usually evergreen but may take on reddish tints for the winter. Fertilizer usually isn't necessary.

Linum

FLAX

Perennial flax is invaluable for a burst of blue in the summer garden.

FLAX PLANTS FORM FEATHERY MOUNDS of slender stems lined with short, slender, blue-green leaves. Blue flax (*Linum perenne*) typically grows 12 to 18 inches (30 to 45 cm) tall, with sky-blue (or sometimes white) flowers. Narbonne flax (*L. narbonense*) tends to be slightly taller — 18 to 24 inches (45 to 60 cm) — with deeper blue flowers. Well-established plants of both species can grow 1 to 2 feet (30 to 60 cm) taller than the usual heights.

Individual flax blooms tend to last only one day or less, often dropping by early afternoon on sunny days, but they appear in abundance over a long season. The winter hardiness of both species can vary widely, depending on the growing conditions. In loose, sandy soil, the plants send down deep taproots and may survive as far north as Zone 4 (possibly even Zone 3); in heavier soil, the root system tends to be more shallow and the plants may survive the winter only in Zones 6 or 7 to 9.

❖ GROWING TIPS

▸ **Light & soil.** Perennial flax thrives in full sun and average, dryish, well-drained soil. It tolerates light shade but may bloom poorly and be floppy there.

▸ **Division & propagation.** In ideal conditions, the plants can be long lived, but it's not unusual for them to last only 2 to 4 years in most gardens. They also don't respond well to being moved or divided. Fortunately, it's easy to grow perennial flax from seed sown outdoors in fall to early spring or indoors in late winter or early spring; barely cover the seed with soil or seed-starting mix. Seedlings bloom their first year. The plants may also self-sow freely, providing their own replacements.

▸ **Potential problems.** Apart from occasional problems with aphids or slugs, the main problem with flax is rot if the soil stays wet in winter.

❖ SEASONAL CARE

◔ Spring

▸ Set out new plants, or attempt to move existing clumps if absolutely necessary, in early spring. Space them about 18 inches (45 cm) apart.

Water new plantings occasionally if rain is lacking. A gravel mulch is usually better choice than an organic mulch, especially in sites that don't have perfect drainage. If your flax plants sprawled last year, try cutting them back by about one-half in late spring to get bushier clumps. Untrimmed plants may begin blooming in late spring.

◔ Summer

▸ Once the first flush of bloom has dropped (usually by midsummer), shear the plants by one-third to one-half to promote regrowth and possible rebloom. If your plants do flower again, repeat the shearing in late summer. It's a good idea to leave at least one plant uncut so the seedpods can drop some seed. Water spring plantings occasionally during dry spells. Established clumps tend to be very drought tolerant, but giving them a thorough watering right after you cut them back can encourage regrowth.

✿ ◉ Fall & Winter

▸ In ideal conditions, perennial flax may continue blooming into fall. The foliage generally remains good looking for at least part of the winter, so wait until late winter to cut off the stems near the base. North of Zone 7, you may want to protect your plants with a lightweight winter mulch, such as straw, pine needles, or evergreen branches. Scatter a general-purpose organic fertilizer or a shovelful of compost around the clumps every other year in late fall to late winter.

❖ **HIGH AND DRY** If you want your perennial flax plants to be truly perennial, give them a spot with loose, sandy, dryish soil. They can perform well as annuals in moist, compost-enriched soil, but don't depend on them surviving the winter in that kind of site.

Linum perenne 'Saphyr'

Lobelia

LOBELIA, CARDINAL FLOWER

Hummingbirds and butterflies aren't the only ones attracted by the tubular blooms of lobelias; gardeners enjoy them, too!

THE SPIKY BLOOM CLUSTERS OF LOBELIA generally appear in mid- to late summer, adding rich color just when many other perennials are taking a break.

Cardinal flower (*Lobelia cardinalis*; plants sold as *L. fulgens* and *L. splendens* now belong here, too) bears bright red blooms in spikes 2 to 5 feet (60 to 150 cm) tall, with deep green to red-tinged leaves. It can be hardy in Zones 2 to 9. Great blue lobelia (*L. siphilitica*), also called blue cardinal flower, blooms in shades of blue (or sometimes white) with bright green leaves; it's usually 2 to 3 feet (60 to 90 cm) tall and grows in Zones 3 to 9. Hybrids between these two species are usually sold as *L. × speciosa* or *L. × gerardii*. They bloom in a range of reds, pinks, and purples in spikes 2 to 5 feet (60 to 150 cm) tall, with green, bronze, or deep red foliage. Their hardiness varies but is usually Zones 5 or 6 to 9.

❁ GROWING TIPS

▶ **Light & soil.** Lobelias can grow in full sun in cooler areas but generally perform best in morning sun and afternoon shade or in light all-day shade. Fertile, evenly moist soil is ideal, but the plants can also grow in average, well-drained soil with regular watering.

▶ **Division & propagation.** Even healthy clumps tend to die out after 3 or 4 years. To keep them vigorous, divide every 2 or 3 years in spring or fall. Lobelias will also self-sow if you leave the spent flower stalks in place and have some bare soil (unmulched) areas near them. To start them yourself, sow the tiny seed outdoors in fall or indoors in late winter; don't cover it. The plants may bloom their first year.

▶ **Potential problems.** Possible problems include aphids, slugs and snails, gray mold (botrytis), leaf spots, rust, and viruses.

❁ SEASONAL CARE

◐ Spring

▶ Set out new plants, or move or divide existing clumps, in early to midspring. Space them about 1 foot (30 cm) apart. If your soil is on the sandy side, dig a shovelful of compost into the hole at planting time.

Water new plantings regularly if rain is lacking. Organic mulch helps to keep the soil evenly moist, but it can also smother the tiny seeds and prevent self-sown seedlings from emerging, so you may want to hold off on mulching until late spring or even later if you want the seedlings.

◉ Summer

▶ Cardinal flower and the hybrids may begin flowering in early summer, but mid- to late summer is usually peak bloom time for perennial lobelias. Once the main spike is done, leave it in place to produce and drop seeds, or snip it off just above the leafy part of the stem to tidy the plants. New, shorter bloom spikes may emerge below the cut, particularly on cardinal flower and the hybrids.

Keep watering spring plantings if rain is lacking. Established plants also benefit from regular watering during dry spells if their soil doesn't naturally stay moist.

✿ ◉ Fall & Winter

▶ In warmer climates (roughly south of Zone 6), you could set out new plants or move or divide existing clumps in early fall. Water new plantings regularly for the first month or so if rain is lacking.

Lobelias may continue flowering into fall. Leave the stalks in place for the winter. Scatter a general-purpose organic fertilizer or a shovelful of compost (or both) around the clumps in late fall to late winter. In Zone 6 and north, consider protecting the clumps with evergreen branches or a pine-needle mulch for winter if you don't have a dependable snow cover. Remove the mulch in late winter to early spring.

❁ TROUBLESHOOTING

▶ **Plants die over winter.** Try to buy cardinal flower plants grown from seed collected in your region to improve the odds of cold hardiness. North of Zone 7, treat hybrids like annuals and plan on replacing them each spring; if they do overwinter, consider it a bonus.

❁ **IT'S IN THE GENES** While the species *Lobelia cardinalis* grows in a wide range of hardiness zones, the cold hardiness and heat tolerance of individual plants can vary. Those with bronzy to purple leaves, particularly, tend to be less tolerant of cold and more adaptable to warm climates.

Lobelia cardinalis

Lupinus

LUPIN, LUPINE

Fantastic in photographs, lupins aren't always as rewarding in reality, unless you live where summer nights are on the cool side.

GROWING FROM THICK, DEEP ROOTS, these clump-forming perennials produce deeply divided green leaves and upright stalks topped with showy bloom spikes. The lupins grown in gardens are primarily hybrids, flowering in a wide range of solid colors, including white, yellow, orange, red, pink, purple, and blue, as well as bicolors. Height is typically 2 to 4 feet (60 to 120 cm), depending on the cultivar or seed strain. Lupins generally grow best in Zones 3 to 6, but they can also perform well in parts of Zones 7 and 8 where summers aren't too hot.

GROWING TIPS

▸ **Light & soil.** Lupins like full sun in cool-summer areas; elsewhere, try them in a site with morning sun and afternoon shade or in light all-day shade. Average, evenly moist but well-drained soil is ideal.

▸ **Division & propagation.** Division in early spring is an option for propagating your favorite lupins, but you also run the risk of killing them; if you really want to try, dig deeply to get as much of the root system as possible. Or, leave the main plant in place but dig out one or two offsets (if there are any) from the base of the plant. Generally, it's easiest to grow new plants from seed sown about ⅛ inch (3 mm) deep outdoors in fall or indoors in late winter. Soaking the seed in water overnight before indoor sowing may speed germination. Some strains bloom the first year. Lupins may also self-sow, but they tend to eventually produce mostly blue and purple blooms.

▸ **Potential problems.** Aphids and powdery mildew are the most common problems; other potential problems include plant bugs, slugs and snails, gray mold (botrytis), leaf spots, rusts, and root rot.

SEASONAL CARE

◐ Spring

▸ Set out new plants, or move or divide existing clumps if really necessary, in early spring. Space them 18 to 24 inches (45 to 60 cm) apart. If your soil is on the sandy side, work a shovelful of compost into the planting hole. Water new plantings regularly if rain is lacking. Apply a generous layer of organic mulch before summer. If you had problems with your lupins sprawling last year, consider inserting stakes next to or setting grow-through supports over the emerging clumps in midspring. In warm areas, lupins often begin blooming in late spring.

◉ Summer

▸ Early summer is prime bloom time for lupins in most areas. In cooler regions, flowering continues into midsummer. Once the flowers drop, you may choose to let the seeds form and drop so you get self-sown seedlings. Or, you may prefer to cut off the whole stalk close to the base, especially if the plant is affected by pests or diseases; fresh new foliage should emerge. Water both new and established lupins regularly if rain is lacking to keep the soil evenly moist.

✿ ◉ Fall & Winter

▸ In cool areas, lupins may produce some new blooms in early to midfall. Leave the stalks to self-sow or remove them to tidy the plants. Scatter a general-purpose organic fertilizer or a shovelful of compost (or both) around each clump in late fall to late winter. You may want to protect the clumps with a winter mulch, especially in areas where you don't get a dependable winter snow cover.

✿ KEEP IT COOL Hybrid lupins tend to perform best where summer nights are on the cool side. Elsewhere, they may bloom well for a year or two and then flower poorly or disappear altogether; in that case, consider buying or starting new plants every other year, so you always have vigorous young plants coming along.

Lupinus hybrid

Lychnis

CAMPION, CATCHFLY

Campions are champions where bright summer color is what you need!

MALTESE CROSS OR JERUSALEM CROSS (*Lychnis chalcedonica*) produces clusters of brilliant scarlet (or sometimes pink or white) flowers over rich green leaves on upright stems reaching 2 to 4 feet (60 to 120 cm) tall. It's usually recommended for Zones 3 to 9. Haage campion (*L. × haageana*) bears clustered, red to orange blooms and green leaves on plants 8 to 18 inches (20 to 45 cm) tall. Arkwright's campion (*L. × arkwrightii*) is a hybrid between Maltese cross and Haage campion, typically with bronzy to purplish foliage and orange-red flowers on stems reaching 1 to 2 feet (30 to 60 cm) tall. The hardiness range for both Haage campion and Arkwright's campion is usually given as Zones 5 to 8, but gardeners as far north as Zone 3 have reported growing them successfully.

Rose campion (*L. coronaria*), also known as mullein pink, looks rather different than its cousins, due to a covering of silver-gray hair on the leaves and stems. The branching stalks, which usually reach 2 to 3 feet (60 to 90 cm) tall, are topped with vibrant magenta, pale pink, or white flowers. It's generally hardy in Zones 3 to 9.

Lychnis coronaria

❋ GROWING TIPS

▶ **Light & soil.** Haage campion generally grows best in full sun or with just a few hours of afternoon shade, with average, evenly moist but well-drained soil. Maltese cross and Arkwright's campion adapt to full sun to partial shade with average, somewhat moist but well-drained soil; rose campion also thrives in those conditions, but it can tolerate even more shade and drier soil.

▶ **Division & propagation.** Maltese cross can live many years without division; the others benefit from being divided every 2 to 3 years. Rose campion, in particular, tends to act like a biennial, producing only leaves the first year and then dying after flowering the second year. Cutting off all the flower stems after the first flush of bloom and dividing the clumps every other year may keep them going longer. Or, let some seeds form and drop to get self-sown seedlings. To grow new plants from seed, sow outdoors in late fall to early spring or indoors in late winter; don't cover it. Arkwright's campion often blooms the first year from seed.

▶ **Potential problems.** Possible problems include slugs and snails, leaf spots, root rots, and rusts but usually aren't serious.

❋ SEASONAL CARE

◐ Spring

▶ In early spring, remove any winter mulch, and snip off any winter-damaged foliage on rose campion. Set out new plants of any of these campions, or move or divide existing clumps, in early to midspring. Space Haage campion plants about 1 foot (30 cm) apart and the others 12 to 18 inches (30 to 45 cm) apart. Water

Lychnis × arkwrightii 'Vesuvius'

new plantings regularly if rain is lacking. Apply an organic mulch before summer. In some areas, rose campion begins blooming in late spring.

◎ Summer

▸ Early to midsummer is prime bloom time for campions. Removing individual flowers or flower clusters as they finish may extend the bloom season for a few weeks and minimizes self-sowing. Once new flowers stop appearing, cut most campions back by about two-thirds to get fresh foliage and possibly some rebloom in fall; on rose campion, cut the flower stalks all the way back to the leafy rosette. In hot climates, Haage campion may die back to the ground in midsummer and might not reappear until next spring, especially if the soil is dry. All campions can benefit from regular watering if rain is lacking, but after their first year, they can get by with occasional soakings during extended dry spells.

✪ ☉ Fall & Winter

▸ South of Zone 6, set out new plants, or move or divide existing clumps, in early fall. Water new plantings regularly for the first month or so if rain is lacking. Campions may produce some additional flowers in early to midfall. Scatter a general-purpose organic fertilizer or a shovelful of compost around each clump in late fall to late winter. Rose campion's leafy rosettes usually look good through at least part of the winter; the others can be cut down in late fall to late winter. North of Zone 6, you may want to protect Haage campion and Arkwright's campion with a winter mulch, especially where you don't have dependable winter snow cover.

Lysimachia

LOOSESTRIFE

The good news about loosestrifes is that they're typically sturdy, adaptable, and easy to grow, traits that make them tempting to gardeners looking to fill space quickly and inexpensively.

THE BAD NEWS IS that they can be a little (actually, a lot) too vigorous, taking over valuable garden space and crowding out less rampant companions. All of the species mentioned here are generally hardy in Zones 3 to 9.

Gooseneck loosestrife (*Lysimachia clethroides*), with arching, tapering spikes of white flowers atop stems 2 to 4 feet (60 to 120 cm) tall, is one of the most notorious spreaders in this group. Yellow loosestrife (*L. punctata*), which grows 1 to 3 feet (30 to 90 cm) tall with clusters of bright yellow flowers from early to late summer, is another strong spreader. Fringed loosestrife (*L. ciliata*) has equally bright but smaller yellow flowers on stems reaching 2 to 4 feet (60 to 120 cm) tall. Most commonly grown in its purple-leaved version (sold as 'Purpurea', 'Atropurpurea', or 'Firecracker'); it's a little less aggressive than yellow loosestrife but can still crowd out less vigorous partners.

Creeping Jenny (*L. nummularia*), also known as moneywort, shares the same spreading tendencies of its cousins. Instead of creeping underground, though, it produces trailing stems that hug the surface of the ground and can take root at each leaf joint and quickly form extensive carpets barely 2 inches (5 cm) tall, with scattered yellow flowers in summer.

Lysimachia ciliata 'Firecracker'

❉ GROWING TIPS

▸ **Light & soil.** Loosestrifes generally thrive in full sun to partial shade with average, moist but well-drained soil.

▸ **Division & propagation.** Divide loosestrifes every 3 years, or more often if you want to control their spread; spring and fall are the best times. Division is so easy that there's really no need to propagate them any other way, but if you really want to try growing them from seed,

sow it outdoors in fall and leave it uncovered.

▸ **Potential problems.** Through the growing season, snip off or dig out any all-green shoots on the variegated cultivars. Besides browned

foliage (leaf scorch) in too-dry soil, possible problems include spider mites, leaf spots, and rusts; these are rarely serious, though.

❉ **A SNIP IN TIME** A post-bloom shearing is especially useful for the purple-leaved form of fringed loosestrife (*Lysimachia ciliata* 'Purpurea'), which tends to turn greenish by late summer if not cut back. The summer trim encourages deep purple new growth that looks great well into fall.

○ Spring

▸ Set out new plants, or move or divide existing clumps, in early to midspring. Space the clumps 18 to 24 inches (45 to 60 cm) apart. Water new plantings regularly if rain is lacking. Apply an organic mulch before summer, if desired.

◎ Summer

▸ Most loosestrifes begin blooming in early summer and continue into mid- or late summer. Gooseneck loosestrife tends to start a few weeks later and flower through late summer. Cutting gooseneck, yellow, and fringed loosestrifes back by one-half to two-thirds as soon as the blooms finish prevents self-sowing, removes tattered foliage, and encourages a flush of fresh new leaves. Water first-year plantings regularly during dry spells; established plantings benefit from occasional watering, too.

✤ ⊙ Fall & Winter

▸ Set out new plants, or move or divide existing clumps, in early fall. Water new plants regularly for the first month or so if rain is lacking. Gooseneck loosestrife and creeping Jenny may continue to bloom into early fall. The foliage of gooseneck loosestrife also changes color — usually to a deep red to reddish brown — as autumn progresses. Cut the upright loosestrifes to the ground when they start to look unattractive, anytime from late fall to late winter. Creeping Jenny tends to hold its leaves through part or all of the winter. Scatter a general-purpose organic fertilizer or shovelful of compost around the clumps every other year in late fall to late winter, if desired.

Lysimachia clethroides 'Geisha'

:: TROUBLESHOOTING

▸ **Plants spread aggressively.**
If you're considering growing a loosestrife but don't have one yet, take the warnings of their spreading nature seriously and consider a better-behaved alternative, such as Culver's root (*Veronicastrum*) for gooseneck loosestrife or a coreopsis (*Coreopsis*) for yellow loosestrife. If you're set on growing a loosestrife, your safest bet is planting it by itself in a space that's surrounded by paving, so it can't escape. Or, try it in a less-than-ideal spot, such as heavy clay, deep shade, or a dry, infertile spot where you can't get other plants to grow. Dividing the plants every year or two may also help to slow their spread. Trying to control loosestrifes by planting them in bot-

tomless buckets sunk into the soil, or with some other type of root barrier, may not be successful, because the rhizomes can leap over the edge if it's too close to the ground. Variegated cultivars of yellow loosestrife, such as 'Alexander' and 'Golden Alexander', and 'Aurea', the yellow-leaved form of creeping Jenny, tend to be better behaved than their parents in most gardens. 'Geisha', the variegated version of gooseneck loosestrife, is slightly less rampant than the green-leaved parent but still spreads too quickly for most borders. If you already have a loosestrife that's taken over part of your garden, it's generally best to cut it to the ground, then cover the area with several layers of cardboard and a thick layer of mulch for a few years to smother it.

Malva

MALLOW

Mallows may not be the best-behaved or longest-lived plants in the garden, but for quick color and a long bloom season, they're tough to beat.

MALLOWS LOOK MUCH LIKE scaled-down versions of their cousins, the hollyhocks (*Alcea*), with spires of cupped blooms from summer into fall on clump-forming plants with rounded to heart-shaped, scallop-edged lower leaves and deeply lobed upper leaves.

Hollyhock mallow (*Malva alcea*) bears pink or white blooms on plants typically 2 to 4 feet (60 to 120 cm) tall. 'Fastigiata' is more narrowly upright than the species. Musk mallow (*M. moschata*) looks basically like hollyhock mallow but tends to be a bit shorter: usually 18 to 36 inches (45 to 90 cm) tall. Both species are usually recommended for Zones 4 to 8. Zebra mallow (*M. sylvestris*) generally grows 3 to 5 feet (90 to 150 cm) tall, with pink, blue, or purple flowers that have darker stripes radiating out from the center. 'Zebrinus' is usually used to describe plants with light pink flowers striped with deep purple. Zones 5 to 9.

✣ GROWING TIPS

▶ **Light & soil.** Mallows perform well in full sun or light shade with average, well-drained soil.

▶ **Division & propagation.** You can divide established clumps every 2 to 3 years in spring, if desired.

Raise vigorous new plants from seed sown (and barely covered) outdoors in fall to spring or indoors in late winter to late spring; they'll begin blooming during their first summer.

▶ **Potential problems.** Mallows are susceptible to a number of problems, including aphids, Japanese beetles, spider mites, leaf spot, and rust. If pests or diseases become a serious issue, pull out and destroy affected plants, then start new ones; they grow quickly.

✣ SEASONAL CARE

◗ Spring

▶ Set out new plants, transplant seedlings, or divide existing clumps if necessary, in early spring. Space them about 18 inches (45 cm) apart. Water new plantings regularly if rain is lacking. Apply an organic mulch before summer. If you're growing the plants in some shade or if they flopped last year, set grow-through supports over the clumps in early to midspring or pinch off the stem tips once in mid- to late spring. Established plants often begin blooming in late spring.

◉ Summer

▶ Established mallows are usually in peak bloom in early summer. First-year seedlings often start a few weeks later, by midsummer. If necessary, prop up leaning stems with linking stakes or Y-stakes. When most of the flowers on a spike are finished, cut it back by one-half to two-thirds to prevent self-sowing and encourage rebloom. Keep watering spring plantings regularly if rain is lacking. Established mallows also appreciate regular watering, or at least occasional soakings, during dry spells.

✪ ◉ Fall & Winter

▶ Mallows may continue to produce at least a few blooms until frost. Keep cutting off the spikes (snip them off close to the bottom) to prevent self-sowing. Leave the foliage growing at the base of the plant for the winter, though. Scatter a general-purpose organic fertilizer or a shovelful of compost around the clumps in late fall to late winter.

✣ TROUBLESHOOTING

▶ **Plants die.** It's not unusual for mallows to die out after 2 or 3 years, even in ideal growing conditions. One way to prolong their life is to cut the plants back by about two-thirds in late summer to encourage a flush of new leafy growth; this prevents them from putting all of their energy into flowers and seeds. Regularly removing finished flowers or flower stalks through the summer and fall can also help. Consider leaving one or two stalks to set seed, though, so you'll get a few self-sown seedlings to replace the parent plants if they die. Or, simply treat mallows as annuals or biennials, starting new plants from seed every spring or every other spring.

✣ **DEFINITELY DEADHEAD** Mallows are beautiful in bloom but can self-sow prolifically, sometimes to the point of becoming weedy. Fortunately, there's an easy way to keep them in check: simply snip off the spent flower stalks.

Malva sylvestris

Monarda

BEE BALM, BERGAMOT

The bright blooms of bee balms are one of the joys of the summer garden.

THESE PERENNIALS PRODUCE creeping rhizomes that spread to form patches of upright stems clad in aromatic leaves and topped in shaggy-looking flower clusters. Common bee balm or Oswego tea (*Monarda didyma*), with brilliant red blooms and deep green leaves, typically grows 2 to 4 feet (60 to 120 cm) tall. Wild bee balm or wild bergamot (*M. fistulosa*) has the same height range but with purplish pink to pale pink flowers and lighter green leaves. There are also many hybrids between these two species, blooming in white or shades of purple, pink, or red. As a group, bee balms are generally recommended for Zones 3 to 8.

Monarda 'Jacob Cline'

❖ GROWING TIPS

▸ **Light & soil.** Bee balms grow well in full sun if the soil doesn't dry out completely; planting in average, well-drained soil, with morning sun and afternoon shade or with light all-day shade, is best. Common bee balm is most dependent on regular moisture; wild bee balm tolerates drier conditions, and the hybrids fall somewhere in between.

▸ **Division & propagation.** Dividing plants every 2 or 3 years keeps them vigorous and helps to control their spread; it's also an easy way to propagate your favorite plants. You can also propogate bee balm by taking stem cuttings in summer. Or, sow seed outdoors in fall to early spring or indoors in late winter; don't cover it.

▸ **Potential problems.** Possible problems include leaf spots and rusts. (Also see Troubleshooting, page 281.) After a few years, dead patches tend to appear in the clump. One option is to dig out the dead parts in spring, then fill the holes with compost or a compost–soil mixture. Usually, though, it's best to dig up the plants, divide them, and replant them into compost-enriched soil.

❖ SEASONAL CARE

◐ Spring

▸ Set out new plants, or move or divide existing clumps, in early to midspring. Space them 18 to 24 inches (45 to 60 cm) apart. Water new plantings regularly if rain is lacking. If the new growth on established clumps looks crowded, you may want to snip out some of the shoots at some point during the spring to leave about 2 inches (5 cm) between the stems. To get lower, bushier summer growth, you could cut the plants back by about one-half in late spring. Apply an organic mulch before summer.

◎ Summer

▸ If you didn't cut the plants back in late spring, or if you did but want to delay bloom until later in the summer, you can shear the plants back by about one-third in early summer. Usually, bee balms are in

❖ **MOIST, RICH SOIL** Simple steps that go a long way in keeping bee balms looking their best include watering regularly during dry spells and dividing the plants frequently to maintain their vigor. Other tricks include working a shovelful of compost into their hole at planting time and using an organic mulch to keep their soil from drying out.

Monarda fistulosa

full flower from midsummer into late summer. Regularly snipping off the flowerheads when their blooms have dropped off may encourage rebloom and prevents self-seeding. Or, you may choose to leave the seed heads to enjoy their interesting form. Water both first-year and established plants regularly during dry spells.

✪ ☉ Fall & Winter

▸ Set out new plants, or move or divide existing clumps, in early fall. Water new plantings regularly for the first month or so if rain is lacking. If you didn't cut back your bee balms in late summer, cut the stems down after frost or leave the seed heads for winter interest and cut in late winter instead. Scatter a general-purpose organic fertilizer or a shovelful of compost (or both) around the plants in late fall to late winter.

❖ TROUBLESHOOTING

▸ **Leaves, stems, and buds with dusty white to gray patches.** Powdery mildew is a fungal disease that often appears on bee balms in mid- to late summer. At the first sign of the disease, pinch off affected leaves and spray the rest of the plant with an organic fungicide. If the disease has already spread, cut the plants back by about three-quarters or to any new growth that's sprouting at the base. Next time you plant bee balm, consider a mildew-resistant cultivar, such as 'Claire Grace', 'Jacob Cline', or 'Marshall's Delight'. Watering regularly during dry spells and keeping the soil covered with an organic mulch can also help bee balms to stay healthy.

Nepeta

CATMINT

Pretty flowers, handsome foliage, and a fuss-free nature make catmints a classic choice for perennial plantings.

USUALLY, THE HARDEST PART of growing catmints is trying to figure out their correct names! One species, commonly called Persian catmint, used to be known as *Nepeta mussinii* but is now classified as *N. racemosa*. It is the parent of the hybrid Faassen's catmint (*N. × faassenii*). Both of these produce mounded plants in the range of 1 to 2 feet (30 to 60 cm) tall, with small, gray-green leaves and spikes of purple-blue flowers. The main difference is that Faassen's catmint is supposed to be sterile, so it should bloom over a longer period and not produce unwanted seedlings. Siberian catmint (*N. sibirica*) tends to form creeping patches of more upright stems with green leaves; it usually reaches 2 to 3 feet (60 to 90 cm) tall. 'Six Hills Giant', which is sometimes listed under *N. sibirica*, can reach 3 to 4 feet (90 to 120 cm) tall. As a group, catmints are generally recommended for Zones 3 to 8.

Nepeta sibirica 'Souvenir d'Andre Chaudron'

❖ GROWING TIPS

▶ **Light & soil.** Catmints thrive in full sun but can also grow in morning sun and afternoon shade or in light all-day shade (especially in hot climates). Dryish, not-especially-fertile soil is ideal. Rich, evenly moist soil encourages lush growth that may be prone to flopping.

▶ **Division & propagation.** Dividing catmint clumps every 3 to 4 years in spring or fall helps to keep them vigorous. It's also a simple way to propagate your favorites. You can also propogate catmint by taking stem cuttings after flowering. If you want to grow catmints from seed,

sow outdoors in fall to early spring or indoors in late winter; barely cover it.

▶ **Potential problems.** Possible problems include plant bugs, slugs and snails, leaf spots, and powdery mildew, but they usually aren't serious enough to require control.

❖ SEASONAL CARE

◐ Spring

▶ Set out new plants, or move or divide existing clumps, in early spring. Space them 18 to 24 inches (45 to 60 cm) apart, or about 30 inches (75 cm) apart for 'Six Hills Giant'. Water new plantings regularly if rain is lacking. Apply a mulch before summer. (Gravel makes a

great mulch for catmints, but you could use an organic mulch instead.) Catmints typically begin blooming by late spring.

◎ Summer

▶ Early summer is peak bloom time for catmints. This first flush of bloom typically finishes by midsummer. At that point, shearing them back by one-half to two-thirds minimizes self-sowing, encourages bushy regrowth, and usually promotes rebloom. If the plants do flower again, you can shear again in late summer, if needed. Keep watering spring plantings occasionally if rain is lacking.

✪ ◉ Fall & Winter

▸ Set out new plants, or move or divide existing clumps, in early fall. Water new plantings regularly for the first month or so if rain is lacking. Catmints often bloom into autumn; if yours do, shear again lightly once the flowers drop. The foliage tends to hold up into early winter, at least, so you could either wait until late winter to cut the stems down or trim them back to the basal growth (if any) in mid- to late fall. Scatter a general-purpose organic fertilizer or a shovelful of compost around the clumps every other year in late fall to late winter.

❖ TROUBLESHOOTING

▸ **Plants self-sow prolifically.** Unfortunately, catmint cultivars are often mixed up in the nursery trade, so the plants you buy as cultivars of sterile Faassen's catmint may actually belong to Persian catmint or other seed-producing species. To further confuse matters, some cultivars that *are* sterile are sold under the name of species that normally produce seed. If it's important to you to have a sterile form, get a division from a friend's plant that you know hasn't set seed. Regardless of what kind of catmint you're growing, shearing the plants back as soon as most of the blooms drop off removes most of the developing seed, if there is any.

Cats generally prefer catnip (*Nepeta cataria*) but may also chew or roll on the ornamental catmints, especially right after planting. If a kitty has access to your garden; consider covering new catmints with chicken wire for a week or so.

Relatively Speaking

Calamints (*Calamintha*) thrive in the same growing conditions as catmints with the same basic care. Large-flowered calamint (*C. grandiflora*) bears bright pink blooms from early to late summer or early fall on spreading plants that generally grow 1 to 2 feet (30 to 60 cm) tall. It's usually hardy in Zones 3 to 8. 'Variegata', with white-speckled foliage, is even showier but tends to revert to solid green; be sure to remove reverted growth as soon as you see it, or the all-green shoots will quickly take over.

Lesser calamint (usually sold as *Calamintha nepeta* or *C. nepetoides*) grows in woody-based, slower-spreading clumps, with an abundance of tiny, white to pale purple-blue flowers from early summer well into fall, even without shearing. It's suggested for Zones 4 or 5 to 8. Both calamints tend to grow 1 to 2 feet (30 to 60 cm) tall and have very aromatic foliage. Both may also self-sow prolifically; shearing in midsummer and again in late summer to early fall can help to minimize unwanted seedlings.

Oenothera

SUNDROPS, EVENING PRIMROSE

From carpeting creepers to knee-high clump-formers, plants in the genus *Oenothera* bring an abundance of easy-care color to the garden.

EACH BLOOM OF *OENOTHERA* lasts only a day or less, but they appear in abundance, creating a showy flower display for weeks or even months, mostly in summer. There are many species and hybrids to choose from.

One classic favorite is common sundrops (sold as *O. fruticosa* and *O. tetragona*), which grows in moderately spreading clumps of leafy rosettes with upright stems usually 1 to 2 feet (30 to 60 cm) tall. Clusters of red-blushed to all-red buds open to cupped, bright yellow, day-blooming flowers. It's usually recommended for Zones 3 to 8.

Day-blooming *O. versicolor* (usually grown as 'Sunset Boulevard') is another upright-grower to about 2 feet (60 cm) tall with reddish stems topped by flowers that open yellow then quickly turn peachy orange to red as they age. It's usually recommended for Zones 5 to 9.

Despite its name, showy evening primrose or Mexican evening primrose (*O. speciosa;* also sold as *O. berlandieri*) flowers during the day, with rosy pink, pale pink, or white flowers atop thin, upright stems usually 1 to 2 feet (30 to 60 cm) tall. The slender green leaves may turn red in hot, dry conditions. It spreads rapidly by underground runners to form large patches. Zones 5 to 9.

O. macrocarpa (also still sold as *O. missouriensis*) is commonly known as either Ozark sundrops or Missouri evening primrose. It forms somewhat sprawling, low clumps of long, narrow, light green to silvery leaves. It reaches 6 to 12 inches (15 to 30 cm) tall in bloom, with large, fragrant, yellow-aging-to-orange flowers that open in mid- or late afternoon and close by the next morning. Zones 4 to 8.

❀ GROWING TIPS

▸ **Light & soil.** Full sun to light shade with average, well-drained soil is fine for these tough, adaptable perennials.

▸ **Division & propagation.** Divide common sundrops and showy evening primrose in spring or fall every 3 to 5 years, or more often (even every year) if you're trying to slow their spread. This is also a simple way to propagate these two species. *O. versicolor* tends to act like a short-lived perennial or even an annual, and Ozark sundrops prefers to be left undisturbed, so division isn't necessary for these two. Sow seed outdoors in fall to early spring or indoors in late winter to early spring; barely cover it. Indoor-started seedlings often bloom during their first growing season.

▸ **Potential problems.** Possible problems include aphids, downy and powdery mildew, leaf spots, and rusts, but they are rarely serious.

❀ SEASONAL CARE

◐ Spring

▸ Set out new plants, or move or divide existing clumps of common sundrops and showy evening primrose, in early spring. Space them 12 to 18 inches (30 to 45 cm) apart. Water new plantings regularly if rain is lacking. Apply an organic or gravel mulch before summer. In mild climates, showy evening primrose may start flowering as early as early spring; elsewhere, it usually starts in mid- to late spring. Established plants of *O. versicolor* and Ozark sundrops generally begin blooming in late spring.

◉ Summer

▸ Common sundrops typically begin blooming in early summer and continue until mid- or late summer. When they finish, you could shear them lightly to remove just the developing seedpods or trim them back all the way to the basal leaves. *O. versicolor* and Ozark sundrops often bloom all through the summer. Pinch or snip off the seedpods, if you wish, to possibly extend the bloom display and prevent self-sowing.

Showy evening primrose may go dormant in early summer where the summers are very hot; elsewhere, it normally keeps flowering through the summer. If the blooms stop or slow down in mid- to late summer, you could shear the patches back by one-half to two-thirds to encourage new growth and flowers.

Water spring plantings occasionally if rain is lacking. Established plants can be quite drought tolerant

Oenothera fruticosa

but flower most freely with an occasional soaking during extended dry spells.

☼ ☉ Fall & Winter

▸ Set out new plants, or move or divide existing clumps, in early fall. Water new plantings occasionally for the first month or so if rain is lacking. The green leaves of common sundrops often turn red to burgundy when cool weather arrives. If you didn't remove the old stems after bloom, cut them back to the basal leaves after frost. *O. versicolor* and Ozark sundrops may flower into fall; keep removing their seedpods if you want to prevent self-sowing. Showy evening primrose may also continue to bloom, or begin again if it took a break in summer, and its foliage may turn red. Shear it back by one-half to two-thirds at some point during the fall to remove the seedpods. Scatter a general-purpose organic fertilizer or a shovelful of compost around the clumps every other year in late fall to late winter.

❖ TROUBLESHOOTING

▸ **Plants spread aggressively.** If you grow sundrops or evening primroses, you can pretty much expect that they'll spread to some extent, either by self-sowing or creeping roots or both. The creepers — common sundrops and showy evening primrose — expand most vigorously in full sun and rich, loose, somewhat moist soil, so to slow them down, you could try them in less-than-ideal conditions, such as partial to full shade, or dry, infertile soil (perhaps on a slope), or heavy clay. Or, plant them within a root barrier (such as a large bottomless pot sunk almost up to its rim in the soil) or in a bed surrounded by paving, where they can spread freely but not creep away. They may still seed around, though, if you don't pick or shear off the seedpods regularly. Of the two spreaders, common sundrops is fairly easily to pull out where it's not wanted, while showy evening primrose can be a real problem to eradicate.

Origanum

OREGANO

Ornamental oreganos add as much zip to your garden as their culinary cousins can to your cooking.

THEIR WOODY-BASED CLUMPS spread outward by creeping rhizomes — usually at a slow to moderate rate, but sometimes fairly quickly in loose, sandy soil — and bear small, oval to rounded leaves that are often aromatic but generally not flavorful. The slender, upright to arching stems are tipped with clusters of small, pink to purple blooms set among green to deep purple bracts (modified leaves).

Origanum laevigatum and its cultivars (such as 'Herrenhausen' and 'Hopleys') normally grow to about 2 feet (60 cm) tall. There are several hybrids (including 'Rosenkuppel' and 'Rotkugel') that are closer to 18 inches (45 cm) tall. Some of these oreganos — particularly 'Herrenhausen' and, to a lesser extent, 'Rosenkuppel' — have purple to purple-flushed foliage in cool weather. Golden oregano (*O. vulgare* 'Aureum') and the hybrid 'Norton Gold' have yellow foliage; there are also white- or yellow-variegated selections. *O. rotundifolium* 'Kent Beauty' is distinctive for its arching to trailing stems, blue-green leaves, and tiny flowers set among showy, pale-green bracts that are strongly blushed with pink. All of these are generally hardy in Zones 5 to 10.

Origanum vulgare 'Aureum'

❋ GROWING TIPS

▶ **Light & soil.** A site with full sun and average, dryish soil is ideal for most ornamental oreganos. Good drainage is critical, especially in winter.

▶ **Division & propagation.** Divide the clumps every 3 or 4 years to keep them vigorous, control their spread, and propagate your favorites. Or, take stem cuttings in spring. Seed-grown plants can vary in height and color, but if you want to try growing oreganos from seed, sow indoors in early spring or outdoors in mid-spring and barely cover it.

▶ **Potential problems.** Aphids, plant bugs, and spider mites occasionally bother the plants but seldom cause serious damage.

❋ SEASONAL CARE

💧 Spring

▶ Set out new plants, or move or divide existing clumps, in early to midspring. Space them about 18 inches (45 cm) apart. Water new plantings regularly if rain is lacking. On established plants, trim off the old stems when new shoots start growing from the base. Mulch usually isn't necessary, but if you choose to apply it, consider using gravel instead of an organic mulch, especially if your soil isn't perfectly drained. In warm areas, ornamental oreganos may begin blooming in late spring.

◎ Summer

▶ Most ornamental oreganos start flowering in early to midsummer and continue through late summer. Snip off the bloom clusters once the flowers drop to possibly extend the flowering period, or leave them for their interesting form. Water spring plantings occasionally if rain is lacking; established oreganos usually don't need it.

✪ ☉ Fall & Winter

▶ South of Zone 6, you could set out new plants, or move or divide existing clumps, in early fall. Water new plantings occasionally for the first month or so if rain is lacking. Flowering may continue into early fall or even until frost. Leave the tops in place through the winter. In Zone 5, you may want to protect the clumps with a loose mulch, such as evergreen boughs, for winter protection. Scatter a general-purpose organic fertilizer around the clumps every other year in late fall to late winter.

Paeonia

PEONY

Peonies have a relatively short bloom display, but the flowers are so lovely that many gardeners wouldn't be without them.

THERE'S AN AMAZING NUMBER of species and cultivars to choose from, but fortunately, the care for the common garden or herbaceous peonies — most of which are hybrids of *Paeonia lactiflora, P. officinalis,* and a few other species — is basically the same. These long-lived, clump-forming perennials sprout from subsurface buds each spring, with deep red to red-tinged shoots that mature into rich green, lobed leaves on upright stems from 2 to 4 feet (60 to 120 cm) tall. The stems are topped with large, single, semidouble, or double flowers, commonly in white or shades of pink, coral, or red.

The hardiness of garden peonies varies depending on the cultivar, but most are hardy in Zones 3 to 7 or 8. They tend to grow poorly in areas where they don't get enough winter cold, but some cultivars, such as 'Festiva Maxima', are better adapted than others to warm areas.

Paeonia 'Little Red Gem'

❉ GROWING TIPS

▸ **Light & soil.** Full sun is usually ideal, but south of Zone 6, a site with light afternoon shade can help the flowers last a little longer. Average, well-drained soil is fine, though the plants really thrive in evenly moist (but not soggy), compost-enriched soil.

▸ **Division & propagation.** Peonies are generally sturdy, long-lived plants that can grow beautifully in one spot for many years. It's best to leave them undisturbed, but if you do need to move or divide them (ideally in late summer to early fall, or in early spring), dig deeply to keep as many of the roots as possible. Use a sharp knife to cut the clump into sections with at least three — and preferably five or six — buds or stems. (Smaller divisions can take several years to recover.) Peonies are very slow from seed, and the hybrids will vary in height and color. But if you want to try, sow outdoors in late summer or early fall; barely cover the seed. Or, sow indoors in fall or winter, keep in a warm place for 2 to 3 months, then enclose the pots in a plastic bag and refrigerate for 3 months before moving them back to a warm place.

▸ **Potential problems.** A number of problems can attack peonies, including aphids, rose chafers, scale, slugs and snails, thrips, anthracnose, leaf spots, powdery mildew, root rots, verticillium wilt, and root-knot nematodes. (Also see Troubleshooting, page 289.)

Paeonia obovata

Most gardeners choose to cut off withered peony flowers to improve their plants' appearance and possibly reduce disease problems. If you decide not to deadhead, the seedpods can add some interest into late summer, when they split to release their seeds.

❉ SEASONAL CARE

◑ Spring

▸ Set out bare-root or container-grown peonies, or move or divide existing clumps if necessary, as early in spring as possible. The plants are going to live in one spot for a long time, so it's worth putting extra effort into preparing their site.

Dig a large planting hole, loosening the soil in an area ideally 12 to 18 inches (30 to 45 cm) square and 1 foot (30 cm) deep, then refill the hole partway with the topsoil you removed mixed with a shovelful or two of compost and some general-purpose organic fertilizer. You want the buds of bare-root peonies to sit about 2 inches (5 cm) below the soil surface in Zone 6 and north,

and about 1 inch (2.5 cm) below the surface south of that. When planting out container-grown peonies, set the stem bases (at the point where they join the crown, not where they emerge from the soil in the pot) at the same level recommended for bareroot plants in your area. Finish filling the hole around the roots. Water new plantings regularly if rain is lacking. Apply an organic mulch around both new and established peony clumps, but be careful not to pile it right on top of the crown or against the stems.

▸ If you're growing tall hybrids, or those with semidouble to double flowers, it's a good idea to set grow-through supports over the clumps in early to midspring. If you forget, consider pinching off the main bud on each stem, if you can bear it, to encourage side buds, which will produce smaller blooms that are less likely to flop. Or, use linking stakes to corral the stems before the flowers open. Species peonies and early blooming hybrids may start flowering in midspring in the South and late spring in cooler areas. Midseason hybrids start about 2 weeks later, and late hybrids may be in flower by the very end of spring.

◎ Summer

▸ In hot-summer regions, the peony show may be finished by early summer, when cooler-climate gardeners are enjoying the peak bloom time. Clip off the spent flowers just above the uppermost leaf on the stem, if desired. The foliage may start to look tired by late summer, but leave it in place as long as you can stand to look at it. Late summer into early fall can be a good time to move or divide your peonies, if necessary. Water spring and late-summer plantings regularly if rain is lacking; established peonies also benefit from occasional watering during dry spells.

✚ ☉ Fall & Winter

▸ Early to midfall is the ideal time to set out bare-root peonies; water them occasionally for the first month or so if rain is lacking. Established plants that still have their leaves may develop attractive fall foliage color. If the leaves look tattered in early fall, you may choose to cut them down early; otherwise, wait until after frost to cut the stalks off at or just below the soil surface. Scatter a general-purpose organic fertilizer or a shovelful of compost (or both) around each clump in late fall to late winter. It's a good idea to mulch late summer– and fall-planted peonies for their first winter, at least. North of Zone 5, consider applying a winter

Peony buds naturally secrete a sticky substance that attracts ants. If ants are present, they'll do no harm; if they don't show up, the buds should still open normally.

mulch to all of your peonies if you can't depend on winter snow cover.

❖ TROUBLESHOOTING

▸ **Shoots wilt; stem bases darkened, softened.** Botrytis blight (also known as gray mold and peony blight) tends to show up around midspring, especially in cool, damp conditions. The stems show the first symptoms; soon after, you may also notice flower buds that turn black and fail to open, or that only open partway. Blooms that do open may turn brown and develop a fuzzy gray mold; leaves may show similar symptoms. Cut off and destroy affected parts or stems; next spring, try dusting around emerging shoots with powdered sulfur or spraying with a biofungicide to prevent further problems. Downy mildew and southern blight can cause similar stem-base damage but also spread into the crown, causing rot; in these cases, dig up and destroy affected plants.

▸ **Plants do not produce flower buds, or produce tiny buds that never open.** It can take several years for peonies to settle in and bloom properly after being planted, transplanted, or divided. If the plants still don't bloom after that, it may be that they're planted too deep. Dig up and

reset the crowns so the buds are no more than 2 inches (5 cm) below the soil surface. Established clumps that used to bloom well may now be overcrowded and need to be divided. Or, it could be that the plants didn't set flower buds the summer before because they were in too much shade (peonies prefer at least 6 hours of sun, and ideally 8 or more), because the soil was too dry, or because they needed fertilizer. Excessive cold may kill the buds during the winter. Also see "Flower buds do not open," below.

▸ **Flower buds do not open.** Besides botrytis (see "Shoots wilt; stem bases darkened, softened," above), a number of other problems can stop already formed flower buds from blooming, including damage from late frost or weather that's unusually hot, cold, wet, or dry. If weather causes the problem, the plants should bloom normally next year. Feeding by tiny insects known as thrips may stop buds from opening altogether or cause distorted, flecked petals. It's tough to control thrips: try spraying with insecticidal soap three or four times, 3 to 4 days apart, as soon as you suspect damage, or snip off and destroy seriously damaged buds and blooms.

Papaver

POPPY

Perennial poppies flower for just a few weeks, but their bold blooms make them a favorite with many gardeners.

THE GIANT-FLOWERED ORIENTAL POPPY is usually listed as *Papaver orientale*, but the plants grown in gardens are mostly hybrids between *P. orientale, P. bracteatum,* and another species. By any name, they're undeniably eye-catching, forming lush clumps of large, deeply cut, hairy, deep green leaves and upright stems topped with bowl-shaped blooms in white or shades of pink, red, scarlet, and orange. Most reach 2 to 3 feet (60 to 90 cm) when they bloom, but they may range from 18 inches (45 cm) for the compact cultivars to nearly 4 feet (1.2 m) for the tallest types. Oriental poppies are generally recommended for Zones 2 to 8. (They can grow in some warmer areas, but they require a period of winter chilling, so they tend to fade away after just a year or two.)

Smaller in scale but equally pretty, Iceland poppy (*P. nudicaule*) produces clumps of lobed, hairy, light green to gray-green leaves and cupped blooms in a range of bright and pastel colors atop stems usually 1 to 2 feet (30 to 60 cm) tall. In areas with cool summers, they can be reliably perennial; elsewhere, they're often short lived. So technically, these plants can grow in Zones 1 to 10, but they tend to act like annuals or biennials south of Zone 5 or so.

✿ GROWING TIPS

▸ **Light & soil.** Full sun is usually best for poppies, but they can tolerate some shade in warmer areas. They thrive in deeply dug soil with a shovelful or two of compost worked into the planting hole. Average moisture levels are fine; they generally don't like very dry sites, but good drainage is critical, especially in winter.

▸ **Division & propagation.** Divide the clumps every 4 to 6 years to relieve overcrowding and to propagate your favorites. Another option is to take root cuttings in mid- to late summer. It's also fairly easy to grow both kinds of poppies from seed. Sow Oriental poppy seed outdoors in late fall to early spring or indoors in late winter; don't cover it. Sow Iceland poppy outdoors in late fall to early spring for flowers the first spring or in summer for bloom the following spring. Poppies also tend to self-sow, and you can move the seedlings fairly easily while they have only a few leaves.

▸ **Potential problems.** Iceland poppies normally aren't bothered by problems, except aphids. Aphids can bother Oriental poppies, too, along with a number of other problems, including leaf hoppers, plant bugs, rose chafers, botrytis blight (gray mold), downy mildew, powdery mildew, root rot, verticillium wilt, and root-knot nematodes. (Also see Troubleshooting, opposite page.) Still, Oriental poppies can be quite long-lived plants. Oriental poppy can leave quite a gap in the garden when it goes dormant in summer, so pair it with a perennial partner that will spread out to fill the space in summer, such as bluestar (*Amsonia*) or Russian sage (*Perovskia*), or set out transplants or direct-sow seeds of fast-growing annuals, such as flowering tobaccos (*Nicotiana*) or salvias, around it.

✿ SEASONAL CARE

◐ Spring

▸ Set out plants of Iceland poppy, spaced about 1 foot (30 cm) apart, in early spring. This is also a good time to set out potted plants of Oriental poppy: space compact cultivars about 18 inches (45 cm) apart and full-size cultivars about 2 feet (60 cm) apart. You could also try moving or dividing Oriental poppies in early spring if really necessary; it's not an ideal time, though. Water new plantings regularly if rain is lacking, and apply an organic mulch in early to midspring.

▸ The foliage of Oriental poppy expands quickly as soon as the weather starts warming up. If you're growing tall Oriental cultivars and they flopped last year, you might consider placing grow-through sup-

✿ **SMALL IS GOOD** Tall cultivars of Oriental poppy can be prone to sprawling and are difficult to stake effectively. Consider choosing a compact cultivar such as 'Allegro' or the Pizzicato strain, which reaches only 18 inches (45 cm) tall.

ports over the clumps in early spring; in most cases, though, if the hoops are low enough to be hidden by the leaves, then they're not tall enough to effectively support the flower stems. Instead, you might consider setting linking stakes around the clumps when the flower buds form to provide temporary support during the short bloom period. Oriental poppy generally opens in late spring in the warmest part of its range.

▸ Iceland poppy may flower through the spring in mild areas, or begin its season in mid- to late spring in cooler regions.

◎ Summer

▸ Early summer is prime time for Oriental poppy bloom in many areas. Once the petals drop off, you may choose to let the attractive seedpods develop or snip off the flowering stems at the base. In many areas, the leaves start to decline as soon as the flowers finish; you can cut the whole plant to the ground then, if you wish, or let it die back to the ground on its own in midsummer. In cool areas, the plants may look respectable all summer. Oriental poppies appreciate occasional watering if rain is lacking, as long as their leaves are growing; if they die back to the ground, don't worry about watering them. If you'd like to plant new Oriental poppies, or if you need to move or divide your existing plants, late summer to early fall is the ideal time (cut them down first, if they're not already dormant). Set the buds of new bare-root plants so they're about 2 inches (5 cm) below the soil surface.

▸ Iceland poppies may continue blooming through the summer where the nights are relatively cool, especially if you water them during dry spells and regularly cut off the finished flower stems. Otherwise, it's common for summer heat to halt

Papaver orientale 'Fruit Punch Mix'

the show by midsummer, even with deadheading. If their leaves stick around, Iceland poppies may flower again next year; if the plants disappear, plan on replacing them in fall or next spring.

◒ ◓ Fall & Winter

▸ Finish planting, moving, or dividing Oriental poppies in early fall. This is also a good time to set out new plants of Iceland poppies for bloom in winter (in the southernmost zones) or next spring. Established Iceland poppies may continue flowering into early fall in cool regions. Oriental poppies send up new foliage in early fall, and they may also surprise you with a flower or two in fall. Water both new and established plantings occasionally during fall dry spells. Leave the foli-

age in place for the winter. Scatter a general-purpose organic fertilizer or a shovelful of compost around your poppy plants in late fall to late winter. First-year plantings of Oriental poppies can benefit from a lightweight winter mulch, such as evergreen branches, especially where winter snow cover isn't dependable; established clumps generally don't need protection.

❖ TROUBLESHOOTING

▸ **Plants with dark spots.** Bacterial blight can cause a variety of symptoms on Oriental poppies, including deep green leaf spots that turn black; dark spots on stems, petals, and pods; dropped foliage; and eventually dead plants. Remove and destroy affected plants.

Patrinia

PATRINIA

If you're looking for something a little different for summer color, the lacy blooms of patrinias may fit the bill. These out-of-the-ordinary perennials bear toothed or deeply divided leaves on upright stems topped in loose clusters composed of many tiny blooms.

GOLDEN LACE (PATRINIA SCABIOSIFOLIA), also known as golden valerian, produces low, dense clumps of light green leaves and taller, slender stems topped with vivid yellow flowers. It commonly grows 4 to 6 (1.2 to 1.8 m) tall, but plants sold as 'Nagoya' are a more compact 2 to 3 feet (60 to 90 cm). Dwarf patrinia (*P. gibbosa*), another yellow-flowered clump-former, generally grows 18 to 24 inches (45 to 60 cm) tall. *P. triloba* is yet another yellow-flowered species, but it's much more of a spreader, forming patches that usually reach 18 to 24 inches (45 to 60 cm) tall. And then there's white patrinia (*P. villosa*), with white flowers typically 2 to 3 feet (60 to 90 cm) tall atop creeping carpets. All of these normally perform well in Zones 4 or 5 to 8.

Patrinia scabiosifolia

❋ GROWING TIPS

▸ **Light & soil.** Patrinias can grow in either full sun or partial shade with average, well-drained soil. Evenly moist (but not soggy), compost-enriched soil is a plus.

▸ **Division & propagation.** Golden lace is best left undisturbed once established, but its seedlings are fairly easy to move. You can divide the other patrinias in spring or fall every 4 to 6 years — more frequently if you need to control their spread. Patrinias grow readily from seed sown outdoors in late fall to early spring or indoors in late winter to early spring; barely cover it with soil or seed-starting mix.

▸ **Potential problems.** Patrinias can host a fungal disease called daylily rust; it doesn't much bother them, but the disease is a very serious problem on daylilies (*Hemerocallis*), so some authorities recommend against planting patrinias.

❋ SEASONAL CARE

◐ Spring

▸ Set out new plants, or move or divide existing clumps, in early to midspring. Space them 18 to 24 inches (45 to 60 cm) apart. Water new plantings regularly if rain is lacking. Apply an organic mulch before summer.

◎ Summer

▸ Dwarf patrinia blooms mostly from early to mid- or late summer. Golden lace starts in mid- to late summer, and *P. triloba* and *P. villosa* begin in late summer. Leave the spent flower clusters for their form or snip them off to prevent self-sowing. Water spring plantings regularly if rain is lacking. Established plantings also appreciate occasional watering during dry spells. If golden lace's leaves look tattered by the end of the summer, cut down the entire plant to get fresh new foliage for fall.

✹ ◉ Fall & Winter

▸ Set out new plants, or move or divide existing clumps, in early fall. Patrinias often continue to flower into early fall, and their foliage often takes on bright colors as cooler weather returns. Snip off the spent flower-heads to prevent self-sowing, but leave the foliage for the winter. Scatter a general-purpose organic fertilizer or a shovelful of compost around the plants in late fall to late winter. In Zone 4, you may want to protect the clumps with a winter mulch.

❋ **START SMALL** Golden lace (*Patrinia scabiosifolia*) tends to transplant most successfully when the plants are small. Older clumps may take several years to bloom after planting, moving, or division, so it's normally best to leave them undisturbed.

Penstemon

PENSTEMON, BEARDTONGUE

Penstemons have a reputation for being fussy, but the fault generally doesn't lie with the plants themselves.

IT'S THE GARDENER'S JOB to choose those that will thrive in his or her climate, rather than trying to force the plants to grow where they're not well suited. Some of the hundreds of species are adapted to hot, arid regions, while others grow best in cool, dry climates; then there are those that can tolerate a wider range of growing conditions.

One of the best known of the widely adapted group is foxglove penstemon (*Penstemon digitalis*), with green, red-tinged, or deep red leaves and loose, spikelike clusters of white to pale pink, tubular flowers atop upright stems anywhere from 2 to 4 feet (60 to 120 cm) tall. Hairy beard-tongue (*P. hirsutus*), blooming a few weeks later with light purple-and-white flowers, is normally 2 to 3 feet (60 to 90 cm) tall, but its popular dwarf version (*P. hirsutus* var. *pygmaeus* or 'Pygmaeus') stays around 6 inches (15 cm) tall. Beardlip penstemon (*P. barbatus*), also known as common beardtongue, is showier and blooms longer, with denser flower spikes mostly in shades of pink to red on stems anywhere from 1 to 5 feet (30 to 150 cm) tall. All of these are generally hardy in Zones 3 to 9. There are also some stunning hybrids, varying widely in flower color, bloom time, height, and hardiness.

✿ GROWING TIPS

▸ **Light & soil.** Penstemons typically thrive in full sun, but most can tolerate light shade, especially in warmer zones. Good drainage is a must for all penstemons. Foxglove penstemon usually grows best in average, somewhat moist (but not soggy) soil; the others are better suited to drier sites.

▸ **Division & propagation.** In ideal sites, penstemons can be relatively long lived, so if the clumps look crowded, consider dividing them every 3 to 4 years. Less-than-ideal conditions, though — such as too-wet or too-fertile soil, winter freezing and thawing, or high humidity — can cause the plants to die out after just a season or two. Take stem cuttings in spring, or to let your plants self-sow, to keep replacements coming along. Or, look for strains that are described as blooming the first year from seed, then grow them as annuals. Sow seed outdoors in late fall to early spring or indoors in late winter to early spring; don't cover it.

Penstemon digitalis 'Husker Red'

Penstemon (continued)

▸ **Potential problems.** Some possible problems include aphids, slugs, crown rot, leaf spots, rusts, and root-knot nematodes; mostly, though, the plants aren't seriously affected.

❖ SEASONAL CARE

○ Spring

▸ Set out new plants, or move or divide existing clumps, in early spring. Space them about 1 foot (30 cm) apart. Water new plantings regularly if rain is lacking. Apply an organic mulch around foxglove penstemon, if desired; leave the others unmulched or use gravel instead. Foxglove penstemon usually flowers in late spring; beardlip penstemon generally starts then, too.

◎ Summer

▸ When foxglove penstemon is finished flowering in early summer, you could leave the seed heads for later interest or remove them to tidy the plant. Snip off the spent clusters just above the uppermost leaves, then cut off the remaining stems at the base when they start to look bad later in the summer; or, simply cut all the stems down to the basal leaves right after bloom. Hairy beardtongue flowers in early to midsummer; when it's finished, treat it the same way.

▸ Beardlip penstemon generally keeps flowering into midsummer, at least; the hybrids bloom at different times and for different periods through the summer. When their first flower clusters fade, snipping them off just above a bloom cluster or developing bud lower down on the stem can extend the flowering season. Or, give them a rest by cutting them back by about one-half or even down to the basal leaves; this may encourage them to bloom again heavily later in the summer.

▸ Water spring plantings regularly if rain is lacking. Established penstemons tolerate dry periods but may flower more abundantly with occasional watering.

◐ ◉ Fall & Winter

▸ Many penstemons rebloom, or continue to bloom, well into fall, especially if you deadheaded or cut them back in the summer. When the show is finished, cut down the flowering stems if you wish. (Consider letting a few stems set seed to get self-sown seedlings.) Leave the basal foliage for the winter, though. Most penstemons stay green through the winter, but a few, such as foxglove and hairy penstemon, tend to turn deep purple. Scatter a general-purpose organic fertilizer or a thin layer of compost around the plants every year or two in late fall to late winter. In cold-winter areas, you may want to protect the plants with a loose winter mulch, such as evergreen boughs, straw, or pine needles.

Penstemon barbatus

Perovskia

PEROVSKIA, RUSSIAN SAGE

Shrubby clumps of perovskia make a stunning statement in the summer and fall garden, and they're attractive in other seasons, too.

THE UPRIGHT TO SOMEWHAT SPRAWLING, woody-based, whitish stems of perovskia carry aromatic, toothed to lacy-looking, gray-green leaves through the growing season, but they're practically obscured by the many-branched, spiky clusters of small, purple-blue flowers. Perovskias typically reach 3 to 5 feet (90 to 150 cm) tall and wide. You may see them sold as *Perovskia atriplicifolia* or *P. abrotanoides,* although most are actually hybrids. Fortunately, the names don't matter much from a maintenance standpoint, because they all share the same growing

Perovskia with *Rudbeckia*

conditions and care needs. Perovskias are usually hardy in Zones 5 to 9, and possibly as far north as Zone 3 with excellent drainage and winter snow cover.

❊ GROWING TIPS

▶ **Light & soil.** Perovskias perform best in full sun and average, dryish soil; good drainage is a must. They can tolerate light shade but are more prone to sprawling there.

▶ **Division & propagation.** Divide them every 4 to 6 years in spring or fall if you just want to reinvigorate large clumps or more frequently to control their spread. Digging up a few offsets is also an easy way to propagate your favorites. Other options include taking stem cuttings in spring to early summer or sowing seed outdoors in early spring or indoors in late winter (barely cover it with soil or seed-starting mix).

▶ **Potential problems.** Perovskias are typically trouble free, as long as their site is well drained.

❊ SEASONAL CARE

◐ Spring

▶ Set out new plants, or move or divide existing clumps, in early spring. Space them 2 to 3 feet (60 to 90 cm) apart. Water new plant-

ings occasionally if rain is lacking. If you wish to mulch the plants, gravel is often a better choice than an organic mulch.

▶ Once new growth appears in spring, cut the previous year's stems back to just above the lowest set of leaves on each stem or shear the whole plant back to about 6 inches (15 cm) tall. If the stems died back completely, new growth may still come up from the ground; in that case, cut the stems back as far as you wish. If your perovskias tend to sprawl in summer, trim them back again by about one-third in late spring (or a few weeks earlier in the warmest parts of their range, where the plants begin blooming by late spring) to promote more-upright growth.

◎ Summer

▶ In warm areas, perovskias can start flowering in early summer; farther north, they begin in mid- to late summer. If early blooming clumps stop flowering in summer, or if your plants sprawl badly, cut them back by one-half to two-thirds for bushy

new grow and later rebloom. (This will also help to prevent self-sowing, which can be prolific in mild areas.) Water spring plantings occasionally if rain is lacking; established plants rarely need it.

✪ ☉ Fall & Winter

▶ South of Zone 5, set out new plants, or move or divide existing clumps, in early fall. Water new plantings occasionally for the first month or so if rain is lacking. Established clumps typically keep blooming into early fall, at least. Eventually, the leaves drop off, but the whitish stems and seedpods remain to provide winter interest. If you wish to tidy the clumps or prevent self-sowing, trim the plants back lightly, but leave at least 1 foot (30 cm) of stem for the winter. Scatter a general-purpose organic fertilizer or a shovelful of compost around the clumps every other year in late fall to late winter. North of Zone 6, consider applying a protective winter mulch, such as evergreen branches or pine needles.

Persicaria

PERSICARIA, FLEECEFLOWER, KNOTWEED, SMARTWEED

If you're looking for a plant that's tough as nails, pick a persicaria.

THERE'S A LOT OF CONFUSION surrounding persicarias. Part of it is about their correct names: many of the plants in this group are often sold under a variety of other botanical names, including *Polygonum, Fallopia,* and *Tovara.*

Then, there's the question of which are safe to grow in gardens and which can spread to the point of being seriously invasive. The summer-to-fall-flowering species described here may creep or self-sow but are generally not classified as invasive.

One of the shortest options is Himalayan fleeceflower (*Persicaria affinis*), which forms spreading carpets of bright green, roughly oval leaves and slender stems topped with dense red, pink, or white flower spikes typically 6 to 8 inches (15 to 20 cm) tall. Clump-forming to moderately spreading snakeweed (*P. bistorta*), also called bistort, has similar but thicker, pink bloom spikes from 18 to 36 inches (45 to 90 cm) tall over broader leaves. Mountain fleeceflower (*P. amplexicaulis*) grows in clumps of tapering foliage topped by slender wands of rosy pink to red-dish flowers usually 3 to 4 feet (90 to 120 cm) tall. Giant fleeceflower (*P. polymorpha*), also called white dragon, reaches to about 6 feet (1.8 m) tall and wide, forming distinct clumps of stout stems carrying lance-shaped leaves and topped with large, creamy white flower plumes. All of these can grow in Zones 3 to 8 or 9.

Other persicarias are prized more for their foliage than their flowers. Jumpseed (*P. virginiana*; also sold as *P. filiformis* or *Tovara virginiana*) typically reaches 2 to 3 feet (60 to 90 cm) tall, with upright stems clad in oval leaves and tipped with wispy spikes of tiny green or red flowers. Some selections have green leaves heavily marked with maroon; others have cream-splashed leaves that may also bear maroon markings (as on 'Painter's Palette'). Zones 3 to 9. *P. microcephala* is generally about the same size and produces loose clusters of white flowers, but it's mostly grown as 'Red Dragon', which offers red stems and deep red, silver-marked new leaves. It can be hardy as far north as Zone 4, but it's generally recommended for Zones 6 to 9.

✿ GROWING TIPS

▶ **Light & soil.** Tough and adaptable, persicarias grow well in full sun to partial shade and average, moist but well-drained soil. If the soil dries out, the leaf edges may turn brown; to prevent this, mulch generously, water regularly if rain is lacking (for the first few years, at least), and consider moving the plants into afternoon shade in hot climates.

▶ **Division & propagation.** Divide persicaria clumps every 3 to 5 years in spring or fall to relieve overcrowding and for propagation. You could also take stem cuttings before the plant flowers, or sow seed outdoors in fall to spring (barely cover it with soil).

▶ **Potential problems.** Persicarias are a favorite with Japanese beetles, but otherwise, they generally aren't both-ered by pests or diseases. Himalayan fleeceflower's ground-hugging stems can creep quickly but are easy to pull out if you need to control the spread.

✿ SEASONAL CARE

◑ Spring

▶ Set out new plants, or move or divide existing clumps, in early to midspring. Space plants of Himalayan fleeceflower about 18 inches (45 cm) apart; snakeweed and jumpseed about 2 feet (60 cm) apart; mountain fleeceflower and *P. microcephala* about 3 feet (90 cm) apart; and giant fleeceflower about 5 feet (1.5 m) apart. Water new plantings regularly if rain is lacking. Apply an organic mulch before summer. Himalayan fleeceflower and snakeweed often begin flowering in late spring. Giant fleeceflower may be a little late to sprout in some years but grows quickly, and it, too, may begin to bloom in late spring in some areas.

Persicaria virginiana 'Painter's Palette'

Persicaria polymorpha

◎ Summer

▸ Himalayan fleeceflower typically flowers through the summer. Snakeweed is at its best in early to midsummer but may produce some blooms later as well. Mountain fleeceflower generally starts in midsummer and continues through the summer. Giant fleeceflower may start in early summer (if not sooner) and bloom into midsummer or start in midsummer and continue through late summer. The flowers on all of these tend to turn rusty brown as they age; snip them off back to the leaves, if you wish, or leave them for their form.

▸ Jumpseed and *P. microcephala* start flowering in late summer. On jumpseed, the blooms aren't very showy, so you may want to keep them

snipped off to prevent self-sowing. On *P. microcephala,* leave them or remove them, as you wish. If the plant starts getting too large for its space, feel free to cut it back by about one-half to control its size; you'll get more colorful new foliage too.

▸ Water spring plantings of all persicarias regularly if rain is lacking. Established plants also appreciate occasional watering during dry spells.

✸ ☉ Fall & Winter

▸ Set out new plants, or move or divide existing clumps, in early fall. Water new plantings regularly for the first month or so after planting if rain is lacking. Many persicarias continue to flower into early fall, at least; mountain fleeceflower, in particular, is often at its best from early

fall until frost. Keep clipping off the flower stalks of jumpseed to prevent self-sowing.

▸ As the weather cools, the leaves of snakeweed, mountain fleeceflower, and (sometimes) giant fleeceflower may take on reddish to purplish colors. The older leaves of Himalayan fleeceflower typically turn rusty brown, while the younger leaves take on reddish tints or stay deep green; shear off the flower stems, if you wish, but leave the foliage in place for winter. As the others die back after frost, cut them to the ground then or wait until late winter (or early spring) to remove the dead stalks. Scatter a general-purpose organic fertilizer or a shovelful of compost around each clump in late fall to late winter.

Phlomis

PHLOMIS, JERUSALEM SAGE

Handsome in leaf and distinctive in bloom, phlomis are an out-of-the-ordinary option for multiseason garden interest.

THEY DIFFER IN SIZE AND COLOR, but they all have similar flower structures: ball-like bloom clusters that appear along the upper parts of the upright stems.

Jerusalem sage is a common name used for two long-blooming, yellow-flowered species with fuzzy, aromatic, gray-green to olive-green leaves. *Phlomis fruticosa* forms shrubby clumps that typically reach 3 to 6 feet (90 to 180 cm) tall. It's most often grown in Zones 7 to 10, but garden-ers several zones farther north have also claimed to grow it successfully. *P. russeliana* tends to be much shorter — to about 3 feet (90 cm) tall — and is generally hardy in Zones 4 to 9. *P. tuberosa* is quite different than the other two, with rich green leaves and light pink to purplish flowers on deep purple-red stems usually 4 to 6 feet (1.2 to 1.8 m) tall. It's recommended for Zones 3 to 9.

❖ GROWING TIPS

▶ **Light & soil.** Full sun brings out the best from phlomis in most areas, but in hot, dry climates, partial shade is often ideal. Good drainage is impor-tant for all three species. *P. fruticosa* and *P. russeliana* tend to grow best in loose, sandy to gravelly, infertile soil. *P. tuberosa* is more tolerant of moist (but not soggy), fertile soil.

▶ **Division & propagation.** Divide *P. russeliana* and *P. tuberosa* every 4 to 5 years in spring or fall, or take stem cuttings of any phlomis in summer. To grow phlomis from seed, sow indoors in late winter or outdoors in spring; barely cover it.

▶ **Potential problems.** Slugs may feed on the foliage of *P. tuberosa,* and crown rot can affect any phlomis growing in too-wet soil, but mostly, the plants aren't bothered by pests or diseases. It can take young phlomis plants a few years to settle in and bloom; and established plants occa-sionally skip flowering for a year.

❖ SEASONAL CARE

◐ Spring

▶ Set out new plants, or move or divide existing clumps, in early spring. Space them about 2 feet (60 cm) apart. Water new plantings regu-larly if rain is lacking. Apply a light organic mulch around *P. tuberosa* before summer; leave the other two unmulched or use gravel instead. In very mild regions, *P. fruticosa* may begin blooming at any point dur-ing the spring. *P. russeliana* can be a little slow to produce new growth in spring. *P. tuberosa* sends up fresh foliage early and may start blooming in late spring.

◑ Summer

▶ *P. fruticosa* and *P. russeliana* flower all through the summer in most areas. If *P. fruticosa* stops producing new flowers, cutting the plants back by one-third to one-half can encour-age fresh growth and more blooms. *P. tuberosa* may continue flower-ing from late spring through early summer or start in early summer and continue through midsummer (sometimes even into late summer). Once its flowers are finished, the flowering stems turn brown; remove them at the base to tidy the plants and prevent self-sowing or leave them for their interesting form. Keep watering spring plantings occasion-ally if rain is lacking. Established plantings can also benefit from occa-sional watering during dry spells.

◐ ◉ Fall & Winter

▶ South of Zone 6, set out new plants, or move or divide existing clumps, in early fall. Water new plant-ings occasionally for the first month or so if rain is lacking. *P. fruticosa* and *P. russeliana* may keep flowering into early fall, and their seed heads and leaves stay attractive through the winter months. Wait until late winter to remove the old flowering stems: cut back to the uppermost leaves, or further down the stems to reduce the size of the clump, on *P. fruticosa,* and close to the base of the stems on *P. russeliana.* Leave the stems of *P. tube-rosa* for winter structure, or remove them at any point in the fall or winter. Scatter a general-purpose organic fertilizer around *P. tuberosa* every year or two in late fall to late winter; the other two species generally don't need fertilizing.

Phlomis tuberosa

Phlox

Phlox are a classic choice for perennial plantings in many regions, and with good reason: they're eye-catching in bloom, and they're often delightfully fragrant, as well.

THERE ARE MANY PHLOX to choose from, but fortunately, they fall into just a few basic groups, which makes figuring out how to care for them relatively straightforward. First, you can separate them into two groups: the upright types and the low-growing types.

Among the upright types, which are also referred to as border phlox, are several clump-formers with relatively large flower clusters produced mainly in summer. Garden phlox (*Phlox paniculata*), also known as summer phlox, blooms mostly in white or shades or pink over matte green leaves on stems usually 3 to 4 feet (90 to 120 cm) tall. Carolina phlox (*P. carolina*) reaches about the same height and flowers in the same color range but has shinier leaves. Meadow phlox (*P. maculata*) tends to be a bit shorter than the other two — typically 2 to 3 feet (60 to 90 cm) tall. It has somewhat glossy leaves, too, but they are narrower than those of Carolina phlox. There are also many hybrids in this group, offering a wide range of plant heights and flower colors. All of these upright phlox are generally recommended for Zones 3 to 8.

The low-growing phlox, which form mats, carpets, or spreading mounds, separate rather neatly into two smaller groups: the sun-lovers and the shade-lovers. All of these typically bloom for several weeks in spring (possibly into summer), though their exact flowering period can vary depending on the climate and on local weather conditions.

One of the best-known low-growing sun-lovers is moss phlox (*P. subulata*), also known as moss pink, which forms ankle-high carpets of needlelike leaves smothered with white, pink, reddish, or lavender-blue flowers. Zones 2 to 9. Some other sun-lovers include narrow-leaved, pink-flowered prairie phlox (*P. pilosa*) — commonly 12 to 18 inches (30 to 45 cm) tall and hardy in Zones 3 to 8 — and sand phlox (*P. bifida*), with needlelike leaves and white to pale purple flowers on carpets about 6 inches (15 cm) tall. Zones 4 to 8.

As you can guess by its name, woodland phlox (*P. divaricata*) is one of the shade-tolerant low-growers. Also known as wild blue phlox, it's a spreader with lance-shaped leaves and upright stalks to about 1 foot (30 cm) tall, topped with light purple-blue or white flowers; Zones 3 to 8. Another shade-lover is creeping phlox (*P. stolonifera*), with roughly oval leaves and blue, pink, or white flowers that typically reach 6 to 8 inches (15 to 20 cm) tall; Zones 2 to 8.

❋ GROWING TIPS

▶ **Light & soil.** Upright types (garden phlox, Carolina phlox, and meadow phlox) grow best in a site with full sun to light shade and compost-enriched, moist but well-drained soil. The low-growing sun-lovers (moss phlox, prairie phlox, and sand phlox) prefer full sun and average to poor, relatively dry sites. Loose, sandy soil is ideal; if your soil is on the heavier side, try growing these phlox in a raised bed or on a slope for better drainage. Woodland phlox thrives with morning sun and afternoon shade or light all-day shade, while creeping phlox is better suited to partial or full shade; compost-enriched, evenly moist but well-drained soil is ideal for both.

▶ **Division & propagation.** Plan on dividing upright phlox every 3 to 5 years in spring or fall. Division is also an easy way to propagate your favorite cultivars; alternately, take stem cuttings in spring to early summer or try root cuttings in fall or early spring. The low-growing sun-lovers also benefit from being divided every 3 to 5 years (or more frequently if you're trying to slow their spread). It's ideal to divide them right after flowering, but you can also do it in early spring or early fall. Taking stem cuttings in summer is another option for propagation. Woodland and creeping phlox generally don't need to be divided to stay healthy, but if you want to propagate them, divide right after flowering (the ideal time), or in early spring or early fall. If you want to try growing phlox from seed, sow outdoors in fall and barely cover it with soil.

▶ **Potential problems.** A number of possible problems can bother the various types of phlox, among them beetles, plant bugs, spider mites, stalk borers, aster yellows, botrytis (gray mold), crown rot (southern blight), leaf spots, mosaic virus, rusts, and stem and leaf nematodes. (See Troubleshooting, page 303,

Phlox subulata

too.) Also, it's not unusual for older clumps of upright phlox to drop their lower leaves as the growing season progresses. Divide and replant them into compost-enriched soil to help restore their vigor, and water them regularly. If the leaf drop still occurs, pair the plants with lower-growing companions to hide the phlox's "bare ankles."

❄ SEASONAL CARE

◐ Spring

▸ Set out new plants in early spring. You can also move or divide existing clumps in early spring, although it's usually best to wait until after flowering for those that bloom in spring (basically, all of the low-growing, spreading types). Space the low-growers about 18 inches (45 cm) apart and the upright, summer-blooming types about 2 feet (60 cm) apart. Water new plantings regularly if rain is lacking.

▸ Early spring is a good time to snip off any winter-damaged shoots on phlox that hold their foliage through the winter. Be aware that it's common for some phlox to have a reddish or purplish tinge to their leaves in spring. Upright phlox and shade-loving low-growers benefit from an organic mulch applied in spring. The low-growing sun-lovers don't really need mulch, but if you wish to use it, apply only a light layer of organic mulch or use gravel instead.

◑ Summer

▸ Some low-growing phlox continue blooming into the summer. Once any low-growing phlox is finished, shear off the flower stems just above the foliage to tidy the plants. (If you had problems with your low-growing phlox clumps flopping open last summer, consider cutting them back a little harder — by about one-half their height — to encourage bushier regrowth.) Early summer is also a good time to move or divide the spring-bloomers, if needed.

▸ Meadow phlox mostly flowers from early to midsummer, while Carolina phlox may bloom from early to midsummer or mid- to late summer, depending on where you live. Garden phlox and the hybrids commonly bloom from mid- to late summer or late summer into fall. Cutting off the spent flower clusters helps to extend the bloom period on all of these upright phlox and helps to prevent self-sowing (particularly important for garden phlox, which can reseed heavily).

If your upright phlox clumps sprawl during or after flowering, or if their leaves get heavily spotted or discolored, cut them back by one-half to two-thirds to shape the plants and get better-looking leaves for the rest of the growing season.

▸ Through the summer, keep watering spring and summer plantings if rain is lacking. Established clumps of upright, summer-blooming phlox and shade-loving low-growers also appreciate watering during dry spells.

✪ ☉ Fall & Winter

▸ Set out new plants, or move or divide existing clumps, in early fall. Water new plantings regularly for the first month or so if rain is lacking.

▸ Summer-blooming phlox may continue flowering into autumn; keep snipping off the spent flower clusters to prevent self-sowing. After frost, cut the stems of upright phlox plants to the ground. Scatter a handful of general-purpose organic fertilizer or a shovelful of compost (or both) around each clump in late fall to late winter.

▸ Low-growing phlox tend to hold their leaves well into winter, if not

Phlox paniculata 'Nora Leigh'

On variegated phlox cultivars like 'Nora Leigh' snip off any solid-green shoots as soon as you notice them. If they return, you'll need to dig up the clump and cut out the all-green section before replanting the rest. Otherwise, the entire clump may be mostly or entirely green within a few seasons, as the vigorous green parts crowd out the weaker-growing variegated stems.

the entire winter season. In colder regions where winter snow cover is lacking, covering the plants with evergreen branches can help to keep the foliage and developing flower buds from being damaged by cold.

Scatter some compost around the shade-lovers (woodland phlox and creeping phlox) in late fall to late winter. The sun-loving types generally don't need fertilizing.

❖ TROUBLESHOOTING

▸ **Leaves, stems, and buds with dusty-looking, white to gray patches.** Powdery mildew is a fungal disease that attacks several types of phlox: particularly garden phlox but also some other types. Carolina phlox and meadow phlox have glossier leaves, which seem to be less susceptible to infection, so these upright species have been crossed to produce a number of hybrids that appear to have better-than-average mildew resistance. Choosing cultivars that are described as being mildew-resistant is a great way to minimize the chance of this problem. Still, these cultivars are not completely immune to mildew, so if the growing conditions favor the fungus, you may still notice some symptoms.

Regular watering during summer dry spells can help the plants to stay healthy; so may dividing overgrown clumps or snipping out all but four to six stems in spring, to allow for good air circulation around the stems and leaves. If you do notice powdery white spots starting to form on a few leaves, pinch off and destroy the affected foliage and spray the rest of the plant with fungicidal soap or a biofungicide to slow further disease development. If you don't notice the damage before the plants are seriously affected, cut off and destroy all of the top growth.

▸ **Flowers change color from year to year.** Garden phlox and some of its hybrids can self-sow prolifically, mostly producing seedlings that flower in shades of pink. Sometimes, these seedlings sprout up right next to their parents, and you may not notice them until you see a plant that suddenly appears to have two bloom colors in one clump. If this happens, dig up the clump right after bloom and divide it to remove the unwanted part. Pull or dig out any other off-color seedlings as soon as you spot them. If your phlox flowers are basically the same color you expected but a somewhat different shade or intensity, it's likely due to the growing conditions. Blooms may be bleached out or lose a contrasting "eye" in intense sun or high temperatures, or they may appear darker than usual in cool weather.

Garden phlox (*Phlox paniculata*) and its hybrids are glorious in full flower, but their large bloom clusters may cause the tall stems to sprawl. Try cutting them back by one-third to one-half in late spring or early summer to get somewhat lower, bushier plants that will be less prone to flopping. Otherwise, you may need to use linking stakes or Y-stakes to prop up the tallest types.

Phlox paniculata 'David'

Powdery mildew

Physostegia

OBEDIENT PLANT, FALSE DRAGONHEAD, DRAGON MINT

If you're already growing obedient plant, you may be more likely to call it by another name — "disobedient plant" — because of its habit of spreading quickly by creeping roots.

STILL, IT CAN BE WORTH PLANTING for its showy spikes of pink, purplish pink, or white flowers, which appear atop upright stems clad in narrow, deep green leaves. It generally grows 3 to 4 feet (90 to 120 cm) tall, although the stems can be as short as 2 feet (60 cm) or as tall as 6 feet (1.8 m), depending on the cultivar. If you like its spiky blooms but are nervous about adding it to your garden, consider trying 'Miss Manners', a white-flowered selection that's distinctive for its tendency to stay in noncreeping clumps. Obedient plant can grow in Zones 3 to 9.

Physostegia virginiana

❀ GROWING TIPS

▶ **Light & soil.** Full sun and moist, compost-enriched soil encourages the most vigorous growth on obedient plant. However, the goal in growing this perennial is more often to slow it down than to encourage its spread, so consider trying it in a less-than-ideal spot, such as a somewhat dry or infertile site, or in tight, clayey soil. Obedient plant can also grow in partial shade, but its stems are more likely to flop there.

▶ **Division & propagation.** Dividing obedient plants every 2 or 3 years (or even every other year) may help to control their spread somewhat, and it's also a simple way to propagate the plants. You can also take stem cuttings in late spring to early summer, or sow seed outdoors in fall to early spring and barely cover it with soil.

▶ **Potential problems.** Possible problems include crown rot (southern blight), leaf spots, and rust, but they're not very common.

❀ SEASONAL CARE

◐ Spring

▶ Set out new plants, or move or divide existing clumps, in early to midspring. Space them about 2 feet (60 cm) apart. Water new plantings regularly if rain is lacking. Apply an organic mulch before summer. If your plants sprawled last year, cut them back by about one-half in late spring to encourage lower, bushier stems.

◉ Summer

▶ In most areas, obedient plant starts flowering in late summer. Clipping off the flower clusters once the blossoms drop can extend the flowering period by several weeks. (This also helps to prevent self-sowing.) If your plants sprawl or start to look tired by the end of the summer, cut them back by two-thirds, or even all the way to the ground, for fresh new growth. Water spring plantings regularly if rain is lacking. Established plants grow most vigorously with occasional watering during dry spells but can get by without it.

❂ ◉ Fall & Winter

▶ Set out new plants, or move or divide existing clumps, in early fall. Water new plantings regularly for the first month or so if rain is lacking. Obedient plant may continue blooming into autumn, especially if you snip off the spent flower clusters. Cut down the stems any time after frost. Scatter a general-purpose organic fertilizer or a shovelful of compost around the clumps every other year in late fall to late winter.

❀ TROUBLESHOOTING

▶ **Plants spread aggressively.** Think carefully about how you're going to control your obedient plant *before* you plant it. Grow it alone where it can spread freely or pair it with equally vigorous partners, and snip off the faded flower clusters regularly to prevent self-sowing. In a mixed border, try planting it in a large, bottomless pot or bucket sunk almost to its rim in the soil, or surround the clump with a strip of plastic or metal about 6 inches (15 cm) deep.

Platycodon

BALLOON FLOWER

Platycodon grandiflorus 'Zwerg'

Whether you prefer their puffed-up buds or their wide-open, star-shaped blooms, balloon flowers are a welcome sight in the summer garden.

THE LIGHT GREEN NEW SHOOTS of balloon flower (*Platycodon grandiflorus*) mature into upright stems clad in rich green, toothed leaves and topped with purple-blue, pink, or white flowers. The plants commonly grow 2 to 4 feet (60 to 120 cm) tall, though some compact cultivars reach just 6 to 12 inches (15 to 30 cm) tall. Balloon flowers are generally recommended for Zones 3 to 9.

❋ GROWING TIPS

▸ **Light & soil.** Balloon flowers can perform well in full sun to light shade with average, somewhat moist but well-drained soil.

▸ **Division & propagation.** If you must move or divide them, dig deeply to preserve as much of the root system as possible. New plants may take several years to settle in and reach their mature size. The easiest way to propagate balloon flowers is by sowing seed (left uncovered) outdoors pretty much any time or indoors in late winter to early spring.

▸ **Potential problems.** Other than occasional feeding by slugs and snails, and possible root rot if their site is too wet, balloon flowers are typically trouble free and can grow well in one spot for many years without needing to be divided.

❋ SEASONAL CARE

○ Spring

▸ Set out new plants, or move or divide existing clumps if you must, in early spring. Space them 18 to 24 inches (45 to 60 cm) apart, or 12 inches (30 cm) apart for the dwarf cultivars. Water new plantings regularly if rain is lacking. Apply an organic mulch before summer. Be aware that balloon flowers are very slow to sprout, sometimes not appearing until the very end of spring. If your plants sprawled last year, consider setting grow-through supports over them in mid- to late spring, or snip off the shoot tips once in late spring to promote lower, bushier growth.

◎ Summer

▸ If you didn't pinch your balloon flower plants earlier, cut the plants back by about one-half in early summer if you want to prevent sprawling. In mild areas, the plants may flower mostly in early to midsummer; elsewhere, they're at their best in mid- to late summer. Carefully pinching or snipping off the dead blossoms encourages the plants to produce more flowers and prevents self-sowing. Water first-year plantings regularly if rain is lacking. Established plantings also benefit from occasional watering during dry spells.

◑ ◉ Fall & Winter

▸ Set out new plants, or move or divide established clumps if you must, in early fall. Water new plantings regularly for the first month or so if rain is lacking. Balloon flowers may bloom into early fall or even until frost. As the temperatures cool, the foliage typically turns bright yellow, sometimes with shades of red or purple as well. Once the leaves drop, it's fine to remove the dead stems. Consider cutting them a bit higher than usual, though — about 4 inches (10 cm) or so above the ground — to mark the location of the clumps. Scatter a general-purpose organic fertilizer or a shovelful of compost around each clump in late fall to late winter.

❋ **START FROM SEED** If you'd like to experiment with growing perennials from seed, balloon flowers are a great plant to start with. Their seedlings are a little delicate, so you need to handle them gently, but they grow quickly and may flower during their first summer. They're so speedy, in fact, that some are sold as annuals, even though they're winter hardy in most areas.

Polemonium

JACOB'S LADDER

Lovely in leaf and even prettier in bloom, Jacob's ladders are an elegant addition to early season beds and borders.

Polemonium careuleum 'Brise d'Anjou'

ALSO KNOWN AS GREEK VALERIAN, the most common Jacob's ladder, *Polemonium caeruleum*, has distinctly upright bloom stems topped with clusters of blue or white flowers. It typically reaches 18 to 24 inches (45 to 60 cm) tall. Creeping Jacob's ladder (*P. reptans*) — which actually doesn't creep, but instead stays in somewhat loose mounds typically 12 to 18 inches (30 to 45 cm) tall — has similar-looking blooms but tends to flower a few weeks earlier. Both species are generally recommended for Zones 3 to 8.

❁ GROWING TIPS

▸ **Light & soil.** Jacob's ladders can grow in full sun in the cooler parts of their growing range, but in most areas, partial shade is best. Compost-enriched, moist but well-drained soil is ideal.

▸ **Division & propagation.** Jacob's ladders generally don't need to be divided and can be slow to recover if you try it, so consider taking stem cuttings in summer if you want to propagate your favorites. Or, sow seed outdoors in fall to early spring or indoors in late winter to early spring; barely cover it.

▸ **Potential problems.** The plants can be long lived where the growing conditions are just right; elsewhere, they may fade away after a few years, so consider letting a few flower stalks set seed to get self-sown seedlings for replacements.

❁ SEASONAL CARE

◗ Spring

▸ Set out new plants, or move or divide existing clumps, in early spring. Space them 12 to 18 inches (45 to 60 cm) apart. Water new plantings regularly if rain is lacking. Early spring is a good time to snip off any winter-damaged leaves. Add a generous layer of organic mulch before summer. Creeping Jacob's ladder usually starts flowering in mid-spring, while the common Jacob's ladder often begins in late spring.

◎ Summer

▸ Creeping Jacob's ladder typically finishes flowering in early summer. *P. caeruleum* may continue from spring or not begin until early summer, then keeps flowering into midsummer. When the blooms are finished, cut off the flowering stems at the base to tidy the plants and prevent self-sowing. A few new flowers may appear later in the summer. Keep watering spring plantings regularly if rain is lacking. Established plants also appreciate watering during dry spells. If the soil dries out in summer, the leaves may develop browned tips; in that case, cut the foliage to the ground and water thoroughly to encourage a flush of fresh new leaves.

✿ ◎ Fall & Winter

▸ Set out new plants, or move or divide existing clumps, in early fall. Leave the foliage in place in winter. Scatter a general-purpose organic fertilizer or a shovelful of compost around each clump in late fall to late winter.

❁ **SUCCESS WITH STRIPES** Both species of Jacob's ladder have variegated cultivars, but those of *P. caeruleum* can be tricky to grow successfully. 'Stairway to Heaven' creeping Jacob's ladder (*P. reptans*), on the other hand, appears to be more widely adaptable to average garden conditions.

Polygonatum

SOLOMON'S SEAL

Solomon's seals aren't especially showy in bloom, but their handsome foliage and form earn them a place as stars of the shade garden.

THEIR CREEPING ROOTS FORM expanding patches of upright-to-arching stems that carry two rows of oval to broadly lance-shaped, light to medium green leaves. Small, bell-shaped blooms hang below the leaves early in the season, maturing into small, rounded, blue-black fruits. Several commonly grown species bear creamy white to greenish white flowers.

Dwarf Solomon's seal (*Polygonatum humile*) is the shortest at 4 to 8 inches (10 to 20 cm) tall; great Solomon's seal (*P. biflorum* var. *commutatum*) reaches 6 to 7 feet (1.8 to 2.1 m). Most others are in the range of 2 to 3 feet (60 to 90 cm) tall, including common Solomon's seal (*P. × hybridum*), fragrant Solomon's seal (*P. odoratum*), and smooth Solomon's seal (*P. biflorum*). Variegated fragrant Solomon's seal (*P. odoratum* var. *pluriflorum* 'Variegatum'; also sold as *P. falcatum* 'Variegatum') is a popular selection with pink new shoots, red to pink stems, and cream-streaked leaf edges. All of these Solomon's seals are generally hardy in Zones 3 to 9.

Polygonatum odoratum 'Variegatum'

❀ GROWING TIPS

▶ **Light & soil.** Solomon's seals can tolerate full sun in cool-summer areas, especially if the soil stays evenly moist; elsewhere, they thrive in morning sun and afternoon shade or light all-day shade with average, somewhat moist but well-drained soil. They can even tolerate full shade with dry soil, if you water them regularly for the first few years to get their roots well established.

▶ **Division & propagation.** The clumps don't require regular division, but if they outgrow their space, or if you want to propagate them, you can divide them in spring (ideally before or just as they begin sprouting) or in early fall. If you want to try growing them from seed, sow outdoors in late summer or fall and barely cover it with soil.

▶ **Potential problems.** Possible problems include slugs and snails, weevils, leaf spots, and rusts; usually, though, the plants are trouble free.

❀ SEASONAL CARE

○ Spring

▶ Set out new plants, or move or divide existing clumps, in early spring. Space dwarf Solomon's seal plants 8 to 12 inches (20 to 30 cm) apart and the others about 18 inches (45 cm) apart. Water new plantings regularly if rain is lacking. Apply a generous layer of organic mulch in early to midspring. Solomon's seals begin blooming in mid- to late spring.

◎ Summer

▶ Flowering generally finishes in early summer. There's no need to bother with deadheading. In dry conditions, the plants may start to look tattered or turn yellow by late summer; in that case, cut them to the ground. Keep watering spring plantings regularly if rain is lacking. Established plantings benefit from occasional watering during dry spells.

✪ ◉ Fall & Winter

▶ Set out new plants, or move or divide existing clumps, in early fall. Water them regularly for the first month or so if rain is lacking. As the weather cools, the plants typically turn yellow, adding color to the fall garden. Once the leaves drop, cut the stems to the ground. Scatter a general-purpose organic fertilizer or a shovelful of compost around each clump every year or two in late fall to late winter.

Potentilla

CINQUEFOIL

Easy-care cinquefoils offer a long season of bright blooms and don't ask for much in return.

CINQUEFOILS FORM HANDSOME, evergreen mounds of multipart leaves, with branching flower stems carrying small but colorful flowers typically 18 to 30 inches (45 to 75 cm) tall.

Himalayan cinquefoil (*Potentilla atrosanguinea*), also known as ruby cinquefoil, typically bears deep red flowers over three-part green leaves with silver undersides. Silver cinquefoil (*P. atrosanguinea* var. *argyrophylla*; also known as *P. argyrophylla*) has similarly shaped leaves that are dis-tinctly more silvery, plus yellow flowers. The blooms of Nepal cinquefoil (*P. nepalensis*) are mostly in the red to rosy purple range, over five-parted green leaves with narrower leaflets. There are also many hybrids between these species, with green to silvery leaves and single to double blooms in a wide color range, including many shades of yellow, orange, red, and pink, as well as white. These cinquefoils are usually recommended for Zones 4 to 8.

❀ GROWING TIPS

▸ **Light & soil.** Give cinquefoils a site with full sun to light shade with average, well-drained soil. These perennials tend to perform best where summers aren't particularly hot and humid.

▸ **Division & propagation.** Divide the clumps every 3 years in spring or fall to keep them vigorous. Division is also a good way to propagate your favorite colors; or, take stem cuttings in spring. If you don't mind that the flower colors can vary, you can easily grow new plants from seed. Sow outdoors in fall to spring or indoors in late winter to early spring, and barely cover the seed.

▸ **Potential problems.** Apart from occasional problems with aphids, strawberry weevils, leaf spots, or powdery mildew, cinquefoils are mostly trouble free.

❀ SEASONAL CARE

◑ Spring

▸ Set out new plants or move or divide existing clumps in early spring. Space them about 2 feet (60 cm) apart. Water new plantings regularly if rain is lacking. Apply an organic mulch in early to midspring. Cinquefoils may begin blooming in late spring.

◎ Summer

▸ Early to midsummer is peak bloom time for most cinquefoils, though they often keep producing new blooms through the rest of the summer. If the flowers slow down, or if the clumps start looking messy or are sprawling too much in mid-to late summer, shear off the spent flowering stems to encourage fresh new growth and possible rebloom. Keep watering spring plantings regularly if rain is lacking. Watering established clumps occasionally during dry spells encourages the most abundant flowering and prevents leaf browning.

✿ ◉ Fall & Winter

▸ South of Zone 5, set out new plants, or move or divide existing clumps, in early fall. Water new plantings regularly for the first month or so if rain is lacking. Cinquefoils often continue blooming into fall, especially if you cut them back in summer. Once they're finished, cut off the flowering stems. The foliage often looks good well into the colder months. North of Zone 6, consider protecting the clumps with evergreen boughs or another lightweight winter mulch. Scatter a general-purpose organic fertilizer or a shovelful of compost around each clump every year or two in late fall to late winter.

❀ **CINQUEFOIL CHANGES** Young cinquefoil plants tend to stay close to the ground, but after a season or two, they typically mound more than sprawl.

Potentilla nepalensis

Primula

PRIMROSE

Primroses grow in rosettes of deeply veined leaves with clustered flowers in a variety of colors.

THERE ARE DOZENS OF SPECIES and hybrids of primroses to choose from, but only a few of them are available outside of specialty nurseries.

Among the best-known primroses are the polyantha primroses (*Primula × polyantha*), a group of hybrids that reach 6 to 12 inches (15 to 30 cm) tall in full bloom, with flat-faced flowers in a rainbow of solid colors and bicolors. Their growing range can be Zones 3 to 8, though individual plants may vary in hardiness. Cowslip (*P. veris*), one of the parents of the polyanthas, has the same height and har- diness range but with relatively narrow, nodding blooms. The fragrant flowers are commonly yellow, but you can also find forms with orange to reddish blooms.

Drumstick primrose (*P. denticulata*) holds light pur- ple, pink, red, or white flowers in spherical clusters atop stems about 1 foot (30 cm) tall. Japanese primrose (*P. japonica*) is the giant of this group, reaching 1 to 2 feet (30 to 60 cm) tall in bloom, with red, pink, or white flowers held in tiered clusters. Both of these primroses are gener- ally hardy in Zones 3 to 8.

❊ GROWING TIPS

▶ **Light & soil.** Primroses can toler- ate quite a bit of sun in spring, but by summertime, they benefit from some shade, especially during the hottest part of the day. Somewhat moist, compost-enriched soil is ideal; drumstick and Japanese primroses, in particular, appreciate constantly moist soil.

▶ **Division & propagation.** Dividing crowded clumps every 2 to 3 years, right after bloom or in early fall, is a good way to help keep them vigor- ous, and it's also an easy option for propagating your favorite plants. If you don't mind that the flower color may vary, you can try growing new plants from seed. Sow outdoors in fall to early spring; don't cover the seed. Or, sow indoors in early winter, then enclose the pots in plastic bags and refrigerate them for 6 to 12 weeks before moving them to a cool, bright spot. Primroses may also self-sow in ideal conditions, if you don't dead- head them right after flowering.

▶ **Potential problems.** A number of problems can bother primroses, including aphids, black vine weevils, flea beetles, slugs, spider mites, aster yellows, leaf spots, mosaic virus, and rusts.

❊ SEASONAL CARE

◐ Spring

▶ Set out new plants in early spring. Space polyanthas and cowslips about 8 inches (20 cm) apart and drumstick and Japanese primroses about 1 foot (30 cm) apart. You can move or divide the plants in early spring, if you must, but it's usually best to wait until right after they are finished flowering. Water new plant- ings regularly if rain is lacking. Apply a generous layer of organic mulch in early to midspring. Polyanthas, cowslips, and drumstick primroses usually bloom in early to late spring; Japanese primroses tend to start a bit later, in mid- to late spring.

◯ Summer

▶ Most primroses are finished flow- ering by early summer, but Japanese primroses often continue through early summer or even into midsum- mer. After bloom, clip off the spent flowering stems to tidy the plants; move or divide the plants then, too, if needed. Polyanthas and cowslips may develop yellowed leaves (snip them off) or lose their leaves altogether in hot-summer areas, then resprout in fall. Regularly watering both new and established plantings if rain is lacking can help to keep primrose plants looking good through the summer.

◒ ◉ Fall & Winter

▶ Set out new plants, or move or divide existing clumps if you didn't do it earlier, in early fall. Water new plantings regularly for the first month or so if rain is lacking. It's not unusual for primroses to produce scattered rebloom in fall. (In fact, in mild regions, polyanthas can be treated as annuals, planted in fall for flowering through the winter.) Scatter a general-purpose organic fertilizer or a shovelful of compost (or both) around each clump in late fall to late winter. Polyanthas and cowslips keep their leaves during the winter; drumstick and Japanese primroses die back to the ground. North of Zone 5, consider protect- ing your primroses with a winter mulch, particularly if you don't have a dependable snow cover through the coldest months.

In ideal growing conditions, primroses are typically trouble free. Elsewhere, it can take some regular attention to keep them in peak condition, but when you see their lovely spring blooms, you'll know they're worth it.

Primula japonica

Pulmonaria

PULMONARIA, LUNGWORT

Superb for beautiful blooms in spring and lovely foliage later, pulmonarias ask relatively little in return for their extended period of garden interest.

THERE ARE SEVERAL SPECIES of pulmonaria to choose from. Those sold as Bethlehem sage (*Pulmonaria saccharata*) and *P. officinalis* typically have broad, spotted leaves; longleaf pulmonaria (*P. longifolia*) is also spotted but has much narrower foliage. The flowers of the spotted-leaf types tend to be pink in bud and when just opened, commonly turning blue as they age.

Of the species with solid-green leaves, red lungwort (*P. rubra*) has relatively wide foliage and reddish flowers, while blue lungwort (*P. angustifolia*) has slender leaves and deep blue flowers.

Most of the pulmonarias sold today are hybrids of these and other species, so they vary widely in their leaf shape and markings (from none at all to silver-spotted to nearly solid silver), as well as in flower color, vigor, and heat tolerance. Generally, though, they all form slowly expanding clumps or patches that reach 12 to 18 inches (30 to 45 cm) tall in bloom. Hardiness varies, too, but most can grow well in Zones 3 to 8.

❁ GROWING TIPS

▸ **Light & soil.** In the coolest parts of their growing range, pulmonarias can grow in full sun, but generally, they thrive with morning sun and afternoon shade or with light all-day shade. They can tolerate full shade but won't flower as abundantly there. Compost-enriched, evenly moist but well-drained soil encourages vigorous growth and lush foliage. Pulmonarias can also adapt to quite dry sites, especially if you water them regularly for the first few summers.

▸ **Division & propagation.** Divide your pulmonarias right after flowering or in early fall every 4 to 6 years, or whenever they look crowded. Division is also the best way to propagate your favorite plants. You'll rarely find seed for sale. If you leave the flowering stems on your plants after bloom, they'll often self-sow; keep in mind, though, that the seedlings can vary in flower color and leaf markings.

▸ **Potential problems.** Aphids occasionally bother the plants, and slugs and snails may feed on tender new leaves. (Also see Troubleshooting, opposite page.)

❁ SEASONAL CARE

◐ Spring

▸ Set out new plants in early to midspring. Space them about 18 inches (45 cm) apart. Water new plantings regularly if rain is lacking. Early spring is a good time to trim away any winter-damaged leaves, if you didn't do it earlier; just be careful not to damage the emerging flower buds. Apply a generous layer of organic mulch before summer. The peak bloom period for pulmonarias is usually early to midspring, though it can continue through late spring. If you need to move or divide your plants, it's ideal to complete the task as soon as the flowers are finished.

◉ Summer

▸ As pulmonarias finish blooming, their flower stems usually sprawl to the ground. You could leave them, because the emerging new foliage will cover them up. Or, you may choose to cut them off at the base, to tidy the clumps and prevent self-sowing. Keep watering spring plantings regularly if rain is lacking. Established clumps also benefit from occasional watering during dry spells.

✿ ◉ Fall & Winter

▸ Set out new plants, or move or divide existing clumps if you didn't do it right after flowering. Water new plantings regularly for the first month or so if rain is lacking. The return of cooler weather brings out

❁ **WHACK IT BACK** As the summer progresses, pulmonaria leaves may appear tattered or discolored. Snip off damaged leaves individually or shear all of the foliage to the ground to get a flush of fresh new foliage (and possibly even a few new flowers) in a few weeks.

Pulmonaria hybrid

new foliage and sometimes scattered light rebloom. The foliage tends to look good into early winter, at least. Late winter is a good time to clip off any dead or winter-damaged leaves. providing a clean backdrop for the new blooms, which may emerge by the end of the winter. At some point between late fall and late winter, scatter a general-purpose organic fertil-izer or a shovelful of compost around each clump.

✿ **TROUBLESHOOTING**

▸ **Leaves and stems with powdery white coating.** Powdery mildew is a common problem on pulmonar-ias, especially during hot weather. Mulching generously and watering regularly to keep the soil moist can help to prevent this fungal disease; so can planting cultivars that are touted as being mildew-resistant. If your plants do show signs of mildew, cut them to the ground, destroy the trimmings, and water the plants thoroughly to promote a flush of clean new leaves.

Rodgersia

RODGERSIA

Have a low spot in your yard where typical perennials don't thrive? Rodgersias may be a perfect solution for that problem area.

THESE STURDY, SLOW-SPREADING PERENNIALS produce substantial mounds of large compound leaves topped with showy flower plumes in white or shades of pink. Fingerleaf rodgersia (*Rodgersia aesculifolia*), usually with creamy white flowers, typically reaches 3 to 6 feet (90 to 180 cm) tall in bloom. Bronzeleaf rodgersia (*R. podophylla*) also has creamy white flowers and generally grows 3 to 5 feet (90 to 150 cm) tall in bloom; unlike fingerleaf rodgersia, this species has distinctly jagged leaflet tips. The foliage of featherleaf rodgersia (*R. pinnata*) looks much like that of fingerleaf rodgersia, but this species commonly blooms in shades of pink to red, reaching 3 to 4 feet (90 to 120 cm) tall. Rodgersias are typically recommended for Zones 4 to 7, although they may adapt to somewhat colder and somewhat warmer areas.

Rodgersia aesculifolia

❁ GROWING TIPS

▶ **Light & soil.** In relatively cool areas, rodgersias can thrive in full sun; elsewhere, they commonly grow best in light, all-day shade. Evenly moist, compost-enriched soil is ideal. These plants thrive with ample moisture while they're actively growing, especially if they're getting some sun. After the first few years, they can tolerate somewhat drier conditions but still prefer that their soil doesn't dry out completely.

▶ **Division & propagation.** Rodgersias spread slowly and seldom need to be divided, unless you want to propagate them in spring or fall. If you'd like to try growing them from seed, sow outdoors in fall or indoors in late winter; don't cover it with soil or seed-starting mix.

▶ **Potential problems.** Apart from possible slug damage on the emerging shoots, the plants are seldom bothered by pests or diseases. It may take 3 years or more for young rodgersias to settle in and begin flowering.

❁ SEASONAL CARE

◐ Spring

▶ Set out new plants, or move or divide existing clumps, in early spring. Space them about 3 feet (90 cm) apart. Water new plantings regularly if rain is lacking. Apply a generous layer of organic mulch before summer.

▶ In the cooler parts of their growing range, rodgersias may not emerge until mid- or late spring; in warmer areas, the plants may be in bloom in late spring. It's common for new rodgersia leaves to be reddish to brown.

◎ Summer

▶ Prime bloom time for rodgersias is usually early to midsummer or mid- to late summer, depending on which species you're growing and where you live. Cut the finished flower plumes back to the foliage or let them stay for autumn interest. The leaves of most rodgersias turn green by midsummer, but they may redevelop a brownish to reddish cast by the end of the summer. To prevent crispy leaf edges, water your plants regularly during dry spells for the first few years. Established patches also appreciate occasional soakings during extended dry spells.

◑ ◉ Fall & Winter

▶ Set out new plants, or move or divide existing clumps, in early fall. Water new plantings regularly for the first month or so if rain is lacking. The leaves typically turn reddish brown to deep red in autumn. Cut them off once they have been killed by frost. Scatter a general-purpose organic fertilizer or a shovelful of compost (or both) around each clump in late fall to late winter. North of Zone 5, consider protecting your rodgersias with a winter mulch.

Rudbeckia

RUDBECKIA, ORANGE CONEFLOWER

Bright daisy blooms borne over a long season have endeared rudbeckias to generations of gardeners. The color range is rather limited — mostly clear yellow to orange-yellow — but the plants vary in height and habits.

BLACK-EYED SUSAN (*Rudbeckia hirta*), also known as gloriosa daisy, tends to grow just 1 to 3 feet (30 to 90 cm) tall. It has very hairy leaves and single to double, dark- to green-centered flowers in shades of yellow, gold, and rust through most of the growing season. Orange coneflower (*R. fulgida*) typically reaches 2 to 4 feet (60 to 120 cm) tall, with dark-centered, golden yellow daisies. *R. fulgida* var. *sullivantii* 'Goldsturm' usually flowers in midsummer to early fall; *R. fulgida* var. *fulgida* tends to start several weeks later and continue well into fall. Three-lobed coneflower (*R. triloba*), also known as brown-eyed Susan, has hairy leaves and dark-centered, golden flowers as well, but the blossoms are much smaller. It tends to bloom from midsummer to midfall, reaching anywhere from 2 to 5 feet (60 to 150 cm) tall.

Among the taller rudbeckias are cutleaf or ragged coneflower (*R. laciniata*), with smooth, deeply lobed to multipart leaves and bright yellow, single to double blooms with green-to-brown centers. Shining or shiny coneflower (*R. nitida*) is similar but with unlobed or shallowly lobed leaves. Both of these can reach anywhere from 3 to 8 feet (90 to 240 cm) tall and usually bloom in midsummer to early fall. Golden glow (*R. laciniata* 'Hortensia'), also known as outhouse plant, and 'Goldquelle' bear double flowers typically 3 to 6 feet (90 to 180 cm) tall.

Distinctly different from the others in this genus is giant or great coneflower (*R. maxima*), also called cabbage-leaf coneflower, with broad, smooth, powder blue leaves. In mid- or late summer to early fall, it bears yellow-petaled daisies with quite large, near-black center cones atop stems typically 5 to 7 feet (1.5 to 2.1 m) tall.

Most of these rudbeckias are hardy in Zones 3 to 9, except for giant coneflower, which is usually recommended for Zones 5 to 9.

Rudbeckia fulgida

Rudbeckia (continued)

The seed heads of orange coneflowers (*Rudbeckia fulgida*), in particular, can hold their form well through most or all of the winter. However, they can also self-sow enthusiastically, so you may choose to clip off the spent flower stems after bloom and enjoy their fresh green foliage through the fall.

⚙ GROWING TIPS

▸ **Light & soil.** For the most part, rudbeckias thrive in full sun to light shade. Three-lobed coneflower tends to be the most shade tolerant of the bunch. Average, well-drained soil is fine. While rudbeckias are often touted as being drought tolerant, most look their best and bloom most abundantly with ample moisture. Giant coneflower, especially, prefers soil that stays evenly moist. Rich soil encourages vigorous growth on all rudbeckias but may lead to sprawling stems, especially on tall-growing cultivars in windy sites.

▸ **Division & propagation.** Usually, you don't need to bother with dividing either black-eyed Susans or three-lobed coneflower. Propagate them by growing new plants from seed, or allow a few of their seed heads to mature and drop seed to get replacement plants. Orange coneflower, cutleaf coneflower, golden glow, and shining coneflower benefit from being divided in spring or fall every 3 to 5 years. (Cutleaf coneflower and golden glow, in particular, tend to expand relatively quickly by creeping roots, so you may want to divide them every 2 or 3 years to slow their spread.) Orange coneflower can self-

sow prolifically, so you may want to keep the spent flowers clipped off to prevent over-abundant "volunteers." Giant coneflower plants tend to be long lived and seldom need division, unless you want to propagate them. To grow rudbeckias from seed, sow indoors in late winter to early spring or outdoors in early to midspring, and leave the seed uncovered.

▸ **Potential problems.** Various species of rudbeckias can be bothered by a wide variety of pests and diseases, including aphids, beetles, borers, caterpillars, plant bugs, aster yellows, leaf spots, powdery mildew, rusts, southern blight (crown rot), and mosaic virus. Generally, though, these perennials are tough enough to shrug off most problems without help. Black-eyed Susans (gloriosa daisies) may act as annuals or short-lived perennials, flowering during their first growing season and then fading out after just a year or two. Three-lobed coneflower tends to be biennial, producing only leaves in its first year, then dying out after flowering during its second growing season.

✣ SEASONAL CARE

◐ Spring

▶ Set out new plants, or move or divide existing clumps, in early to midspring. Space most of them about 18 inches (45 cm) apart; allow 2 to 3 feet (60 to 90 cm) between clumps for the tall-growing types. Water new plantings regularly if rain is lacking. Apply an organic mulch before summer.

◯ Summer

▶ If you wish to encourage lower, bushier growth on your coneflowers, consider cutting them back by one-third to one-half in early summer. Black-eyed Susans (gloriosa daisies) usually begin blooming in early summer; other species generally start in mid- to late summer and flower through late summer, at least. Snip off the finished flowers to extend the bloom period and prevent self-sowing, or leave them for their attractive seed heads. If the stems of tall-growing rudbeckias sprawl after bloom, cut them to the ground. Keep watering spring plantings regularly if rain is lacking. Established plants also appreciate occasional watering during dry spells.

Rudbeckia maxima

◑ ◉ Fall & Winter

▶ Set out new plants, or move or divide existing clumps, in early to midfall. Water new plantings regularly for the first month or so if rain is lacking. Rudbeckias often flower into early fall, or even until frost. Keep clipping off the finished flowers to prevent self-sowing, or leave them for their interesting form and as a seed source for birds. Others may start to sprawl or break down by early to midwinter, so feel free to cut them down then. The basal foliage of some coneflowers also stays handsome through much or all of the winter, so leave it in place unless it looks unattractive. Scatter a general-purpose organic fertilizer or a shovelful of compost around each clump in late fall to late winter.

Relatively Speaking

Prairie coneflower (*Ratibida pinnata*), also known as gray-head coneflower, looks much like a rudbeckia, with long, bright yellow petals that droop from a prominent gray-green to brownish center through the summer months, and possibly into fall. It's usually 3 to 5 feet (90 to 150 cm) tall. Red prairie coneflower (*R. columnifera*), also known as Mexican hat, is similar but with shorter red-and-yellow or solid-yellow petals; it grows 2 to 3 feet (60 to 90 cm) tall. Both are hardy in Zones 3 to 10. They thrive in full sun to light shade and average, well-drained soil. Remove the flowers when the petals drop to prevent self-sowing or leave the seed heads for the birds. These plants are long lived and seldom need to be divided.

Ruta

RUE

Rue isn't just for herb gardens anymore!

A BEAUTY IN ORNAMENTAL BEDS and borders, rue (*Ruta graveolens*) forms shrubby mounds anywhere from 1 to 3 feet (30 to 90 cm) tall, with deeply cut, gray-blue to blue-green foliage that's accented by clustered yellow flowers in summer. It's usually recommended for Zones 4 to 10.

From a maintenance standpoint, the most important thing to know about rue is that you should *always* wear gloves — and ideally long sleeves and long pants as well — when working around the plants. Otherwise, if you get some of the oil from the leaves and stems on your skin and then expose it to sunlight, you may end up with a nasty blistered rash. Some people have reported having this reaction when handling wet rue on cloudy days, too.

Ruta graveolens

❖ GROWING TIPS

▸ **Light & soil.** Rue thrives in full sun to light shade in average, well-drained soil. It can adapt quite well to hot, sandy, relatively infertile sites; heavy clay or constantly moist soil can be fatal.

▸ **Division & propagation.** Rue doesn't usually recover well from being moved or divided, due to its deep roots. To propagate, leave a few seedpods on the plants to get self-sown seedlings, or start replacement plants by sowing seed (barely cover it) outdoors in fall or indoors in late winter.

▸ **Potential problems.** Usually, the only insects that feed on rue are the larvae of giant swallowtail and black swallowtail butterflies, so if you notice caterpillars feeding on your plants, just leave them alone. Diseases are rarely an issue. It's not unusual for rue plants to die out after a few years, though.

❁ SEASONAL CARE

◐ Spring

▸ Set out new plants, or move existing clumps if you must, in early spring. Space them about 2 feet (60 cm) apart. Water new plantings regularly if rain is lacking. In early to midspring, trim established plants back to about 8 inches (20 cm) tall to encourage dense, well-branched growth. Apply a light layer of organic mulch before summer, if desired, or try a gravel mulch instead.

◉ Summer

▸ If you're growing rue primarily for its foliage color, feel free to shear off the developing flower buds in early to midsummer. If you choose to let the plants bloom, then clip off the developing seed heads after the petals drop to tidy the clumps and prevent self-sowing. Keep watering spring plantings if rain is lacking. Established clumps generally don't need supplemental water.

✿ ◉ Fall & Winter

▸ Set out new plants in early fall; water them regularly for the first month or so if rain is lacking. Rue leaves usually look good well into winter and can even be "ever-blue" in mild climates. In Zone 4, it's a good idea to protect the roots with a winter mulch. Rue seldom needs to be fertilized.

❖ **THE GLOVES ARE ON** The yellow summer blooms of rue are pretty, but it's the cool-colored foliage that really catches the eye — and catches the nose, too, with its strong, bitter scent. Wearing gloves when working around rue protects your skin from a potentially irritating oil in the leaves and stems.

Salvia

SALVIA, SAGE

Spiky-flowered salvias add welcome contrast to companions with rounded blooms or mounded forms.

Salvia × superba 'East Friesland'

MOST SALVIAS ARE STURDY, trouble-free plants that can grace your garden with beautiful blooms or lovely leaves (or both) for many months, or even all year-round, with a minimum of fussing from you. There are many hundreds of species and countless cultivars and hybrids to choose from, so it's not possible to cover more than a sampling of some popular perennial choices here: several beloved for their blooms and a few prized mostly for their foliage.

Among the best-known hardy salvias for perennial borders are those grown for their abundance of slender flower spikes — mostly in shades or blue to purple, but sometimes in pink or white. These include violet sage (*Salvia nemorosa*), meadow sage or meadow clary (*S. pratensis*), and hybrids of these and other species, usually listed as *S. × sylvestris* or *S. × superba*. There's a lot of confusion with the names, and you may see the same cultivar name attached to several different species names. From a maintenance standpoint, though, it doesn't matter much, because they all need the same basic care. They grow in bushy clumps of rich green leaves and can reach anywhere from 1 to 3 feet (30 to 90 cm) in bloom. Lilac sage (*S. verticillata*) produces somewhat plumper spikes of purple-blue or white blooms usually 18 to 36 inches (45 to 90 cm) tall, with broader, fuzzy, grayish green leaves. These salvias are generally recommended for Zones 4 to 9, though they may be somewhat more winter hardy if your soil is very well drained or a zone or two less hardy in wet winter sites.

For foliage that's colorful *and* flavorful, consider culinary or garden sage (*S. officinalis*). The species typically bears gray-green leaves (and purple-blue flowers, too), but

there are also cultivars with purple, bright silver, or variegated foliage. They grow in shrubby mounds usually 18 to 36 inches (45 to 90 cm) tall. The species is generally recommended for Zones 5 to 9; but the colored-leaf selections may be a zone or two less hardy.

Lyreleaf sage (*S. lyrata*) is distinctly different, forming low rosettes. The species isn't widely grown in gardens, but selections with purple-blushed to solid-purple foliage are becoming more popular for Zones 5 to 10. The upright flower stalks, typically 1 to 2 feet (30 to 60 cm) tall, may bear bluish to pinkish white flowers. (Sometimes, few or no blooms are evident, although seeds still form.)

❧ GROWING TIPS

▸ **Light & soil.** Salvias thrive in full sun but can also tolerate light shade. (Afternoon shade is a plus in the warmest zones.) Average, well-drained soil is fine for most salvias; in a site with too much shade or in one with too-rich or too-moist soil, the stems are more prone to flopping. Lyreleaf sage is an exception, in that it usually grows best in evenly moist soil.

▸ **Division & propagation.** Perennial sages benefit from being divided every 3 to 5 years, ideally in early spring (or in early autumn where winters aren't especially cold). Division is also an easy way to propagate your favorites; stem cuttings in spring or summer are another option. If you want to raise salvias from seed, sow indoors in late winter to early spring or outdoors in spring or summer; leave the seed uncovered.

▸ **Potential problems.** A few pests and diseases that occasionally bother

Salvia (continued)

salvias include aphids, beetles, plant bugs, leaf spots, and powdery mildew, but they're rarely serious enough to need control.

❧ SEASONAL CARE

○ Spring

▸ Set out new plants, or move or divide existing clumps, in early to midspring. Space most of them 18 to 24 inches (45 to 60 cm) apart; space lyreleaf sage plants about 1 foot (30 cm) apart. Water new plantings regularly if rain is lacking. Cut back culinary sage plants by about one-half when new growth appears to encourage dense, bushy new growth. Most of these salvias benefit from an organic mulch applied before summer; for culinary sage, a gravel mulch may be a better choice. In mild areas, salvias may be in bloom by late spring.

◎ Summer

▸ Early summer is typically peak bloom time for perennial salvias, but flowering can continue well into mid- or even late summer. Once the first flush of blooms is over on the bushy types, trim the plants back lightly (by about one-third) to remove the finished spikes, prevent self-sowing, and encourage rebloom in a few weeks. Or, on violet sage, meadow sage, their hybrids, and lilac sage, snip off the finished stems close to the base of the plant: fresh new foliage will develop, if it hasn't already, and some cultivars may be in bloom again by the end of the summer.

▸ On lyreleaf sage, consider clipping off the emerging flower stems before the buds open to better show off the colorful foliage and prevent self-sowing (which can be prolific to the point of weediness). You'll probably need to repeat this process every few days through the summer to completely stop seed formation.

▸ Keep watering spring salvia plantings if rain is lacking. Established clumps of culinary sage seldom need watering; the others can tolerate moderate dry spells but grow and flower best with occasional watering to keep the soil from drying out completely.

◯ ◉ Fall & Winter

▸ South of Zone 6, set out new plants, or move or divide existing clumps, in early fall. Water new plantings regularly for the first month or so if rain is lacking. It's not unusual for perennial salvias to produce at least a few flowers into early or midfall. Leave the spent flowering stalks in place for the winter to enjoy their form, or cut them back to the basal leaves to tidy the plants and prevent self-sowing. Culinary sage tends to holds its foliage well into winter; leave it untrimmed until spring. North of Zone 6, consider protecting salvias with a winter mulch. In late fall to late winter, scatter a general-purpose organic fertilizer or a shovelful of compost around each plant.

Salvia officinalis 'Berggarten'

Sanguisorba

BURNET

Burnets form dense clumps of multipart leaves with oblong, toothed leaflets, creating a delicate, ferny appearance.

ALTHOUGH THEY LOOK DELICATE, burnets are quite sturdy, spreading by rhizomes to form broad patches. Their tiny flowers are grouped into dense clusters atop slender, multibranched stems.

Alaskan burnet (*Sanguisorba menziesii*) bears short, fuzzy-looking, cylindrical, deep red bloom clusters reaching 2 to 3 feet (60 to 90 cm) tall, over blue- to grayish green leaves. Zones 2 to 9. Great burnet (*S. officinalis*) is the same color in bloom but starts flowering about a month later, with light green leaves on stems that are often red-tinged. It reaches 3 to 4 feet (90 to 120 cm) tall in bloom; Zones 3 to 9. Japanese burnet (*S. obtusa*) is one of the more eye-catching burnets in bloom, with gray-green foliage and fluffy-looking pink flower clusters usually 3 to 4 feet (90 to 120 cm) tall; Zones 4 to 8.

Oriental or narrowleaf burnet (*S. tenuifolia*), for Zones 4 to 8, has elongated green leaflets and commonly reaches 4 to 6 feet (1.2 to 1.8 m) tall in bloom. 'Purpurea' has deep red flower clusters that are either upright or nodding; 'Alba' has drooping white clusters. Canadian burnet (*S. canadensis*), another later-season bloomer with a similar height range, bears gray-green leaves and white flower spikes that are distinctly upright; Zones 2 to 8.

Sanguisorba tenuifolia 'Purpurea'

Sanguisorba (continued)

❊ GROWING TIPS

▸ **Light & soil.** A site with full sun and average soil is normally best for burnets, but they benefit from some afternoon shade in the warmer parts of their growing range. A site where the soil stays evenly moist is ideal; too-dry conditions can lead to leaf browning.

▸ **Division & propagation.** Burnets usually need division only every 4 to 6 years, but you can divide them more often if you wish to slow their spread.

Division is also a quick and easy way to propagate burnets. To raise them from seed, sow outdoors in fall to early spring or indoors in late winter to early spring; don't cover the seed.

▸ **Potential problems.** The only pest that's a serious problem is Japanese beetles; powdery mildew can also affect the foliage. Burnets may take a few years to settle in, but after that, they start creeping outward, usually at a moderate rate.

❊ **LEAN ON ME** Compost-enriched soil encourages vigorous growth on burnets, but then their stems can be prone to sprawling. If moving them to a less-fertile site isn't an option, pair them with ornamental grasses or other sturdy companions to lean on, or prop them up with linking stakes.

❊ SEASONAL CARE

◐ Spring

▸ Set out new plants, or move or divide existing clumps, in early spring. Space them about 2 feet (60 cm) apart. Water new plantings regularly if rain is lacking. Apply a generous layer of organic mulch before summer. Alaskan burnet may be in bloom by late spring.

◎ Summer

▸ Alaskan burnet is usually in full flower through early summer. Japanese burnet and great burnet generally start in midsummer; Oriental burnet and Canadian burnet usually begin in late summer. Snipping off the spent flower stalks at the base of the plant prevents self-sowing and may extend the bloom season. Or, consider leaving them in place, because the seed heads have the same interesting form as when in bloom, and those on dark-flowered species retain the deep red color for many weeks. Keep watering spring plantings regularly if rain is lacking. Established burnets also benefit from watering during dry spells.

✪ ◉ Fall & Winter

▸ Most burnets continue flowering into early fall, at least, and their foliage often takes on bright colors as temperatures cool. It's fine to set out new plants in early fall, and you can move or divide existing clumps then, too, if you don't mind cutting short the autumn display. Water new plantings regularly for the first month or so if rain is lacking. Once frost turns the plants brown, you can cut them down any time. Scatter a general-purpose organic fertilizer or a shovelful of compost around each clump in late fall to late winter.

Saponaria

SOAPWORT

Soapworts aren't nearly as popular as their close cousins, dianthus, but they can be just as useful for adding cheerful color to dryish sites.

THESE VIGOROUS PERENNIALS can fill a good bit of space quite quickly, by creeping or sprawling as well as by self-sowing. Rock soapwort (*Saponaria ocymoides*), in particular, can make a great groundcover, forming carpets of small leaves with pink or white blooms that reach 6 to 12 inches (15 to 30 cm) tall. It's usually recommended for Zones 3 to 7 or 8. Hybrid soapwort (*S. × lempergii*) — most often available as the pink-flowered selection 'Max Frei' — has a similar height and habit but tends to be somewhat less hardy; it's normally rated for Zones 5 to 8.

Bouncing Bet (*S. officinalis*), with pink to white flowers and upright to sprawling stems that reach 1 to 2 feet (30 to 60 cm) tall, is an exceptionally vigorous spreader; in fact, it's considered invasive in some areas. Bouncing Bet can grow in Zones 2 to 8.

Saponaria officinalis 'Rubra Plena'

✿ GROWING TIPS

▶ **Light & soil.** Soapworts thrive in full sun to light shade and average, dryish soil. They'll also grow in moist, nutrient-rich soil, but they'll be more prone to sprawling there.

▶ **Division & propagation.** Divide plants in spring or fall every 3 to 5 years, or more often if you want to slow their spread. Division is also an easy propagation method. Other options include taking stem cuttings in spring or summer or sowing seed outdoors in fall to spring; leave the seed uncovered.

▶ **Potential problems.** Soapworts normally aren't problem prone, except for rot in too-moist sites and occasional damage from slugs and snails or leaf spots.

✿ SEASONAL CARE

◐ Spring

▶ Set out new plants, or move or divide existing clumps, in early spring. Space them about 18 inches (45 cm) apart. Water new plantings regularly during dry spells. Consider using gravel instead of an organic mulch to keep the crowns dry and minimize the chance of rot, especially in sites where the soil is on the clayey side. Rock soapwort and bouncing Bet may begin blooming in late spring.

◎ Summer

▶ Early summer tends to be peak bloom time for the soapworts, although in some areas, hybrid soapwort may not start flowering until midsummer. When the first flush of bloom is finished, shear the plants back by about one-half to get bushier regrowth, prevent self-sowing, and possibly encourage another set of flowers as well. Keep watering first-year plantings occasionally if rain is lacking; established clumps seldom need watering.

◑ ◉ Fall & Winter

▶ Set out new plants, or move or divide existing clumps, in early fall. Water new plantings regularly for the first month or so if rain is lacking. It's not unusual for soapworts to produce at least a few flowers in fall; keep cutting off the spent blooms to prevent self-sowing. Bouncing Bet generally dies back after frost; cut it down any time. Rock soapwort and hybrid soapwort are usually evergreen so wait until late winter to trim them back. Scatter a general-purpose organic fertilizer or a handful or two of compost around each clump every other year in late fall to late winter.

✿ **SPRAWLING CHARM** The spreading nature and somewhat sprawling habit of Bouncing Bet (*Saponaria officinalis*) make it a poor choice for a high-visibility border. Its old-fashioned sort of charm can look good in less formal sites, though, and you can find some selections with double flowers or variegated foliage, which tend to be slightly less rampant.

Scabiosa

With an extended bloom season rivaling that of many annuals, pincushion flowers are a favorite with many gardeners.

THESE PERENNIALS PRODUCE dense basal clumps of deeply cut leaves that are typically grayish green, with upright stems topped in blooms composed of domed centers surrounded by a ruff of short petals.

The best-known one of the bunch is the selection 'Butterfly Blue' (often listed under *Scabiosa columbaria*), with lavender-blue flowers atop stems typically 12 to 18 inches (30 to 45 cm) tall. 'Pink Mist' reaches about the same height, with pinkish blooms. Both of these are recommended for Zones 3 to 8. *S. caucasica*, for Zones 4 to 9, is similar but slightly larger in scale, reaching 2 to 3 feet (60 to 90 cm) tall with flowers in shades of lavender-blue to white. Yellow scabious (*S. columbaria* subsp. *ochroleuca*) adds a different color to the mix, with ivory to pale yellow flowers that reach 2 to 3 feet (60 to 90 cm) tall over ferny, grayish foliage. It's recommended for Zones 3 or 4 to 10.

❀ GROWING TIPS

▸ **Light & soil.** Full sun is normally best, but pincushion flowers can take light shade, too; in fact, they may perform best there in the warmest parts of their range. Average, well-drained soil is fine; a soil pH that's near-neutral to slightly alkaline is ideal.

▸ **Division & propagation.** Divide pincushion flowers (ideally in spring) every 3 to 4 years for propagation or to keep them vigorous and flowering freely. You could also take cuttings of the basal shoots in spring. Or, sow seed (barely cover it) outdoors in fall to spring or indoors in late winter to early spring. Yellow scabious may bloom during its first year from seed.

▸ **Potential problems.** Pests typically aren't a serious issue, but powdery mildew may discolor the foliage. Other potential disease problems include aster yellows, root rot, and southern blight.

❀ SEASONAL CARE

◐ Spring

▸ Set out new plants, or move or divide existing clumps, in early spring. Space them 12 to 18 inches (30 to 45 cm) apart. Water new plantings regularly if rain is lacking. On established clumps, clip off any winter-damaged leaves in early spring, if desired. If your pincushion flower plants tend to sprawl in summer, set grow-through supports over them, or insert "pea stakes" (pieces of twiggy brush) around the clump, in early to midspring. Apply an organic mulch before summer. The first blooms may open in late spring.

◐ Summer

▸ Pincushion flowers are usually in full flower in early summer and continue into late summer, at least, especially if you regularly remove the spent blooms. (Deadheading also helps to prevent self-sowing.) Snip off the finished flowers individually,

Relatively Speaking

Knautia (*Knautia macedonica*) looks very much like a pincushion flower and thrives with the same general care and siting; the main difference is its deep red flower color. It grows 1 to 2 feet (30 to 60 cm) tall. Zones 4 to 8. If you like the look of pincushion flowers but would prefer them closer to eye level, consider giant scabious (*Cephalaria gigantea*; also sold as *Scabiosa gigantea*). Recommended for Zones 3 to 8, its yellow flowers appear through most of the summer atop stems typically 6 to 7 feet (1.8 to 2.1 m) tall. It thrives in the same conditions and with the same basic care as pincushion flowers. When you cut down the finished flower stems in late summer, cut off any tattered or discolored leaves at the same time to tidy the clumps.

down to a bloom or bud — if there is one — lower down on the stem, or cut at the base of the stem. Or, shear off all the stems at once in mid- or late summer; this removes some blooms, too, but it's a much quicker process. Water spring plantings regularly if rain is lacking. Established plants can tolerate dry spells but bloom most abundantly with occasional watering.

◐ ◉ Fall & Winter

▸ Set out new plants in early fall. You can move or divide existing clumps then, too, if you must, but that cuts short the bloom display, which often continues well into fall. Water new plantings regularly for the first month or so if rain is lacking. Keep deadheading to prevent self-sowing. Once all the flowers are finished, cut off the spent stems at the base, but leave the foliage; it stays green for most or all of the winter. Scatter a general-purpose organic fertilizer or a shovelful of compost around each clump in late fall to late winter. Pincushion flowers usually don't need winter protection, but you may want to cover them with evergreen boughs in the coldest parts of their growing range.

❖ **HIGH AND DRY** Pincushion flowers may die out after just a year or two in sites that are too wet in winter, or in heavy, compacted soil. Digging deeply before planting, or growing them in a raised bed, may solve the problem. In other cases, such as with yellow scabious (*Scabiosa columbaria* subsp. *ochroleuca*), the plants are just naturally short lived.

Scabiosa 'Pink Mist'

Sedum

If regular watering isn't one of your favorite gardening chores, sedums may be a great choice for your garden.

THERE ARE MANY DOZENS of species, cultivars, and hybrids of sedum to select from, in a wide range of heights, habits, and flower and foliage colors. While it's not possible to highlight more than a few of them here, it's not really necessary to give details about every kind of sedum, because they generally fall into one of two groups: those with trailing stems and those with mostly upright stems.

Sedums with trailing stems tend to form broad patches or carpets, because the stems can take root wherever they touch the soil. The tips of the stems, however, eventually turn upright, and they produce their flower clusters at the top. One of the best-known species in this group is two-row sedum (*Sedum spurium*), with rounded leaves — which may be light green, reddish, or variegated — and red, pink, or white flowers. Woodland stonecrop (*S. ternatum*) bears white flowers over small, light green leaves. Kamschatka stonecrop (*S. kamtschaticum*) has narrower, toothed leaves that may be bright green or variegated, plus yellow flowers. *S. rupestre* 'Angelina' (also listed under *S. reflexum*) is distinctive for its bright yellow to greenish yellow, needle-like foliage; it too bears yellow flowers. Goldmoss sedum (*S. acre*), also known as biting stonecrop, is yet another

yellow-flowered species with very small, narrow, light green foliage along fast-spreading stems. (This sedum creeps so readily, in fact, that it can be too aggressive in the garden and even invasive in natural areas.) All of these typically reach 4 to 6 inches (10 to 15 cm) in bloom and are recommended for Zones 3 or 4 to 8 or 9.

The more upright sedums tend to stay in distinct clumps. They typically have thick, oval leaves that may be light green, grayish to bluish green, purplish green to deep purple, or variegated with white or yellow. Their stems are topped with flattened to domed flower clusters, usually in shades of pink to rosy red but sometimes white or light yellow. Heights can range from 1 to 3 feet (30 to 90 cm) tall, depending on the cultivar. Some species that fall into this group include *S. erythrostictum* (*S. alboroseum*), showy stonecrop (*S. spectabile*), and orpine (*S. telephium*). There are many hybrids as well, among them 'Autumn Joy' and 'Autumn Fire', 'Matrona', 'Purple Emperor', and 'Vera Jameson'. (Note that you may see these upright-growers sold under the genus name *Hylotelephium* instead of *Sedum*.) This group is generally rated for Zones 3 to 9.

❁ GROWING TIPS

▶ **Light & soil.** Full sun and average to poor, well-drained soil is best for most sedums, but most can tolerate light shade, too. (Woodland stonecrop is an exception, usually growing best in partial shade and moist but well-drained soil.)

▶ **Division & propagation.** Upright sedums can be very prone to sprawling if the soil is too rich or too moist, if they get too much shade, or if they need to be divided. It's easy to divide sedums (ideally in spring or fall). Trailing sedums usually don't require it. Upright types may need it every 2 to 3 years to stay sturdy and vigorous.

Sedums can be propagated by division. It's also a simple matter to propagate sedums by stem cuttings; even trimmings that fall to the ground may take root. To grow them from seed, sow outdoors in fall to spring or indoors in late winter to early spring and leave it uncovered.

▶ **Potential problems.** Rot may be a problem in too-moist sites, and aphids may cause distorted shoot tips or damage the developing flower buds. Other possible problems include slugs and snails, powdery mildew, and rust, but the plants are seldom seriously affected.

❁ SEASONAL CARE

○ Spring

▶ Set out new plants, or move or divide existing clumps, in early to midspring. Space the trailing types 12 to 18 inches (30 to 45 cm) apart and the upright types about 2 feet (60 cm) apart. Water new plantings occasionally if rain is lacking. Mulch usually isn't needed, but if you wish to add it, you could use either organic mulch or gravel.

▶ Trim off any dead top growth on established plants in early to midspring. Upright sedums can be prone to flopping later in the season,

Sedum spectabile 'Neon'

so consider setting grow-through supports over the emerging clumps, or try pinching or shearing back the shoots to about one-half their height in mid- to late spring. Woodland stonecrop usually flowers in mid- to late spring, and some of the other trailers may begin blooming by the end of the spring.

☀ Summer

▸ Most of the trailing sedums bloom in summer, but their specific flowering period varies depending on the species, the cultivar, and the climate. It's not necessary to remove the spent flowers, but if you wish to do it, you could snip them off by hand or use a string trimmer for large patches.

▸ The upright sedums usually start forming flower buds in midsummer and begin blooming in late summer. If your upright sedums sprawled in previous years and you didn't divide or support them in spring, it's a good idea to cut them back by about one-half in early summer (either for the first time or as a follow-up to a spring pinching or shearing).

▸ Water first-year plantings occasionally if rain is lacking. Established sedums seldom need supplemental water.

❖ **LEAN ON ME** Upright sedums have a habit of looking full and sturdy right up until bloom time, then suddenly sprawling in all directions. It's best to prevent this with spring staking or a spring or summer trim, but if you forget, corral the clumps with linking stakes as soon as you notice the stems starting to lean.

Sedum kamtschaticum 'Variegatum'

Sedum (continued)

✪ ⊙ Fall & Winter

▸ Set out new plants, or move or divide existing clumps, in early to midfall. Midfall (or spring) may be better to move or divide the upright types in all but the coldest zones, so you don't cut the bloom display short; their flowers usually last well into early fall, then darken as the seed heads form. Water new plantings occasionally for the first month or so if rain is lacking. The leaves of many trailing sedums remain through part or all of the winter, often turning purplish to reddish.

The foliage of upright types tends to turn yellow before dropping. Leave their dried seed heads in place for winter or cut the dead stems off at the base after frost. Don't add fertilizer or compost.

✿ TROUBLESHOOTING

▸ **Leaves or flowers are not the color you expect.** Foliage color can vary depending on the amount of light and on the temperature. Purple-leaved sedums, for instance, may look more greenish if they don't get full sun, or they may be deep bluish green when they emerge and take several weeks to darken to purple. Green-leaved and variegated cultivars may take on reddish tints in either cold or hot weather, or if the soil is dry. Variegated sedums often produce all-green shoots; in this case, dig up the plant, divide out the all-green portion, and replant the variegated part. Upright sedums that bloom in shades of pink can also vary in flower color depending on the site conditions: the same cultivar may appear distinctly pink in one part of your yard and closer to brick red in another. It's also possible for self-sown seedlings to pop up close to the parent plant, making it appear that a single clump has multiple flower colors.

In sunny sites, 'Angelina' sedum (*Sedum rupestre* 'Angelina') develops rich orange at the tips in winter, then turns back to bright yellow for the growing season. In partial shade, it stays more of a greenish yellow color year-round.

Sedum rupestre 'Angelina'

Solidago

GOLDENROD

Goldenrods are limited in the flower colors they offer — essentially, just shades of yellow — but their range of heights and bloom times extends their versatility.

THERE ARE OVER A HUNDRED SPECIES of goldenrods, though only a few of them are commonly grown in gardens. One of the most popular selections is 'Fireworks' rough-stemmed goldenrod (*Solidago rugosa*), which spreads moderately to form patches of deep green leaves topped with slender, arching to nearly horizontal bloom clusters. It grows 3 to 4 feet (90 to 120 cm) tall. 'Golden Fleece' autumn goldenrod (*S. sphacelata*) looks something like a very dwarf form of 'Fireworks', but with thicker bloom clusters and broader leaves. It, too, is a moderate creeper but reaches just 1 to 2 feet (30 to 60 cm) tall. Both of these are recommended for Zones 4 to 9. In between the two, heightwise, is wreath goldenrod (*S. caesia*), with narrow leaves on deep purple stems anywhere from 1 to 3 feet (30 to 90 cm) tall; Zones 4 to 8. You can also find a number of plume-flowered hybrid goldenrods, most of which stay in well-behaved clumps and are recommended for Zones 4 to 9.

❀ GROWING TIPS

▶ **Light & soil.** Full sun to light shade with average, well-drained soil is generally ideal. Wreath goldenrod, though, usually prefers partial shade. And while most goldenrods can be quite drought tolerant, 'Fireworks' seems to perform best with a bit more moisture. (If it dries out too much, it tends to drop its lower leaves.) Too much shade or too-rich soil may lead to sprawling stems.

▶ **Division & propagation.** Divide clump-forming goldenrods every 4 to 6 years. More frequent division (every 2 to 3 years) may help to control the spread of creepers, such as 'Fireworks' and 'Golden Fleece'. Division in spring is one way to propagate your favorites; stem cuttings in early summer are another option. To grow from seed, sow outdoors in fall to early spring or indoors in late winter to early spring; barely cover it with seed-starting mix.

▶ **Potential problems.** A number of insect pests, as well as leaf spots, powdery mildew, and rust, may affect the leaves, but these usually aren't serious enough to require control.

❀ **A BOUNTY OF BUGS** A variety of bugs, beetles, and caterpillars can feed on goldenrods, but they're seldom troublesome enough to cause serious damage, probably because the flowers attract so many beneficial insects as well.

❀ SEASONAL CARE

◯ Spring

▶ Set out new plants, or move or divide existing clumps, in early to midspring. Space most of them 12 to 18 inches (30 to 45 cm) apart, or about 2 feet (60 cm) apart for 'Fireworks' and the tall-growing hybrids. Water new plantings regularly if rain is lacking. Apply an organic mulch before summer.

◎ Summer

▶ If you want to reduce the ultimate flowering height of 'Fireworks' and the tall-growing hybrids or try to prevent sprawling if your goldenrods have done that in the past, cut their stems back by one-third to one-half in early summer. Taller goldenrods tend to start blooming by late summer.

▶ On the low-growing hybrids, a light trim (by one-quarter to one-third) at the very beginning of the summer can also help to delay the bloom for a few weeks. Left untrimmed, compact hybrids may begin flowering by midsummer or even earlier. Clipping off the flower plumes as they drop their blossoms can encourage rebloom and prevents self-sowing. Or, if the leaves look bad, cut the spent flowering stems off close to the base to get new foliage.

▶ Water spring plantings if rain is lacking. Established plants usually don't need watering, except for 'Fireworks', which benefits from occasional watering during dry spells. And remember — don't blame your goldenrods if hay-fever symptoms start appearing around the time they're blooming; instead, blame the much lighter, wind-blown pollen of ragweeds (*Artemisia*), which is released in abundance around this time.

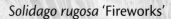

Solidago rugosa 'Fireworks'

✪ ☉ Fall & Winter

▸ Many goldenrods continue flowering into autumn, while others, such as 'Golden Fleece' and wreath goldenrod, may not even begin until early fall. Because of their late bloom season, it's usually best to set out, move, or divide them only in spring. Goldenrods generally hold their form well into the colder months, but if you leave the seed heads for winter interest, the plants may self-sow. If you want to minimize the chance of seeding, then cut the stems back to the basal leaves after frost. Scatter a general-purpose organic fertilizer or a shovelful of compost around each clump every year or two in late fall to late winter.

Stachys

LAMB'S EARS, BETONY, WOUNDWORT

Soft to the touch and easy on the eye, too, the fuzzy foliage of lamb's ears (*Stachys byzantina*) is a favorite with many gardeners.

ALSO KNOWN AS WOOLLY BETONY, the plants form dense, spreading carpets of silvery white leaves, with small, purplish pink flowers on upright, equally fuzzy flower stalks that can reach 1 to 2 feet (30 to 60 cm) tall. If you prefer a uniform carpet of foliage with few or no flower spikes, look for the selections 'Silver Carpet' or the larger-leaved, gray-green 'Big Ears' (also known as 'Countess Helene von Stein'). Lamb's ears are recommended for Zones 4 to 8.

With the lesser-known species big betony (*S. macrantha*; also sold as *S. grandiflora*) and wood betony (*S. officinalis*), the key feature is their spiky clusters of pinkish purple, pink, or white flowers, which can reach 1 to 2 feet (30 to 60 cm) tall. Their foliage is bright to deep green and grows in dense, slow-spreading mounds. These betonies are usually rated for Zones 4 to 8.

❁ GROWING TIPS

▸ **Light & soil.** Full sun to partial shade (especially afternoon shade in hot climates) is generally fine. Betonies usually grow best in evenly moist but well-drained, compost-enriched soil. Lamb's ears tend to perform best in dryish sites where the soil isn't very rich.

▸ **Division & propagation.** Divide the clumps every 3 or 4 years in spring or fall to remove dead centers or more frequently to control their spread. Division is also an easy way to propagate these plants. Or, sow seed (left uncovered) outdoors in fall to early spring or indoors in late winter to early spring.

▸ **Potential problems.** Occasional problems include slugs and snails, leaf spots, and powdery mildew. (See Troubleshooting, opposite page.)

❁ SEASONAL CARE

◐ Spring

▸ Set out new plants, or move or divide existing clumps, in early spring. Space lamb's ears 18 to 24 inches (45 to 60 cm) apart and betonies 12 to 18 inches (30 to 45 cm) apart. Water new plantings regularly

Stachys 'Big Ears'

if rain is lacking. On established clumps, snip off or rake out any winter-damaged leaves in early spring. Apply an organic mulch before summer. In mild regions, flowering may begin in late spring.

◎ Summer

▸ Early to midsummer is typically peak bloom time for both lamb's ears and betonies, but they may continue to flower through late summer. If you don't like the flowers of lamb's ears, snip off the bloom stalks as they emerge; otherwise, cut them off at the base once the flowers are done to tidy the planting and prevent self-sowing. On betonies, trim off the finished flower stems at the base or leave the developing seed heads for later interest. If the foliage on either species starts to thin out or look tattered, shear the plants back to about 2 inches (5 cm) to get fresh new leaves. Keep watering spring plantings regularly if rain is lacking. Established lamb's ears can tolerate moderate dry spells without supplemental water; betonies benefit from occasional watering.

❂ ◉ Fall & Winter

▸ Set out new plants, or move or divide existing clumps, in early fall. Water new plantings regularly for the first month or so if rain is lacking. Established plants may produce some flowers into early fall. Trim off their flower stems, if desired, but leave their foliage in place; it usually looks good through most or all of the winter. Scatter a general-purpose organic fertilizer or a shovelful of compost around betony clumps in late fall to late winter; lamb's ears usually don't need fertilizing.

Lamb's ears (*Stachys byzantina*) may spread quickly — sometimes enough to be considered aggressive in some gardens — and those thick, leafy carpets can be prone to disease problems. After a while, you may notice some parts of the patch dying out. Cutting off all the foliage close to the ground may encourage healthy new leaves to form.

✿ TROUBLESHOOTING

▸ **Foliage turns yellow or brown.**
The dense, woolly foliage of lamb's ears can be prone to rotting, particularly during spells of humid or rainy weather. Thinning the clumps once or twice during the summer (or in other seasons, as needed) by pulling or raking out the older, dying leaves can freshen up the plants' appearance and minimize disease problems. If necessary, cut the whole clump to the ground. 'Big Ears' tends to be less prone to rotting, because its leaves aren't quite as hairy as the very silvery types.

Stokesia

STOKES' ASTER

The shaggy-petaled, daisy-form flowers of Stokes' aster (*Stokesia laevis*) add a touch of whimsy to summer beds and borders.

THE PLANT FORMS MOUNDS of relatively slender, deep green leaves, with flowers mostly in shades of blue to purple (often changing color as they age) but sometimes in white, pink, or light yellow. Most Stokes' asters reach 1 to 2 feet (30 to 60 cm) tall in bloom, but a few selections, such as 'Omega Skyrocket', may reach 3 to 4 feet (90 to 120 cm). These perennials are usually recommended for Zones 5 to 10.

Before you decide to fill your garden with Stokes' asters, be aware that their performance can vary greatly. In some areas, for instance, the plants flower from late spring to frost, while in others, they bloom for just a few weeks in summer, or sometimes don't bloom at all. And in some gardens, the flowering stems stay tidily upright, while in others, those of the very same cultivar are weak and sprawling. Unfortunately, there doesn't seem to be much reason as to why they're so variable, so it's difficult to predict how they'll behave. Don't let that deter you, though: experiment with different cultivars until you find a good match for your garden.

Stokesia laevis 'Blue Danube'

🌸 GROWING TIPS

▸ **Light & soil.** A site with full sun to light shade and average, somewhat moist but well-drained soil is ideal for Stokes' asters.

▸ **Division & propagation.** Divide the clumps (ideally in spring) every 4 to 6 years to keep them vigorous; this is also an easy way to propagate your favorites. Other options include taking root cuttings in late fall or early spring or sowing seed (barely covering it) outdoors in fall to early spring or indoors in late winter or early spring.

▸ **Potential problems.** Possible problems with Stokes' asters include botrytis blight (gray mold), leaf spot, and powdery mildew, as well as rot in too-wet soil, but these usually aren't common.

🌸 SEASONAL CARE

◐ Spring

▸ Set out new plants, or move or divide existing clumps, in early to midspring. Space them 12 to 18 inches (30 to 45 cm) apart. Water new plantings regularly if rain is lacking. Early to midspring is also a good time to snip off any damaged or discolored leaves. Add an organic mulch before summer. In some areas, Stokes' aster may begin flowering in late spring.

◎ Summer

▸ Early to midsummer is generally prime bloom time for Stokes' aster, though it may keep flowering through the summer, especially if you remove the spent blossoms. Trim them off just above a lower bud, if there is one, or snip off the whole stem near the base. Keep watering spring plantings regularly if rain is lacking. Established clumps can tolerate moderate dry spells but usually look their best with occasional watering.

✤ ◉ Fall & Winter

▸ Stokes' asters may continue flowering well into fall (or even into winter in areas that don't get hard frosts), so it's usually best to divide them in spring. But if you need to move or divide them, or if you want to set out new plants, do it in early fall. Water new plantings regularly for the first month or so if rain is lacking. Clip off any remaining stalks after frost, or leave the seed heads for winter interest. The foliage stays green through the winter. Scatter a general-purpose organic fertilizer or a shovelful of compost around the plants in late fall to late winter. North of Zone 6, consider protecting the clumps with a loose winter mulch, such as evergreen boughs or pine needles.

🌸 **SPRAWLING STOKES** The flowering stems of Stokes' asters can be prone to sprawling, but it's difficult to stake them effectively to prevent the problem. If it happens repeatedly, try moving your plants to a different site, or try a different cultivar.

Symphytum

COMFREY

With comfreys, you need to think carefully about where you want them *before* you plant.

Symphytum × uplandicum
'Axminster Gold'

IT'S NOT BECAUSE they're impossible to move, but because any root pieces left behind are likely to sprout again, making them tough to get rid of permanently. Still, they can be practical and handsome in the right site, forming clumps or patches of broad, hairy leaves with clusters of nodding flowers that dangle from the tips of the upright, branching flower stems.

Symphytum ibericum (also sold as *S. grandiflorum*) spreads readily, making it too aggressive for most mixed borders but excellent as a groundcover. It reaches 12 to 18 inches (30 to 45 cm) in bloom, with deep green leaves and reddish buds that open to pale yellow flowers. There are also several hybrids in the same height range, offering different flower colors (such as 'Hidcote Blue') or variegated foliage (as on 'Goldsmith'). Russian comfrey (*S. × uplandicum*), mostly grown in its variegated forms, is much larger in scale, reaching 2 to 4 feet (60 to 120 cm) tall in bloom, with reddish pink buds that open to purplish to blue flowers. Its roots grow deeper but tend to stay in tight clumps, although its large leaves spread out to fill a wide space. As a group, comfreys are commonly recommended for Zones 4 to 8.

❀ GROWING TIPS

▸ **Light & soil.** Comfreys may grow in full sun if the soil stays evenly moist (though not soggy). Usually, though, a site with morning sun and afternoon shade or light all-day shade and somewhat moist but well-drained, compost-enriched soil is ideal. After a year or two of regular watering, comfreys can even perform well in dry shade.

▸ **Division & propagation.** Division is a good way to propagate your favorite comfreys, and the creeping types can benefit from it any time they start looking overcrowded. Root cuttings taken in fall or early spring can work for propagating the green-leaved types; variegated comfreys, however, will turn out solid green from root cuttings, so you might want to try taking cuttings of the flowering stems instead. You'll seldom find comfrey seed for sale, but established plants may self-sow.

▸ **Potential problems.** Apart from slugs or snails and rust, the plants are mostly problem free.

❀ SEASONAL CARE

◐ Spring

▸ Set out new plants, or move or divide existing clumps, in early spring. Space *S. ibericum* and the compact hybrids about 18 inches (45 cm) apart; allow a space 2 to 3 feet (60 to 90 cm) across for Russian comfrey. Water new plantings regularly if rain is lacking. Apply a generous layer of organic mulch in early to midspring. In some areas, comfreys may be in bloom by late spring.

◯ Summer

▸ Early summer is usually peak bloom time for comfreys. Once the flowers drop, cut off just the bloom stalks at the base to tidy the plants and prevent self-sowing, or shear the entire clump back to about 4 inches (10 cm) to encourage a batch of fresh new foliage. (It's a good idea to wear gloves when working with comfreys, by the way, because handling the bristly leaves can cause skin irritation.) Water spring plantings regularly during dry spells. Established clumps can tolerate some drought, especially in shady sites, but the variegated cultivars may develop brown leaf edges if they dry out too much. If this happens, snip off the affected leaves and water thoroughly to encourage lush new leaves.

◑ ◉ Fall & Winter

▸ Set out new plants, or move or divide existing clumps, in early fall. Water new plantings regularly for the first month or so if rain is lacking. The foliage often stays fresh looking well into winter, so feel free to wait until late winter to cut it off. Scatter a general-purpose organic fertilizer or a shovelful of compost around each clump in late fall to late winter.

Tanacetum

This diverse group of perennials includes several old-fashioned flowering favorites.

TANSY (*Tanacetum vulgare;* also known as *Chrysanthemum vulgare*), for one, bears clusters of bright yellow, buttonlike blooms that can reach 2 to 4 feet (60 to 120 cm) tall. The strongly scented, lacy leaves are usually deep green (or yellow on the cultivar 'Isla Gold') and grow in vigorously creeping clumps that can quickly crowd out less rampant companions. Hardy in Zones 3 to 8, tansy can also self-sow freely and is considered invasive in some regions.

Like tansy, feverfew is as widely grown as an herb as it is an ornamental, and it's sold under a number of different names, including *T. parthenium, C. parthenium, Matricaria parthenium,* and *Pyrethrum parthenium.* It, too, bears deeply cut, aromatic leaves but stays in distinct clumps, with single or double, white, daisy-form flowers reaching 1 to 3 feet (30 to 90 cm) tall. The leaves are usually medium green, but 'Aureum' has yellow foliage. Feverfew can grow in Zones 2 or 3 to 10.

The showiest of this bunch, bloomwise, is commonly called painted daisy or pyrethrum daisy (*T. coccineum;* also sold under *C. coccineum* or *Pyrethrum coccineum*). Its relatively large single to double flowers bloom in white or shades of red, pink, or magenta atop stems reaching 1 to 3 feet (30 to 90 cm) tall over low clumps of ferny, rich green leaves. It's usually recommended for Zones 3 to 7 or 8.

❂ GROWING TIPS

▸ **Light & soil.** A site with full sun, or morning sun and afternoon shade, and average, well-drained soil is fine for all three of these adaptable perennials. (Feverfew is the most shade tolerant of the three.)

▸ **Division & propagation.** Tansy and painted daisy can be divided every other year to slow tansy's spread, maintain the vigor of painted daisy, or propagate either. You may want to wear gloves, because handling tansy or feverfew foliage may irritate sensitive skin. Feverfew tends to be short lived, often acting more like an annual or biennial than a perennial. You could try dividing it every year to keep it going, let a few flowers set seed to get self-sown replacements, or start new plants from seed. Sow seed outdoors in fall to early spring or indoors in late winter to early spring; don't cover it.

▸ **Potential problems.** They're prone to sprawling in too-rich soil and rot in too-moist sites. Other possible problems include aphids, slugs and snails, spider mites, aster yellows, botrytis (gray mold), and powdery mildew.

❂ SEASONAL CARE

◑ Spring

▸ Set out new plants, or move or divide existing clumps, in early spring. Space them 12 to 18 inches (30 to 45 cm) apart. Water new plantings regularly if rain is lacking. Apply an organic mulch before summer, if desired. Painted daisies can be prone to flopping when in full bloom, so you may want to set a grow-through support over each clump in early to midspring. Painted daisies and feverfew may begin flowering in late spring.

◎ Summer

▸ Painted daisy generally blooms in early to midsummer, feverfew can flower through the summer, and tansy usually blooms in mid- and late summer. Once the flowers are finished, shear off the stems close to the base to get new leaves and possible rebloom later in the season (especially on feverfew). On painted daisy, you could wait until all of the flowers are finished, but on feverfew and tansy, you may want to cut them back even before all of the blooms are done so the earliest flowers don't have time to drop seed. Water spring plantings regularly if rain is lacking. Established clumps need only occasional watering during extended dry spells.

✛ ⊙ Fall & Winter

▸ Set out new plants, or move or divide existing clumps, in early fall. Water new plantings regularly for the first month or so if rain is lacking. Established clumps may bloom sporadically until frost. Keep the finished flower stems trimmed off, except for leaving one or two on feverfew to get a few replacement seedlings in case the original plants die. Feverfew foliage usually sticks around through the winter; the others generally go fully dormant by early winter. Scatter a general-purpose organic fertilizer or a shovelful of compost around the plants every year or two in late fall to late winter. You may want to protect fall divisions with a winter mulch.

Tanacetum parthenium

Thalictrum

MEADOW RUE

With their fernlike, multipart foliage and fluffy-looking flower clusters, meadow rues have a delicate and dainty appearance.

ONE OF THE MOST COMPACT OPTIONS is dwarf or Kyosho meadow rue (*Thalictrum kiusianum*), which spreads slowly to form carpets of deep green leaves accented with purplish pink flowers to about 6 inches (15 cm) tall; Zones 4 to 8. Columbine meadow rue (*T. aquilegiifolium*), usually reaching 2 to 4 feet (60 to 120 cm), has bluish green leaves and rosy purple, pink, or white flowers; Zones 5 to 8. Yunnan meadow rue (*T. delavayi*), generally growing 3 to 5 feet (90 to 150 cm), bears light green to blue-green foliage and purplish pink or white flowers; Zones 4 to 8. Dusty meadow rue (*T. flavum* subsp. *glaucum*) carries blue-gray leaves topped with yellow flowers from 3 to 6 feet (90 to 180 cm) tall; Zones 3 to 8.

Among the tallest options in this genus are lavender mist (*T. rochebrunianum*), growing anywhere from 4 to 8 feet (1.2 to 2.4 m) tall with medium green leaves, and hybrid 'Elin', towering up to 10 feet (3 m) with powder blue foliage; both bear pinkish purple blooms. They're usually recommended for Zones 4 or 5 to 8.

Thalictrum flavum subsp. *glaucum*

GROWING TIPS

▶ **Light & soil.** In the coolest parts of their growing range, meadow rues can tolerate full sun with ample moisture. In most areas, though, they thrive in partial shade and somewhat moist but well-drained soil that's enriched with compost.

▶ **Division & propagation.** Meadow rues don't often need division, but you can divide them in spring or fall for propagation or to reduce the size of large clumps. Or, sow seed outdoors in fall and lightly cover it with soil.

▶ **Potential problems.** Leaf miners, slugs, leaf spots, powdery mildew, and rusts are occasional problems but seldom serious.

SEASONAL CARE

○ Spring
▶ Set out new plants, or move or divide existing clumps, in early spring. Space dwarf meadow rue

about 8 inches (20 cm) apart, the medium-sized species about 18 inches (45 cm) apart, and lavender mist and 'Elin' 2 to 3 feet (60 to 90 cm) apart. Water spring plantings regularly if rain is lacking. Apply a generous layer of organic mulch before summer. Dwarf and columbine meadow rues may begin flowering in late spring.

◎ Summer
▶ Dwarf and columbine meadow rue tend to be at peak bloom in early summer but may continue into midsummer. Yunnan and dusty meadow rues usually start in early to midsummer and continue through late summer; lavender mist and 'Elin' generally begin in mid- to late summer. The seed heads can be interest-

ing, but you may want to trim them off to prevent self-sowing. If the top growth looks browned or tattered, you can cut it back to the base. Keep watering new plantings regularly if rain is lacking. Established clumps also benefit from occasional watering during dry spells.

◐ ◉ Fall & Winter
▶ Set out new plants, or move or divide existing clumps, in early fall. Water new plantings regularly for the first month or so if rain is lacking. Yunnan meadow rue, lavender mist, and 'Elin' may bloom into autumn. Cut down the stems in mid- to late fall. Scatter a general-purpose organic fertilizer or a shovelful of compost around each clump in late fall to late winter.

SUPPORT SYSTEMS You may need to prop up tall meadow rues if they start to sprawl. For a more permanent solution, give them sturdy companions, such as shrubs or tall grasses, for support.

Thymus

THYME

Their small, oval leaves offer a range of colors and scents, and the plants may be accented with clusters of red, pink, light purple, or white flowers.

MOTHER-OF-THYME (sold as *Thymus serpyllum* or *T. praecox*), also called creeping thyme or wild thyme, creates carpets of deep green leaves barely 4 inches (10 cm) tall. Woolly thyme (*T. pseudolanuginosus*; also sold as *T. serpyllum* 'Lanuginosus') forms ground-hugging, grayish green mats barely 2 inches (5 cm) tall; it seldom flowers.

Other thymes form bushy micro-shrubs typically 6 to 12 inches (15 to 30 cm) tall. These include plants known as common, garden, English, or French thyme (usually sold as *T. vulgaris*) and lemon thyme (commonly sold as *T.* × *citriodorus*).

As a group, thymes may be hardy as far north of Zone 3 with excellent drainage and winter snow cover, but they're most commonly recommended for Zones 5 to 9.

Thymus serpyllum

✿ GROWING TIPS

▶ **Light & soil.** Give thymes a site in full sun to light shade with average, well-drained soil.

▶ **Division & propagation.** They usually don't need to be divided, unless you want to propagate them; in that case, dig and divide the entire clump in spring or fall or simply dig and transplant a few rooted sections. To grow thymes from seed, sow outdoors in fall to spring or indoors in late winter to early spring; don't cover it.

▶ **Potential problems.** Apart from occasional problems with slugs and snails, leaf spots, and dieback in damp sites or humid weather, thymes are typically trouble free.

✿ SEASONAL CARE

◐ Spring

▶ Set out new plants, or move or divide existing clumps, in early to midspring. Space them about 1 foot (30 cm) apart, and water them regularly if rain is lacking. On established thymes, trim off any winter-damaged tips once new growth begins. Mulch usually isn't necessary, but you could use a light layer of organic mulch if desired; gravel can also be a great mulch for thymes.

◎ Summer

▶ Thymes that flower typically produce their blooms in early to midsummer. It's not necessary to shear off the spent flowerheads on creeping thymes, unless you want to tidy the plants. Cutting back the bushy types by one-third to one-half either before or after flowering helps to keep them bushy and compact.

Water spring plantings occasionally if rain is lacking. Established thymes can tolerate drought but also benefit from occasional watering during extended dry spells.

◑ ◉ Fall & Winter

▶ Set out new plants, or move or divide existing clumps, in early fall. Water new plantings regularly for the first month or so if rain is lacking. Thymes normally hold their leaves through most or all of the winter, often taking on purplish tinges during cold weather. North of Zone 6, you may want to protect fall plantings with evergreen boughs or another lightweight mulch for their first winter. Fertilizer isn't necessary.

✿ **WHACK IT BACK** Every few years, cut your thyme plants back by one-half to two-thirds once you see new leaves forming in spring to encourage vigorous new shoots. This also helps to prevent sprawling on bushy types.

Tiarella

FOAMFLOWER, FALSE MITREWORT

Spiky clusters of small, white to pinkish flowers give foamflowers their name, but the heart-shaped to deeply lobed foliage, often marked with red to deep purple, is just as attractive.

FOAMFLOWERS SOLD AS *Tiarella cordifolia* tend to form rosettes that send out trailing stems, which produce new plantlets and create a ground-covering carpet. Those sold as *T. wherryi* or *T. cordifolia* var. *collina* stay in more distinct, runner-less clumps. And then there are numerous hybrids, which may be either creeping or clumping; with these, you'll need to read their pot tags or catalog descriptions to determine their specific habits. Foamflowers usually reach 12 to 18 inches (30 to 45 cm) tall in bloom and are commonly rated for Zones 3 to 8.

✿ GROWING TIPS

▸ **Light & soil.** A site with some morning sun and afternoon shade or light all-day shade tends to bring out the best flowering, but foamflowers can grow in partial to full shade, too. Evenly moist but well-drained, somewhat acid soil that's been enriched with compost is ideal.

Tiarella 'Heronswood Mist'

▸ **Division & propagation.** The plants generally don't need regular division, unless you want to propagate your favorites in early spring or early fall. To start foamflowers from seed, sow outdoors in summer or fall and leave it uncovered.

▸ **Potential problems.** Foamflowers aren't prone to many pests or diseases, except for occasional problems with black vine weevils (also see Troubleshooting in the *Heuchera* entry on page 246), powdery mildew, or rust.

✿ SEASONAL CARE

◐ Spring

▸ Set out new plants, or move or divide existing clumps, in early spring. Space them 12 to 18 inches (30 to 45 cm) apart. Water new plantings regularly if rain is lacking. Foamflowers benefit from a generous layer of organic mulch applied in early to midspring. They usually begin flowering in mid- to late spring.

◐ Summer

▸ Foamflowers generally keep blooming into early summer. Pinching or snipping off the finished flower stems at their base improves the appearance of the clumps and can extend the bloom period a bit. Keep watering spring plantings regularly if rain is lacking. Established plantings perform best with occasional watering during dry spells.

◑ ◑ Fall & Winter

▸ Set out new foamflowers, or move or divide established ones, in early fall. Water new plantings regularly for the first month or so if rain is lacking. It's not unusual for a few flowers to appear in autumn, and the foliage can take on rich shades of red, bronze, burgundy, and gold as the weather cools. The leaves usually stick around for most or all of the winter. You may want to protect fall plantings with a winter mulch; established plantings usually don't need it. Scatter a shovelful of compost around the plants in late fall to late winter.

✿ **OLDIES BUT GOODIES** The newer foamflower hybrids offer amazing foliage shapes and patterns, but don't overlook some of the older, tried-and-true selections, such as clump-forming 'Oakleaf' or spreading 'Running Tapestry'.

Tiarella 'Spring Symphony'

Relatively Speaking

Foamy bells (× *Heucherella*) are hybrids of heucheras (*Heuchera*) and foamflowers (*Tiarella*), forming clumps or carpets of lobed leaves that are often marked with red or silver. Their white, pink, or red, foamflower-like blooms reach 12 to 18 inches (30 to 45 cm) tall and usually appear in early to midsummer. They thrive with the same general care as foamflowers. Foamy bells are rated for Zones 4 to 9 but tend to perform best in cool-summer regions.

Tradescantia

SPIDERWORT, WIDOW'S TEARS

Spiderworts tend to draw mixed reviews from the gardeners who grow them.

THE FLAT-FACED FLOWERS of spiderworts (*Tradescantia* Andersoniana Group; also sold as *T. × andersoniana*), which bloom in white or shades of pink, purple, blue, and rosy red, are quite beautiful up close — the main point in their favor. Unfortunately, each flower lasts less than a day, opening in early morning and usually closing by early afternoon.

The blooms are held in clusters at the tips of upright stems, among slender, somewhat arching leaves that may be bright green, grayish green, purple-tinged, or even bright to greenish yellow. Spiderworts form grasslike clumps that grow anywhere from 1 to 3 feet (30 to 90 cm) tall. They're usually recommended for Zones 4 to 9.

Tradescantia 'Blue and Gold'

❀ GROWING TIPS

▸ **Light & soil.** Sites with full sun and moist to wet soil tend to encourage abundant flowering, but spiderworts can also grow well in partial shade with average, well-drained soil.

▸ **Division & propagation.** In ideal growing conditions, the clumps can expand quickly, so you may need to divide them as often as every 2 to 3 years to control their spread. Division is also an easy way to propagate your favorites. To grow them from seed, sow outdoors in fall to early spring or indoors in late winter to early spring; barely cover it.

▸ **Potential problems.** Possible problems include slugs and snails, various caterpillars, botrytis blight (gray mold), leaf spots, and rust.

❀ SEASONAL CARE

◐ Spring

▸ Set out new plants, or move or divide existing clumps, in early spring. Space them about 18 inches (45 cm) apart. Water new plantings regularly if rain is lacking. Apply an organic mulch before summer.

Flowering may start in late spring (even earlier in mild climates).

◉ Summer

▸ Early summer tends to be prime bloom time for spiderworts. Once you notice that few or no new flowers are opening, cut them back by about one-half, or even all the way to the ground if they have sprawled. Water spring plantings regularly if rain is lacking. Established clumps may also benefit from watering during dry spells.

✿ ☉ Fall & Winter

▸ Set out new plants, or move or divide existing clumps, in early fall. Water new plantings regularly for the first month or so if rain is lacking. New leafy growth often appears on established clumps in early fall, along with scattered rebloom on some cultivars. The new foliage may hold up well into winter, or the plants may die back after frost; feel free to cut back dead top growth at any point. Spiderworts usually don't need fertilizing (it just encourages them to grow faster and sprawl more).

❀ TROUBLESHOOTING

▸ **Stems sprawl; leaves look tattered or die back altogether.** Spiderworts simply don't thrive in very hot weather, so it's common for them to look bad by midsummer in many areas. One way to minimize later sprawling is to cut the clumps back by one-third to one-half in mid- to late spring (ideally before the flower buds form). Or, wait until after bloom and cut them to the ground in midsummer. Be aware, though, that they may not resprout new leaves until early fall.

❀ **THINK BEFORE YOU PLANT** Spiderworts are very prone to sprawling in summer, smothering smaller companion plants and generally looking ugly, and they can self-sow prolifically as well. Still, if you have lots of space to fill and don't mind doing some extra maintenance, they can be useful for cool-season color in out-of-the-way spots.

Tricyrtis

TOAD LILIES

The attractive form and intricate flowers of toad lilies earn them a place of honor in many shady gardens.

FORMOSA TOAD LILY (*Tricyrtis formosana*; sometimes sold as *T. stolonifera*) is one well-known species, typically growing in creeping patches with upright stems reaching 2 to 3 feet (30 to 90 cm) tall, glossy leaves, and loose flower clusters at the stem tips. It's usually rated for Zones 5 or 6 to 9. Common toad lily (*T. hirta*) has the same height range but tends to stay in tighter clumps, with arching stems, hairy leaves, and clustered flowers held more closely at the stem tips and along the upper parts of the stems as well. It's usually rated for Zones 4 to 9.

There are also many hybrids between these and other species, so you can choose from toad lilies in a range of heights and flower colors (from the common purple-spotted white to pure white, pink, lavender, or yellow), with hardiness ranges from 4, 5, or 6 to 8 or 9. The names are often mixed up in the nursery trade, which further confuses the issue. Fortunately, almost all have the same needs, so it's not critical to know exactly which ones you're growing to care for them successfully.

Tricyrtis hirta 'Miyazaki'

❖ GROWING TIPS

▶ **Light & soil.** Toad lilies thrive in light to partial shade with evenly moist but well-drained, compost-enriched soil. North of Zone 6, a site with morning sun and afternoon shade may increase the odds of your toad lilies flowering before frost.

▶ **Division & propagation.** Toad lilies generally don't need to be divided, but if you want to separate or propagate them, early to mid-spring, just as they begin growing, is the best time. To grow them from seed, sow outdoors in fall to early spring or indoors in late winter to early spring; don't cover it. Where the growing season is long enough for the seed to ripen, toad lilies may self-sow.

▶ **Potential problems.** Slugs and snails may damage the foliage, but otherwise, the plants are usually trouble free as long as their soil doesn't dry out.

❖ SEASONAL CARE

◖ Spring

▶ Set out new plants, or move or divide existing clumps, in early to midspring. Space them about 1 foot (30 cm) apart, or 18 inches (45 cm) apart if you know you have a spreading type. Water new plantings regularly if rain is lacking. Apply a generous layer of organic mulch before summer. Toad lilies may be a little slow to sprout, possibly not emerging until midspring.

◯ Summer

▶ Some toad lily hybrids begin blooming in mid- to late summer.

Keep watering spring plantings regularly if rain is lacking. Established toad lilies also benefit from regular watering to keep the soil evenly moist; otherwise, the leaves may develop brown edges.

✿ ◉ Fall & Winter

▶ Early to midfall tends to be peak bloom time for toad lilies. Once a hard freeze has killed the stems, you can cut them down at any point. Scatter a general-purpose organic fertilizer or a shovelful of compost around each clump in late fall to late winter.

❖ **NIPPED IN THE BUD** Where fall frosts come early, the flower buds of toad lilies can be nipped before they even open. It's worth protecting your plants with a box or some other covering overnight if frost is predicted; that way, if the weather gets milder again, the flowers may still have time to bloom.

Trollius

GLOBEFLOWER

Colorful and elegant, globeflowers are invaluable for adding bright blooms to moist soil borders.

THEY GROW IN DENSE CLUMPS of lobed to deeply cut, bright to deep green leaves, with upright stems that carry single, semidouble, or double cupped flowers in shades of bright to light yellow, orange, or ivory. You'll see globeflowers sold under a variety of botanical names, including *Trollius chinensis, T. × cultorum, T. europaeus,* and *T. ledebourii;* many of the plants are hybrids. They can vary in height and bloom time, but they all have the same basic care needs. Globeflowers generally grow best where summers aren't too hot and are usually recommended for Zones 3 to 7.

Be aware that some single-flowered globeflowers look very much like buttercups (*Ranunculus*). So if your globeflower plants start creeping far and wide, it's likely that you really have buttercups instead, and you'll probably want to remove them as soon as possible so they don't take over. True globeflowers tend to stay in tight clumps (though they may spread lightly to moderately by self-sowing).

Trollius 'Orange Globe'

❖ GROWING TIPS

▶ **Light & soil.** Globeflowers can grow in full sun if their soil stays dependably moist to wet. In partial shade, they still prefer evenly moist soil but can also tolerate average, well-drained conditions if you mulch them in spring and water during the summer.

▶ **Division & propagation.** Divide the clumps every 4 to 6 years, ideally right after flowering; spring and fall are acceptable, too. Division is also the best way to propagate your favorites. If you want to try raising globeflowers from seed, sow outdoors in late summer; don't cover it with soil.

▶ **Potential problems.** Other than occasional problems with leaf spots or powdery mildew, they're usually trouble free.

❖ SEASONAL CARE

◐ Spring

▶ Set out new plants in early spring, spaced about 18 inches (45 cm) apart. Water new plantings regularly if rain is lacking. Apply a generous layer of organic mulch in early to midspring. Some globeflowers may begin blooming in early spring, but most start in mid- to late spring.

◑ Summer

▶ Globeflowers typically finish flowering in early summer, but some may bloom into mid- or even late summer, especially where summers are relatively cool. Snip off spent flowering stems at the base if you want to prevent self-sowing. If needed, divide the clumps after flowering. Keep watering spring plantings and summer divisions regularly if rain is lacking. Established clumps also benefit from regular watering if their soil doesn't naturally stay moist.

✣ ◉ Fall & Winter

▶ Set out new plants, or move or divide existing clumps, in early fall. Water new plantings regularly for the first month or so if rain is lacking. Established globeflowers may produce scattered rebloom in fall. Once the tops die back after frost, cut them down at any point. Scatter a general-purpose organic fertilizer or a shovelful of compost around each clump in late fall to late winter.

❖ **KEEP IT COOL** Gardeners in cool-summer areas may enjoy globeflower blooms through most of the summer. In warmer areas, dry spells can cause the leaves to turn yellow and die back; if that happens, trim them to the ground.

Verbascum

MULLEIN

The dramatic spikes of mulleins are stars in the summer garden, and their low, broad foliage rosettes are handsome through the growing season and beyond.

PURPLE MULLEIN (*Verbascum phoeniceum*) has deep green leaves and purple, pink, or white flower spikes from 2 to 3 feet (60 to 90 cm) tall. It's usually recommended for Zones 6 to 9, but gardeners as far north as Zone 4 have reported success overwintering it. Nettle-leaf mullein (*V. chaixii*) is about the same height but more grayish green in leaf, with yellow or white flowers; Zones 4 or 5 to 9. Olympic mullein (*V. olympicum*), also known as Greek mullein or candlewick, and Turkish or giant silver mullein (*V. bombyciferum*) have hairy, silvery gray leaves and branched spikes of yellow flowers reaching 5 to 8 feet (1.5 to 2.4 m) tall. They too usually perform best in Zones 4 or 5 to 9.

Verbascum phoeniceum

Along with these and other species, there are a number of hybrids, mostly with grayish leaves and flowers in shades of yellow, orange, peach, and pink. They can grow anywhere from 1 to 6 feet (30 to 180 cm) tall and are usually rated for Zones 5 or 6 or 9.

❖ GROWING TIPS

▸ **Light & soil.** Mulleins generally grow best in full sun and average, well-drained soil. A soil pH on the alkaline side is a plus.

▸ **Division & propagation.** Mulleins seldom need to be divided, and they usually don't recover easily from being moved, except in the seedling stage. Propagate them by taking root cuttings in fall or early spring, or sow seed (barely cover it) outdoors in fall to early spring or indoors in late winter to early spring. Purple mullein may bloom the first year from seed.

▸ **Potential problems.** Soil that's too rich may lead to weaker, sprawling stems, and rot can be a concern in too-moist sites. Other possible (but not very common) problems include spider mites, leaf spots, powdery mildew, and root-knot nematodes.

❖ SEASONAL CARE

◐ Spring

▸ Set out new plants in early spring, spaced about 2 feet (60 cm) apart. Trim off any winter-damaged leaves on established clumps. Water new plantings regularly if rain is lacking. Apply an organic or gravel mulch before summer. Some kinds — particularly purple and nettle-leaf mulleins — begin flowering in late spring.

◯ Summer

▸ Early to midsummer is usually peak bloom time for purple and nettle-leaf mulleins, while Olympic and Turkish mulleins tend to be at their best in mid- to late summer. The hybrids usually bloom from early to late summer. Tall-growing mulleins may need staking to support their flower stalks, especially in windy sites. Cut off the finished flower stalks at the base to help

extend the life of the plant and to prevent self-sowing, which can be abundant. (The hybrids are sterile, so they won't self-sow.) Water spring plantings occasionally if rain is lacking. Established clumps tolerate drought but also bloom best with occasional watering.

◑ ◉ Fall & Winter

▸ Set out new plants in early fall and water them regularly for the first month or so if rain is lacking. Olympic and Turkish mulleins may flower into early fall, and other kinds may produce a few flowers, too. Cut down any remaining spikes by late fall if you want to prevent self-sowing, but leave the foliage in place. North of Zone 6, you may want to protect the plants with evergreen boughs or another lightweight winter mulch. There's usually no need to fertilize mulleins.

Verbena

VERBENA, VERVAIN

The long-lasting flowers of verbenas add months of color to hot, sunny gardens, and their interesting forms and persistent foliage stick around to add some zip in winter as well.

BRAZILIAN VERVAIN or purple-top verbena (*Verbena bonariensis*; also known as *V. patagonica*) grows anywhere from 3 to 6 feet (90 to 180 cm) tall, with sparse, narrow, deep green leaves and slender stems tipped in dense clusters of lavender-purple flowers. It may survive the winter as far north as Zone 5, but it's commonly rated for Zones 7 to 10. Brazilian vervain self-sows freely, even in colder climates, and is considered invasive in a few areas.

Rose verbena (*V. canadensis*; also known as *Glandularia*

canadensis) is much lower, growing 6 to 18 inches (15 to 45 cm) tall, with domed clusters of pink, red, white, or purple flowers and toothed or divided, rich green leaves on trailing stems that may take root where they touch the soil. There are cultivars with purple, pink, red, or white flowers, held in domed clusters. Hybrid 'Homestead Purple' is especially vigorous, with vibrant purple flowers. These verbenas may overwinter with protection in Zone 5 but are mostly rated for Zones 6 or 7 to 10.

❀ GROWING TIPS

▸ **Light & soil.** Verbenas tend to grow best in full sun with average, well-drained soil, but they may benefit from a bit of afternoon shade were summers are very hot.

▸ **Division & propagation.** Sow verbena seed outdoors in fall to early spring (barely cover it), or sow indoors in late winter, place the pot in a plastic bag, and refrigerate it for about 3 weeks before moving it to a warm, bright place to sprout. To propagate the trailing types, you could instead use the easier route of taking stem cuttings any time during the growing season. If you take cuttings in fall, treat them as houseplants for the winter north of Zone 8, then plant them outdoors after the last frost date the next spring.

▸ **Potential problems.** Some problems include spider mites, leaf spots, and especially powdery mildew; mostly, though, the plants are

vigorous enough to shrug off these challenges.

❀ SEASONAL CARE

◐ Spring

▸ Set out new plants, or move or divide existing clumps, in early to midspring. Space most of them 12 to 18 inches (30 to 45 cm) apart; allow about 2 feet (60 cm) between clumps of 'Homestead Purple'. Water new plantings if rain is lacking. Apply an organic or gravel mulch before summer. Cut established clumps of Brazilian vervain to about 2 inches (5 cm) in early spring, and give the trailing verbenas a very light trim, if desired. The plants often begin blooming by late spring and may start even earlier in the mildest zones. Cutting Brazilian vervain back by one-third to one-half, or pinching off the shoot tips of the trailing types, once in mid- to late spring promotes bushier, more compact growth.

◔ Summer

▸ Verbenas are commonly in full bloom through the summer. Keep the flower heads clipped off of upright verbenas if you want to prevent self-sowing. Brazilian vervain plants that started flowering in spring may start to look a bit floppy and tired by mid- to late summer; in that case, cut them back by about one-half for later rebloom. Keep watering spring plantings if rain is lacking. Established verbenas can tolerate some drought but also tend to stay healthier and bloom most abundantly if their soil stays somewhat moist.

◑ ◉ Fall & Winter

▸ These verbenas commonly continue blooming until frost. You may want to keep most or all of the spent flowerheads of Brazilian vervain clipped off to minimize self-sowing; otherwise, leave them for winter interest. Leave the trailing types untrimmed for the winter; north of Zone 7, consider protecting them with a winter mulch. Scatter a general-purpose organic fertilizer or a shovelful of compost around each clump in late fall to late winter.

❀ **LET IT SOW** It's not unusual for verbenas to die out after just a year or two, especially in the colder parts of their range. Brazilian vervain (*Verbena bonariensis*) self-sows readily, though, so you can simply transplant self-sown seedlings where you want them in spring.

Verbena bonariensis with fountain grass (*Pennisetum*) and goldenrod (*Solidago*)

Vernonia

IRONWEED

If you're looking to add eye-level color to late-season plantings, ironweeds can be a great choice.

THESE PERENNIALS GROW in broad, dense clumps of sturdy, upright stems clad in deep green, lace-shaped leaves and topped with fuzzy-looking clusters of reddish purple to rich purple flowers. Prairie ironweed (*Vernonia fasciculata*) usually grows 3 to 4 feet (90 to 120 cm) tall. New York ironweed (*V. noveboracensis*) can reach 4 to 8 feet (1.2 to 2.4 m) tall, while tall ironweed (*V. gigantea*; also sold as *V. altissima*) grows anywhere from 4 to 10 feet (1.2 to 3m) tall. These ironweeds are usually recommended for Zones 4 to 9.

Vernonia noveboracensis

✺ GROWING TIPS

▸ **Light & soil.** Full sun to light shade and somewhat moist but well-drained soil is ideal. The more moist and rich the soil, the taller the plants are likely to get.

▸ **Division & propagation.** The plants are long lived and usually don't need to be divided, but if you do wish to reduce their size or propagate them, you could divide them in spring. Other options include taking stem cuttings in early summer or sowing the seed (barely covered) outdoors in fall.

▸ **Potential problems.** Ironweeds have a few problems — including leaf miners, leaf spots, powdery mildew, and rust — but they're seldom serious enough to need control.

✺ SEASONAL CARE

◐ Spring

▸ Set out new plants, or move or divide existing clumps, in early to midspring. Space them about 2 feet (60 cm) apart. Water new plantings regularly if rain is lacking. Cut down any remaining top growth on established plants in early spring. Apply an organic mulch before summer. If your ironweeds tend to get taller than you'd like, try cutting them back by about one-half in late spring to reduce their mature height.

◑ Summer

▸ If you forgot to cut back your ironweeds in late spring, or if you did cut them but want to reduce their bloom-time height even more with a second trim, cut them back by about one-half in early summer. In some climates, ironweeds may begin blooming in midsummer, but they commonly start in late summer. Keep watering spring plantings regularly if rain is lacking. Established ironweeds can tolerate some drought but tend to look their best with occasional watering during dry spells.

✪ ◉ Fall & Winter

▸ Set out new plants in early fall and water them regularly for the first month or so if rain is lacking. Ironweeds flower into early fall and sometimes even later. Clip off the spent flowerheads to prevent self-sowing; otherwise, leave them for winter interest. Scatter a general-purpose organic fertilizer or a shovelful of compost around each clump in late fall to late winter.

✺ **DEFINITELY DEADHEAD** The dried stems and seed heads of ironweeds hold up well into winter, but the plants can also self-sow freely, so you may choose to clip off the spent flower clusters regularly during the bloom season to prevent unwanted seedlings.

Veronica

The spiky blooms of veronicas grace sunny gardens with months of color — mostly shades of blue and purple, but sometimes pink or white — on upright or creeping plants.

ONE OF THE BEST-KNOWN upright species of Veronica is spike speedwell (*Veronica spicata*), with green to gray leaves on stems anywhere from 8 to 24 inches (10 to 60 cm) tall. Longleaf speedwell (*V. longifolia*) tends to be slightly larger, reaching 1 to 3 feet (30 to 90 cm) tall in bloom. There are also many hybrids in a variety of heights. These upright veronicas are generally recommended for Zones 3 to 8.

A few creeping veronicas can be aggressive spreaders, to the point of being considered weeds, but several make lovely garden plants. They tend to bloom earlier than the upright types, with a flowering season that may span just a few weeks. Hungarian speedwell (*V. austriaca* subsp. *teucrium*; also sold as *V. teucrium*), which can reach 1 to 2 feet (30 to 60 cm) tall, is usually rated for Zones 3 to 8. Prostrate speedwell (*V. prostrata*), which stays closer to 6 inches (15 cm) tall, is recommended for Zones 4 or 5 to 8. 'Georgia Blue', often listed under *V. peduncularis*, is a selection appreciated for its glossy, green to bronzy foliage as much as its flowers. It grows to about 8 inches (20 cm) tall and is rated for Zones 5 or 6 to 8.

❖ **MILDEW MANAGEMENT** Keeping the soil evenly moist in summer can help prevent powdery mildew, a common disease problem, especially on the upright veronicas. If powdery mildew is a problem every year, consider trying selections that seem to be resistant, such as 'Goodness Grows' and 'Blue Charm'.

Veronica 'Goodness Grows'

Veronica (continued)

❋ GROWING TIPS

▸ **Light & soil.** A site with full sun to light shade and somewhat moist but well-drained soil is generally ideal for veronicas. Soggy soil is fatal, especially in winter.

▸ **Division & propagation.** Divide the plants every 3 years (or more often for the creeping types) in spring or fall to keep them vigorous, or to propagate them. Taking stem cuttings in summer is another propagation option. Or, sow seed outdoors in fall to early spring or indoors in late winter to early spring; don't cover it.

▸ **Potential problems.** Possible problems include downy and powdery mildew, leaf spots, root rot, rust, and root-knot nematodes.

❋ SEASONAL CARE

◐ Spring

▸ Set out new plants, or move or divide existing clumps, in early spring. Space the upright kinds 12 to 18 inches (30 to 45 cm) apart and the creeping kinds 18 to 24 inches (45 to 60 cm) apart. Water new plantings regularly if rain is lacking. Apply an organic mulch in early to midspring. (The creeping types also look great with a gravel mulch instead.) The taller upright veronicas tend to sprawl in summer, so you may want to set grow-through supports over their emerging clumps. Creeping veronicas can start blooming in early spring in mild climates but are usually at their peak in mid- or late spring. Some of the upright veronicas may start flowering by late spring.

◎ Summer

▸ Creeping veronicas commonly finish flowering in early summer, if they didn't before. When their flowers are done, shear the plants back by about one-half to keep them dense and bushy. Upright veronicas are generally at their best in early to midsummer. Snipping off the finished flower spikes (just above a bud or leaf set lower on the stem) can prolong the bloom well into late summer. Keep watering spring plantings if rain is lacking. Established veronicas also tend to look best with occasional watering during summer dry spells.

❋ ◎ Fall & Winter

▸ Set out new plants, or move or divide existing clumps, in early fall. Water new plantings regularly for the first month or so if rain is lacking. It's not unusual for any veronica to produce scattered rebloom in early to midfall. The basal foliage of many kinds can hold up into at least early winter, so leave it alone if it looks good. But if the top growth all dies after frost, feel free to cut it down. Scatter a general-purpose organic fertilizer or a shovelful of compost around each clump in late fall to late winter.

If your veronicas have sprawled or simply look ratty in summer, just shear them back to 1 to 2 inches (2.5 to 5 cm) above the ground to promote a flush of new foliage.

Veronicastrum

CULVER'S ROOT, BLACK ROOT

The elegant and eye-catching bloom spires of Culver's root are ideal for pepping up later-season beds and borders.

THE PLANTS FORM broad clumps of upright stems clad in whorls of lance-shaped leaves and tipped with tiny blooms grouped into branching clusters of tapering spikes. *Veronicastrum virginicum* (also sold as *Veronica virginica*) typically has white to pink-tinged flowers. *V. sibiricum* more commonly has pale blue to lavender-blue flowers and tends to start blooming several weeks earlier. Both can reach anywhere from 3 to 7 feet (90 to 210 cm) tall but are typically in the range of 4 to 6 feet (1.2 to 1.8 m). Culver's roots are usually recommended for Zones 3 to 8.

Veronicastrum virginicum

✿ GROWING TIPS

▸ **Light & soil.** Culver's roots thrive in full sun but can also perform well in light shade (especially in warmer zones), though they may be more prone to leaning or sprawling there. They can grow in average, well-drained soil but really shine in moist to wet sites with compost-enriched soil.

▸ **Division & propagation.** Culver's roots seldom need division, but you could divide them every 5 years or so for propagation, or take stem cuttings in summer. To grow them from seed, sow outdoors in fall to spring or indoors in late winter to early spring; don't cover it.

▸ **Potential problems.** Possible problems include plant bugs, leaf spots, and powdery mildew, but they're rarely serious enough to require control. Young plants can take several years to fill out.

✿ SEASONAL CARE

◐ Spring

▸ Set out new plants, or move or divide existing clumps, in early to midspring. Space them 2 to 3 feet (60 to 90 cm) apart. Water new plantings regularly if rain is lacking. Apply an organic mulch before summer. It's not unusual for the new foliage of Culver's roots to be tinged with red.

◎ Summer

▸ In the warmer parts of their growing range, Culver's roots may begin flowering as early as early summer. In most areas, though, *V. sibiricum* starts in midsummer and *V. virginicum* begins a few weeks later, in mid- to late summer. Snip off the spent flower clusters just above a set of leaves near the top of the stem to encourage rebloom and prevent self-sowing, or leave them for their interesting seed heads. Usually, the plants look great through the summer, but if they drop their lower leaves, you could cut them to the ground at the end of the summer. Keep watering spring plantings regularly if rain is lacking. Established plants can also benefit from occasional watering during dry spells if their soil isn't naturally moist.

◑ ◉ Fall & Winter

▸ Set out new plants in early fall, or move or divide existing clumps once they are finished flowering. Water new plantings regularly for the first month or so if rain is lacking. The dried stems and seed heads of *V. virginicum* tend to hold their form through most of the winter, so you can either wait until late winter to cut it down or remove the stems during fall cleanup if you want to prevent self-sowing. *V. sibiricum* tends to break down by early to midwinter anyway, so you may want to go ahead and cut it down after frost. Scatter a general-purpose organic fertilizer or a shovelful of compost around each clump in late fall to late winter.

✿ **SUPPORT SYSTEMS** If your Culver's root plants are prone to sprawling, install stakes in spring for later support or add sturdy companions, such as tall grasses, for the stems to lean against. Another option is to trim the stems back by one-third to one-half in mid- to late spring.

Viola

VIOLA, VIOLET

Violets are a classic favorite for spring gardens. It's possible for those sold as annuals — those commonly called pansies and violas — to last for more than one year, but mostly, the perennial species best known by gardeners is the sweet violet (*Viola odorata*) and its hybrids.

SWEET VIOLET PLANTS SPREAD by runners to form patches of rich green, heart- to kidney-shaped leaves, with small but sweetly scented purple, blue, pink, or white flowers typically 4 to 8 inches (10 to 20 cm) tall. Sweet violets are usually recommended for Zones 5 or 6 to 8.

Labrador violet (*V. labradorica*) is even shorter, reaching just 4 inches (10 cm) in bloom, with tiny purple-blue flowers and heart-shaped foliage. It's most commonly grown in its distinctly purple-leaved form and sold as 'Purpurea', *V. labradorica* var. *purpurea*, or *V. riviniana* Purpurea Group. It can grow in Zones 3 to 9.

Viola labradorica with *Sedum ternatum*

❖ GROWING TIPS

▸ **Light & soil.** Violets tolerate some sun in spring, fall, and winter but generally prefer partial to full shade, especially in summer. They adapt to average, well-drained sites but thrive in evenly moist (but still well-drained), compost-enriched soil.

▸ **Division & propagation.** Every 3 years (or more often, if necessary), divide the clumps in spring or fall to control their spread, or to propagate them. To grow them from seed, sow outdoors in late summer or fall; barely cover the seed with soil. The plants will also self-sow freely, sometimes to the point of becoming weedy.

▸ **Potential problems.** Violets may be bothered by a wide range of pests and diseases, among them aphids, cutworms, slugs and snails, spider mites, botrytis blight (gray mold), leaf spots, root rots, rusts, southern blight, and various nematodes. Mostly, though, the plants can tolerate the damage without intervention.

❖ SEASONAL CARE

◐ Spring

▸ Set out new plants, or move or divide existing clumps, in very early spring or just after flowering. Space them about 8 inches (20 cm) apart. Water new plantings regularly if rain is lacking. Apply an organic mulch in early to midspring. Both sweet and Labrador violets may bloom from early through late spring. Clipping off individual flowers can extend the bloom season but usually isn't practical unless you have just a few plants.

◎ Summer

▸ In most areas, violets finish blooming by early summer, and their foliage may start to look bad. (Purple-leaved Labrador violets also tend to turn greenish in warm weather.) At this point, you may want to shear the patches back by one-half to two-thirds to encourage fresh leafy growth. Both spring-planted and established violets look their best with regular watering if rain is lacking, though established violets can tolerate some dryness.

✿ ◉ Fall & Winter

▸ Set out new plants, or move or divide existing clumps, in early fall. Water new plantings regularly for the first month or so if rain is lacking. Early fall is also a good time to shear off the foliage if it has been damaged by pests or diseases. Both sweet and Labrador violets start growing again as the weather cools and may bloom through the fall, and even through the winter in mild climates. Scatter a general-purpose organic fertilizer or shovelful of compost around the clumps in late fall to late winter.

❖ **WATCH OUT** Both sweet violets (*Viola odorata*) and Labrador violets (*V. labradorica*) spread freely, especially in ideal conditions. Clipping off the fading flowers won't completely prevent self-sowing, but maintaining a thick layer of mulch may help to prevent some of the seeds from sprouting.

Yucca

YUCCA, ADAM'S NEEDLE

Easy to grow and definitely dramatic, yuccas are a common sight in gardens and landscapes across the country.

THEY PRODUCE CLUMPS of stiff to arching, sword-shaped leaves often edged with curly fibers and usually 1 to 3 feet (30 to 90 cm) tall. In some species, the rosettes are held atop even taller, thick stems; in others, they form at or close to ground level. Mature rosettes send up stout stalks that may be anywhere from 3 to 10 feet (90 to 300 cm) tall, topped with clusters of large, nodding white flowers.

There are a number of species well suited to warm climates, and a few are winter hardy surprisingly far north. Among the hardiest species are soapweed (*Yucca glauca*), for Zones 3 to 10; Adam's needle (*Y. filamentosa*; sometimes sold as *Y. flaccida*), for Zones 4 to 10 — this one includes many of the most popular variegated yuccas; and beaked yucca (*Y. rostrata*), also known as big bend yucca, for Zones 5 or 6 to 10. It's not necessary to know exactly which yuccas you're growing, though, because they all take the same basic care.

Yucca filamentosa 'Gold Sword'

❖ GROWING TIPS

▸ **Light & soil.** Yuccas thrive in full sun and average, well-drained to dry soil but can grow in partial shade, too. Established plants tolerate salt and drought.

▸ **Division & propagation.** Division usually isn't necessary, but if you want to propagate your favorites, dig up one or more of the offsets in spring or fall. If you want to try growing them from seed, sow outdoors in spring or indoors in late winter or early spring; barely cover it.

▸ **Potential problems.** Possible problems include aphids, mealybugs, plant bugs, scale, crown rot, and leaf spots, but they're rarely serious enough to need control.

❖ SEASONAL CARE

◐ Spring

▸ Set out new plants, or move or remove offsets from existing clumps, in early to midspring. Space them about 3 feet (90 cm) apart. Water new plantings regularly if rain is lacking. On established plants, trim off any winter-damaged foliage at the base in early spring. (Be sure to wear long sleeves and heavy gloves while doing this, and work carefully, because the leaves may be tipped with sharp spines.) Also cut out any reverted (nonvariegated) rosettes on clumps that are supposed to have variegated foliage. Yuccas don't require mulching, but if you wish to, apply either an organic or gravel much in spring.

◎ Summer

▸ Some species, such as soapweed, bloom mostly in early to midsummer, while others are in full flower in mid- to late summer. Once the flowers are done, you could simply cut off the stalk at the base, but it's best to cut out that entire rosette, because it won't bloom again. The smaller rosettes around it may take several more years to reach flowering size, so your clumps may not bloom every year. Established yuccas don't need watering, but you may want to water spring plantings occasionally if rain is lacking.

✿ ☉ Fall & Winter

▸ Set out new plants, or move or separate offsets from existing clumps, in early fall. Water new plantings regularly for the first month or so if rain is lacking. Some yuccas may continue flowering into early fall. Remove any rosettes that have already flowered; otherwise, leave the foliage alone. Variegated yuccas may take on pinkish tinges.

❖ **TOUGH CUSTOMER** Before planting any yucca, choose its site carefully, because established plants can be very difficult to remove. You can dig out the visible parts, but they'll often return from any roots left in the soil.

USDA Hardiness Zone Map

The United States Department of Agriculture (USDA) created this map to give gardeners a helpful tool for selecting and cultivating plants. The map divides North America into 11 zones based on each area's average minimum winter temperature. Zone 1 is the coldest and Zone 11 is the warmest. To locate your zone, refer to the map here, or for the most up-to-date information, visit the National Arbor Day Foundation's Web site: www.arborday.org/media/zones.cfm.

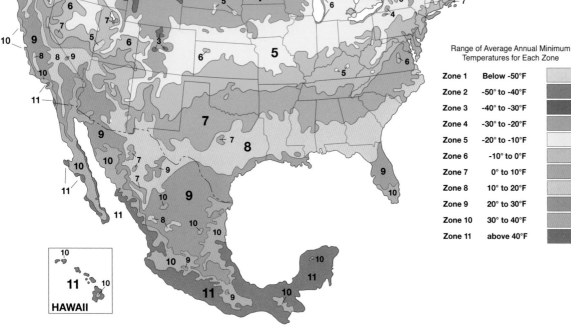

ALASKA

HAWAII

Range of Average Annual Minimum Temperatures for Each Zone

Zone 1	Below -50°F	
Zone 2	-50° to -40°F	
Zone 3	-40° to -30°F	
Zone 4	-30° to -20°F	
Zone 5	-20° to -10°F	
Zone 6	-10° to 0°F	
Zone 7	0° to 10°F	
Zone 8	10° to 20°F	
Zone 9	20° to 30°F	
Zone 10	30° to 40°F	
Zone 11	above 40°F	

Resources

Plant Conservation Alliance's Alien Plant Working Group

www.nps.gov/plants/alien

USDA Cooperative Extension Service

www.csrees.usda.gov/Extension

Index

Page references in **bold** indicate main entries; page references in *italics* indicate photos.

G

Gaillardia (blanket flower), 62, *62*, **222–23**
 × *grandiflora*, 222
  'Goblin', 223
Galanthus (snowdrops), 171–72
Galeobdolon luteum (yellow archangel), 258
garden cleanup, 11, *11*, 234, *234*
 "3 R's" for, 90
 approaches to, 49, 51, 54
 calendar for, 50
 foliage and flowers, 17, *17*
 off-season cleanup, 17
 trimming plants, *49*, 49–51, 54
 See also debris handling
gardener's garters. See *Phalaris arundinacea* var. *picta*
gas plant. See *Dictamnus*
Gaura (gaura, wand flower, bee blossom, appleblossom grass), **224–25**
 lindheimeri, 224
  'Siskiyou Pink', 225
gayfeather. See *Liatris*
Geranium (hardy geranium, cranesbill), **226–27**
 'Brookside', 226, 227
 cantabrigiense (Cambridge geranium), 226, 227
 cinereum (grayleaf geranium), 226
 clarkei (Clarke's geranium), 226, 227
 endressii (Endress's geranium), 226
 'Gerwat' (Rozanne), 226, 227
 'Johson's Blue', 226
 maculatum (wild geranium), 226
 macrorrhizum (bigroot geranium), 226, 227
 phaeum (mourning widow), 226
 pratense (meadow cranesbill), 226
 sanguineum (bloody cranesbill), 226, 227
  'New Hampshire Purple', 226
 trimming of, 77, *77*, 227
Geum (geum, avens, Grecian rose), **228**
 × *borisii*, 228
 chiloense (G. *quellyon*), 228
 coccineum, 228
 'Georgenberg', 228
Gillenia (Bowman's root, Indian physic, American ipecac), **229**
 stipulata, 229
 trifoliata, 229, *229*
Gladiolus, 173
 communis subsp. *byzantinus*, 173

Glandularia canadensis (rose verbena), 346
globeflower. See *Trollius*
globe thistle. See *Echinops*
gloriosa daisy. See *Rudbeckia*
goat's beard. See *Aruncus*
goldenray. See *Ligularia*
goldenrod. See *Solidago*
Goniolimon tataricum. See *Limonium*
granny's bonnet. See *Aquilegia*
grasses, **230–34**
 cleanup for, 234, *234*
 "clumpers" and "creepers," 230
 dividing in place, 88, *88*
 growing tips for, 230–31
 invasive types of, 118
 ornamental grasses, 230
 removal of, *14*, 14–15
 seasonal care for, 231, 234
 troubleshooting, 234
Grecian rose. See *Geum*
Greek valerian. See *Polemonium*
grooming perennials, **67–77**
 calendar for, 71
 disbudding, 71, 75, *75*
 to extend/delay bloom, 73
 layered look, 70, *70*
 light, frequent trimming, 70
 shearing perennials, 77, *77*
 for size and shape, 69–71
 testing methods and, 72
 thinning, crowding and, 72
 See also deadheading
groundsel. See *Ligularia*
Gypsophila (baby's breath), **235**
 'Bristol Fairy', 235
 double-flowered cultivars, 235
 paniculata (common baby's breath), 235, *235*
 repens (creeping baby's breath), 235
 'Viette's Dwarf', 235

H

Hakonechloa macra (Hakone grass), 232
hardening off perennials, 64
hardiness zone, 7
hardiness zone map, 355, *355*
hardy ageratum. See *Eupatorium*
hardy geranium. *See Geranium*
hardy hibiscus. See *Hibiscus*
harebell. See *Campanula*

Other Storey Titles You Will Enjoy

Designer Plant Combinations, by Scott Calhoun.
More than 100 creative combinations, planted by top garden designers across the country, to inspire home gardeners to put plants together in unexpected but stunning groupings.
240 pages. Paper. ISBN 978-1-60342-077-8.

Fallscaping, by Nancy J. Ondra and Stephanie Cohen.
A comprehensive guide to the best plants for brightening late-season landscapes.
240 pages. Paper with flaps. ISBN 978-1-58017-680-4.

Foliage, by Nancy J. Ondra.
An eye-opening garden guide to the brilliant colors and textures of dozens of plants, all chosen for the unique appeal of their leaves.
304 pages. Paper with flaps. ISBN 978-1-58017-648-4.
Hardcover with jacket. ISBN 978-1-58017-654-5.

Garden Stone, by Barbara Pleasant.
A best-selling guide to 40 enchanting, creative projects for landscaping with plants and stone.
240 pages. Paper. ISBN 978-1-58017-544-9.

The Gardener's A–Z Guide to Growing Flowers from Seed to Bloom,
by Eileen Powell.
An encyclopedic reference on choosing, sowing, transplanting, and caring for 576 annuals, perennials, and bulbs.
528 pages. Paper. ISBN 978-1-58017-517-3.

Grasses, by Nancy J. Ondra.
Photographs and plans for 20 gardens that highlight the beauty of grasses in combination with perennials, annuals, and shrubs.
144 pages. Paper with flaps. ISBN 978-1-58017-423-7.

The Perennial Gardener's Design Primer,
by Stephanie Cohen and Nancy J. Ondra.
A lively, authoritative guide to creating perennial gardens using basic design principles for putting plants together in pleasing and practical ways.
320 pages. Paper. ISBN 978-1-58017-543-2.
Hardcover with jacket. ISBN 978-1-58017-545-6.

These and other books from Storey Publishing are available
wherever quality books are sold or by calling 1-800-441-5700.
Visit us at *www.storey.com*.